Never Say I

edited by
Michèle Aina Barale,
Jonathan Goldberg,
Michael Moon, and
Eve Kosofsky Sedgwick

Never Say I

Sexuality and the First

Person in Colette, Gide,

and Proust

MICHAEL LUCEY

Duke University Press   Durham & London   2006

This project was partially supported by
funding from the President's Research
Fellowships in the Humanities, University
of California.

Additionally, Duke University Press
gratefully acknowledges the support of the Arts
and Humanities Division at the University of
California, Berkeley, which provided funds
toward the production of this book.

Contents

Acknowledgments

Interlocution, intersubjectivity, and the importance of a surrounding social context are major themes throughout these pages, beginning here. To all who helped create the context and conditions in which this work came to seem doable and exciting, my heartfelt thanks. Four of the chapters in *Never Say I* got going or got finished thanks to invitations to speak or to write from various people including Remi Lenoir, Françoise Gaspard and Didier Eribon, Tom Conner, Naomi Segal, and Elisabeth Ladenson. An earlier version of chapter 4 was published in English as "Practices of Posterity: Gide and the Cultural Politics of Sexuality," in *Andre Gide's Politics: Rebellion and Ambivalence*, ed. Tom Conner (New York: Palgrave, 2000), and is reprinted with permission. An earlier version of chapter 5 appeared as "Proust's Queer Metalepses" in *MLN* 116 (2001): 795–815, © The Johns Hopkins University Press. It is reprinted with permission of The Johns Hopkins University Press. The participants in a Berkeley graduate seminar on Proust and the first person helped me out a good deal, as did various members of the audiences for lectures drawn from these chapters. The good fortune of time in which to read, think, and write came thanks to a fellowship from the John Simon Guggenheim Memorial Foundation, which enabled an extended research stay in Paris. Further essential support came from a University of California President's Research Fellowship in the Humanities, and a Humanities Research Fellowship from the University of California, Berkeley. I am immensely grateful for this support. David Copenhafer provided research assistance for some of these chapters. Librarians and the collections at Berkeley and Stanford and the Bibliothèque Nationale de France were essential to the research that went into this book. It's been a pleasure to work with Ken Wissoker,

Justin Faerber, Sage Rountree, and everyone else at Duke University Press again. Elizabeth Povinelli pointed me in the direction of some helpful reading at a crucial moment. Monique Nemer offered a set of pertinent comments on a couple of chapters and some key references. Eve Kosofsky Sedgwick and Ann Smock showed their support generously. Tim Hampton, Leslie Kurke, and Celeste Langan, invaluable intellectual companions of many years, trained their canny eyes on a good number of these pages. Ross Chambers, Elisabeth Ladenson, and Sharon Marcus troubled themselves to comment extensively on the whole manuscript, much to its betterment. Most essential and beloved enabler of all, Gerry Gomez, thank goodness, has been there most every day.

Introduction: Referring to Same-Sex Sexualities in the First Person

"Listen, dear, now you must make me a promise. Your *Nourritures terrestres* is fine . . . very fine, even. . . . But dear, from now on never again write 'I.' "

And as I didn't seem to understand him fully enough, he went on: "In art, you see, there is no *first* person."

[«Écoutez, dear, il faut maintenant que vous me fassiez une promesse. Les *Nourritures terrestres*, c'est bien . . . c'est très bien . . . Mais, dear, promettez-moi: maintenant, n'écrivez plus jamais JE».

Et comme je paraissais ne pas suffisamment comprendre, il reprenait:—«En art, voyez-vous, il n'y a pas de *première* personne».]
—ANDRÉ GIDE, *Oscar Wilde* (1910)

He is fat, or rather puffy; he reminds me somewhat of Jean Lorrain. I am taking him *Corydon*, of which he promises not to speak to anyone; and when I say a word or two about my Memoirs:

"You can tell anything," he exclaims; "but on condition that you never say: *I*." But that won't suit me.

[Il est gras, ou plutôt bouffi; il me rappelle un peu Jean Lorrain. Je lui apporte *Corydon* dont il me promet de ne parler à personne; et comme je lui dis quelques mots de mes Mémoires:

«Vous pouvez tout raconter, s'écrie-t-il; mais à condition de ne jamais dire: *Je*.» Ce qui ne fait pas mon affaire.]
—ANDRÉ GIDE, speaking of Proust in the May 14, 1921, entry to his *Journal*

Fortunately I have no opinion, what would I have an opinion with, with my mouth perhaps, if it's mine, I don't feel a mouth on me, if only I could feel something on me, I'll try, if I can, I know it's not I, that's all I know, I say I, knowing it's not I, I am far.

[Moi je n'ai pas d'opinion, avec quoi aurais-je une opinion, avec ma bouche peut-être, si c'est la mienne, je ne me sens pas une bouche, ça ne veut rien dire, si je pouvais me sentir une bouche, si je pouvais me sentir quelque chose, je vais essayer, si je peux, je sais que ce n'est pas moi, c'est tout ce que je sais, je dis je en sachant que ce n'est pas moi, moi je suis loin.]

—SAMUEL BECKETT, *L'Innommable* (1953)

When I began writing *La Bâtarde*, I had read Colette's *Break of Day*. It is a book I admire. And then I had read the series of "Claudine" novels, and found that Colette lacked courage, was timid. So I said to myself: "I am going to try to be frank, because there is no reason that only men should be able to talk about intimate matters . . ." In any case, when I write, it's all the same to me. I can recount anything. Nothing embarrasses me. You could say that I don't think about the reader. I am alone with myself. I say everything, but make an effort to do so tastefully and tactfully.

[Quand j'ai commencé *La Bâtarde*, j'avais lu *La Naissance du jour* de Colette. C'est un livre que j'admire. Et puis, j'avais lu la série des *Claudine*, et j'avais trouvé que Colette manquait de courage, qu'elle était timorée. Alors, je me suis dit: "Je vais essayer d'être franche, car il n'y a aucune raison qu'il soit réservé aux hommes de parler de questions d'intimité . . ." D'ailleurs, quand j'écris, tout m'est égal. Je peux tout raconter, rien ne me gêne. Si vous voulez, je ne pense pas alors au lecteur. Je suis seule avec moi-même. Je dis tout, mais je m'efforce d'y mettre du goût, du tact.]

—VIOLETTE LEDUC, *Lettres françaises*, October 15, 1964

Linguistically, the Author is never more than the instance writing, just as *I* is nothing other than the instance saying *I*: language knows a "subject," not a "person," and this subject, empty outside of the very enunciation which defines it, suffices to make language "hold together," suffices, that is to say, to exhaust it.

[Linguistiquement, l'Auteur n'est jamais rien de plus que celui qui écrit, tout comme *je* n'est autre que celui qui dit *je*: le langage connaît un «sujet», non une «personne», et ce sujet, vide en dehors de l'énonciation même qui le définit, suffit à faire «tenir» le langage, c'est-à-dire à l'épuiser.]
—ROLAND BARTHES, "The Death of the Author" (1968)

Even before "I" knows it, "I" is made a prisoner, it becomes the victim of a fool's deal. What it has mistaken for absolute liberty, the necessary reciprocity, without which language is impossible, is but the surrender, a deal that overthrows the "I" at the mercy of the slightest word.

[Avant même que *je* le sache *je* est fait prisonnier, le voici la victime d'un marché de dupes, ce qu'il a pris pour la liberté absolue, la réciprocité nécessaire sans quoi on ne peut pas comprendre pourquoi . . . n'est que la reddition, un marché qui le jette à la merci du moindre mot.]
—MONIQUE WITTIG, "The Site of Action" (1984)

There is the experience of writing, and that is the moment when once again I become Hervé Guibert as a character in my books. I often have the impression of leading a double life. When people in the street ask me, "*Are you Hervé Guibert?*" I want to respond, "Not just at the moment." Because in that moment I am not caught up in the wave of immodesty, in that strange relationship that there is between experience and writing.

[Il y a l'expérience de l'écriture, et c'est le moment où je redeviens Hervé Guibert comme personnage de mes livres. J'ai souvent l'impression de mener une double vie. Quand des gens me demandent dans la rue: «*Vous êtes Hervé Guibert?*», j'ai envie de répondre: «Non, je ne le suis pas en ce moment.» Parce qu'à ce moment-là je ne suis pas dans une vague d'impudeur, dans cet étrange rapport qu'il y a entre l'expérience et l'écriture.]
—HERVÉ GUIBERT, in *Le Nouvel Observateur*, July 18, 1991

The "one," stigmatized by philosophy and discredited by literature, but which we all are, tries with its desperately "inauthentic" means to say something which, for the "I" that in our most common claim to uniqueness we believe ourselves to be, is the most difficult to hear.

[Ce que le «on», philosophiquement stigmatisé et littérairement déconsidéré, que nous sommes tous tente de dire, avec ses moyens, désespérément «inauthentiques», est sans doute, pour les «je» que nous croyons être, par la plus commune des revendications de singularité, ce qu'il y a de plus difficile à écouter.]

—PIERRE BOURDIEU, "Comprendre," *La Misère du monde* (1993)

CHRISTINE ANGOT: In point of fact I do not write about myself, and it's not autobiography.

FRÉDÉRIC BEIGBEDER: Then who is *Sujet Angot* about?

CA: It's not about anyone, it's about people, it's about people.

FB: Okay, fine, sorry, sorry, really sorry.

[CHRISTINE ANGOT: Le fait est que je ne me mets pas en scène, et que c'est pas de l'autobiographie.

FRÉDÉRIC BEIGBEDER: *Sujet Angot*, ça parle de qui?

CA: Mais ça parle de *personne*, ça parle des gens, ça parle des gens.

FB: D'accord, bon, pardon, pardon, excusez-moi.]

— *Bouillon de culture*, France 2, October 20, 2000

From the beginning of the twentieth century to the end, the first person is a problem in French literature. It poses problems—both theoretical and aesthetic—in French literature in general, of course, but the problems become especially acute, and acutely sociological, in the tradition of writing about same-sex relations that is galvanized toward the beginning of the century by writers such as André Gide and Colette and, a bit later, Marcel Proust. It is from Proust's supposed remark to Gide—"You can tell anything . . . as long as you never say 'I' "—that I take the title for this first of two volumes considering the itineraries of what we might call the queer first person in twentieth-century French literature. The present volume deals with the crucial interventions in this tradition that were made by Colette, Gide, and Proust, in whose ambit or in whose wake most other writers from the century (including, say, Jean Cocteau and Marguerite Yourcenar; Marcel Jouhandeau, Jean Genet, Simone de Beauvoir, and Violette Leduc; Robert Pinget, Monique Wittig, Pierre Guyotat, Guy Hocquenghem, and Tony Duvert; Roland Barthes, Marguerite Duras, and Hervé Guibert; Christine Angot, Mathieu Lindon, Guillaume Dustan, Rachid O., and Nina Bouraoui, as well as many others) all find themselves working.

Whatever Proust may have said to Gide in 1921 about using "I," it's worth remembering that he was himself in the midst of writing a long novel in the first person. As Gide's journal entry from May 1921 makes clear, he saw himself and Proust as developing divergent, not to say opposing, strategies for using the first person to write about same-sex sexuality. One characterization of the difference between them has been to say that Gide's writing was marked by the fact that he was willing to be "out," whereas Proust's was marked by the fact that he remained "closeted."[1] Such an opposition falls short of capturing the full complexity of their situations and their practices, as we shall see. It also ignores a lot of history. There are certain prerequisites to the act of "coming out." It is a social ritual with a certain form, and that form required time to be developed.[2] Gide experimented a great deal with the kinds of acts and statements that we have come to recognize as constitutive of the ritual of coming out. The ritual as it became codified in the later twentieth century required a certain set of modern sexual identities to be firmly in place, and it required (and still requires) that those identities be recognizable by anyone performing and anyone observing or otherwise participating in the ritual. For the ritual to be successful, people have to recognize the ritual itself as something in which they might be asked to participate. Certainly, early in the twentieth century in France, these kinds of recognition could not be taken for granted. Indeed, the same could be said about plenty of circumstances that arise here and there today.[3]

Building on some recent work by Ross Chambers and Anne Freadman, we might also productively consider that ritual situations in which a sexual identity is assumed, qualified, or refused could be thought of as *genres*. As Chambers puts it:

> It is helpful to describe any given local culture as a specific array of genres, where genre is understood as a conventional habitus entailing understandings and agreements that don't need to be specifically negotiated concerning the "kinds" of social interaction that are possible under the aegis of that culture. Interactions that are nongeneric in a given culture are those that are culturally "out of bounds," although they may be generic—that is, they may be regarded as appropriate—in another culture, including one quite proximate to the culture in question. . . . What genres regulate, with varying degrees of rigidity and flexibility, is the social appropriateness of discursive behavior.[4]

In the course of the codification of the coming out ritual or genre, certain kinds of statements would become standard and would assume a certain degree of appropriateness; they would employ a certain vocabulary; they would involve a practice of the first person, an assumption of a particular first person. Such statements (and the contexts for them), however simple and self-evident they might seem to some of us today, were clearly rather difficult to construct and enunciate for their early practitioners. The choice of words that would come to be characteristic of them was far from self-evident; the availability of interlocutors to understand them was not a foregone conclusion; the very social protocols that would enable them to occur were far from widely established. And there is no reason to assume that everyone involved in same-sex sexualities felt (or feels) any compulsion to utter such statements or to enact such scenes. Many people interested in using the first person to write about same-sex sexualities in the early decades of the twentieth century (think of Marguerite Yourcenar) had no interest in participating in any ritual use of language that could have been construed as coming out. This does not necessarily mean that such writers were closeted. The social and historical landscapes in question are much too complicated, as is the array of generic possibilities available to any author, to be well analyzed using any such overly simplistic categorical division, the pertinence of which is always and everywhere open to question. At stake are, in many ways, different practical understandings of the role of the first person in relation to sexuality, different relations to the social, ritual, and referential functions of that first person when it comes to making statements about sexuality.

Authors such as Proust, Gide, and Colette contribute to a complicated and often contradictory project of imagining a first person in which to speak about the same-sex sexual identities that were themselves falling into shapes and forms that achieved easy recognizability in much of Western culture across the twentieth century. These authors are part of a history (not necessarily a unilinear or a progressive or a coherent one) of the *institution* of novel social categories (the homosexual, the gay man, the lesbian, and so on) and of the *constitution* of new social groups—for instance, those that will form what has come to be called the lesbian and gay community, a community that will, in its own time, come to demand certain kinds of representation of its own (both literary and political). In works by the authors studied here, we will see posed not only the questions *Who will speak for a given group?* and *How will that speech be structured?*, but also the questions *Of what group are we speaking?* and *How does speaking of and for a group help bring it into existence or dictate its contours?* Finally, a whole set of questions will arise concerning how a group speaks back to its representatives once it has been constituted.[5]

In an essay called "Description and Prescription," Pierre Bourdieu writes that political action "aims to make or unmake groups—and, by the same token, the collective actions they can undertake to transform the social world in accordance with their interests—by producing, reproducing or destroying the representations that make groups visible for themselves and for others."[6] In this sense, literary works by authors such as Proust, Gide, and Colette can be understood as having political and social import in relation to same-sex sexuality. They contributed to the work of defining social groups (publics) that could be publicly recognized, that could speak and be spoken for. One need not presume that the conceptual categories and terms that such authors used to understand sexuality are the same as (or even developmental precursors to) the forms of sexual identity we often take for granted today. Yet it is still possible to evaluate the contribution these authors and their writings have made to the large cultural process through which modern sexual identities have become both recognizable and somewhat naturalized. Bourdieu speaks in that same essay of the "*labour of enunciation* which is necessary in order to externalize the inwardness, to name the unnamed and to give the beginnings of objectification to pre-verbal and pre-reflexive dispositions and ineffable and unobservable experiences" (129). That labor of enunciation is what I will be tracing in this volume, by examining the efforts of Proust, Gide, and Colette to promote the categories they favor for groups of people involved in same-sex sexualities, to create portraits of people who fit those categories, and to create suitable points of view and narrative practices from which to write about such people, or to speak or write for them or even as them, to assert that they have experience, and to make that experience both valuable and available. How will the first person be mobilized in order to convey the authority, the legitimacy, or the authenticity of the representation? By whom and to whom would the appeal for legitimacy, authority, or authenticity in representation be addressed? I begin here by laying out some of the general preoccupations that guide my study.

My own first person, it will be noted, evinces a certain reluctance about using words like *homosexual* or *gay* or *lesbian* as if they could function as historically neutral designators of some given sexual identity. (This first person also sometimes resorts to the word *queer* as an index of that reluctance and to indicate a sense of the complexity of the set of variables in a social field that would cause an utterance or a sexual practice to be experienced as somehow out of kilter with the norm.) In any case, the preference you will find here for locutions such as "same-sex sexuality" is not based on any sense that these locutions could themselves have any enduring neutrality about them. Let's say that I use *same-sex* not so much for its own illusory neutrality as to mark the nonneutrality of the word *homosexual* and its cognates.[7] Affect and a sense of social position play their part in the word choices that contribute to the figuring of a first person; those choices and the affect involved are indexes of more general social contentions. In this, my own first person is no different from those we will encounter in these pages who find themselves disturbed by or at home in words such as *invert* or *uranist* or *lesbian* or any number of others.

John J. Gumperz and Jenny Cook-Gumperz commented in an article from 1982 that "we customarily take gender, ethnicity, and class as given parameters and boundaries within which we create our own social identities. The study of language as interactional discourse demonstrates that these parameters are not constants that can be taken for granted but are communicatively produced."[8] Much the same could be said of sexual identities. "Talk itself is constitutive of social reality," Gumperz and Cook-Gumperz note. "Where communicative conventions and symbols of social identity differ, the social reality itself becomes subject to question" (3). Such observations will be helpful to keep in mind as we consider a variety of materials dealing with the evolution—the shifting conventions—of social identities tied to sexuality in the early part of the twentieth century. "Social identity and ethnicity are in large part established and maintained through language" (7). So it is with sexual identities: they are produced interactively, through spoken language as well as other forms of social interaction—including obviously, but not exclusively, sex.

Literature is itself a kind of interactional discourse, although it clearly takes place in a slower time frame than conversational or other face-to-face interactions. To analyze the kinds of interaction that occur in this slower time frame requires attention to the larger social context in which literary discourse evolves, to the interrelations between the social context and the particular linguistic interventions that come to be thought of as literature. Literature itself is also a parameter, a field, whose borders are constantly being reestablished by means of the discursive interventions of "works of literature" themselves, as well as by means of the interventions of critics, or by means of other kinds of interactions between publishers and writers, between writers and readers, between booksellers and customers, between critics, journalists, writers, readers and publishers, between professors and students, and so on.[9]

The representation of sexuality, and, in particular, of same-sex sexual relations and of actors in them, is central to the evolution of literary prose forms in twentieth-century France. Throughout the century, the topic of sexuality plays a key role in claims as to what is literature. One finds a consistent ambition—one that is often claimed by writers as essentially a literary ambition—to (in the words of both Proust and Leduc) *tout raconter* or *tout dire*, to tell it all. Robert de Montesquiou would write to Proust in 1921 about how pleased he was, seeing the announced title (*Sodom and Gomorrah*) of a forthcoming volume in Proust's *À la recherche du temps perdu*, that Proust had managed, unlike anyone before him, to "s'être fait revêtir d'avance du *sacer esto* qui permet de *tout dire*," to "have himself cloaked ahead of time in the *sacer esto* that allows one to *say everything*."[10] Montesquiou understands it to take careful preparation, preparation of one's social image as a writer, in order to be accepted as a person who has the permission or the authority to enunciate certain statements, to represent certain subjects, and to be taken seriously in doing so.

At the end of the first part of his memoirs, *Si le grain ne meurt* (*If It Die . . .*), Gide comments, "Roger Martin du Gard, to whom I have shown these Memoirs, finds fault with me for never saying enough in them, and for leaving the reader unsatisfied. And yet I have meant all along to say everything. [*Mon intention pourtant a toujours été de tout dire.*] But in making confidences, there is a limit which cannot be overstepped without artifice, without strain; and what I aim at above all is to be natural."[11] Gide (like Proust) understands that it takes not only the work of creating a certain authoritative public image, but also a work of style to be allowed to "say everything." *Tout dire* becomes one of those catchphrases representing a moving target, a target that shifts precisely as the literary field and the social field in which it is embedded evolve. Both stylistically and in terms of content, *tout dire* will remain a literary value, but it will not be the same for Proust as for Gide; it will have changed its meaning for Genet and Leduc, yet again for Duvert, Guyotat, and Wittig, yet again for Duras, Guibert, Angot, and Dustan.

In twentieth-century French literature frequently *tout dire* is closely, we might say generically, linked to the representation of same-sex sexual relations and the people who engage in them.[12] Writers will consistently argue that both the broaching of this subject matter and the stylistic work surrounding it are key parts to a claim to literary value.

When Violette Leduc spoke on the radio in 1949 of composing the sexually explicit scenes between women that she intended for her novel *Ravages*, she said:

> My effort is to describe as exactly as possible, as minutely as possible, the sensations one experiences in physical love. Without a doubt something is found there that every woman can understand. I am not trying to provoke a scandal, but rather simply to describe precisely what a woman experiences in such moments. I hope this will not seem any more scandalous than the reflections of Mrs. Bloom at the end of Joyce's *Ulysses*. Any sincere psychological analysis, it seems to me, deserves a hearing.[13]

Gallimard would in 1954 refuse to publish *Ravages* unless certain passages were removed, demanding the suppression of certain sexually explicit passages as well as parts of a passage representing an abortion. The censure of the sexually explicit passages would be undone by the publisher only in 2000, with the publication of the complete text of what it then titled *Thérèse et Isabelle*.[14] One sees in Leduc's comments from 1949 what we might call, using Pierre Bourdieu's terminology, an appeal to the autonomy of the literary field, an effort to insist that literature itself be the arbiter of its own forms of value.[15] And we might generalize to say that the representation of same-sex sexualities served throughout the twentieth century as a way in which the French literary field continually tested the limits of its autonomy. Yet if the argument would be made many times throughout the century that saying something previously unsayable or representing something previously unrepresentable about sexuality can ground a claim to literary seriousness, another argument can be heard at least as frequently: that representing sexuality in literature in a way that is advertised as transgressive is also the effect of a market for the louche, a kind of selling out of literature to the prurience of its audience.

Consider the case of Pierre Guyotat's *Eden, Eden, Eden* (a book published in 1970 that was placed under various forms of legal interdiction in France until 1981). As the editors of Foucault's *Dits et écrits* point out, the French government was especially rigorous around 1970 in its use of legal means to censure sexually unruly texts. (Laws penalizing sexual acts that were "against nature" had been imposed in France during World War II and would remain in effect until 1982.)[16] In an unsuccessful effort to protect Guyotat's novel from legal sanctions, Michel Leiris, Roland Barthes, and Philippe Sollers would write prefaces for it, and Michel Foucault would publish an open letter in support of the novel in the newsweekly, *Le Nouvel Observateur*. Foucault discussed the affair and the novel in a long interview from December 1970, commenting on what a curious thing it was that

> in France, in order for a certain vocabulary, and turn of phrase, image, or fantasy to be included in a text, such words have to have a literary alibi. . . . No one had yet spoken of what Guyotat describes in his book. Given that in his text the limits of what is expressible in our vocabulary are crossed, we could say precisely that the text is transgressive. Yet at the same time, in our society, literature has become an institution in which transgressions impossible anywhere else become possible. This is why bourgeois society shows itself to be so tolerant of what happens in literature.[17]

Transgression in literature and in literary representations of sexuality has become almost ordinary, expected, Foucault suggests. It often produces the very sense that something *is* literature; and it occasionally (but not for Guyotat as it turns out, at least not in the long term) guarantees a certain marketability. Foucault goes on to draw a contrast between the legal perils of *Madame Bovary* and those of *Eden, Eden, Eden*: it sufficed for Flaubert to portray the mundane daily reality of bourgeois adultery in order to be scandalous and for his book to be put on trial; Guyotat shows sexual acts between men that go beyond "what gay men actually do in Paris." And yet, in 1970, the novel will be sanctioned but not banned outright, whereas during the same period gay men could be sent to prison for having sex.[18]

Here is the broad history Foucault is sketching: "Literature was normative in the seventeenth century, where it claimed for itself a social function. In the nineteenth century it stepped over to the other side. But today it seems to me that literature is returning to its normal social function by way of a certain cheapening of itself or because of the enormous power of assimilation that the bourgeoisie holds" (119). Yet perhaps the history Foucault offers here is a bit too schematic, for the threat (if that's what it is) of the assimilation of "transgressive" sexualities by a literary market is hardly new to the later twentieth century. It was well known in the nineteenth and early twentieth centuries as well. In Montesquiou's 1921 letter to Proust, for instance, the "*sacer esto* that allows one to *say everything*" also, Montesquiou suggests, allows one "to draw *large dividends*." Proust would feel obliged to insist in his reply that "my books earn me nothing."[19] The marketability of Colette's risqué Claudine novels would be another prime example from the early twentieth century: the novels were bestsellers; they were turned into successful stage productions; there were marketing tie-ins such as hats, cigarettes, and perfumes.[20] For some this meant that Colette should not be taken seriously as a literary artist. When, in 1907, Gide heard of Colette appearing on stage at the Moulin Rouge with her cross-dressed lover Missy, he referred to this "scandal" as an "exhibition éhontée," a shameless exhibition.[21] He would prefer at this point in time to imagine her contributions to culture (specifically her way of insisting on a place in public discourse for a consideration of same-sex sexualities) and his own to have nothing in common.

In his postscript to *The Rules of Art*, Bourdieu reminds us that "commercial literature has not just come into existence recently; nor is it new that the necessities of commerce make themselves felt at the heart of the cultural field. But the grip of the holders of power over the instruments of circulation—and of consecration—has undoubtedly never been as wide and as deep as it is today—and the boundary has never been as blurred between the experimental work and the *bestseller*." Bourdieu distinguishes between "autonomous" producers and "heteronomous" ones. He writes, "the heteronomous producer, whom the Italians magnificently call *tuttologo*, is the Trojan horse by means of which all forms of social stranglehold—that of the market, of fashion, of the state, of politics, of journalism—are imported into the field of cultural production" (347). The autonomous producer (the aspiration of a Proust or a Gide) is the one cloaked with sacer esto and whose books often earn nothing. The heteronomous producer (Colette's husband Willy most certainly, and Colette to a greater or lesser extent) specifically endeavors to draw dividends. Yet there are many cases in which the distinction drawn in Bourdieu's paradigm would seem not to apply, or not to explain very much—Colette being a primary example early in the century, and Hervé Guibert and Christine Angot being potential examples from the century's end. (Marguerite Duras is another interesting writer to think about in these terms.) That is to say, under certain circumstances in the twentieth century, the "experimental" or autonomously literary work and the bestseller or the work of the heteronomous producer have been one and the same or, better, it has been the ability to trouble this distinction that has marked the importance of certain works. In works dealing with same-sex sexuality these categories have overlapped to the point that it is the ability to confuse them that often takes on salience, and the principle of categorization in question that sometimes seems thereby to lack pertinence. This may be one of the effects of sexuality's ambiguous place in the literary field. In another passage in *The Rules of Art*, Bourdieu describes the opposition between heteronomous and autonomous producers in slightly different terms that are also helpful for the present analysis. He speaks of "the difference (ordinarily described in terms of *value*) between works that are the pure product of a milieu and a market, and those that must produce their market and may even contribute to transforming their milieu, thanks to the work of emancipation of which they are the product and which is accomplished, in part, through the objectivation of that milieu" (104). Sometimes literary works dealing with sexuality don't respect this difference: they can fall into or arise from a ready-made market and yet perturb people within that market while also acting strongly on the literary field itself.

Now, if the matter of sexuality, and of same-sex sexuality in particular, poses a conundrum regarding the structure of the twentieth-century French literary field, the manner of writing in the first person poses another, and the two come on numerous occasions to be intimately related. That is, the use of the first person interacts with the representation of same-sex sexuality to produce the curious effects of confusion in the literary field that Foucault points to via a vocabulary of transgression and assimilation and that Bourdieu designates with his distinction between the experimental work and the bestseller or heteronomous and autonomous producers. Especially strong in the elite areas of the French literary field at the end of the nineteenth century is the set of practices and beliefs that authorizes and is encapsulated in Wilde's remark to Gide that "in art there is no *first* person." Wilde there gives voice to a literary current that has Flaubert and Mallarmé among its major representatives. (Proust's "You can tell anything on condition that you never say: *I*" shows that he understands himself to belong to this same tradition even if his first-person novelistic practice might initially seem to contradict this.) This is, to turn to another moment in Bourdieu's analysis, the literary current that produced the concept of the "pure gaze," one which "requires a posture of impassivity, indifference and detachment, if not a cynical casualness" (110). Bourdieu associates this gaze with "the very movement of [a] field towards autonomy." He continues:

> The assertion of the autonomy of the principles of production and evaluation of the work of art is inseparable from the assertion of the autonomy of the producer, that is, of the field of production. . . . The evolution of different fields of cultural production towards a greater autonomy is ac-

companied . . . by a sort of reflexive and critical turning back by producers upon their own production, which leads them to distinguish its own principle and its specific assumptions. In so far as it manifests a rupture with external demands and a desire to exclude artists suspected of obeying them [think here of Wilde's cautionary remark to Gide, or Gide's dismissal of Colette], the affirmation of the primacy of form over function, of mode of representation over the object of representation, is the most specific expression of the claim to the autonomy of the field and of its pretension to produce and to impose the principles of a specific legitimacy as much in the order of production as in the order of reception of the work of art. (299–300)

The autonomy of literary art is for many to be found in the refinement of formal literary practices—whatever the subject matter. The refined consumer of art is one capable of appreciating the formal work that is valued by the autonomous literary field itself. The presence of a first person—especially when the author is a woman—has sometimes been suspected as being an indication of a failure of autonomy, or—especially when that first person speaks of sexuality—an indication that the object of representation is taking precedence over the mode of representation, or a sign that a "reflexive and critical turning back by producers upon their own production" is in remission. The "«on» que nous somme tous," to recall the epigraph from Bourdieu, "the 'one' which we all are," is harder to hear—and, it would seem, aesthetically more demanding to produce—than "the 'I' that in our most common claim to uniqueness we believe ourselves to be." The "I," the "je" is, it sometimes seems, the less rigorous formal path.[22]

Yet there is no reason to think that the formal work that someone like Flaubert brought to such a high pitch could not direct its attention to the first person itself. Understanding that there can be formal work done on the first person itself is the clearest way to apprehending how someone like Proust belongs to the ongoing intellectual tradition in novel writing (a tradition in which there is a strong relation between sociological analysis and experiments with form) in which Balzac and Flaubert precede him, just as it is the clearest way of understanding how Beckett fits into that tradition as one of Proust's followers. Beckett's most interesting relation to Proust is not to be found in the essay he dedicated to him but in the work on pronouns, in particular the first person, that he takes over from him and renders ever more explicit. For the work of abstraction on the first person pronoun that is explicit in

Beckett's *L'Innommable* is, as we shall see in a later chapter, palpable already in Proust's *À la recherche du temps perdu*.[23] Certainly it is the work of abstraction done on the first person, an abstraction that takes many forms across the century, that links the really remarkable first person works of twentieth-century French literature to the Flaubertian tradition of pure aesthetics, autonomous literature, and an analytical attention to form as a critical practice.[24]

Of the manifold ways of working in, on, and with the first person in literature (on JE or *je* or "je"),[25] of understanding it in an abstract way, one way (and, while interesting enough, not always the most interesting) is to work fairly strictly within linguistic terms: thinking about the first-person pronoun's function as a shifter. Certainly this is one of Barthes's launching pads in "The Death of the Author" (1968), which resonates, for instance, with contemporary work by linguists such as Oswald Ducrot, who writes in *Dire et ne pas dire* (1972): "What is remarkable about the pronoun *I* is not just that it constitutes a shorthand way of speaking about oneself. It is more that it obliges the person speaking to refer to herself with the same word that her interlocutor will use in turn for the same task. The use of *I* (and much the same could be said of *you*) thus constitutes an apprenticeship in and a constant practice of reciprocity" (3). Ducrot notes that what he designates reciprocity is a version of the intersubjectivity to which Benveniste refers at the end of his classic essay on "Subjectivity in Language," where he writes that it is "the condition of intersubjectivity which alone makes linguistic communication possible."[26] Barthes clearly has Benveniste in mind as well. Consider Benveniste's equally famous essay on "The Nature of Pronouns," where he writes that "these 'pronominal' forms do not refer to 'reality' or to 'objective' positions in space or time but to the utterance, unique each time, that contains them. . . . *I* . . . can be assumed by each speaker on the condition that he refers each time only to the instance of his own discourse."[27] This particular form of abstraction of the first person can be found regularly in Barthes's writing as in certain other literary work. Along with "The Death of the Author," the sections from *Roland Barthes by Roland Barthes* titled "Le Shifter comme utopie" ("The Shifter as Utopia") and "Moi, je" ("Myself, I") would be pertinent examples.[28] In a related vein, Tony Duvert indicates how novelists might think of the first person as even more appropriate than the third person for abstract work. Duvert notes that Pinget's novel *Le Libera* shows to what an extent "the first person, if we refuse it any introspective or autobiographical implications, can efface, much more successfully than a 'he' (which always presupposes someone who is enunciating it) any human reference within a fiction, any presence that would preexist the novel. . . . The 'I' becomes the person of indetermination, of stubborn silence [*mutisme*], of absence."[29]

Yet there are aspects of an apprenticeship—never ending, and full of missteps—in the first person that are less purely linguistic, that are more clearly linked to the social and sociosexual forms of contestation that are part of pronoun usage, and they also prove to be a rich vein to be mined in the tradition of writing I will be investigating here. One well-known account of this apprenticeship focusing on the childhood acquisition of pronouns comes in Roman Jakobson's essay "Shifters and Verbal Categories," where we learn:

> Pronouns belong to the late acquisitions in child language and to the early losses in aphasia. If we observe that even linguistic scientists had difficulties in defining the general meaning of the term *I* (or *you*), which signifies the same intermittent function of different subjects, it is quite obvious that the child who has learned to identify himself with his proper name will not easily become accustomed to such alienable terms as the personal pronouns: he may be afraid of speaking of himself in the first person while being called *you* by his interlocutors. Sometimes he attempts to redistribute these appellations. For instance, he tries to monopolize the first person pronoun: "Don't dare call yourself I. Only I am I, and you are only you." Or he uses indiscriminately either *I* or *you* both for the addresser and the addressee so that this pronoun means any participant of the given dialogue. Or finally *I* is so rigorously substituted by the child for his proper name that he readily names any person of his surroundings but stubbornly refuses to utter his own name: the name has for its little bearer only a vocative meaning, opposed to the nominative function of *I*. This attitude may persevere as an infantile survival. Thus Guy de Maupassant confessed that his name sounded quite strange to him when pronounced by himself. The refusal to utter one's own name may become a social custom. (389)

Jakobson's linking of acquisition to aphasia reminds us that our control of pronouns is always in danger of slipping, and that it is taken as a sign of *social* inadequacy when the slip reveals itself. Michel Butor provides us with a related example of the continual missteps that dog our ways of employing or understanding the first person: "Each one of us has found ourselves speaking to a child, an infant, even an animal, using the first person to refer to it: 'So, have we been behaving ourselves this morning?' " [Chacun d'entre nous s'est surpris sans doute à parler à un enfant, un bébé, un animal même, en employant pour le désigner la première personne: «Eh bien, est-ce que j'ai été sage ce matin?»].[30]

Along with the limit cases for the first person that are infants and animals, and their ongoing tendency to produce distortions in the pronominal usage of even well-trained speakers, we might think of both literature and sexuality as arenas in which pronominal usage requires special attention. Trained readers of literature often forget how much training they have had in order to understand (and to accept as natural, or as literature) pronominal usage they would probably never speak.[31] Perhaps more to the point here, most trained readers of literature have learned it is incorrect to assume an author and a first-person narrator can be thought of as the same entity. For, as Erving Goffman succinctly points out (in a different context) in *Frame Analysis*, "authoring a remark and making it are quite different matters."[32] Every *je* in a first-person novel is, in fact, a JE, or maybe a "je." Even so, trained readers seem to enjoy (in private, in classes, and in books and articles) making this mistake, taking a JE or a "je" for a *je* (especially, for instance, when reading Proust or Colette), and other trained readers feel obliged or entitled to try, and perhaps succeed, in making them feel foolish about their mistake.[33]

Shame or embarrassment are often the signs of social hierarchies being reproduced or enforced. It is not sophisticated to confuse authors and their narrators, even when they set out to confuse you. (Consider Proust: "Then she would find her tongue and say: 'My—' or 'My darling—' followed by my Christian name, which, if we give the narrator the same name as the author of this book, would be 'My Marcel,' or 'My darling Marcel.' ")[34] Learning to speak sophisticatedly about pronouns in literature is a small part of what Aaron Cicourel calls, in the title of one of his essays, "The Acquisition of Social Structure."

To work abstractly on the first person in a literary text can mean to think critically about what we might call the social assumption or enactment of a first person. When it comes to a literary representation of same-sex sexualities, this kind of work becomes especially salient. Verbal interactions concerning sexuality outside of literature are certainly often charged situations for testing the adequacy of one's acquisition of both social structure and pronominal usage. As Cicourel says: "When a speaker commits himself to linguistic and social categories, he provides the hearer, himself, and an observer or researcher with information about what he intends. The commitment, however, may be a compromise between what the speaker felt had to be said, what he did not want to say, what he was incapable of saying because of limited vocabulary, intelligence, or the constraints of speaking with a stranger."[35] A sense of acceptable pronominal usage, and specifically, a nuanced sense of the kinds of referentiality that pronouns enact in different contexts, are important factors in deciding what can be said, and when, regarding one's own or someone else's sexuality—and without embarrassment. Here again, some remarks by Goffman can be helpful:

> Although certainly the pronoun, "I," refers to the speaker, and although certainly the speaker is a specific biographical entity, that does not mean that the whole of this entity in all of its facets is to be included on each occasion of its being cited. For he who is a speaker might be considered a whole set of somewhat different things, bound together in part because of our cultural beliefs about identity. Thus, the referent "I" in the statements: "I feel a chill," "I will take responsibility," and "I was born on a Tuesday" shifts, although in no easily describable way.[36]

In the final sentence of this passage, Goffman distinguishes helpfully between the referent of the first-person pronoun in statements of sensation, statements of responsibility, and statements of fact about oneself. Such statements involve sufficiently different aspects of a same speaker that it could be argued (and Goffman points out that Wittgenstein in fact has made this argument) that the referent of the pronoun—even though it is the "same" pronoun—is not the same.[37] But we could also take Goffman's observation about our "cultural beliefs about identity" in another direction. For such patterns of belief, and the practices that arise from them, shape discourse on sexuality. In what circumstances do we think of or do we end up referring to this or that aspect of "our" sexuality—or of someone else's—with this or that pronoun? In what circumstances do we *not* think of doing so? Apprenticeships in the hierarchies of the social order, in sexuality, and in the use of the first person are often not separable from each other. Proust, in his *Recherche*, for instance, works carefully and extensively on this topic. His novel thereby uses literary form to offer a *sociological* abstraction of the functioning of the first person.

At the end of *The Weight of the World*, Pierre Bourdieu notes, regarding fieldwork in sociology, that "constant control over one's point of view is never as necessary, nor so difficult, as when the social distance that has to be surmounted is only minimal" (625n19). Now the social distance between Proust and the narrator of his novel may be quite small, and yet all the more significant because of its smallness.[38] Indeed, it is perhaps the very smallness of that distance that encouraged so much work within Proust's novel on the functioning of the first person. Bourdieu notes of sociologists (but we might think the same applies to novelists such as Proust) that they

> cannot be unaware that the specific characteristic of their point of view is to be a point of view on a point of view. They can re-produce the point of view of their object and constitute it as such by resituating it within social space. . . . It is solely to the extent that they can objectify themselves that they are able, even as they remain in the place inexorably assigned to each of us in the social world, to imagine themselves in the place occupied by their objects (who are, at least to a certain degree, an alter ego) and thus to take their point of view, that is, to understand that if they were in their shoes they would doubtless be and think just like them.[39]

Both sociological and novelistic experience might then involve a critical experimentation with both appropriation and disappropriation in relation to the first person.

Two more introductory observations about the first person. First of all (as a way of summing up much of what has been said so far), it is a figure. "As speaker," Goffman reminds us, "we represent ourselves through the offices of a personal pronoun, typically 'I,' and it is thus a *figure*—a figure in a statement—that serves as the agent, a protagonist in a *described* scene, a 'character' in an anecdote, someone, after all, who belongs to the world that is spoken about."[40] That figure, that "I," we hope, successfully and intelligibly enacts social relations, keeps face, lays claims, achieves recognition. This is how language functions when it functions well. To understand the use of "I" as always figural is to insist on the pragmatics of pronoun usage. This is a manner of abstraction with which literary texts often work, as we will see regularly in the chapters ahead.

Finally, to get at the abstracting work on the first person in many literary texts, we need to be able to talk in some detail about the links between a given first person (its particular figuration) and the acts of explicit or implicit social enforcement (say, acts of nomination or categorization) it feels authorized to undertake. We need to be able to think pragmatically about the links between a first person in discourse and the social structures that are enacted or brought to bear in the enunciations in which that first person figures. In his essay "Metapragmatic Discourse and Metapragmatic Function," Michael Silverstein notes that "using language in a socioculturally understandable way is, in a sense, the very medium, sometimes the exclusive medium, of what are called enactable social relations among people in groups and societies" (34). Enactable social relations exist culturally prior to any given interaction. Thus the insistence, in pragmatic approaches to understanding linguistic interactions, that a given utterance necessarily takes some of its sense from the larger social universe in which it occurs. Charles Peirce described a version of this idea in his 1907 essay "Pragmatism" when he referred to cases in which "the whole burden of the sign must be ascertained, not by closer examination of the utterance, but by collateral observation of the utterer" (406), or by investigation of the shared understandings that exist in context and to which implicit reference is being made, by investigation of what Bourdieu would call the "pressure of the socially qualified objective situation."[41] It is, of course, not only philosophers, sociologists, and linguistic anthropologists who show us the contextual difficulties in the enactment of a first person in a socially charged situation. That has been the work of literature as well.

At the end of his essay "Indexical Order and the Dialectics of Sociolinguistic Life," Silverstein comments that "language use lives at once in both a micro-sociological and a macro-sociological order which it 'articulates' through us" (293). What will be of most interest in the pages immediately ahead is the understanding we can gain regarding the articulation between one's *personal* understanding of how people are organized into sexual classes, and the larger, official, *macrosociological* understanding of that same question of classification. Silverstein's work is extremely helpful in establishing how what he refers to as *nonreferential indexicality*, a phenomenon closely related to Peirce's "collateral observation," is the main process by which one's own speech and understanding interact dynamically with the macrosociological context.

Indexicality, of course, is the linguistic term to refer to the functioning of parts of speech that often have little or no semantic content of their own, but that serve to point to something within a particular speech context. Deictics are the usual examples of indexes: *this, that, I, you, now, yesterday,* the parts of verbs that indicate tense, and so on. Deictics don't mean much semantically. They are "constituted by a connection between sign and object in the context of speech" and "contribute to the referential content of discourse."[42] Thus deictics can be called referential indexes. They refer within their context in order to perform their function. But there is another kind of indexicality that points not so much to anything in the present referential context as to something in the larger social context. An example would be the choice, in French, of *tu* or *vous*, as Elizabeth Mertz notes: "A switch from *tu* to *vous* in addressing the same person does not signal a change in referent (person referred to); the semantic content of the utterance actually remains identical (*you*—single addressee). What changes is information about the social context."[43] A favorite and slightly more complex example of nonreferential indexicality among scholars working on the topic is taken from the Dyirbal language from Northern Queensland:

> There is an "everyday" set of lexical items, and a "mother-in-law" set, which had to be used by a speaker only in the presence of his classificatory mother-in-law or equivalent affine. In other words, the mother-in-law vocabulary, totally distinct from the everyday one, indexes the specified affinal relation between speaker (*x*) and some "audience"—not the socially defined addressee (*y*)—in the speech situation. . . . It is interesting that the grammatical structure in the traditional sense remains exactly the same in these two kinds of situations. What changes is the entire set of nongrammatical lexical items.[44]

Thus the use of a particular set of lexical items points to the presence within hearing range of a particular person of a particular social relation to the speaker. Silverstein refers to such kinds of indexicality as "functionally independent of reference as such." Yet these are the "indexical modes that link speech to the wider system of social life."[45]

In general, we might posit that in a moment when it is difficult to say something, a moment in which it is difficult among all the available manners of speech to find the one manner that suits a particular context, that very difficulty is an index (a nonreferential one) of some larger social contention. That is, the choice one makes of the way of saying something will point in a nonreferential way to some implicit assertion being made by the speaker regarding an understanding of the social universe and an understanding of the relative positions of the people present in the speech situation within that social universe. (Consider the relative unintelligibility or the relatively undecidable affective or pragmatic import of the following statements in the absence of collateral observation: "I'm a fag," "He's a fag," "He's gay," "What a fairy!" "I'm a lesbian," "She's gay," "I'm a dyke," "How butch!" "They are homosexual," "That's queer," "That's gay," "She's a trannie," and so on.) As Silverstein puts it, defining his interest in a study of the *pragmatics* of language use: "'appropriate' linguistic forms occur as indexes of (pointers to) the particularities of an intersubjective communicative context and . . . 'effective' linguistic forms occur as indexes of (pointers to) intersubjective consequences of communication. . . . Pragmatics includes the notion of how systematic variations in 'saying the same thing' in discourse constitute *social identity markers* of participants in the communicative act."[46] Thus examining the pragmatics of nonreferential indexes is one way of understanding the ritual function of face-to-face linguistic interactions in producing and sustaining the social identities of the participants. And as Silverstein observes, "Ritualized contexts of indexical licensing or authorization are themselves always potentially shifting in a social system, historical change or at least dialectical dynamism being inherent in the way semiosis seems to operate."[47] An apprenticeship in the first person is an apprenticeship in acts of self-authorization or in the assumption of a social identity. It seems evident that across the twentieth century access to self-authorization in statements regarding same-sex sexuality would constitute a complicated arena in which to examine the "intersubjective consequences of communication," in particular to watch the consequences for the sustainability of a first person that tries *effectively* or *appropriately* to say something about same-sex sexualities.

"A genre is a way of speaking," Anne Freadman and Amanda Macdonald tell us. "It organizes the relative position of the interlocutors, what they do for one another, possible uptakes and consequences."[48] What I am calling the work of abstraction on the first person in relation to sexuality might sometimes be thought of as a recourse to that particular genre which consists in calling attention to the work of genre in regulating social life, a genre that strives to index the workings of indexicality that stabilize or shake up a social field. We might also think that abstracting work on the first person in relation to sexuality is sometimes the work of generic innovation, forcing new genres into existence by reworking old ones, calling attention to their limits. In *Untimely Interventions*, Ross Chambers notes that "what makes language *feel* adequate to its users is generic appropriateness, and conversely I've argued that a situation in which generic catachresis becomes necessary generates in witnessing subjects the sense that language is inadequate to their purposes" (32). The writers I am treating here are often involved in the generic work necessary to overcoming an experience of language's inadequacy.

When certain literary creators figured themselves, or figured a first person, in certain statements regarding same-sex sexual relations they participated in semiosis in ways that were socially and politically very pointed. They necessarily called attention not only to the new things they were trying to enunciate, but also to the social implications and the formal characteristics of their enunciation. Chambers refers to this as the work of figuration or, borrowing from Gilles Deleuze and Félix Guattari, *agencing*:

> The interpretation of an utterance includes the utterance's object—the context in which the event of the utterance becomes meaningful—as well as its subject (say, the psychology and/or motivation of the utterer). Agencing, in those terms, could be described, then, as the means whereby readerly (interpretive) attention is diverted both from the subject of the statement and from the subject of the utterance (i.e., from the author), so as to focus instead on the *object* of the *utterance*, what the event of the discourse's utterance is "all about"—something that can best be only surmised. (37)

The authors studied in the following pages performed a work of abstraction on the relation between first-person utterances and same-sex sexualities for practical reasons: in order to find the means to say new things, to produce semiotic dynamism within their social world. In so doing they called (sometimes implicitly, sometimes explicitly) for interpretive attention to be paid to the work of abstraction itself, to the very forms and devices in which and through which the struggle for semiotic dynamism occurs.

The first two of the six chapters that follow develop by way of specific examples some of the theoretical material presented here. Chapter 1 looks at some representations from Gide's *Journal* of verbal interactions between literary figures in which same-sex sexuality is a topic. It takes seriously the claim that a pragmatics of word choice is a crucial element in the figuration of an authoritative first person. Another goal of the first two chapters is to begin to weave a web of relations in which Gide, Proust, and Colette can be seen as mutually implicated. Into that web I will also weave a number of "lesser" literary figures, among them Paul Bourget, Catulle Mendès, Jean Lorrain, Rachilde, Liane de Pougy, and Lucie Delarue-Mardrus.[49] The particular set of literary relations I propose here offers as highly significant some forms of association that are perhaps less commonly dealt with in literary criticism than they might be. Consider the case of Colette. In a contribution to *A New History of French Literature* (the 1989 volume edited by Denis Hollier) titled "1929: 'Odor di Femina' [Sic]," Elaine Marks discusses a book by Jean Larnac from 1929, *Histoire de la littérature féminine en France*, a chapter of which was devoted to Colette. Marks notes that Larnac assumes women to be fundamentally different from men, and therefore, he asserted, so is their writing. Paradoxically, some of Larnac's separatist approach to literary traditions is replicated in *A New History* in 1989. Marks's is the only substantive mention of Colette in the volume; Colette is thus primarily situated not in any relation to her contemporary literary field, but rather in a tradition of women's writing. Marks notes: "It seems reasonable to conclude that in 1929, while Larnac was making order in what he believed to be *the* official tradition of female writers in France, Colette was actively, if unconsciously, disrupting the b(i)ases of that tradition" (891).

Traditions are tricky constructions, tricky habits of thought. There is certainly much to be learned by reading Colette within a tradition of French women's writing. Has it become too much of a received habit of mind to imagine that her writing practice existed primarily in relation to other women's writing? Or, conversely, when writing about other traditions of literary writing or other literary movements extant in her moment (say, that baggy monster some call "modernism"—a habit of categorization at least as likely to be unhelpful to critical thought as enabling of it) to imagine one needn't think of her? I will be working to imagine Colette, Gide, Proust, and others as mutually responsive to each other's writings, reputations, and careers without much concern to place them within more commonly evoked structures of literary affiliation that often serve to obscure truly interesting forms of relation.

Different literary traditions traverse the same literary field at any given literary moment. Individual writers, imagining themselves as belonging to particular traditions (or imagined by later critics to belong there), use traditions as a way of establishing an identity and a status, a way of establishing distinctions between themselves and their contemporaries. Efforts to perpetuate traditions in a given moment will show the traces of these diacritical impulses, these battles for distinction, among contemporaries.

The classic description of a literary field is, of course, Pierre Bourdieu's "Le Champ littéraire," an article whose insights were developed in *The Rules of Art*. I make no attempt in the present study to reconstruct a given state of an entire literary field. My interest is more specifically in what Bourdieu calls "position-taking"—diacritical efforts of given writers—around the question of the literary representation of same-sex sexualities. "The space of works always appears as a field of position-takings," Bourdieu writes in *The Rules of Art*, "which can only be understood in terms of relationships, as a system of differential variations" (205).

Thus chapter 2 will hold Gide, Colette, and Proust within the same thought and show how looking at them together with other contemporaries can reveal certain kinds of position-taking that were going on. I use the question of linguistic register (different ways of saying the same thing) as an avenue of approach to their position-taking efforts in regards to same-sex sexualities. This means I will be discussing works by Gide, Colette, and Proust alongside works of authors of unquestionably lesser quality or lesser status who also dealt with same-sex sexualities in their work. It is important to acknowledge differences in status or quality (as Gide himself felt compelled to do, publishing a denunciation of Catulle Mendès's work in the *Nouvelle Revue Française* very shortly after Mendès's death in 1909). But it is also important to note that writers of different status or quality are part of the same literary field and that they affect each other's strategies for literary production. They write works of different stature, but they are also fighting over stature. I don't know if there is much point in approaching a sloppy novel by Mendès or Lorrain as if it could or should be read with precisely the same techniques one would use to approach a crafted literary production by Proust or Gide or Colette. (Which isn't to say that sloppy novels should be read sloppily. They can and often need to be read with care, but there are many kinds of care.) Forms of critical attention need to adjust themselves to the object to which attention is being paid. Yet it is also worth noting that it is by convincing different critics to read his work differently (indeed, by convincing different critics to read his work) that someone like Gide establishes his difference from someone like Mendès. And there is no doubt that people like Gide, Proust, and Colette were conscious, when they came to those acts of literary position-taking that involved writing about same-sex sexuality, that they existed in some kind of relation (even if they preferred it to be a purely negative relation) both to the figures of and to the works by people like Rachilde or Mendès or Lorrain.

While chapters 1 and 2 develop techniques of reading that allow me to explore relations between Proust, Gide, and Colette, and between them and their contemporaries in relation to the representation of same-sex sexualities and speech about those sexualities, chapters 3 and 4 are more closely focused case studies. Chapter 3 considers Colette's position-taking in the years 1907–9, paying attention in particular to the relations between some of her stage appearances, her journalistic

writing, and her volume titled *Les Vrilles de la vigne*. In chapter 4 I turn
to Gide's own position-taking in the early 1920s, his way of refiguring
posterity for himself and his manner of presenting his own person in his
attempts to justify the publication of a number of "explicit" texts, such
as *Si le grain ne meurt* and *Corydon*.

Chapters 5 and 6 are devoted more exclusively to investigating the
first-person work within one novel, Proust's *À la recherche du temps
perdu*. What, in particular, are its techniques for constructing and purveying a context for queer speech, content for that speech, the value of
that speech, and speaking positions in regards to it? Proust's novel includes a careful, abstract study of impersonation, understood in a strong
sense to designate the ongoing act, the ongoing practice, of assuming
one's first person. The novel also includes a social history of evolving
contexts for and forms of queer speech. (Proust's textual relations with
previous writings by Balzac and Wilde are important in this regard.)
Those two projects, of studying queer impersonation and of investigating the social history of discourses on same-sex sexuality, are, of course,
interwoven. Deleuze and Guattari suggest in *A Thousand Plateaus* that
"there is only individuation of the utterance, there is only subjectivation of the utterance to the extent that the impersonal and collective
assemblage (arrangement) demands and determines it."[50] They are aiming here to get a handle on the abstract function "that connects a
language to the semantic and pragmatic contents of statements, to collective assemblages of enunciation, to a whole micropolitics of the
social field" (7), and their development of the term *agencement collectif
d'énonciation* (a collective arranging or assembling of utterances or
enunciation) is part of that pragmatic project. A book is, for Deleuze
and Guattari, one such *agencement*, a space of crossings in which various
kinds of collective agencies emerge into discourse, in which various
kinds of discursive assemblages sometimes produce new places from
which to speak about new things, in which "those people who are in us
and who make us speak" (as Deleuze puts it elsewhere) find their
expression by producing new kinds of speech.[51] But an *agencement* is not
just a given product of a signifying practice, a specific token of speech,
or a particular novel. It is the speech produced in interrelation with the
social configuration that allows that speech to be produced, to be
meaningful, and to be effective. Thus, "the social character of an utterance is intrinsically founded only if one succeeds in demonstrating how
that utterance in and of itself points to [indexes, one might say] *collectively produced arrangements*" [le caractère social de l'énonciation n'est

intrinsèquement fondé que si l'on arrive à montrer comment l'énonciation renvoie par elle-même à des *agencements collectifs*]. Silverstein titled one of his articles "Indexical Order and the Dialectics of Sociolinguistic Life." Deleuze and Guattari, like Proust, like the pages that follow, share an interest in that topic, an interest in the social character and function of utterances about same-sex sexuality (the work they do on the social order, the work the social order does on them, the indexical relations that are the signs and the instruments of this work), and specifically, an interest in what it means, or what it does, to put such utterances in the first person.

one

Gide, Bourget, and Proust Talking

> The learning of exemplars is part of the process of constituting a community.—MARY DOUGLAS, "Rightness of Categories"

> Identification rests upon organization into entities and kinds. The response to the question "Same or not the same?" must always be "Same what?" Different soandsos may be the same such-and-such: what we point to or indicate, verbally or otherwise, may be different events but the same object, different towns but the same state, different members but the same club or different clubs but the same members, different innings but the same ball game.—NELSON GOODMAN, *Ways of Worldmaking*

In his essay "Social Space and the Genesis of 'Classes,'" Pierre Bourdieu writes of what he refers to as "the power of naming," a power one strives for in "the symbolic struggle for the production of common sense or, more precisely, for the monopoly of legitimate *naming* as the official—i.e. explicit and public—imposition of the legitimate vision of the social world." In this struggle, Bourdieu tells us, "agents bring into play the symbolic capital that they have acquired in previous struggles, in particular all the power that they possess over the instituted taxonomies, those inscribed in people's minds or in the objective world, such as qualifications [*titres*]."[1] In France (as elsewhere), the period from roughly the 1870s to the 1940s can be seen as a reasonably fierce episode in the ongoing social and taxonomic struggle over the modalities of reference that would be permissible as regards same-sex sexualities. How these sexualities could be named and perceived was at stake, as was how the sexualities would be conceptualized—by means of what categories and social divisions. That everybody one might today identify as belonging to the category of "homosexual" would end up in the same category was not a foregone conclusion, and many of the people remembered as major participants in bringing into being a discourse on homosexuality did not themselves understand that category in the way it is frequently understood today. Indeed, many of them had no interest in the establishment of the category with which we now work. I propose here to look at some of the evidence of this social struggle of denomination, which is also a struggle for access to self-expression and self-representation, by way of an examination of two episodes described in André Gide's *Journal*, one from 1915 and the other from 1921.

The people we will encounter in these episodes occupy a kind of middle ground regarding social acts of denomination. In "Social Space and the Genesis of 'Classes,'" Bourdieu mentions first of all, "the world of particular perspectives, of individual agents who, on the basis of their particular point of view, their particular position, produce namings—of themselves and others—that are particular and self-interested (nicknames, insults, or even accusations, indictments, slanders, etc.), and all the more powerless to gain recognition, and thus to exert a truly symbolic effect, the less their authors are *authorized*, either personally . . . or institutionally . . . and the more directly they are concerned to gain recognition for the point of view that they are seeking to impose" (239). The three particular individuals we will mainly be considering here, André Gide, Paul Bourget, and Marcel Proust, captured in two scenes of private conversation, each represent varied sets of interest, and varying degrees of authority. The scenes we will be considering are not ones in which they try to exercise any kind of symbolic authority on a macrosocial level, but this does not mean we will not be able to extract from these scenes information about the large social processes that form the context for their exchanges.

To "the world of particular perspectives" Bourdieu opposes "the authorized point of view of an agent who is personally authorized, such as a great critic or a prestigious preface-writer or established author (Zola's *'J'accuse'*), and above all the legitimate point of view of the authorized spokesperson, the delegate of the state" (239). In certain other contexts, Bourget (1852–1935), around the moment of his conversation with Gide in 1915, might justifiably have laid claim to some kind of title to authority. He had been elected to the Académie Française in 1894, and was well known for novels that invariably set out to diagnose the moral perils and perversions of the modern world and to advocate for the salutary influence of religious faith. He would be instrumental in launching the careers of writers such as Maurice Barrès and François Mauriac and would count among his admirers writers such as Francis Carco, a minor literary figure who holds a significant place in the French tradition of writing about same-sex sexualities. In 1915 Proust could not quite yet be thought to possess any convincing claim to enduring literary authority; Gide was further along the path to becoming a celebrated author but would solidly achieve that status only in the 1920s. Yet both authors were in the process of writing works meant to produce a recognizable claim to authority, in particular via their representations and discussions of same-sex sexuality. One of the interesting aspects of the two private scenes I want to examine here, then, is that they bring together writers fully engaged elsewhere in the struggle to gain or to maintain literary authority as a way of speaking to social issues, and in both of these private scenes there is a palpable sense of the struggle to maintain a sense of self, a sense of "face" that might guarantee or sustain that ascription of authority. It is the pragmatic uses being made by Gide, Proust, and Bourget of the ritual context of face-to-face interaction, in particular in regards to social identity markers tied to sexuality, that I propose to consider here.

Gide, Bourget, and Wharton

André Gide describes his conversation with Paul Bourget in his journal entry for November 26, 1915. He is spending a few days touring together with the American novelist Edith Wharton in the south of France, taking a break from the work they were both doing for the Foyer Franco-Belge during World War I. Wharton had met Bourget in 1893 when he was visiting the United States and had kept up a friendship with him ever since. It is she who takes Gide to see the older novelist. Gide writes:

> I have made the acquaintance of Paul Bourget. He received me most cordially at Costebelle, at his estate named Le Plantier, to which Mrs. Wharton had taken me. He felt a great need to captivate someone he knows to represent another generation, another side of the fence, another point of view. The introduction took place in the garden. (2:110)

> [J'ai fait la connaissance de Paul Bourget. Il m'a reçu avec la plus grande amabilité à Costebelle, dans sa propriété du Plantier, où m'introduit Mrs. Whar-

ton. Grand besoin de séduire celui qu'il sait d'une autre génération, d'un autre camp, d'un autre bord. C'est dans le jardin qu'eut lieu la présentation. (907)]

Bourget has an agenda for this meeting with the younger writer. (Gide is 46, Bourget 63; Gide has recently published *The Vatican Cellars* (*Les Caves du Vatican*—also titled *Lafcadio's Adventures* in translation), his latest hesitant step toward the writing with the explicit reference to homosexuality that will characterize his publications in the 1920s: *The Counterfeiters*, *If It Die . . .* , *Corydon*.) Bourget wants to question Gide about Gide's book from 1902, *The Immoralist*. That book, along with his 1897 volume, *The Fruits of the Earth*, referred to same-sex sexual relations in ways that seemed direct to some and indirect to others.[2]

Of the people who considered *The Immoralist* to be a text explicitly about same-sex inclinations, one was Rachilde in the review of the book she published in the *Mercure de France* in July 1902. She did not take the protagonist of *The Immoralist*, Michel, to be essentially drawn to same-sex relations: "He sets snares in the woods of Sodom. But he is only a poacher, and only dares follow the cruel Eros who is a hunter of males at night."[3] Rachilde here refers to the scenes in the novel in which Michel, fascinated by the masculine beauty of one of the workers on his country estate, prowls the estate with him in the dark, poaching off of his own lands. In general, Rachilde's opinion of Gide's book seems to have been that it is not entirely successful precisely because Gide avoids taking on same-sex erotic tendencies directly, the way other writers of the time (say Georges Eekhoud) were doing. He hedges his bets by portraying Michel as a "pseudo-poitrinaire," someone who may or may not truly have tuberculosis. Rachilde suggests that people afflicted with tuberculosis are well known for giving way to any and all forms of carnal excess. Michel is thus, in her eyes, an exceptional case of same-sex tendencies and not a typical one. As she puts it:

> Written with the charming scruple that it is dealing with a clinical case and not the real sources of desire, the book sheds no light on the normal *immoralism* of man. For a doctor, what we will refer to as a "uranist" is someone who is sick. For a poet of as much delicacy as the creator of Michel, such a person is, well, a convalescent. There is a difference, and we are obliged to be content with what we get, hoping for the day when fine poets will be cured of their dilettantism, which itself is a bit abnormal.
>
> [Écrit avec le joli scruple de traiter un cas de clinique et non pas les sources même du désir, il n'éclaire pas l'*immoralisme* normal de l'homme. Pour un

médecin un . . . uraniste est un malade. Pour un poète aussi délicat que le créateur de Michel, c'est un . . . convalescent . . . Il y a une nuance et nous devons nous en contenter, en espérant mieux le jour où les bons poètes se guériront de leur toujours trop anormal dilettantisme. (184, ellipses in original)]

The wickedness of Rachilde's gesture here is to suggest that Gide's abnormal dilettantism, from which he needs to be cured in order to become a truly interesting writer, is part of what identifies him as afflicted by the very condition (uranism) that doctors consider to be an illness. Rachilde's own opinion whether or not that condition is best thought of as an illness remains dilettantishly vague.

It is almost impossible to imagine that Bourget had not read Rachilde's 1902 review of *The Immoralist*. It appeared in the column in the *Mercure de France* in which she regularly reviewed a group of novels, the first two or three getting extensive commentary, the last five or six a sentence or two. To *The Immoralist* she granted the honor of being the first book reviewed in the July 1902 column. The book that was reviewed second, and quite unfavorably, was Bourget's *L'Etape* (The Phase of Development), a "social" novel that conjoined, as was usual for Bourget, a hostility toward democracy and social mobility with an expression of the admirable forms of stability to be found in a return to the Catholic faith. Rachilde called it both "a well constructed book" and "a book of bad faith due to excessive craft" (184).

Of the many kinds of "social problems" that were of interest to Bourget were those presented by nonnormative sexualities. The durable curiosity Bourget shows for Gide's 1902 novel when they meet in 1915 is evidence enough of this. But it is a subject to which Bourget turns only, as Gide puts it, "after Mrs. Wharton had left us for a moment to go and see Mme Bourget, who was kept in her room by a slight indisposition" [après que Mrs. Wharton nous eut laissés quelques instants pour aller voir Mme Bourget qu'une indisposition retenait dans sa chambre]:

"Now that we are alone, tell me, Monsieur Gide, whether or not your immoralist is a pederast."

And, as I seem somewhat stunned, he reinforces his question:

"I mean: a practicing pederast?"

"He is probably more likely an unconscious homosexual," I replied as if I hardly knew myself; and I added: "I believe there are many such."

At first I thought that he had taken this way of showing me that he had read my book; but he especially wanted to develop his theories:

"There are," he began, "two classes of perversion: those that fall under the head of sadism and those that belong to masochism. To achieve sexual pleasure both the sadist and the masochist turn to cruelty; but one, and so on . . . while the other," and so on . . .

"Do you class homosexuals under one or the other of these perversions?" I asked just to have something to say.

"Of course," he replied, "for, as Régis points out . . ."

But at this moment Mrs. Wharton returned and I never learned whether, according to him, the homosexual fell under the head of sadism or of masochism. I was sorry that he turned the conversation into another channel; it would have amused me to have Mrs. Wharton's opinion, if indeed she might have had one. (2:110–11)

[«Maintenant que nous voici seuls, apprenez-moi, monsieur Gide, si votre Immoraliste est ou n'est pas un pédéraste?»

Et, comme je reste un peu interloqué, il insiste:

«Je veux dire: un pédéraste pratiquant?

—C'est sans doute plutôt un homosexuel qui s'ignore», répondis-je, comme si je n'en savais guère trop rien moi-même; et j'ajoutai: «je crois qu'ils sont nombreux.»

Je pensais d'abord qu'il voulait ainsi me montrer qu'il avait lu mon livre; mais il tenait surtout à m'exposer ses théories:

«Il y a, commença-t-il, deux catégories de perversions: celles qui ressortissent au sadisme, et celles qui se rattachent au masochisme. Le sadique et le masochiste, pour atteindre la volupté, ont recours l'un et l'autre à la cruauté; mais l'un, etc. tandis que l'autre, etc.

—Rangez-vous les homosexuels parmi les dépravés de l'un des deux genres? demandai-je pour dire quelque chose.

—Nécessairement, reprit-il; car, ainsi que le fait observer Régis . . .»

Mais, à ce moment, Mrs. Wharton rentra et je ne pus connaître, si selon lui, l'homosexuel se rattachait au masochisme ou au sadisme. Je regrettai qu'il détournât alors la conversation; il m'eût amusé de connaître l'avis de Mrs. Wharton, si tant est qu'elle en eût un. (907–8)]

The scene and its description are rich in material for analysis. I would like to turn in a moment to the ritual aspects of the scene and to the way it both indexes and instantiates larger forms of social contention related to the representation of same-sex sexualities, but before doing so, there are two different but related questions I wish to address, that of synonymy and that of practicing.

Of course, to wonder if someone is a "practicing pederast" is to link pederasty metaphorically to religion (as in the phrase "practicing Catholic"). I suppose that link opens up the possibility one might be a "lapsed homosexual,"[4] but the more common opposition that Gide invokes here is that of a "latent" one, a pederast not practicing because the desire remains suppressed. The other interesting category opened up by the notion of a nonpracticing pederast is that of the practicing nonpederast—the person who engages in pederasty without "being" one. We should probably assume that a good number of Gide's sexual partners throughout his life belonged to this category—one that it is hard to articulate and perhaps especially hard to speak from. When Gide, in a passage we will look at shortly, says that he never imagined Proust to be "so exclusively" a uranist, he also designates a slippery categorical space, one that can be discerned in writings throughout the century and that explains, for instance, why certain characters in Proust's novel (Morel, Saint-Loup) prove so frustratingly difficult to contain within the most readily available sexual-identity categories of today. Under certain circumstances, one can belong to a category without following the practices that characterize it exclusively (or at all), just as under other circumstances one can follow its practices without belonging to it. About such matters, people are likely to disagree. (Bourget, being interested in the etiology of perversion, would probably not wish to endorse—at least not publicly—the category of the practicing nonpederast.)

Synonymy is another topic that brings us face to face with the question of how categories are produced and maintained. When Gide first drafted this scene for his journal, he used a slightly different vocabulary. In the manuscript version, Bourget asks Gide, "Was your Immoralist a homosexual?" [Votre Immoraliste était-il un homosexuel?], after which Gide comments, "The question was so blunt that at first I was disconcerted, and as I was slow to respond, he insisted: 'I mean to say, a practicing homosexual?'" [La question était si brutale que j'en fus d'abord désarçonné et comme j'hésitais à répondre, il insista: «Je veux dire un homosexuel pratiquant?»]. Later in the manuscript version of the scene, he writes "But at this very moment Mrs. Wharton returned and I was unable to discover if, having said that there were only two categories of perversions, he was about to establish a third, or if he was claiming that uranism belonged to one of the two previous categories, and which" [Mais, à ce moment, Mrs. Wharton rentra et je ne pus connaître si, après avoir dit qu'il n'y avait que deux catégories de perversion, il allait en établir une troisième, ou s'il prétendait faire rentrer l'uranisme dans une des deux catégories précédentes; et dans laquelle].[5]

These changes might seem minor. What would it matter if Bourget said *pédéraste* or if he said *homosexuel*? What would it matter if Gide said *l'homosexuel* or *l'uranisme*? It turns out to be worthwhile to pause over the fact that Gide chose to make these revisions. Was he aiming at accuracy, correcting a faulty memory? Did he see a distinction between these different terms that would help him create the particular rhetorical effect he was looking for? I'm not sure we can answer that question with absolute accuracy, but we can learn something about the importance of register and about the dynamic evolution of the pragmatics of register from scenes like this one. To put things slightly differently, in this ritualized encounter between two novelists and in the choices of words that Gide portrays them making, we can see "worldmaking" (to use Nelson Goodman's term) in action. At stake is whose version of the world will prevail (or simply survive) during this conversation.

In an essay called "On Likeness of Meaning," Nelson Goodman lays down a sort of challenge: "Can we accept the conclusion that a word has the same meaning as no other word than itself?"[6] This is an interesting question for anyone thinking about sexuality in historical moments in which nomenclature is a serious issue for the actual people involved. France in the last decade of the nineteenth and the first decades of the twentieth century is in the midst of one such moment. *Invert, pederast, uranist, unisexual, homosexual, ambisexual, tribade, lesbian, sapphist*—what's the difference?[7] Goodman observes that "in ordinary speech, when we say that two terms have the same meaning, we usually indicate only that their kind and degree of likeness of meaning is sufficient for the purposes of the immediate discourse" (229). This suggests a complementary question: in what circumstances does the likeness of meaning of two terms no longer suffice for them to be interchangeable? As Goodman reminds us regarding words that seem to have the same meaning, "we must remember that the requirements vary greatly from discourse to discourse" (229). What set of discursive circumstances might have made Gide want to substitute the word *pédéraste* for the word *homosexuel* as he revised this journal entry? The significance of Gide's choice cannot be understood simply at the semantic level of communication. It must be understood pragmatically as well.

The words *pédéraste* and *pédérastie* have been current in French since at least the sixteenth century. Words such as *homosexuel* and *homosexualité* entered the language in the early 1890s, and *uranisme* and *uraniste* followed a few years later. The earliest attestations of *homosexuel* and *homosexualité* offered by the *Trésor de la langue française* come from the *Annales médico-psychologique* and of *uranisme* and *uraniste* from the *Archives d'anthropologie criminelle*. One of the first authors to use the word *uraniste* in the *Archives d'anthropologie criminelle* was Marc-André Raffalovich, who would collect a number of his articles from the *Archives* and expand them into an 1896 book he titled *Uranisme et unisexualité: Étude sur différentes manifestations de l'instinct sexuel*.[8] Raffalovich was more a literary than a scientific fellow, and indeed, the *Archives d'anthropologie criminelle* were themselves read in literary circles and also took account of literary publications. In 1897 Raffalovich published in the *Archives* an article about Rachilde's novel of the same year *Les Hors Nature* (Those Nature Excludes), which had at the center of its plot an androgynous and incestuously inclined pair of brothers. The article included extensive excerpts from Rachilde's novel, and Raffalovich comments, "Despite the obligation to write a novel, despite what is romantic and novelistic, Rachilde, as far as the psychic side of uranism is concerned, may well know more than do many doctors or professors." In 1905, Rachilde, writing in the *Mercure de France* about a novel titled *Les Pervertis* (Perverts), encourages her readers to read a recent article by Raffalovich in the *Archives* that deals with Uranist groups. (The title of Raffalovich's 1904 article is "Uranist Groups in Paris and Berlin.")

Literature, medical science, and criminology overlap considerably in the late-nineteenth- and early-twentieth-century circles in which "official" ways of referring to same-sex sexual relations were being worked out.[9] The "expert" Bourget mentions, Dr. Régis, for example, can be found writing an article on "A Case of Sexual Perversion of the Sadistic Form" in the *Archives* in 1899. A person claiming to be a student of Régis, Dr. Cazanove, will write an article in 1906 titled "Sexual Depravation among the Members of the Penal Colony at Saint-Jean-du-Maroni (French Guyana)" in which he will catalogue all the different kinds of relations between men to be found in that prison colony:

Soup-makers, a slang term that designates two individuals who act reciprocally as man and as woman.

Households, an intimate union of two individuals in which one is exclusively active, the other exclusively passive.

Unattached individuals, active or passive, who turn now to this person, now to that in order to satisfy their passions.

Passive subjects, of whatever variety, carry the slang name of *kid*.

[*Les faiseurs de soupe*, terme d'argot pour désigner deux individus qui se servent réciproquement d'homme et de femme.

Les ménages, union intime de deux individus où l'un est exclusivement actif, l'autre exclusivement passif.

Les individus sans attache, actifs ou passifs, s'adressant tantôt à l'un, tantôt à l'autre, pour satisfaire leur passion.

Les sujets passif, quels qu'ils soient, portent en argot le nom de *mômes*.]

Of the *soup-makers*, Cazanove will note that they are not many and that "in fact, pederasts are rarely both active and passive; rather they are exclusively one or the other. Doubtless this is why the soup-makers are held in such low esteem by their comrades" [Les pédérastes, en effet, sont rarement actifs et passifs à la fois; ils sont plutôt exclusivement l'un ou l'autre. C'est pour cela, sans doute, que les faiseurs de soupe sont si mal considérés par leurs camarades].[10]

Cazanove's summary of prison slang is helpful in a number of ways. It calls our attention to the extent to which questions of acts and positions in their relation to identities troubled thinking about male same-sex sexual relations at the turn of the century (as they would continue to do in following decades—and still do today), and troubled efforts at categorization. We see Cazanove using *pédéraste* as an umbrella term to capture groups of people who, while experiencing some sense of interrelation, also experience important divisions among themselves. We see that battles around categorization and nomenclature created oppositions between people supposedly within the groups being forged and named, as well as between them and people on the outside.

Clearly it is not only nomenclature that is being debated. The categorical divisions themselves are unstable, and the borders of the groups being referred to are volatile. It almost does seem to be a question, as Goodman has it, of "different members but the same club or different clubs but the same members," were it not for the fact that certain clubs are actively trying to exclude certain members while certain outside observers are trying to force their acceptance. Also volatile are the protocols that would establish "appropriate" reference to such subjects and people. The protocols needed to establish who can talk to whom about such topics, when, and using what language are very much under negotiation.

As the scene with Bourget attests, Gide had an acute experience of the struggles regarding the *pragmatics* of reference to these sexual categories. But he is also well known for his struggle on the semantic level (not that these two levels can be held entirely distinct from each other). If Dr. Cazanove lists for us in ethnographic fashion the terms of self-nomination and self-categorization of the prisoners in French Guyana, Gide will himself try to intervene in activist fashion on the question of semantic usage, most famously in a passage from his journal from 1918 in which he is writing about his book *Corydon* (a book over which he worried for many years before finally publishing it in a commercial edition in 1924):

I call a *pederast* the man who, as the word indicates, falls in love with young boys. I call a *sodomite* . . . the man whose desire is addressed to mature men.

I call an *invert* the man who, in the comedy of love, assumes the role of a woman and desires to be possessed.

These three types of *homosexuals* are not always clearly distinct; there are possible transferences from one to another; but most often the difference among them is such that they experience a profound disgust for one another, a disgust accompanied by a reprobation that in no way yields to that which you (heterosexuals) fiercely show toward all three.

The pederasts, of whom I am one (why cannot I say this quite simply, without your immediately claiming to see a brag in my confession?), are much rarer, and the sodomites much more numerous, than I first thought. . . . As to the inverts, whom I have hardly frequented at all, it has always seemed to me that they alone deserved the reproach of moral or intellectual deformation and were subject to some of the accusations that are commonly addressed to all homosexuals. (2:246–47)

[J'appelle *pédéraste* celui qui, comme le mot l'indique, s'éprend des jeunes garçons. J'appelle *sodomite* . . . celui dont le désir s'adresse aux hommes faits.

J'appelle *inverti* celui qui, dans la comédie de l'amour, assume le rôle d'une femme et désire être possédé.

Ces trois sortes d'*homosexuels* ne sont point toujours nettement tranchées; il y a des glissements possibles de l'une à l'autre; mais le plus souvent, la différence entre eux est telle qu'ils éprouvent un profond dégoût les uns pour les autres; dégoût accompagné d'une réprobation qui ne le cède parfois en rien à celle que vous (hétérosexuels) manifestez âprement pour les trois.

Les pédérastes, dont je suis (pourquoi ne puis-je dire cela tout simplement, sans qu'aussitôt vous prétendiez voir, dans mon aveu, forfanterie?), sont beaucoup plus rares, les sodomites beaucoup plus nombreux, que je ne pouvais croire d'abord. . . . Quant aux invertis, que j'ai fort peu fréquentés, il m'a toujours paru qu'eux seuls méritaient ce reproche de déformation morale ou intellectuelle et tombaient sous le coup de certaines des accusations que l'on adresse communément à tous les homosexuels. (1092)]

The most obvious difference between Gide and Cazanove is that for Cazanove *pédéraste* is the umbrella term that *homosexuel* is for Gide. For Cazanove, the typical members of the overarching category are a pair, one of whom is exclusively "passive" and one of whom is exclusively "active," whereas Gide more or less disavows men given to passive sexual relations with other men. The most obvious similarity between the passage from Gide and the passage from Cazanove has to do with their representations of the discomfort produced by the official effort to group together people who hold themselves distinct, and who think of certain people as being outcasts with whom they especially do not wish to be associated. Cazanove tells us that the outcasts are those "soupmakers" who, within their couple, do not distinguish between "active" and "passive" partners.[11] Gide would make the inverts into the outcasts. We could take these rather different categorical arrangements as in themselves indices (nonreferential ones) of other social characteristics of the people giving voice to the divisions. They tell us, and they are meant to tell us, something about the divergent social locations from which differing categorical divisions can be voiced, experienced, enacted, enforced, maintained, or dismissed.[12]

For Gide, and for the social point of view he represents, all "passivity" would be assigned to the inverts. Apparently it would be possible to be a *pédéraste* or a *sodomite* without engaging in sexual acts in which someone "plays the role of the woman in the comedy of love." For Gide, age distinctions between partners are crucial in establishing categorical distinctions, whereas age is not even mentioned as a variable in Cazanove's inquiry. For the culture about which Cazanove writes (perhaps not so distant from the culture represented in a number of Genet's novels), what is important in order not to lose esteem is that one not switch between "masculine" and "feminine" roles. The feminine role itself is not the most disreputable category; those who fall into disrepute are those whose roles in the "comedy of love" are variable. To belong to the culture Cazanove describes involves both experiencing and enacting this way of assigning repute and disrepute. Gide is interested in neither the experience nor the enactment in question.

Up until the end of his life, Gide would occasionally take the time to insist that the divisions he experienced as pertinent within the category of the homosexual were more significant and more telling than the umbrella grouping itself, even though he never found himself in a set of cultural circumstances in which his insistence could amount to much. In one of the last entries in *So Be It* (*Ainsi soit-il*), the notebook he was writing in at the time of his death, he comments:

> The great number of confidences I have been in a position to receive has convinced me that the variety of cases of homosexuality is much greater than that of cases of heterosexuality. And, furthermore, the irrepressible loathing a homosexual may feel for another whose appetites are not the same as his is something of which the heterosexual has no idea; he lumps them all together so as to be able to throw them all overboard at one and the same time, and this is obviously much more expedient. I tried in so far as I could to make the distinction between pederasts in the Greek sense of the word (love of boys) and inverts, but no one deigned to see anything in this but a rather groundless discrimination, and I had to give it up. (163–64)

> [Le grand nombre des confidences que j'ai été appelé à recevoir m'a persuadé que la diversité des cas d'homosexualité est plus grande, et de beaucoup, que celle des cas d'hétérosexualité. Il y a plus: l'irrépressible dégoût que peut éprouver un homosexuel pour un autre dont les appétits ne sont pas les mêmes est chose dont l'hétérosexuel ne peut se rendre compte: il les fourre tous dans le même sac pour les jeter par-dessus bord en bloc, ce qui est évidemment beaucoup plus expédient. J'ai tenté pour ma part de faire le départ entre pédérastes selon l'acception grecque du mot: amour des garçons, et les invertis, mais on n'a consenti à y voir qu'une discrimination assez vaine, et force m'a été de me replier. (194–95)]

Gide was certainly correct in stating that his categorical distinctions failed to convince many people of their pertinence. Putting aside for a moment his seemingly irrepressible phobia regarding effeminate men or men who enjoy various forms of penetrative sex, we can appreciate his point that the durability of certain kinds of social categories has little to do with their "truth."[13] And there is perhaps something we can understand about his confrontation with Bourget if we grasp what that scene has to teach us about the struggle around categories that Gide spent his life losing. Why do some systems of categorization have the force to impose themselves, whereas others, with varying degrees of alacrity, fall by the wayside? What does it take for someone to impose his or her own categories in any given situation?

Think about the dialogic observation that Gide inserts parenthetically into his journal entry from 1918: "The pederasts, of whom I am one (why cannot I say this quite simply, without your immediately claiming to see a brag in my confession?), are much rarer." Gide reveals a certain malaise, placing himself in front of a critical public and expressing in a paradoxical manner his inability simply to say, "I am a pederast." This inability is surely linked to his impression (doubtless a correct one) that almost no one would understand by that word what he means it to mean. One answer to his question as to why he cannot just simply say what he wishes and produce in his interlocutors (imaginary or otherwise) the response he would wish for is that not many (if any) interlocutors ready to take his meaning exist within his cultural ambit—where things are understood, in general, differently.

Gide brings into play the same problem when he chooses to have Paul Bourget say "pédéraste" instead of "homosexuel" so that he can then make the switch to the word *homosexual* in his reply. Pronounced by Bourget, "pédéraste" would refer without distinction to a general category of people. If it was simply a matter of a friendly conversation on any old topic, Gide might have been able to respond to the question as to "whether or not your immoralist is a pederast . . . I mean: a practicing pederast?" with an observation something like this:

> Perhaps, Monsieur Bourget, the protagonist of *The Immoralist* was unconscious of his sexual inclination and so did not practice it, but I might also tell you that as far as I am concerned the word *pederast* has a very specific meaning of which your usage seems to indicate you are unaware. It refers to a man who is drawn to adolescents, with whom he limits himself to a certain number of specific sexual acts. The use you make of this word, where you seem to refer without distinction to any homosexual man, seems erroneous to me. Moreover, I myself, being a pederast in the strict sense of the term, am ideally situated to clarify this matter for you.

If Gide is in no position to say any such thing in this particular conversation, at least in the written account of it that he produces later he is able to show himself making an effort to oppose the word *homosexuel* to the word *pédéraste* in order to indicate, at least on some subliminal level, that there are certain distinctions that do exist for him, even if they are difficult to talk about.

The availability of a whole range of words to refer to "the same thing" allows for the possibility of certain people—when they insist on semantic distinctions between the words—trying to enforce certain social distinctions. This is one of the things Gide's hesitations over the words *homosexuel*, *pédéraste*, and *uraniste* reveal. But the scene with Bourget also shows that in this particular context Gide's semantic distinctions cannot prevail—doubtless for pragmatic reasons.[14]

"In general," writes Erving Goffman in his essay "On Face-Work," "a person determines how he ought to conduct himself during an occasion of talk by testing the potential symbolic meaning of his acts against the self-images that are being sustained. In doing this, however, he incidentally subjects his behavior to the expressive order that prevails and contributes to the orderly flow of messages. His aim is to save face; his effect is to save the situation."[15] Gide, in describing the interaction that takes place between him and Bourget, gives us a good example of what Goffman theorizes in his essay. It is Bourget who defines the circumstances of the conversation, and Gide who finds himself obliged to follow the flow of the messages that Bourget originates. Bourget broaches the subject of homosexuality abruptly, leaving Gide "somewhat stunned," speaking "as if I hardly knew myself," asking Bourget questions simply to save face, "just to have something to say." Surely, when he asks Gide a question regarding the sexuality of one of Gide's characters, it is nearly as if he asks Gide a question about his own sexuality—and certainly Bourget would have been quite capable of asking people he knew for information on this subject. It is clear why the interaction would become intensely uncomfortable quite quickly. If, despite Gide's initial confusion, the painful situation is finally saved (to use Goffman's word), it is because Gide finds a figure, a personage, for himself that serves the situation. Obviously, the personage he constructs is not able to assume his "pederasty" in any overt fashion in front of Bourget, nor to defend the categorical specifics in which we have seen Gide invest himself elsewhere.

"Instead of stating a view outright, the individual tends to attribute it to a character who happens to be himself, but one he had been careful to withdraw from in one regard or another," writes Goffman in *Frame Analysis*. "When he does cite himself," Goffman has noted a few pages earlier, "when he does use 'I,' this I is likely to be different in some respects from the speaker himself-at-the-moment, thus ensuring that he will be speaking with reduced weight and in a special frame, parenthesizing himself from the cited figure in his own reporting of his own experience."[16] Goffman's analysis is suggestive for understanding the

Gide, Bourget, and Proust Talking   43

ways in which various aspects of certain sexual identities—being "in the closet" or "coming out," interactions with strangers—involve practices of the first person that require constant improvisation as well as a resourcefulness accumulated out of painful experience.

If Gide experiences a certain difficulty in speaking of homosexuality, or of *his* homosexuality, or of his *version* of homosexuality, in front of Bourget, such is not necessarily the case in all contexts, and it is worth pausing over some of the reasons why the context established by Bourget is so problematic. We have already seen the interests that certain linguistic anthropologists take in the functioning of nonreferential indexes in the Dyirbal language, in which there exists a specific lexicon that is to be used when the mother-in-law is present. Now, in the scene between Gide and Bourget, it is precisely in the moment following Edith Wharton's leaving their presence that Bourget chooses to turn to the topic of homosexuality in *L'Immoraliste*: "Now that we are alone," Bourget begins. It would thus seem that for Bourget Wharton's departure authorizes the broaching of a topic and the use of a lexicon that one is not permitted to use in her presence. "But at this moment Mrs. Wharton returned and I never learned whether, according to him, the homosexual fell under the head of sadism or of masochism." Wharton's return apparently obliges Bourget to end the conversation abruptly. Are we (is Gide) therefore to imagine that for Bourget the fact that certain words are pronounced is an indication that one is among men, or indeed that pronouncing these words in the absence of women is a ritualistic performance of masculinity? Gide seems forced to accept this version of their circumstances. He is, in a certain way, forced to be the man that Bourget requires him to be. The personage in which he figures himself is, under these circumstances, not in a position to assert his way of linking pederasty and masculinity in the face of Bourget's speculations about sadism and masochism.[17] The "Wharton-absent" language that Bourget speaks indicates that he is speaking to Gide *as a man*. It would seem to indicate also that he is *not* speaking to Gide *as a pederast*. In fact, Gide's near speechlessness faced with Bourget's question is a sign of his need to find a footing on which to speak as a man whose same-sex tendencies are not on display, are out-of-frame. His interesting hesitation in composing his journal entries as to into whose mouth to put the word *pédéraste* is an indication that self-possession and license to speech are not easily granted to someone who wishes to take up that particular word in certain ways. Perhaps what we can read in the scene is a sense, beyond Gide's control, but not beyond his perception, that speech via the word *homosexual* would come more easily—especially in the context of speaking to someone such as Bourget.

If Gide had his way, there would come into being a widely shared and durable semantic distinction between *pederast* and *invert*, two categories that are for him collocated inappropriately by the word *homosexual*. But he cannot speak that situation into being. Rather, speech here seems to teach Gide that the difference between *pederast* and *invert* will not be semantic, it will be pragmatic—it will have to do with the person speaking, the person being addressed, the people in earshot, and what indications regarding social status are to be made about any or all of them.[18]

One final comment on the scene between Gide and Bourget before turning to the scene between Gide and Proust that Gide describes five and a half years later. If Gide seems obliged to submit to the terms of the interactional contract that Bourget offers at the moment of the interaction, the writing of the scene in his *Journal* is, of course, a moment in which he can take some revenge for the insulting experience he has undergone. It would seem, for instance, in the writing of the scene, that he rebels against the form of masculinity he is called upon to enact, just as he rebels against the form of femininity to which Wharton is assigned: "I was sorry that he turned the conversation into another channel," he says, speaking of the moment when Wharton reenters the scene. "It would have amused me to have Mrs. Wharton's opinion, if indeed she might have had one." Gide's tone here seems slightly ambiguous, but even if Wharton might have had no particular opinion on the question of whether "the homosexual fell under the head of sadism or of masochism," we might imagine that she would have had no difficulty in many contexts in speaking of sexual relations between people of the same sex. It was, in fact, through Paul Bourget that Wharton had met Vernon Lee, for instance. Wharton herself was the friend not only of Gide, but also of Henry James who, in 1907, had introduced her to Morton Fullerton, a man with whom she would subsequently have an intense intimate relationship, a man also well known for his seductions of other men as well as other women.[19] In any case, a bit further along in this journal entry, Gide shows himself and Wharton making fun together of Bourget's intellectual and scientific pretensions. Clearly Gide would have had an easier time speaking to a woman like Edith Wharton about sexual questions (for his masculinity would have been played out differently in such a context—one in which there may well also have been more shared background beliefs about sexuality) than he had with Bourget (where he was called upon to be a certain kind of man and therefore found himself tongue-tied).

Gide, Proust, and Uranism

Up to this point I have focused on the kinds of pragmatic and semantic differences that might be in play in the different uses of the words *pédéraste* and *homosexuel* in the scene between Gide and Bourget. There remains the question of the use of the word *uranisme*, present in the manuscript version, where Gide writes, "I was unable to discover if, having said that there were only two categories of perversions, he was about to establish a third, or if he was claiming that uranism belonged to one of the two previous categories, and which." He modified the published version to read, "I never learned whether, according to him, the homosexual fell under the head of sadism or of masochism." What pragmatic difference might there be to explain this switch?

My suggestion would be that in the case of the substitution of *homo-sexuel* for *uraniste*, just as in the case of the nonequivalence of *pédéraste* and *homosexuel*, the presence of a lexical variant can be considered as the remaining trace of a kind of ritual work on the self that takes place in private as well as public spaces. Gide notes in his journal in the second half of May 1921, while speaking of a visit to Proust that he had made, "We scarcely talked, this evening again, of anything but uranism" (2:267, 1126). He says "this evening again" because he had also visited Proust earlier that month, on May 13, and wrote in his journal the next day, "As soon as I arrived," Proust began "to talk of uranism." Gide notes as well that, "Far from denying or hiding his uranism, he exhibits it, and I could almost say boasts of it." A few lines further on, he adds:

> He tells me his conviction that Baudelaire was a uranist: "The way he speaks of Lesbos, and the mere need of speaking of it, would be enough to convince me," and when I protest:
> "In any case, if he was a uranist, it was almost without his knowing it; and you don't believe that he ever practiced. . . ."
> "What!" he exclaims. "I am sure of the contrary; how can you doubt that he practiced? He, Baudelaire!"
> And in the tone of his voice it is implied that by doubting I am insulting Baudelaire. But I am willing to believe that he is right; and that uranists are even a bit more numerous than I thought at first. In any case I did not think that Proust was so exclusively so. (2:265)

[Il me dit la conviction où il est que Baudelaire était uraniste: «La manière dont il parle de Lesbos, et déjà le besoin d'en parler, suffiraient seuls à m'en convaincre», et comme je proteste:

«En tout cas, s'il était uraniste, c'était à son insu presque; et vous ne pouvez penser qu'il ait jamais pratiqué . . .

—Comment donc! s'écrie-t-il. Je suis convaincu du contraire; comment pouvez-vous douter qu'il pratiquât? lui, Baudelaire!»

Et, dans le ton de sa voix, il semble qu'en en doutant je fasse injure à Baudelaire. Mais je veux bien croire qu'il a raison; et que les uranistes sont encore un peu plus nombreux que je ne le croyais d'abord. En tout cas je ne supposais pas que Proust le fût aussi exclusivement. (1124–25)]

There are some remarkable similarities between the scene Gide describes between himself and Proust and the one he describes between himself and Bourget, especially if one considers the two scenes as interaction rituals. Notice first the frequency of the use of the words *uraniste* and *uranisme* in the passages relating to Proust.[20] As we have seen, the word *homosexuel* and the word *uraniste* arrived in the French language at more or less the same moment in the 1890s. Gide will use the word *uraniste* on and off again up until the end of his life as a synonym for homosexual. Yet perhaps, as the scenes at Proust's reveal, he will favor *uraniste* in more private situations or when speaking with people who share in this sexuality.[21] (Thus, while he might be willing to entertain the thought of Bourget assigning homosexuals to either a sadistic or a masochistic camp, he may perhaps wish to keep the word "uranist" free for more sympathetic speakers and contexts.) That is to say, the words *homosexuel* and *homosexualité* will slowly become (at least for Gide) the preferred choices for official and public discussions, whereas *uraniste* and *uranisme* will become the preferred choices in informal situations, and will also be easier words to assume personally, easier words with which to craft ways of speaking of oneself to others like oneself.[22] Yet if Gide's journal entry would seem to indicate that he and Proust both felt at ease together with the word *uranist*, that they communed in their use of the word, that it existed in a comfortable register for their private conversations, this is not to say that they communed in much else regarding the representation of same-sex sexualities.

One way of speaking of oneself is to speak of others, and we see in the scene with Proust (as in the scene with Bourget) that a topic of conversation sufficiently common to be considered a ritual practice is one that consists in a debate regarding the supposed sexual practices of another individual: "Tell me . . . whether or not your immoralist is a pederast. . . . I mean: a practicing pederast?" "How can you doubt that he practiced? He, Baudelaire!" Obviously, the more important function of this ritual is not to establish the truth about this or that person, but rather to define the limits of the category to which the person is being tentatively assigned. As Mary Douglas commented, "The learning of exemplars is part of the process of constituting a community." When Gide concedes that perhaps Proust was right as far as Baudelaire was concerned, that "uranists are even a bit more numerous than I thought at first," and that "I did not think that Proust was so exclusively so," we see quite precisely that it is through ritually structured conversations such as the one he is having with Proust that a person maintains or modifies the boundaries of the categories through which he or she perceives the world, to which he or she affiliates, and in which he or she communes. Such conversations—different, and with different effects, depending on whether they are official or informal, on where they take place, on the respective social positions of the people participating— belong among the acts by which and through which someone tries to realize and validate a vision of the world.

Within Parisian literary circles, the month of May 1921, the month in which Gide and Proust spoke of uranism and of Baudelaire, was apparently filled with these kinds of conversations. It was on May 2, 1921, that the second part of Proust's *The Guermantes Way* had been put on sale. At the end of that volume Proust adjoined the first brief section of *Sodom and Gomorrah*, which was to be the next major division of Proust's novel. In part 1 of *Sodom and Gomorrah*, the first-person narrator of the *Recherche* observes a sexual encounter between two men, Charlus and Jupien. The conversation between Gide and Proust on Baudelaire takes place on the evening of May 13. Proust had sent a message to Gide on May 12, with an invitation to come see him that evening, but Gide had been unable to accept. On the morning of the thirteenth, he sends Proust a note of apology:

> It is true that I was late returning home for dinner (around quarter past 8), having been tied up at Madame M.'s by a conversation about *Guermantes* and about what follows it—and I would have loved to have been able to report this conversation to you in all its freshness.—Wherever I go, everyone is speaking only of you. Princess Murat is giving readings of certain excerpts of Charlus—on the telephone!
>
> But my nephew [Mark Allégret], with whom I was dining, and who is

leaving this evening for Upper Silesia, is even sadder than I. Had he been able to come with me to your doorstep, and had you not thought it too much of an imposition to bid him enter, he would have told you of the scene of consternation to which your book gave rise within his family—a scene that perhaps he finds a bit too amusing.

[Il est vrai que je ne suis rentré dîner qu'assez tard (vers 8 heures et quart) m'étant laissé retenir chez Madame M. par une conversation sur *Guermantes* et sur ce qui suit—dont j'eusse bien voulu vous apporter tout frais les échos.—Où que j'aille on ne parle plus que de vous. La princesse Murat donne des lectures de certains morceaux de Charlus—par téléphone!

Mais le plus désolé sera mon neveu [Marc Allégret] qui précisément dînait avec moi et qui part ce soir pour la Haute Silésie. M'accompagnant jusqu'à votre seuil et si peut-être vous n'aviez trouvé trop importun qu'il le franchisse, il vous eût raconté la consternante scène de famille à laquelle votre livre a donné lieu—dont peut-être il s'amusa un peu trop.][23]

It would seem that Charlus, now explicitly labelled a "man-woman" in the novel, was a hit among people interested by same-sex culture (the Princess Murat and her friends, for instance), and that among literate families such as the Allégrets, some of whose members might have been suspicious of those sexualities, dinner-table conversations on this topic sparked by Proust's book may have been a bit testy.

The conversations Gide had been hearing about the scene between Charlus and Jupien in Proust's novel were perhaps not all to his liking. This would explain one of the notes to the preface he wrote for *Corydon* in 1922:

Certain books—Proust's in particular—have accustomed the public to be less alarmed by, and to consider more deliberately—what it previously pretended or preferred to ignore. For how many of us suppose they can suppress what they ignore! . . . But such books have greatly contributed, I fear, to our current confusion. The theory of the woman-man, of the *Sexuelle Zwischenstufen* (intermediate degrees of sexuality) advanced by Dr. Hirschfeld in Germany quite some time before the war—and which Marcel Proust appears to accept—may well be true enough; but that theory explains and concerns only certain cases of homosexuality, precisely those with which this book does not deal—cases of inversion, of effeminacy, of sodomy. (xx)

[Certains livres—ceux de Proust en particulier—ont habitué le public à s'effaroucher moins et à oser considérer de sang-froid ce qu'il feignait d'ignorer, ou préférait ignorer d'abord. Nombre d'esprits se figurent volontiers qu'ils suppriment ce qu'ils ignorent. . . Mais ces livres, du même coup, ont beaucoup contribué, je le crains, à égarer l'opinion. La théorie de l'homme-femme, des «Sexuelle Zwischenstufen» (degrés intermédiaires de la sexualité) que lançait le Dr Hirschfeld en Allemagne, assez longtemps déjà avant la guerre, et à laquelle Marcel Proust semble se ranger—peut bien n'être point fausse; mais elle n'explique et ne concerne que certains cas d'homosexualité, ceux dont précisément je ne m'occupe pas dans ce livre— les cas d'inversion, d'efféminement, de sodomie. (8)]

Proust and Gide were perfectly aware that they were not pursuing the same strategies in the struggle for the representation of same-sex sexualities, just as they were aware of not being invested in exactly the same set of categories for these sexualities. In a letter to Jacques Boulenger dated May 16, 1921, Proust comments, "You know that my final chapter has angered many homosexuals. I am quite sad about this. But it is hardly my fault if M. de Charlus is an older man. I couldn't suddenly give him the look of a Sicilian shepherd" [Vous savez que j'ai fâché beaucoup d'homosexuels par mon dernier chapitre. J'en ai beaucoup de peine. Mais ce n'est pas ma faute si M. de Charlus est un vieux monsieur, je ne pouvais pas brusquement lui donner l'aspect d'un pâtre sicilien].[24] Proust's reasons for employing the word homosexual here, as opposed to the word *pederast*, say, or *uranist*, seem clear. He (unlike Gide in *Corydon*) has no interest in invoking a heroic Greek or Mediterranean heritage for the sexuality he is representing. Perhaps he is being slightly disingenuous when he tries to make his excuses by insisting he was dealing with his character's particularities more than he was seeking any form of exemplarity. For him, as for Gide, writing about same-sex sexualities was a question of exemplification and of the exemplarity of exemplification. Gide's discomfort with what Proust writes is the result of his perception that Proust's representational work runs the risk of being perceived as perfectly exemplary.

Proust and Gide obviously had an acute awareness of the gaps between the two paradigms for male same-sex sexuality they were offering. Gide apparently even lost sleep over the difference. Maria Van Rysselberghe mentions Gide telling her in August 1921 that "the man-woman conception of Proust kept me from sleeping last night." When Van Rysselberghe asks if he finds Proust's notion to be mistaken, he replies, "No, but to use it as the basis for all of uranism is revolting" [Non, mais bâtir là-dessus tout l'uranisme me révolte].[25] Yet if the distinctions between Gide and Proust's conceptualizations weighed heavily on Gide's mind, it is also the case that he could not avoid understanding that he and Proust were somehow writing about "the same thing"—for certainly everyone else around them thought so, whether that "same thing" was referred to as uranism or pederasty or inversion or homosexuality. This commonsensical understanding of "the same thing" is a powerful *social* phenomenon. Nelson Goodman can certainly insist, with all the logical rigor in the world, that "the response to the question 'Same or not the same?' must always be 'Same what?' "[26] Still, asking such a critical question will do little good in a social context configured in such a way that no one cares to hear the question.[27] When François Mauriac reads *Corydon*, for instance, he writes to Gide, "I cannot really grasp your distinction between homosexuals and inverts" [j'entends mal votre distinction entre homosexuels et invertis]. Mauriac's wording is interesting, in that he takes note of Gide's distinction between upright and moral pederasts and the morally more problematic inverts, but he does not keep to Gide's terminology. Nor is he interested in lending credence to the part of Gide's distinction relating to sexual practices. He is interested only in refuting the idea of the moral elevation of anyone who gives way to same-sex sexual inclinations: "When I call to mind all such men I know, I only see unhappy, diminished, fallen creatures, to the extent that they are not struggling against it" [Quand je songe à tous ceux que je connais, je ne vois que des malheureux, des diminués, des êtres déchus, dans la mesure où ils ne luttent pas].[28]

Mauriac was, in the early 1920s, trying to work out some relation between his sexuality, his Catholicism, and his sense of appropriate moral behavior. He was trying to construct a suitable speaking position for himself in regard to these issues. Writing both to and about Gide and Proust was one way he worked on the construction of this position. Even in 1931, Gide would comment in his journal on the amount of courage Mauriac demonstrated simply by speaking about Gide in the Catholic circles within which he moved.[29] Mauriac had shown that courage already in December 1921, when he wrote an article in defense of Gide, who had recently been attacked in print by the Catholic critic Henri Massis, in an article titled "The Influence of M. André Gide." Mauriac justified Gide in part by reference to his aesthetic achievement: "He [Gide] serves France by writing better French than anyone else in the world. Were his language somehow put in the service of a moral goal it could only be less pure. The value of this exquisite art lies in its disinterestedness" [Il sert la France en écrivant le français mieux que personne au monde; asservie à une fin morale, sa langue serait peut-être moins pure; cet art exquis vaut par son désintéressement].[30] It is a little difficult to understand what disinterestedness might mean here, except a set of strategies meant to justify the representation of a certain subject matter by way of the refinement of its manner of presentation. Yet Mauriac was clearly drawn to the specific subject matter of Gide and Proust as much as he was to their style.

Consider in this light a letter that Proust receives from Mauriac on May 15, 1921, on the subject of Proust's recently published book:

As for the last twenty pages . . . I experienced on reading them a host of contradictory feelings: admiration, repulsion, terror, disgust . . . But what can one do? I believe in the fatality of the work of art: There was no way you could not bear this terrible fruit. It was to you and no one else that was to fall the role of the angel who raises the accursed cities from their ashes, and who separates the waters of the Black Sea. I tremble, my friend—in spite of the carefully crafted horror of the portrait you have painted— to think of all those who were holding their eyes closed in order not to see themselves and whose secret and shameful wound you have bluntly touched with your finger. They will be like those medical students who believe themselves to be afflicted by everything they read about in their books—I am thinking of all those young people hesitating at the accursed frontier who will be pitilessly pushed towards Sodom by your diagnosis . . . As far as I am concerned, I believe that for many this is a fearful form of election, a condemnation to purity, to Holiness . . . In any case, it was inevitable. There was no way you could not write this.

[Quant au vingt dernières pages . . . J'ai éprouvé à leur endroit tous les plus contradictoires sentiments: admiration, répulsion, terreur, dégoût . . . Mais quoi? Je crois à la fatalité de l'oeuvre d'art: Vous ne pouviez pas ne pas porter ce fruit terrible. C'était à vous et non à un autre que devait échoir le rôle de l'ange qui fait surgir les villes maudites de leur cendre et qui écarte les eaux de la mer Noire. Je frémis, mon ami—en dépit de l'horreur voulue de votre peinture—en songeant à tous ceux qui fermaient les yeux pour ne pas se voir et dont vous touchez d'un doigt brutal la secrète et honteuse plaie. Pareils à ces étudiants de médecine qui se croient atteints de tout ce que décrivent leurs manuels—je pense à tant de jeunes êtres hésitant sur la frontière maudite et que votre diagnostic impitoyable rejettera vers Sodome . . . Pour moi, je crois que chez beaucoup, c'est une élection terrible, une condamnation à la pureté, à la Sainteté . . . Mais enfin, c'était inévitable. Vous ne pouviez pas ne pas écrire cela.][31]

Mauriac vests Proust with the double-edged *sacer esto* of which we have already seen Montesquiou speak. His rhetoric of *sainteté* prefigures the rhetorical position Genet will construct in his early novels, in which he seeks out the same *sacer esto* effect as Proust in order to ground his literary authority. Mauriac claims to appreciate the "horror" Proust built into this section of his novel, and certainly others have followed him here. Antoine Compagnon describes the scene between Charlus and Jupien as "une caricature impitoyable" [an unpitying caricature] and "une violente étude de moeurs" [a shocking study of behavior].[32] Perhaps. Perhaps not. It probably all depends on the context in which you read. As Mauriac also notes (and claims to be chagrined by), there are those who, reading these pages, will be able to use them to make something new of themselves. The long critical tradition of either reveling in the "horror" of the depiction in Proust's novel, or else, inversely, castigating it as a phobic or derogatory depiction—a tradition that has yet to run out of steam—shows to what an extent the particular instance of social categorization in evidence in it (and the fierce concerns of exemplarity it provokes) continue to preoccupy us. Yet, just conceivably, these pages are not, nor ever were, intrinsically unpitying or horrifying, and perhaps someday a context will present itself in which that social fact can be more readily appreciated.[33]

In any case, the publication of Proust's volume is a big event. People cannot seem to put it down. They buy and read it within a week or so. It causes them to talk, even to lose sleep. It makes speech available to them, or it forces them to speak in ways they would rather not. Mauriac writes to Proust as if both of them were outside the sexual category in question. Of course, Mauriac knew better. A bit later in this same letter, he writes: "I know from Gide that your health is no better and I am very sad to hear that you are suffering so badly." That is to say that Gide and Mauriac had probably spoken together about Gide's recent visits to Proust, about the conversation between Proust and Gide on uranism that had taken place only two days earlier. Perhaps the recognition, the perhaps unconscious gratitude, that Mauriac expresses to Proust in his letter for the representational work Proust has done comes from the simple fact that Proust has provided the occasion for so many in the circles in which Proust, Gide, and Mauriac moved to take up the question of "homosexuality," and to take it up in some kind of first person, even if it is often not a first person that assumes that sexuality directly.

As Goffman reminds us in the passage I quoted earlier, "As speaker, we represent ourselves through the offices of a personal pronoun, typically 'I,' and it is thus a *figure*—a figure in a statement—that serves as the agent, a protagonist in a *described* scene, a 'character' in an anecdote, someone, after all, who belongs to the world that is spoken about, not the world in which the speaking occurs. And once this format is employed, an astonishing flexibility is created."[34] Goffman is one of the great theoreticians of the first person and its uses. He subtly indicates how hard it is to present the full extent of his critical thinking in the language we have at hand. "I" is a figure that never fully grasps us, and that we never fully grasp, whose reference is transient in the extreme. "Howsoever we feel obliged to describe ourselves, we need not include in this description the capacity and propensity to project such descriptions. (Indeed, we cannot entirely do so)," says Goffman, a page later. That is, in describing oneself, the agent of the description is neither obliged, nor equipped, to assume that the description of self fully attains or pertains to the agent of the description. Goffman continues: "When we say, 'I can't seem to talk clearly today,' *that* statement can be very clearly said. When we say, 'I'm speechless!,' we aren't. (And if we tried to be cute and say, 'I'm speechless—but apparently not enough to prevent myself from saying that,' our description would embody the cuteness but not refer to it.) In Mead's terms, a 'me' that tries to incorporate its 'I' requires another 'I' to do so."[35]

As early as 1908 Proust had begun work on the pages that would become the first part of *Sodome et Gomorrhe*, published in 1921. One might think of saying that he spent his time finding a way to say "I am speechless on the subject of my sexuality, but apparently not enough to prevent myself from saying that." And perhaps in the process of learning to say something like that, he would be learning to think abstractly about the first person and about its role in utterances dealing with dissident sexuality. It is during that same evening in which Gide and Proust spoke of Baudelaire, Gide tells us, that he told Proust of his plans for his memoirs (*If It Die . . .*) which caused Proust to cry out: "You can tell anything . . . but on condition that you never say: *I*," and Gide to comment in his journal, "but that won't suit me." Proust and Gide each spent many years fashioning a first person in order to speak of uranism, or of pederasty, or of inversion, or of homosexuality. In part they were fashioning a public personage who would be taken seriously speaking of such things. In part they were involved in an ongoing apprenticeship, both literary and social, in the functioning of the first person. They, along with other writers around them, would instantiate what they learned in their literary works, both practically and abstractly. The chapters immediately ahead will deal with both the practical and the abstract halves of this project in writings by Gide, Proust, and Colette. Note that what I am aiming at showing here thus cannot be reduced to the portrayal of the struggle of certain sexual outsiders to escape from an imposed silence, to wrest the means of expression away from a normatively homophobic social order. The vectors within a social world of what is normative and what is a dissident or subversive opposition to it can never be satisfactorily assigned in such a simplistic way. We are dealing with position-taking and self-figuration within a large group of people who all are finding ways to speak of same-sex sexualities differently and to different ends.

To be able to set as one's literary objective to *tout dire* about a certain sexuality involves for all three of these authors an understanding both of the literary act of saying as well as of precisely what is said. It is as much a problem of crafting the forms of representation as of crafting the matter to hand. All three authors, in a certain way, aim to be authorized spokespeople on the subject, and this is a privilege they clearly know they need to work to win. As Bourdieu says in "Rites of Institution": "The authorized spokesperson is the one whom it behooves and on whom it is incumbent to speak on behalf of the collectivity. It is both his privilege and his duty, his proper function, in a word, his competence (in the legal sense of the term)."[36] The recognized competence that Colette, Gide, and Proust, among others, will seek, is as much aesthetic and critical as it is social. They configure their projects so that their success depends not only on their abstract grasp of and practical instantiation of the first person but also on their abstract grasp of and practical instantiation of the social problems of categorization. To achieve recognition as a spokesperson, as Bourdieu points out, is an act of social magic:

> Acts of social magic . . . can only succeed if the institution—meaning to institute in an active way someone or something endowed with this or that status or property—is guaranteed by the whole group or by a recognized institution. Even when the act is accomplished by a sole agent . . . it rests fundamentally on the belief of an entire group . . . that is, on the socially

fashioned dispositions to know and recognize the institutional conditions of a valid ritual. (125)

The scenes from Gide's journal that I have been reading here, between Gide, Bourget, and Wharton, and between Gide and Proust, the letters between Gide, Proust, and Mauriac, are all skirmishes in a long social struggle for representation that is inextricably intertwined with a struggle for aesthetic authority. Representation of what? Of whom? By whom? By what means? Everything is at stake, and the long labor of people such as Gide and Proust and Colette is to learn to speak and to be heard to offer a particular version of what is to be represented, of who is to be represented, and of how representation happens—just as they labored to become themselves people who were entitled to speak their point of view. They fashioned themselves in fashioning a way of speaking.

two

Questions of Register in and around 1902

Nevertheless, in spite of these ridiculous social affectations, M. de Charlus was extremely intelligent, and it is probable that if some remote marriage had established a connexion between his family and that of Balzac, he would have felt (no less than Balzac himself, for that matter) a satisfaction on which he would yet have been unable to resist preening himself as on a praiseworthy sign of condescension.

[D'ailleurs, malgré ces habitudes mondaines ridicules, M. de Charlus était très intelligent, et il est probable que si quelque mariage ancien avait noué une parenté entre sa famille et celle de Balzac, il eût ressenti (non moins que Balzac d'ailleurs) une satisfaction dont il n'eût pu cependant s'empêcher de se targuer comme d'une marque de condescendance admirable.]

— MARCEL PROUST, *Sodom and Gomorrah*

Balzac, Literature, and Linguistic Registers

We all know that there exist different registers within a single language providing for different ways of saying what we call "the same thing." To know which register to use in a given situation is an aspect of the linguistic competence we all possess, if unevenly. Literature invokes these registers as well. Sometimes a literary work will simply reproduce this or that register without it having been given much thought; sometimes it knowingly displays its virtuosic manipulation of a register that is understood to be particularly literary; sometimes it uses the phenomenon of contrasting registers to give a certain truthfulness to its representations (to the speech of its characters, for instance); sometimes it takes the occasion to analyze in a more abstract way the very phenomenon of registers, their uses and effects. Consider, in this latter regard, the use of the word *tante* in Balzac's *Splendeurs et misères des courtisanes*. (The English translation goes by the title *A Harlot High and Low*.) *Tante* means "aunt," but its slang usage is roughly equivalent to "fairy" or "fag" or "fruit." Balzac has characters use it in the sense of "boyfriend" or "lover" or perhaps "catamite." The major literary precursor for those late-nineteenth- and early-twentieth-century writers who wish to take up the subject of same-sex sexualities, Balzac in some ways authorizes the interest other writers might choose to show in such subjects, and his novelistic practice offers a model for how to broach them. By examining in a bit of detail Balzac's way of working with the word *tante* we will be able to approach a number of more general theoretical and historical issues regarding ways of speaking about different forms of same-sex sexuality. What we learn from Balzac will also provide the initial elements of a context in which to read certain of Colette's early texts alongside texts by a number of her contemporaries, including Proust, Gide, and Jean Lorrain.

It is in the fourth and final part of *Splendeurs et misères des courtisanes*, "The Final Incarnation of Vautrin," that Balzac uses the word *tante* for the first time in its slang sense.[1] The protagonist of the first three parts of the novel, Lucien de Rubembré, has just killed himself, and the authorities are trying to establish the true identity of Lucien's accomplice, the priest Carlos Herrera, whom they suspect (correctly) of being the escaped criminal known sometimes as Vautrin, sometimes as Jacques Collin. The prison in which this part of the novel is set houses certain of Vautrin's former accomplices, and the authorities send Herrera / Vautrin out into the prison yard in the hopes of producing an interaction between him and his friends that will betray his true identity to them. Also in the prison at the moment is a former lover (*tante*) of Vautrin's, Théodore Calvi, who is awaiting execution.

Vautrin's former accomplices do, of course, recognize him, but without giving him away to the officials who are secretly watching. They speculate among themselves as to why Vautrin might have allowed himself to be captured by the police. "I know what the plan is!" one of them exclaims. "He wants to see his *tante* who's due to be executed."[2] When Balzac published this text for the first time in 1847, was he able to assume that his public would understand this particular usage of the word *tante*? Given that he follows the character's remark with a digression explaining the usage, we can assume that he wanted at least to give the appearance of imagining that his public required an explanation. There thus follows a passage in which the narrator takes it upon himself to enlighten the reader as to the slang sense of this word, a sense familiar to prisoners, police agents, and prison guards, if not to a general public. He proceeds by recounting a scene from the tour an English lord is making of the French prison system. During one prison visit, the following conversation takes place:

> The governor, having shown him round the whole prison, the yards, the workshops, the dungeons, etc., pointed to one building with an expression of disgust.
>
> "I shan't take Your Lordship there," he said, "for that's the quarters of the *tantes* . . ."
>
> "Really!" said Lord Durham, "and what are they?"
>
> "That's the third sex, my lord." (453–54, 6:840)

The narrator then moves on, oddly assuming that the phrase "the third sex" will have served to clear up any confusion for a reader of 1847 confounded by the particular use of the word *tante* to be found among the prisoners.

Balzac is surely one of the first, if not the first author to use *tante* in this way in what we might refer to as "polite" literature, but he was hardly making any discoveries regarding prison slang. In 1837, for example, Eugène-François Vidocq (the famous criminal who became chief of the secret police) had published his book *Les Voleurs* (Thieves), which contained a dictionary of thieves' slang including a definition of *tante*: "Man who has the tastes of women, the woman of men's prisons. . . . It should not be believed that pederasty is always caused by a vicious constitution; phrenologists, who have found the bumps on our skulls corresponding to all the forms of love, have yet to find the bump of Socratic love. . . . Sometimes prison wardens and guards have even allowed marriages to be celebrated with a certain amount of pomp and circumstance."[3] Balzac may have discovered this slang meaning in reading Vidocq or someone else, or he may have encountered it in his own daily life—for perhaps this particular meaning, in wide usage today, was already well-known in 1847. In any case, his way of manipulating the word's usage (or avoidance) within *Splendeurs et misères* reveals that he is interested in more than merely displaying his knowledge of prison slang. He turns out to be intrigued by the patterns of circulation of an impolite word referring to sexual relations between two men. Once the word *tante* has been introduced into his novel, it refuses to disappear. Vautrin, for instance, has another aunt besides Théodore Calvi. She is Jacqueline Collin, a woman the police would be happy to arrest because they believe her to be in possession of some incriminating letters exchanged between Lucien de Rubempré and three of his female aristocratic lovers. Yet now, to speak of Vautrin's *tante*, one is obliged to use metasemantic locutions, such as: "Jacques Collin has a *tante*, a natural *tante*, not an artificial one" (507, 6:892). Vautrin himself participates in this game: "The person is my aunt, quite a convincing aunt [une tante vraisemblable], a woman, an old one" (513, 6:897), thereby emphasizing that not all *tantes* are women, and not all of them are old.

Balzac clearly takes pleasure in the play with this word in which he and his characters indulge. He makes a point of showing that certain people intentionally avoid using this word when in the act of referring to Lucien de Rubempré. When the magistrate Camusot tells his superior that Vautrin has been put into contact with Calvi, he says: "At the moment he [Vautrin] is with your condemned man [Calvi], who was formerly, at the penitentiary for him, what Lucien was in Paris . . . his protégé" (506, 6:891, ellipses in original). Given that Camusot will, on the very next page, refer to Vautrin's aunt, and clarify that he means a "natural" one and not Calvi, it is noteworthy that he here employs the word *protégé* rather than *tante* to refer to Lucien. Doubtless, it is a question of register. A bit earlier in the book, Camusot's wife had been trying to curry favor with the Duchess Maufrigneuse by warning her that the monstrous Vautrin must still possess incriminating letters: " 'Monsieur Camusot knows for a certainty that that monster has put away in a safe place the most compromising [compromet*tantes!*] letters from the mistresses of his . . .' 'Of his friend,' interjected the Duchess quickly" (493, 6:878, ellipses in original). The Duchess moves quickly to control the register from which they will be choosing the word that refers to Lucien. In both of these instances, the three dots in the text stand as the sign of the brief moment in which a choice of words is being made, a moment and choice palpable to the interlocutors, and freighted with significance. In this latter case, just before the three dots, Madame Camusot in fact uses the possessive pronoun *son*, which could not grammatically be followed by *tante*, but could apparently be followed by some other word (*amant*, lover, perhaps) that the Duchess clearly does not wish to hear. In any case, Balzac has craftily left the hint of a *tante* in the passage, at the tail end of the word *compromettantes*, to remind us that it is a word ever ready at hand to refer to Lucien but never in fact used to do so.

Michael Silverstein refers to the phenomenon in evidence here as the "enregisterment of forms" in a language. A great deal of social force can be perceived at work in the way this enregisterment comes to govern the linguistic practices of speakers of a given language.[4] In order to understand the sociological function of registers, we need once again to distinguish between the *semantic* content of speech (the "meaning" of the words spoken) and the *pragmatic* aspects of the same discourse (the functioning—not always semantic—of linguistic signs to establish and do work in and on their particular context). It is by way of its pragmatic aspect that a discourse participates in the creation and the perpetuation of a social universe with all of its divisions into classes. It is through the pragmatic function of a discourse that interlocutors either indicate their well-established places within their social universe, or make implicit claims upon a place that is not yet established as theirs, or else *put* somebody in their place. Calvi cannot really be a protégé. Lucien must not be a *tante*.

Proust and the *Tantes* of Montesquiou

Here is another example to help us understand what is at stake. Once again it has to do with the use of the word *tante* within literary discourse. It is 1905, and Marcel Proust and Robert de Montesquiou spend the month of May writing each other a series of letters in which Montesquiou agrees to participate in an evening party hosted by Proust. He is to give a reading from a chapter of his new book, *Professionnelles Beautés*. The negotiations are a bit complicated: Montesquiou very much wants for the event to take place, but cannot allow himself to exhibit too much eagerness. Proust wants to organize the evening according to his own designs, but knows he has at least to pretend to defer to Montesquiou as far as who will be on the guest list. Montesquiou opens his letters with "Cher Marcel"; Proust with "Cher Monsieur." (Montesquiou is usually taken to be one of the key models for Proust's character Charlus.) The soirée takes place on June 2, 1905, and both seem afterward to be quite content with how the event transpired. In the correspondence following the evening, Proust suggests a bit timidly that he might perhaps write an article on Montesquiou's book, an idea for which Montesquiou expresses real enthusiasm—in an appropriate register, of course. Montesquiou's book contains a chapter called "Le Pervers" (Perversity), devoted to the English artist, Aubrey Beardsley. In one of his letters to Montesquiou Proust makes mention of this chapter:

> An article on this book in which one did not cite all that which peoples and furnishes the special universe of *"Perversity,"* would deny itself the choicest of citations. Yet how could one, in a respectable publication, transcribe the word that follows "actresses"?

> [Un article sur ce livre, où on ne citerait pas ce qui peuple et meuble l'univers spécial du «*Pervers*», se refuserait la plus belle des citations. Mais comment pourrait-on dans une feuille respectable transcrire le mot qui suit «des actrices».][5]

The word that follows "actresses" in Montesquiou's book is, of course, *tantes*, a fetish-word for Proust, a word it would seem that in 1905 he dare not even write in a letter. Here is the passage from Montesquiou's book, in which effects of register are particularly notable. Montesquiou is giving a list of the subjects Beardsley portrayed in his works:

> Bit players and actors . . . naked gnomes . . . madams who are busy reading; nightwalking women, livid in the darkness; epileptic marionettes and sinister-looking café waiters; hairdressers who resemble Louis-Philippe; gallant aged attendants; actresses; fairies [tantes]; groups of Wagnerians expectantly awaiting the satisfaction of their hysteria from a combination of music and obscurity; dressed-up monkeys, undressed ephebes . . . a wild, gay, and grotesque world. . . . I know not if this nomenclature in its seeming incoherence, but in fact quite precise if incomplete, will suffice, while angering those it is intended to anger, to please those it suits, and, by means of its very incoherence succeed in evoking for them this whole sarabande.

> [Ces comparses et ces comédiens . . . des gnomes nus . . . des maquerelles faisant la lecture; des rôdeuses de nuit, blafardes dans l'obscurité; des marionnettes épileptiques, des garçons de café patibulaires; des coiffeurs à la tête de Louis-Philippe; de vieux sigisbées; des actrices; des tantes; des assemblées de wagneriens attendant, de la musique et de l'obscurité combinées, la satisfaction de leur hystérie; des singes habillés, des éphèbes dévêtus . . . tout un monde follet et falot. . . . Je ne sais si cette nomenclature, en apparence incohérente, mais en réalité assez exacte, bien que fort incomplète, saura, tout en fachant ceux qu'il faut, réjouir ceux qu'il convient,

et, de par son incohérence même, évoquer, pour eux toute cette sarabande.][6]

Proust, in his own ever so precious fashion, calls Montesquiou's attention to what is obviously the carefully placed use of *tantes* to be found in *Professionnelles Beautés*. The pragmatic functions of Proust's gesture are multiple. He indicates a certain complicity with Montesquiou regarding their sexuality. He shows himself to be a reader attentive to certain kinds of details. He expresses an admiration for a certain kind of daring in Montesquiou's writing. He admits the impossibility of himself being so daring. One might further imagine that he is here revealing his desire to find a discursive form in which it would be possible for him to use this word. It is, of course, not only a question of finding the appropriate form, it is also a question of becoming the person who has the right to produce that discourse without losing face, without risking too much of who one is or wishes to be. When Proust writes the article on *Professionnelles Beautés* that is published in August 1905, no mention will be made of the chapter on Beardsley.[7]

Montesquiou himself was not at all concerned about losing face or about risking too much in using the word *tantes*. He thereby confirms some of the observations of Pierre Bourdieu regarding the market in linguistic goods:

> As the degree of formality in an exchange situation and the degree to which the exchange is dominated by highly authorized speakers diminish, so the law of price formation tends to become less unfavourable to the products of dominated linguistic habitus. It is true that the definition of the symbolic relation of power which is constitutive of the market can be the subject of *negotiation* and that the market can be manipulated, within certain limits, by a metadiscourse concerning the conditions of use of discourse. This includes, for example, the expressions which are used to introduce or excuse speech which is too free or shocking ("with your permission," "if I may say so," "if you'll pardon the expression," "with all due respect," etc.) or those which reinforce, through explicit articulation, the candour enjoyed on a particular market ("off the record," "strictly between ourselves," etc.). But it goes without saying that the capacity to manipulate is greater the more capital one possesses, as is shown by strategies of condescension.[8]

The capital of someone like Montesquiou is sufficiently great, and the literary context of his discourse sufficiently rarefied, that he could easily conceive himself to be above any form of "negotiation" at all. His entitlement to use the word *tante* is something he seems to take for granted. Proust, wishing to establish himself as a "highly authorized speaker" working literarily with a high degree of formality, is fearful of the down-market effect and the forms of self-implication that might be involved were he to take up the word in print.

Nonreferential Indexes

The word *tante* would seem to function in the contexts we have seen so far as what linguists such as Silverstein have referred to as a nonreferential index. Its use points to something outside the immediate referential context. If I say *tante* in this or that discursive context, I indicate something about what I understand that context to be, about what I understand my own social situation and those of my interlocutors to be, about what I hope to accomplish with my enunciation. As Silverstein has said, in making a useful distinction between what such indexes *presuppose* and what they *entail*: "Indexical meaning is composed of both indexical 'appropriateness-to' at-that-point autonomously known or constituted contextual parameters and indexical 'effectiveness-in' creating contextual parameters that are brought into being."[9]

Mastering a linguistic situation means knowing what you *can* presuppose about the context, what you *must* presuppose, what kinds of shifts you might be able to entail in the shared understanding of the context through what you say, and what kinds of shifts you would never be allowed to get away with. The use we all make of registers that are subject to more or less adroit manipulation implies that we all have a more or less developed sense of what can be called the *metapragmatic* functions at work in a given instance of discourse. We pursue pragmatic goals through our discursive interactions. In pursuing those goals in a given interaction we demonstrate how much awareness we have of the fact that certain discursive choices will or will not work well in pursuit of our goal. Sometimes this is something like a question of genre. Certain things are allowed in a conversation that are unseemly in a letter. A diary is different from either a conversation or a letter. An e-mail is different still, as is a novel. A review of a novel is different from an article in a scholarly journal. A treatise on legal medicine is not a society column, and so on. Gide speaking to Bourget is not Gide speaking to Proust, who is not Gide writing *Corydon*, who is not Gide writing *Si le grain ne meurt*. To quote Silverstein again, "Without a metapragmatic function simultaneously in play with whatever pragmatic function(s) there may be in discursive interaction, there is no possibility of interactional coherence."[10] If Proust is hoping to find a discursive moment, a literary moment, in which he can use the word *tante* while mastering both the semantic and the pragmatic meanings of that usage, he needs to build a discourse that is recognizable and recognized as a suitable means for *someone like him* to say something close to what he wants to say while using that particular word. Obviously Proust is not alone in his discursive universe, and so he must include in his calculations the efforts of other writers who are also working to entail certain modifications of their own in that universe.

Official discourses on sexuality (of which Montesquiou's is not one, whatever his social entitlements might be), and especially on same-sex sexuality, are highly ritualized, at least at the turn of the 1900s. Thus one is required to be invested with a certain authority, to be consecrated, before being able to speak on this subject and be widely heard. Rites of consecration can vary from discipline to discipline. To speak with authority as a doctor and to speak with authority as a novelist would not necessarily require the same form of consecration nor produce the same forms of discourse, although the different discourses may share common gestures. It would be a rare doctor, for instance, who would set out to speak of "pederasty" or "sapphism" without first pronouncing some kind of ritual formula such as the one we find under the pen of a certain Dr. Martineau, at the outset of his 1884 book, *Les Déformations vulvaires et anales produites par la masturbation, le saphisme, la défloration et la sodomie* (Deformations of the Vulva and the Anus Produced by Masturbation, Sapphism, Defloration, and Sodomy):

> This study is rife with difficulties; it demands extreme delicacy of expression; it uncovers a social wound so extensive that perhaps it would be better left secret, just as perhaps it would be best not to reveal the shameful facts on which it is based.

> [Cette étude est hérissée de tant de difficultés; elle exige une délicatesse d'expression si grande; elle révèle une plaie sociale si étendue qu'il vaudrait peut-être mieux la tenir secrète et ne pas divulguer les faits honteux sur lesquels elle repose. (2)]

Such sentences (versions of which can indeed be found at the outset of many novels—perhaps the framings of Gide's *The Immoralist* might count as a literary example) could also be thought of as functioning as nonreferential indexes. Beyond their semantic function (which is, in any case, rather limited), their pragmatic function is to make a claim that the person speaking is in fact consecrated to speak on these subjects, and that he (or, much more rarely, she) can be trusted to do so appropriately. Yet in order not to lose this consecration, the speaker is then obliged to pronounce a discourse that varies in only the most limited ways from previous discourses on the subject, a discourse that corresponds in most every detail to an already well recognized vision of the world. It sometimes seems that the rites that allow one to speak of same-sex sexualities, the rites through which people garner the authority to speak of them, also work to establish and perpetuate the set of epistemological categories according to which one is allowed to understand those very sexualities. The ritual function of speaking about sexuality thus participates in what Nelson Goodman has called "worldmaking": the attempt to found, to impose, to perpetuate an epistemological vision or version of the world. This would be why many discourses on sexuality from the end of the nineteenth century through today are so repetitive: rites function by way of repetition. In highly ritualized discursive arenas, the quota of what one *presupposes* in entering pragmatically into speech acts predominates over what one is allowed to imagine *entailing* by those acts. Yet this is not to say that nothing changes in these discourses or these epistemologies. As Silverstein has noted, "Ritualized contexts of indexical language licensing or authorization are themselves always potentially shifting in a social system, historical change or at least dialectical dynamism being inherent in the way semiosis seems to operate."[11] I am here trying to point to examples of this indexical dynamism within literary discourse on same-sex sexuality.

It is Montesquiou's pleasure to use the word *tante* in describing the "perverse" work of Beardsley, his pleasure to run the risk of angering certain readers in order to reach those who are well suited to appreciate Beardsley (and Montesquiou). Proust lets Montesquiou know he is one of those well suited to Montesquiou's prose even if it is not a prose he would or could himself write. He is, we might say, not as unconcerned about the opinion of people of the likes of Dr. Martineau as Montesquiou appears to be. In any case, it is through the intervention of authoritative speakers (Balzac) or highly entitled ones (Montesquiou) and through the interactions of speakers of different entitlements (Proust and Montesquiou, Camusot and his superior, Madame Camusot and the Duchess Maufrigneuse) that semiotic dynamism can make itself felt. (*Tante* had no place in the Duchess's lexicon. The Count Robert de

Montesquiou finds, a certain number of decades later, that he has purposes it can serve.) I pursue this question of semiotic dynamism by now turning briefly to a discussion of Catulle Mendès's 1890 novel, *Méphistophéla*, gradually providing more context for my ultimate focus in this chapter, on the year 1902, in which both Gide's *The Immoralist* and Colette's *Claudine Married* were published.

Méphistophéla

Literature, as we know, has its own rites of consecration and its own pragmatic and metapragmatic traditions. How is one to write about same-sex forms of desire and same-sex sexual relations? From what ideological point of view? At what point in a career? Within which genre? Drawing on which precursors? Will editors, critics and the public be receptive to publishing and reading what you write? Within which literary current, which literary circles would you do best to situate yourself? How, in what you write, will you indicate who your precursors are, what your ideological position is, what your literary intentions are, who your friends and foes are within the literary world as within the wider social world? All of these are questions regarding the metapragmatic aspect of your writing.

For almost everyone in French literary circles at the end of the nineteenth century, Balzac is the great consecrated figure when it comes to same-sex sexualities. Balzac is the richest source for those for whom one of the functions of literature is to be a discursive place for broaching the topic of same-sex sexualities. (I am here speaking mostly of prose; obviously for poetry one might rather think of Baudelaire.) The sequence at the end of *Splendeurs et misères des courtisanes*, in particular, is exemplary thanks to its evocation of (and investigation of) the registers available for speaking of same-sex sexualities. *Splendeurs et misères* is also exemplary in its way of associating different representations of these sexualities with the confrontation of two disparate social worlds. For many years literary representations of male same-sex relations and of female ones will locate themselves at the conjunction of these two problems: on the one hand the uncomfortable meeting of divergent registers of discourse, on the other the confrontation of conflicting social worlds that harbor conflicting sexual cultures and identities.

Consider the case of Catulle Mendès's *Méphistophéla*. There has been enough social and semiotic dynamism between the 1847 of *Splendeurs et misères des courtisanes* and the 1890 of *Méphistophéla* that Balzac's world of aristocratic friends and protégés has been transformed into a world of aristocratic households in degeneration, their blood exhausted. Balzac's prison-based world of *tantes* has, in parallel fashion, become the world of the Paris slums, the compost from which readers will have grown accustomed to seeing figures such as Zola's Nana arise. Throughout several decades, many French novels will hover ritualistically over the confrontation of these two worlds, aristocratic families and the lowest of low culture, and in particular over the question as to which of these two locales should be thought of as the proper home of errant sexualities. It is precisely around 1902 that one sees, in authors such as Gide and Colette—who at that time were not yet consecrated figures, and would not become so until much later—attempts to break with the set of pragmatic and metapragmatic conventions that governs this schema of representation. The effects of their attempts to renovate the literary forms within which it is permitted to address the subject of same-sex sexualities would require several decades to become firmly established in the literary field, and the older paradigm would retain its utility and viability at least through the 1950s.

Let us spend a moment with Mendès's trashy novel.[12] The central character of *Méphistophéla* is known during her childhood as Sophie Luberti. As an adult she will come to be known as the Baroness Sophor d'Hermelinge. The offspring of a theater girl and the last representative of a line of degenerate Russian aristocrats, she is raised in Fontaine-bleau, shielded from all knowledge about her sordidly mixed origins. She has as a childhood friend, her neighbor, Emmeline d'Hermelinge, for whom she feels deep emotions and mysterious desires that she is unable to represent to herself. One day, the older brother of Emmeline, who had been absent performing military service, returns to the family home, and a marriage is arranged between Emmeline's brother and her friend Sophie. Sophie's lack of understanding of sexuality in general and of her own sexuality in particular becomes more and more pointed, culminating in the events of her wedding night, which the novel luridly describes as an extremely violent rape scene. That horrific experience provides Sophie with the means to arrive at an initial fragmentary comprehension of her feelings for her childhood friend:

> Now that she was grown and that one horrific moment had transformed her into a woman, had revealed to her the frightful nature of masculine desire—so different from what she herself felt, yet somehow also resem-

bling it, now that, having experienced its shamelessness, she could conceive of that passion that forces one mouth upon another, one set of loins against another, she wondered, sometimes proudly, and also with a certain inner turmoil, if there was not, in her own adoration of the sleeping Emmeline, something that while not exactly being the same, was yet somehow analogous to the ardor of the spouse who had thrown himself upon her; and it was as if she had caught a brief glimpse of the chimeric possibility of being the husband of her friend.[13]

Having been cruelly beaten by her husband, who had realized the direction of her inclinations almost before she did, Sophie then convinces Emmeline to escape with her, and they flee to a small house on an island in the Seine not far from Paris. Emmeline will stay for one week before leaving Sophie to return to her family. The two women attempt to make love the last night they spend together, or rather, Sophie attempts to make love to Emmeline, without exactly knowing how to go about it:

Alas, she lacked knowledge of the rites pertaining to the form of worship of which she was the instinctive oblate. Was she absolutely ignorant? No. She had inklings, glimmerings; she could almost guess, but these rites—nearly impossible, at least so they seemed to her—were so strange that she was worried about taking a false step, and so, for fear of committing a sacrilege, was unable to proceed. Emmeline had therefore been right to run away, just as a god would abandon an altar at which prayers were not performed properly. (209)

Now, by a chance that is both literary and ideological, it turns out that this same island to which Sophie and Emmeline have fled is host to a whole household of women from the Parisian demimonde who share Sophie's sexual inclination. Mourning the loss of Emmeline, leaving the island en route for Paris, Sophie finds herself disturbed by the presence of these strange women as they all wait together for the train:

She had never seen creatures like these before. They were so different from Emmeline! Unappealing? No, not all of them. There was one—wearing a great deal of make-up, it has to be said—who was pretty, with red curls covering her forehead right down to her eyes. They were all saying strange things that Sophie could barely understand. One might have been excused for thinking that the French they spoke was a foreign language. Yet in these words that Sophie was hearing for the first time she already perceived something reprehensible. Sounds, even when they are not understood, still carry meaning. . . . What Sophie felt for them in the midst of all her anxiety was a kind of disgust. . . . It did occur to her that these women—bad women, dressed eccentrically—were not as different from her as one might believe. And the suspicion of this inspired in her a certain self-disgust. (217–18)

Of course that young redhead, who is named Magalo, will become Sophie's lover. Yet Sophie will use her, learn from her, and then quickly abandon her once she learns from her all the "science," all the knowledge, all the practices she is curious about. Before sleeping with Magalo, Sophie is totally ignorant: "Now, amid her anger, shame, and disgust, an ardent curiosity appeared in Sophie, established itself, and began to grow—a desire to learn all their science, so close at hand" (227). In a single night she seems to learn all there is to know:

Since only yesterday, how many delicious hours had she lived, yet with what terrible moments! How much knowledge had she gained, and how quickly! At last, to put all of her being into that extraordinary act of pleasure for which she had always longed without being able to imagine its exquisite yet also frightful attainment! Immediately, from the first lesson— not like a student, but like someone who suddenly recovers her memory— she had understood, dared, realized, and, with eyes scorched by glances, nostrils scorched by odors, a mouth filled with another's breath . . . she had conquered, vanquished Magalo, reduced her to those tears that ask for grace without wishing for it to be granted. (277–78)

At one level, what we have here is simply a representation (even if an oversimplified one) of the difficulties often experienced in the transmission of the sexual practices of a minority culture. (We also see here the image of a very specific form of female same-sex sexuality, with one "passive" woman and one "active" one, and in which the distribution of roles would seem to be permanently fixed, where one woman provides physical pleasure to the other.) Yet also interesting for our purposes is the way these passages reveal for us what might be called the topic of slumming (in French, *encanaillement*). The topic was already strongly present in Balzac. One was not to use the word *tante* where *protégé* or *ami* was more appropriate—not because there were no commonalities in the objects designated by the two words, but because there were also important differences, and when one speaks certain social distinctions need to be respected; indeed, when one speaks it is often in order to contribute to the reproduction of social distinctions. In Mendès's writing, we can observe the slow semiotic evolution of a category coming into being, that category that will come to be referred to as *homosexuality*. (The *Trésor de la langue française* gives 1891 as the date of the first appearance of that word in French, the year after the publication of *Méphistophéla*.) This new category eats away at the distinction between *tantes* and *protégés* (or the similar distinction that separates Magalo from the more suitable female partners Sophie will find as the years go by), a difference that was so important to Balzac's aristocrats and that was still palpably functioning in works by Mendès and others like him. In fact, we might say that it was one of the functions of the word *homosexual* to encourage the forgetting of previously quite real and quite practical distinctions having to do with the intersection of social and sexual identities, distinctions that mattered in daily life and that were designated by way of other terms.[14]

Encanaillement / Slumming

In order to speak of same-sex sexualities at the end of the nineteenth and the beginning of the twentieth centuries, writers often seem to have felt obliged to speak of the slow, steady, and dangerous wearing down of the distinction between high society and low society. It was as if one could feel allowed to represent these sexualities only by taking a position regarding the impending loss of important social distinctions, a loss that was often thought to be the fault of the sexual practices in question. Consider a few further examples of the structuring force of the topic of slumming.

At the outset of Liane de Pougy's novel *Idylle saphique* (1901), when the young Miss Florence Temple-Bradfford arrives dressed as a page to declare her love to Annhine de Lys and to suggest that they undertake "to live a little in the burning, feverish atmosphere of Sodom and Gomorrah . . . , that place where, nearly free, the divine embraces of lascivious modern faunnesses can be realized," her interlocutor interrupts her to exclaim, "So . . . that's what it is! . . . You are a . . ." (We stumble across those three dots again.) But Flossie quickly interrupts in turn to cry, "Oh! I beg of you not to inflict any name at all upon that feeling that has had me in its grips ever since I first had feelings, that feeling that devours me here in your presence, Annhine."[15] Flossie interrupts Annhine much in the way that the Duchess interrupted Madame Camusot, to prevent a vulgar word from being applied to practices that had another home elsewhere in the cultural imaginary.

A little further along in the same novel, Flossie explains to Annhine that she has a rich fiancé named Will who, thanks to the reading of Swinburne and Pierre Louÿs that she and he undertook as a couple, allowed himself to be convinced never to sleep with her. As a concession, she has granted him the right to watch while she makes love to other women. Annhine replies:

> I myself have never loved women, and if ever . . . if ever that should happen, well, first of all, I'm not sure it would be with you, and, in any case, no indiscreet observers, that's wrong, debauched, foul! It's filthy. Here we call that a three-party affair, or else another name much too ugly for me to pronounce.
>
> "Oh yes, I know . . . voyeurs . . ." (and Flossie pronounced prettily, and without any shame or embarrassment, with her delicious and faintly foreign accent, that word from the gutter [ce mot canaille]). (56)

Flossie, in her earlier aristocratically inflected fantasy (dressed as a page) had preferred that her desire not be named, labeled, for the word chosen would doubtless have been too vulgar. Yet in another moment this same young bourgeois woman from the States feels no shame or embarrassment around the apparently low-class word *voyeur*.[16] In this small way, as a modern American, she contributes to the destabilization of certain already dated French social distinctions—distinctions already a bit out of kilter within the novel given that Annhine herself is a courtesan and not a lady of social distinction. The novel demonstrates that the questions of slumming, of encanaillement, of the confusion of registers, of the confrontation of different social classes, provide the frames for the literary forms in and through which same-sex sexualities are spoken of, even when "true" aristocrats are not themselves present. (The identity of the novel's author, the Belle Epoque's famous courtesan Liane de Pougy, of course brings up the question of encanaillement in other ways. I will have more to say about Liane de Pougy in the next chapter.)

Consider now the example of a letter from J.-K. Huysmans to André Raffalovich, the author of *Uranisme et unisexualité* (1896) mentioned in chapter 1. Huysmans was the author of the 1884 novel *À Rebours* (*Against Nature*), whose hero (also often said to be based on Robert de Montesquiou) experimented with his own sexuality. (The novel itself would exert an important influence over the title character of Oscar Wilde's *The Picture of Dorian Gray*.) Vernon Rosario has suggested that Raffalovich "enunciated positions so divergent from dominant French medical opinion that they appeared radically prohomosexual." Rosario also notes of Raffalovich that "his campaign to normalize homosexuality was fought by sacrificing a stigmatized group of 'perverse' inverts. In many ways his scientific opinion was the forerunner of the political strategy employed by current homosexual apologists who campaign for the rights of 'good' homosexuals by perpetuating the marginalization of 'bad' ones: cross-dressers, sadomasochism enthusiasts, flamboyant effeminates, and so on."[17] It might be a bit of an exaggeration to refer to Raffalovich's opinions as scientific. He was a man of letters who, over a period spanning roughly ten years, wrote many articles for the *Archives d'anthropologie criminelle*. In his articles, he fought against the use of a conception of "inversion" to explain involvement in same-sex sexualities. His wish was to establish a distinction between "inverts" and what he called "unisexuals" or "uranists." To be absolutely accurate we would have to say that, while he showed a strong preference for the words *unisexual* and *uranist*, he was also at times capable of using the word *invert* as a synonym for them, but he did insist, "(and this is a fairly general rule) that the more a unisexual is morally worthy, the less he will be effeminate."[18]

In the *Archives d'anthropologie criminelle* of December 1904, Raffalovich published a letter he had received from Huysmans after he had read *Uranisme et unisexualité*. In that letter Huysmans recounts his experience as a tourist in the gay world of a certain moment (the 1890s), where his guide was probably Jean Lorrain. Huysmans uses his letter effectively to disavow any sexual kinship with the protagonist of his own novel or with people such as Lorrain:

> The world of the sodomites—your book and your letter bring back to me a number of terrifying evenings I spent in that world, where I was shown around by a talented fellow whose deviant joys are a mystery to no one. I spent several days there; then it was discovered I was there under false pretenses, and I just barely managed to escape with my skin.
>
> It seemed to me a kind of hell. Imagine this: the man who has this vice leaves himself and common man behind. He eats in restaurants, has his hair cut, and lives in a hotel, all of which are run by older sodomites. It is a life on the margins, a restricted life, a secret society whose members recognize themselves by their voices, a fixed gaze, a singing and affected tone that they all share.
>
> Moreover, this vice is the *only* one that effaces the boundaries of castes. A decent man and a lackey are equals—they converse together normally, live

as if without difference in education. This vice achieves what charity cannot, the equality of mankind. This is strange and disturbing.

And what a life for a decent young fellow, like my guide, devoured by this vice, risking the permanent jealousy of blows from a knife.

One evening, in a cabaret on the rue des Vertus that is frequented by this set of people and where sixty-year-old fairies [*tapettes*, a synonym for *tantes*] wearing as much makeup as old actors run a business behind curtains, I saw a well-known man of the theater enter. He had come to find a partner in this place. I had never seen anything so sinister. The man's face, livid, sad enough to make you weep, driven by his vice as if it were a hand pushing at his back, disgusted at himself, resisting and yet proceeding even so, with the collar of his jacket turned up! Once you have seen such things you thank Heaven you have not been afflicted with such tastes! And chastity seems unquestionably great and the only appropriate choice.[19]

Hardly what you would want to call an unprejudiced witness, Huysmans here shows himself rather to be someone who replicates all of the past and present commonplaces that permit one to speak appropriately and "decently" about these matters (matters, it must be said, others would prefer not be spoken of at all): the condemnation of the effacement of social distinction, of the practice of slumming by decent people, a critique of the "gay ghetto" (to update Huysmans's terminology slightly). We also see clearly in Huysmans's performance here the determining (though perhaps unconscious) presence of pragmatic and metapragmatic functions. What Huysmans does, in writing what he writes to Raffalovich, is not simply to describe or to refer. His writing, by way of his use of easily recognizable cultural forms, also indicates *who* he wants to be.

As Silverstein says, "One dimension of the 'meaning' of every speech form is pragmatic, exactly like any social action. From a semiotic point of view, all such meanings can be described as rules linking certain culturally-constituted features of speech situations with certain forms of speech."[20] Different aspects of the pragmatic implications of what we say are more or less readily available to our immediate consciousness. That you choose, in speaking French, to say *vous* to someone or to say *tu* is a pragmatic decision that is probably not entirely conscious, for example, but the choice is easily enough explained after the fact. Many of our choices as we put together what we say are probably less easy for us to make immediate sense of. That you would choose to say *sodomite* at a given moment instead of *invert* or *unisexual* or *uranist*; that you would find yourself in the midst of explaining that it is impossible not to notice the effacement of social distinctions in sodomitical circles; that you feel obliged to point out that decent people demean themselves when they frequent sodomitical locations: these are all discursive decisions whose reasons are probably a bit more opaque to the immediate conscious mind of the speaker. Yet taken all together they indicate who it is you wish to be in the face of your interlocutors. By means of such choices we endeavor to establish not only who we are, but by what right, because of what expertise, from what point of view we speak when we speak about these questions. Our practical decisions situate us ideologically and socially; they determine the alliances we would make, the camp to which we would belong. In literary contexts, they also help make the case for the aesthetic merit of our choice of topic and our way of treating it.

Here is one final example, from a few decades later, of this problem of slumming in relation to literature and sexuality. It is an example that shows to what an extent certain discursive gestures become cultural habits, to what an extent such gestures endure over time. (We should probably also keep in mind that sometimes the indexical value of a given gesture shifts dramatically with the passage of time.) In 1936, Gide has just read Colette's recently published *Mes apprentissages* (*My Apprenticeships*), and writes the following comments in his journal:

> Read Colette's latest book with very keen interest. There is in it much more than a literary gift: a sort of very peculiarly feminine genius and a great intelligence. What choice, what order, what happy proportions in an account apparently so unbridled! What utter tact, what courteous discretion in confidence (in the portraits of Polaire, of Jean Lorrain, of Willy above all, of "Monsieur Willy"); not a touch that fails to hit the mark and to mark itself in one's memory, sketched as at random, as if while playing, but with a subtle, accomplished art. I constantly skirted, brushed against that society that Colette depicts and that I recognize here, artificial, tainted, hideous, and against which, most fortunately, an unconscious residue of puritanism put me on guard. It does not seem to me that Colette, despite all her superiority, was not somewhat contaminated by it.

> [Lu le dernier livre de Colette avec un intérêt très vif. Il y a là bien plus que du don: une sorte de génie très particulièrement féminin et une grande intelligence. Quel choix, quelle ordonnance, quelles heureuses proportions, dans un récit en apparence si débridé! Quel tact parfait, quelle cour-

toise discrétion dans la confidence (dans les portraits de Polaire, de Jean Lorrain, de Willy surtout, de «Monsieur Willy»); pas un trait qui ne porte et qui ne se retienne, tracé comme au hasard, comme en se jouant, mais avec un art subtil, accompli. J'ai côtoyé, frôlé sans cesse cette société que peint Colette et que je reconnais ici, factice, frelatée, hideuse, et contre laquelle, fort heureusement, un reste inconscient de puritanisme me mettait en garde. Il ne me paraît point que Colette, malgré toute sa supériorité, n'en ait pas été quelque peu contaminée.][21]

This passage reveals how over time Gide came to accept Colette as one of his literary peers, as a stylist whose skill rivaled his own. It also reminds us of the fact that in the early years of the century, Gide imagined his literary project (and the role of sexuality in that project) in opposition to what were for him the literarily and morally inferior and inappropriate efforts of people like Colette. From his *Immoralist* in 1902 to *The Vatican Cellars* in 1914 to *The Counterfeiters* in 1925 (and in other works as well), Gide's thinking on sexuality often seems to turn on an opposition between the sincere and the artificial, and his writings on the subject will always, in one way or another, take up the subject of a certain kind of slumming even if he wrenches it far away from the paradigm we find in Balzac and his naturalist followers. What we might see in Gide's reference here to that "unconscious residue of puritanism" would be not only an indication about his social behavior, but also a reflection on his choice of literary register, a choice of register implicating both manner and matter, both what is said and how it is said. Let us then juxtapose Gide's *The Immoralist* and Colette's *Claudine Married*, two works published at almost the same moment in 1902, to see what we can learn about the work of register and position taking in their literary field and about how such concerns affected the representational and formal strategies of Gide and Colette. Rachilde can be our initial guide, for she reviews the two novels in successive issues of the *Mercure de France*, *Claudine Married* in June 1902 and *The Immoralist* in July of the same year.

Gide and Colette in 1902

The *Mercure de France* was well known for its interest in literary attempts at representing same-sex sexualities—homosexual, unisexual, uranist, sapphist, lesbian, and so on. The journal published Pierre Louÿs's novel

Aphrodite in 1896 and Georges Eekhoud's *Escal-Vigor* in 1899. In *Aphrodite* we read of a land in which "when two young and nubile virgin girls . . . love each other, they are permitted by law to marry . . . they have all the rights of a married couple; they can adopt baby girls and include them in their intimate circle. They are respected. They are a family."[22] Louÿs's novel is one that the teenage Claudine reads in *Claudine at School*; she also precociously reads the *Mercure de France*.

For Rachilde (at least in 1902) the terms of the comparison to be made between Gide and Colette are the same as the ones found in Gide's journal entry on Colette from 1936, but reversed. (She even uses a number of the same words—*factice*, artificial, and *frelaté*, tainted.) She comments of the protagonist of *The Immoralist*: "Michel would not be so revolting if only he would either die or else overcome his prejudices. . . . It is impossible to admire Michel. Despite all the trappings of a bookworm who is troubled by the happy ignorance of the lowlife around him, he seems artificial, constructed, cowardly . . . sick [factice, composé, lâche . . . malade]."[23]

On the other hand, *Claudine Married* is, for Rachilde, "a sincere work, so deliciously written that it brings tears of joy to the eyes of those taken with natural art. This ultramodern morality tale is not, however, a book from the Parisian boulevards. Its roots lie further afield than the adulterated life [la vie frelatée] of our time. They are to be found in some ancient forest where a young and virgin druidess wildly offers herself to the embrace of God even before she has known man." Yet if, for Rachilde, the heroine of Colette's novel is perfectly natural, her dalliance during the course of *Claudine Married* in what Rachilde calls "the paths of Lesbos" is not. Claudine, according to Rachilde, takes this queer detour not from any natural penchant, but because she is mystified by her husband and by the attractive Rézi, who is "more a perverse and pallid stuffed figure than a real woman, vice-ridden, fearful, and childish. . . . Claudine believes she is in love with this woman when she is in fact only in love with love."[24]

For Rachilde, Gide's book is a bit out of date and written by an author who is altogether too stuffy, whereas *Claudine Married*, following upon the two previous Claudine novels (*Claudine at School* and *Claudine in Paris*) succeeds in placing Willy (for Rachilde writes her article as if she believes that Colette's husband Willy wrote the book—which is, after all, what the cover stated)[25] "at the forefront of French novelists." Such evaluations might surprise those among us today who are perhaps more used to thinking of *The Immoralist* as one of the first major works in the career of an important modernist artist—a slightly Nietzschean text that stands at the outset of a project that involved simultaneously a quest to represent one kind of sexual liberation and a quest for an endlessly refined approach to literary forms. We might also be used to thinking of the Claudine novels as lightweight, commercialized works, a bit off-color—early works in the career of a writer whose consecration has always been slightly problematic, whose profile has always had enough of a popular quality about it that her literary seriousness has remained open to question. As Bourdieu has said, in speaking of cultural goods, "in dissociating temporal success and specific consecration and in assuring the specific profits of disinterestedness to those who submit to its rules, the artistic (or scientific) field creates the conditions for the constitution (or emergence) of a veritable interest in disinterestedness."[26] It is Gide who (with greater success than Colette in any case) managed to incarnate literary disinterestedness, and surely this partly explains why his literary reputation over the years has sometimes seemed the surer one.

Of course, if Colette disdained to invest her interests in playing a disinterested writerly role, if she sometimes made no bones about writing for money, this is also because she often needed money, whereas Gide never did. If she chose not to disguise her economic situation, if she turned women's work into a major topic of her writing (as in *The Vagabond* or *Music Hall Sidelights*) it might well be said that in so doing she found a way to play with the very terms we find in Bourdieu's analysis, revealing how a woman's (and especially a married woman's) relation to disinterestedness was necessarily different from a man's—this being the result of the way gender structured the social field, and of the different property rights allowed to married women and married men. (Under the Napoleonic Code, women by marrying relinquished most of their property rights to their husbands. Only in 1907, for instance, were married women granted the right to dispose freely of their own earnings and their own inheritances. This was obviously of immediate importance to Colette. Also, it was not only a matter of property rights. Married Frenchwomen were officially granted the legal right to exercise a profession without the authorization of their husbands only in 1965.)[27]

I do not mean to suggest that we should now change our minds and accept the terms of the comparative evaluation of Gide and Colette that Rachilde offers. Her evaluations in any case underestimate and misconstrue aspects of both Gide's and Colette's projects. Yet her remarks can help us to appreciate to what an extent our own evaluations (indeed our own critical practices, our habits of reading) can turn out to be the effects of the structure and history of the literary field itself, produced by the work of various categories and divisions within the field across time.

Gide, as one might imagine, found Rachilde's article extremely annoying. "Those who are hard of hearing are even more dangerous than the deaf," he wrote to his friend Henri Ghéon about Rachilde on July 6, 1902. "If I do not want my book to be taken as an apologia, my only choice is to affirm that it is merely a satire. Is there no space in between the two for the work of art? Must the artist preach either on behalf of or else against his heroes?"[28] The bulk of *The Immoralist* is narrated in the first person by its protagonist Michel. That first-person account is framed by another first-person text written by a friend of Michel's, and that first-person text is further framed by a preface by André Gide. In his preface, Gide writes of the unspecified "problem" being treated in his book: "I make no claim to have invented this 'problem'; whether Michel triumphs or succumbs, the 'problem' continues to exist, and the author offers neither triumph nor defeat as a foregone conclusion. . . . I have tried to prove nothing, but to paint my picture well and light it properly." Formal artistry takes precedence over subject. Certainly the interplay between the three first persons in *The Immoralist* has something to do with Gide's concerns over appropriate ways of speaking about same-sex sexuality. It also has to do with a claim for literary sophistication. In her review, Rachilde notes, a bit unkindly, that the book is filled with "the trickiest kinds of cerebral traps that can be laid for feeble modern minds." Turning immediately away from such questions of formal artistry, Gide's badges of sophistication, Rachilde instead focuses on what she sees as the book's failure to confront same-sex sexualities directly, and the "dilletantisme" resulting from that failure. The book is thus for Rachilde entirely too moral. It is, she says—and she apparently means this to be taken as a criticism—"far from being a perverse work."

Yet it would also be possible to see in Gide's interwoven first persons the indication of a critical awareness of the functioning of first persons, born out of the difficulty of expressing oneself regarding certain kinds of sexuality. The novel exemplifies in its form hard lessons regarding what can appropriately or effectively be said by different first persons in different contexts about their or about someone else's sexuality. If Gide is looking, as he says to Ghéon, for a space between satire and apologia, this is surely because those two modes of speaking about sexuality are both culturally authorized forms of expression and inadequate ones for his purpose. Rachilde's implied imperative—be perverse!—is not what he aims for either. For Rachilde, perversion is the truth of certain sexualities. Her reviews make clear that she preferred to countenance those particular literary works dealing with same-sex sexualities that struck precisely the correct perverse note. When we consider that her praise for the "ultramodern" *Claudine Married* includes a reading of the lesbian episode in that novel as a truthful portrayal of a temporary deviation into perversion by a protagonist only momentarily corrupted by her jaded husband and the equally jaded Rézi, it becomes easier to appreciate the many reasons for Gide's resistance to the kinds of expressive imperatives we hear Rachilde voicing. We should also hold open the possibility that Rachilde's review does not lead us to a full appreciation of the critical work on the first person in relation to same-sex sexuality of which Colette was capable in these years, nor to an accurate sense of the sexual values to be found in the Claudine novels.

Rachilde claims Gide's text to be more reticent in its approach to same-sexuality than one was obliged to be at the time. The Claudine novels are much less reticent, as are all the texts that form the background to them—Mendès's *Méphistophéla*, Louÿs's *Aphrodite* and *Chansons de Bilitis*, and Pougy's *Idylle saphique* are a few of the titles to which more or less explicit reference is made in the *Claudine* series. These are, of course, mainly texts dealing with female same-sex relations. For male same-sex relations, we could consider the writings of Jean Lorrain— not only his novels, but his journalism as well. Take as an example the final paragraph of an article he published on the front page of *Le Journal* on February 4, 1902, a few months before the publication of the novels by Gide and Colette. It was one in a series of articles on figures from popular culture in the south of France and was called "La Petite à François" (François's Little Girl). The article recounts a conversation overheard by the author between four wrestlers on a tour of some villages. One of them, François, is preparing to return home to his wife and newborn baby girl, and his companions are asking him questions about the presents he will be taking back to them. Then one of the friends asks a final question:

> "And the little fellow who was sleeping with you, François, are you taking him home?"
>
> "What little fellow?" the wrestler from the Ardèche region asked, blushing right to the tips of his ears.

"Why the Parisian, the peddler who was selling knives and wallets at the fair and had such cute eyes, Jacques Pretty-Eyes."

"He's going with me to the train station, but, poor fellow, has to stay here for the rest of the season. What would he do back in my village?"

"More importantly, where would he sleep in your house?"

"Stop it, you rascals! When I picked him up for the first time he had nowhere to sleep and had eaten nothing all day, poor kid, and such an excellent fellow! Ah, he knew how to take care of my laundry, and after all, what's wrong with sleeping together? We're poor; the room is cheaper when there are two of you, and you don't get as bored."[29]

[«Et le petit qui couchait avec toi, François, tu l'emmènes?

—Quel petit? faisait l'Ardéchois, rouge jusqu'aux oreilles, quel petit?—Mais le Parisien, le camelot qui vendait des couteaux et des porte-monnaie sur la Foire, et qui avait de si belles mirettes, Jacques les Beaux-Yeux—Il me conduit à la gare, mais reste ici pour la saison, le pôvre. Que ferait-il au village?—Et puis où le logerais-tu chez toi?—Taisez-vous, méchants! Quand je l'ai cueilli la première fois, il ne savait où coucher et n'avait rien mangé de la journée, le môme, et puis si brave! Ah! il m'a bien soigné mon linge, et puis où voyez-vous le mal qu'on ait dormi ensemble! On est des pauvres: la chambre, elle coûte moins cher, et à deux on ne se languit pas tant.»]

Lorrain is famous for his wicked pen. He was particularly wicked, as one of his biographers puts it, "towards those well-placed people who kept their penchants a secret." The story of his duel with Proust (in February 1897) is well known: it resulted from the malicious way in which he spoke of Proust's *Les Plaisirs et les jours* (*Pleasures and Days*) and, in the same article, of the nature of Proust's relations with Montesquiou and Lucien Daudet. Lorrain enjoyed making fun of Montesquiou (and of his poetry), sometimes calling him "Grotesquiou," sometimes "Robert Machère." He nicknamed the actor de Max the "Monsieur aux camélias."[30] But his article about the conversation overheard between the wrestlers has no notable meanness in it. Rather, it seems full of amused sympathy. It's tempting to say that it takes up the question of sexual relations between men in a way that is much more straightforward, much less mannered than the way we find instantiated in Gide's *The Immoralist*, published only a few months after Lorrain's article—tempting, but probably not wholly accurate, for there are doubtless nearly as many enormously varied manners as there are texts. Lorrain's manner, and his reputation as one of the leading journalists in Paris, had both been carefully calculated and constructed over decades of practice. Again it is a question of registers and of the pragmatic and metapragmatic functions brought into play in different kinds of texts. Authors such as Lorrain, Gide, Colette, or Proust were experimenting with these functions whenever they tried out new approaches to the representation of same-sex sexualities. They were certainly all aware of each other—each other's reputations as well as writings.[31] We might even say that they were in some kind of extended conversation or debate with each other, that they were all contributing to a social dynamic in which manners for speaking about same-sex sexual relations—and the effects those manners would have when taken up by different people—were evolving.

Gide's comments in his journal in 1936 about the "artificial, tainted, hideous" society in which Colette and Lorrain moved reveal how much an effort *not* to be—or to write—like them must have been part of his social and literary aims earlier in the century. On the same day (February 4, 1902) that Lorrain published his article about the wrestlers in *Le Journal*, Gide described in his own journal an anecdote Édouard de Max had told him about Lorrain regarding Lorrain's sexual indiscretions:

> "In Nice," he [de Max] tells me [Gide], "I had no sooner gotten into town—the very first day, my dear—than a little coachman leans over to me from his perch and asks: 'A Lorrain special, sir?' "
>
> "So I ask him what he means by a 'Lorrain special,' and he pretends to giggle: 'Well sir, it means to drive out to the end of the Rocher, and then come back.' "
>
> "The coachman wasn't at all bad looking!"
>
> "So what happened," I ask.
>
> "Well, I wanked him for a little while, and then we came back . . . But Lorrain has an incredible reputation down there."

> [«À Nice raconte-t-il, je n'étais pas plus tôt descendu en ville—le premier jour, mon cher,—un petit cocher se penche vers moi du haut de son siège:
>
> «"Un complet Lorrain, m'sieur?"
>
> «Alors je lui ai demandé ce qu'il entendait par "complet Lorrain." Il a fait celui qui veut rigoler:
>
> «"Oh! m'sieur, ça veut dire, aller jusqu'au bout du rocher et puis revenir."
>
> «Le cocher n'était pas vilain.»
>
> MOI: Et alors?

«Et alors je l'ai branlotté un tout petit peu et puis nous sommes revenus
. . . Mais Lorrain a là-bas une renommée fantastique.»]

Gide's next sentence shifts topic slightly: "Passed by the rue O. in order
to prepare for Ghéon's imminent return" [Passé rue O. préparer le
retour de Ghéon].[32] Rue O. refers to a public bathhouse on the rue
Oberkampf. Gide's journal in these years is punctuated by references to
his visits to this establishment, to which he and his friend Ghéon seem
to have repaired regularly in search of their own coachmen, yet apparently with a greater concern for the protection of their names than
Lorrain ever showed.

Gide, in the first person figure he constructs, is clearly working out
an approach not only to a public self but also to writing. The approach
is stylistic (a careful balancing act of "artifice" and "the natural," of
indiscretion and discretion, of confession and reticence); it is also strategic. He is strategizing both about his future reputation (posterity) and
his contemporary literary profile. It's not often done, but it is interesting
to think that Colette (and Lorrain) might be taken as peers for Gide
within the literary field of the first decade of the twentieth century,
figures whose strategies contrast markedly with his even as their projects of representation and experimentation with subject matter overlap
and probably help determine his in interesting ways.

In thinking about Gide's relation to Colette in these terms, using
concepts such as "strategy," comparing the different trajectories of contemporaneous literary careers, I rely on some of Bourdieu's useful
thinking about both biography and literature. In a short essay titled
"L'Illusion biographique," Bourdieu suggests:

> To try to understand a life as a unique and self-sufficient series of successive
> events without any connection other than their association with a "sub-
> ject" whose consistency is undoubtedly only that of a proper name, is just as
> absurd as attempting to make sense of a subway ride without taking into
> account the structure of the system, that is to say, the matrix of objective
> relations among the different stations. Biographical events take shape as so
> many placements and displacements in social space, that is, more precisely,
> in the different and successive states of the structure governing the distribu-
> tion of different kinds of capital which are at stake in the given field.[33]

To invoke Bourdieu's concept of the *field* is to insist on the relational
aspect of each event that contributes to the shaping of a literary career.[34]
To outline a few episodes in the *relationship* between Gide and Colette

or between Gide and Lorrain is to begin to outline the social and literary space in which each of them is making complicated decisions about what it means to be a literary figure associated with the representations and practices of same-sex sexualities. Such decisions are heavily mediated by all sorts of forces within the social and literary fields.

Let us consider one more person in order to further our understanding of the pragmatic struggle under way in this particular "conversation": Lucie Delarue-Mardrus. She launched herself in the Parisian literary world in 1902, at the age of twenty-one, both as a poet (a protegée of Robert de Montesquiou) and as a literary critic. In June, she reads Gide's *The Immoralist*. Her husband (Joseph-Charles Mardrus, well-known for his translation of the *Arabian Nights* [1898–1904]) had detested Gide's book; she adores it. In particular, she appreciates the way it constitutes an application of Nietzsche's teachings (everyone in Paris seems to be reading Nietzsche at this point). But she also especially appreciates what she calls the book's "reticence," a quality she finds strongly expressed in its portrayal of sexuality. She writes to Gide, conveying her enthusiasm for his achievement: "It seems to me that even with Candaule you have never before gone so far into the drama of complication and of thirst. And this muted adventure of a soul is even more complicated because of the adventures of the flesh with which you cause us to shiver, adventures that are full of sweat and blood." Speaking of Gide's protagonist Michel, she adds, "I am pleased that he only barely cracks open the egg . . . I am pleased that he cannot fully shake off the frightful nets of atavism, of education, of habit. . . . It is this reticence, Reticence!, to which I am attached. If Michel freed himself, he would cease to interest me. . . . Michel must remain a slave if Gide is to continue to be of interest to us."[35] In other words, even given all the complicated sexual experiences and the inventive reorganizing of their personal and intimate lives that people like her, people like Gide, like Lorrain, like Colette, like Liane de Pougy, were engaged in—their variety, their range, their experimental feel—even given all of this, Delarue-Mardrus is still happier that a clear expression or representation or assumption of sexual errancy remain beyond the grasp of Gide's protagonist, beyond the reach of literary expression.[36]

Gide was quite struck by Delarue-Mardrus's letter; he writes of it in very favorable terms to his friend Henri Ghéon on June 20, 1902.[37] He goes even further and convinces Delarue-Mardrus to turn her letter into an article for *La Revue blanche*, where it appears on July 15, 1902, under the title "Essai sur «*l'Immoraliste*»." At the same moment that Rachilde is accusing Gide of a "rather too abnormal dilettantism" in the *Mercure de France*, Delarue-Mardrus is praising his "reticence" in the *Revue blanche*.

If Delarue-Mardrus is a fan of Gide and of *The Immoralist*, Lorrain, on the other hand, is unsurprisingly a fan of Colette and of *Claudine Married*. He writes an article about the novel on the front page of *Le Journal* on May 29, 1902, under the title "Should One Read It?" [Doit-on le lire?]. After spending some time recounting the plots of the two previous Claudine novels, dwelling a bit on the character of Marcel, the effeminate young man we first met in *Claudine in Paris*, a "young ephebe who can't seem to leave behind the translations of Greek authors," mentioning Claudine's curiosity regarding the "uranistic correspondence of the handsome Charlie," he then, with a typical inversional rhetorical flourish, suggests that the present installment in the Claudine series should be counted among those "a mother could not allow her sons to read." Describing how, in *Claudine Married*, Claudine's husband Renaud not only encourages his wife to pursue a relationship with the beautiful Rézi, but actively assists her in doing so, he notes, "we find ourselves at quite a distance from *Mademoiselle Giraud, ma femme*, whose husband, having been deceived by his wife, drowns her with his own hands."[38] Lorrain's register is clearly different from that of Delarue-Mardrus (and from that of Rachilde, when she expressed her disapproval of the same-sex affair between women in *Claudine Married*). Instead of speaking in elevated tones about the novel's philosophical antecedents and its classical qualities of discretion and reticence (and instead of referring somewhat disdainfully to the "artificial" quality of sexual relations between two women), Lorrain situates *Claudine Married* forthrightly in its full relation to the subject of same-sex sexual relations, and compares it favorably to a popular and melodramatic novel from 1869 that had had great commercial success and that, despite its portrayal of an obsessive and murderous hostility to sexual relations between women, probably had (as did Mendès's *Méphistophéla*) a great deal of importance in disseminating information about and images of those very relations.[39]

In *Mes apprentissages*, Colette cites a letter she received from Lorrain in October 1902. Lorrain wrote from Marseille, where he had just seen the play based on the first two Claudine novels, a play that was proving immensely successful. Colette's editors have furnished us with a more exact version of that letter than the one provided by Colette herself:

Nine thirty in the morning

And I am just getting back to the hotel

That's what happens when you go out to see *Claudine*. I lived it up like there was no tomorrow . . . Luce, Marcel, and Charley, and all the Claudinettes and all the Claudes (don't believe a word of it, I'm bragging . . . blowing my own horn).

The simple truth is that I'm just getting home . . . it shouldn't matter to you where I spent the night.

[Neuf heures et demie matin

Et je rentre à l'Hôtel

Voilà ce que c'est que de voir jouer *Claudine*. J'ai fait la fête et toute la lyre . . . Luce, Marcel et Charley et toutes les Claudinettes et tous les Claudins (n'en croyez rien, je me vante . . . il faut cultiver sa légende).

La vérité est que je rentre . . . il vous importe peu n'est-ce pas de savoir où j'ai passé la nuit.][40]

What Lorrain sees in Colette is a person who, like him, participates both in the representation and in the perpetuation of a certain kind of popular queer culture, one in which he obviously felt quite at home and to which he had strong allegiances. If he became such a significant but troubling figure, an unavoidable one, for Gide, for Proust, for Montesquiou, for Colette, for Rachilde, for Francis Carco, it is precisely because of his openly avowed affiliation with this "insalubrious" cultural milieu, an affiliation of which he made careful use in constructing his public image and in constructing a strategy for expressing his sexuality and same-sex sexuality in general. His strategies and his image were ones that many others felt were inadmissable or off-limits.[41]

Tantes and Vrilles

Colette's work, as we shall see, retains an affiliation with Lorrain that writers such as Gide and Proust would shun (although Gide and Proust would both in later years testify to their respect for Colette). Writers such as Lorrain and Colette may be working to establish traditions and possibilities of expression that are in tension with those being sought after by writers such as Proust and Gide; nonetheless they are all collectively involved in the search for the appropriate pragmatic and metapragmatic means to link together (1) *a social position* from which one is entitled as a literary figure to express oneself on the question of same-sex sexualities, (2) *forms of literary expression* that are valued, recognized as noteworthy or exceptional, and finally (3) *a particular vision of the sexual order*, of the divisions and categories of the social world through which same-sex sexualities are perceived. Obviously these writers diverge among themselves regarding their relation to those sexualities. Gide is concerned with maintaining a certain kind of dignity. The others mostly are not. Colette and Lorrain are probably not particularly interested in any attempts at theoretical conceptions (however vague and idiosyncratic) of these sexualities, whereas Gide is—as is Proust. Lorrain and Colette seem more interested by the forms these sexualities take in popular culture, and in their transversal relations with a whole range of other marginalized social identities and activities that are found in popular cultural regions; Gide's interest is mainly in bourgeois culture; Proust's in the borderlands between bourgeois and aristocratic culture, with an occasional popular figure thrown in.

In relation to our starting place in Balzac (for Proust and Gide and Colette and Lorrain all write in Balzac's wake when it comes to same-sex sexualities) we could certainly say that all these authors to a greater or lesser extent are trying to rid themselves of the ideological baggage that had accrued to this topic in the naturalist moment—discourses of corrupt or weakened blood, of a society menaced from below by a stew of corruption—baggage that is always in clear evidence in the novels of someone like Mendès.[42] Their work in writing is always structured by the question of register—of the appropriate register for representing same-sex sexualities and for representing them by way of various kinds of cultural confrontations such as the one I have been calling the problem of encanaillement. Gide will strive to take up and renew the discourse of amis and protégés, turning it to his own ends. Proust will renew the specifically sociological project of Balzac, studying bourgeois and aristocratic same-sex sexualities in their imbrication with other kinds of social transformations. Authors like Lorrain and Colette, with their particular interest in sexual countercultures, specifically pursue the compromising (*compromettante*) line sketched out by Balzac. In doing so, they contribute to a reformulation of questions of class and of social and sexual categories. They open new avenues of experimentation for "literature" in terms of its registers and its subjects. When these authors fail to respect certain sexual categorical divisions that are trying to impose themselves or to retain their authority, when they violate rules of propriety (literary and social), when they put words like *tante* (or like *vrille*, as we are about to see) into circulation, they abet the kinds of transformations that are paving the way for the work of later authors such as Jean Genet and Violette Leduc.

Consider in this light a highly Balzacian passage from Lorrain's novel *La Maison Philibert* (1904), which contains a number of characters who might be thought of as descendants of Vautrin, in particular *le Môme l'Affreux* and *la Mélie*:

> These were the names given to these two creatures by those in their circle. There was a strange form of solidarity between them, forged by the admiration each one had for the other's criminal nature. This street girl and this procurer had never had any other kind of relation than a nonsexual friendship formed out of the hatreds and the rebellious feelings they shared regarding laws, the police, and society. They were, in an unconscious kind of way, two anarchical souls at war with all that was part of an established order.

> [C'étaient les deux noms que dans leur milieu on donnait à ces deux êtres. Une mutuelle admiration pour leurs natures de criminels les avait longtemps associés l'un à l'autre dans une étrange solidarité; la fille et le souteneur n'avaient jamais eu d'autres rapports entre eux qu'une espèce d'amitié insexuée faite des mêmes haines et des même révoltes contre les lois, la police et la société. C'étaient, dans leur inconscience, deux âmes d'anarchie en lutte contre tout ce qui est établi.][43]

Like *Splendeurs et misères des courtisanes*, *La Maison Philibert* contains scenes of police interrogations, here principally involving the courtesan Ludine de Neurflize (a character Lorrain based on his friend Liane de Pougy). Ludine and a few other members of her circle had employed the services of le Môme in order to find them some lower-class same-sex partners for their pleasure, and they had all spent an afternoon together on the Île de Robinson sampling the pleasures of the Parisian popular classes and their sexual cultures. Unfortunately for them, one of the boys that le Môme procured for a duke at the party, a boy named Thomas, is la Mélie's sweetheart, and she comes looking for him, full of ill will: "What's it to be, Thomas? Are you a man or not? Do I have to put up with these insults? Aren't you embarrassed to be hanging about with this band of *vrilles* and of *tantes*?" [Allons, Thomas, es-tu un homme? Vas-tu me laisser insulter plus longtemps? T'es pas honteux de traîner avec cette bande de vrilles et de tantes!] (255). In her effort to cause a scene, she becomes angrier and angrier, in the end nearly starting a riot on the island:

"Hey! You over there," she cried out, turning to a group of about twenty working class folk who had gathered about to hear the noisy discussion, "come see what le Môme l'Affreux is up to. He's turned himself into a circus tour guide for high-flying faggots and high-society lezzies. He's pimping in his spare time. Keep on your toes, everyone! They've come to steal your gals; as for you, ladies, sharpen your nails, for it's the males they've come to steal." . . . The moment was becoming dangerous. All the hatred of the lower classes in the face of the luxury and the insolence of the rich, all the accumulated exasperation of old wounds, was about to burst forth. . . .

"Kill the faggots! Kill the bitches! Kill them! Kill them!" la Mélie was screaming.

[Hé! vous autres, criait-elle en se tournant vers une vingtaine de filles et de gars accourus au bruit de la discussion, venez voir le Môme l'Affreux opérer. Il s'est fait cornac pour lopes de la haute et gousses du grand monde et procureur à ses moments perdus; ouvrez l'oeil, l'équipe! on vient vous lever vos femmes, et vous, les gonzesses, aiguisez vos ongles, c'est vos mâles qu'on vient vous souffler. . . . La minute devenait critique, toute la haine sourde des bas-fonds contre le luxe et l'insolence des riches éclatait, exaspérée des rancunes des anciens maux souffert. . . .

—Hou! les tantes, hou! les vaches, tuez-les, tuez-les, hurlait la Mélie. (255–56)]

La Maison Philibert is full of violence, and, in other moments, of a wicked sense of humor. It takes great pleasure in putting into play slang discourse on same-sex sexuality: in this passage, *tantes* and *lopes* for men, *vrilles* and *gousses* for women. The scene in question does manage to end without anyone being killed, even if Thomas, who slaps la Mélie in order to cause her to desist, will live only a few hours longer before falling victim to her murderous vengeance. Rather than dwelling on the 1904 novel's plot, its Balzacian tendencies, or its documentary value regarding popular culture, prostitution, and the sexual underworld of its time, and rather than dwelling on the fact that Lorrain here, unlike Balzac, insists on allowing the word *tante* to be generally applicable to all classes of society, I would like to consider the pragmatic aspect of the text, the indexical value of its use of the word *tante*, and the repercussions such usage could have on the strategies of other authors. This novel, surely as interesting as any of the earlier decadent ones for which Lorrain is better known, has not been as well remembered as it might deserve to be. Yet it was surely read by contemporaries such as Gide,

Colette, Montesquiou, Mendès, and Proust. It forms part of their context. Given that it is part of the context, we can more easily appreciate the slightly ridiculous side of Proust's hesitancy around putting the word *tante* into print in his 1905 article on Montesquiou's *Professionelles Beautés*, or the equally ridiculous side of certain letters that Proust wrote to different publishers around this time, regarding the possible publication of the novel he was beginning to write. In August 1909, five years after the appearance of *La Maison Philibert*, Proust writes to Alfred Vallette, Rachilde's husband and the editor of the *Mercure de France* (which had published both *The Immoralist* and *Claudine Married*): "I am just finishing writing a book which, even though the provisional title is *Against Sainte-Beuve: A Remembrance of a Morning*, is a true novel, one that is sexually extremely immodest in certain parts. One of the main characters is homosexual" [Je termine un livre qui malgré son titre provisoire: *Contre Sainte-Beauve, Souvenir d'une matinée*, est un véritable roman et un roman extrêmement impudique en certaines parties. Un des principaux personnages est un homosexuel].[44] To claim in 1909 that a novel would be "extremely immodest" because one of its characters was homosexual—and to make that claim in a letter to Vallette—hardly made sense (except as a gesture that positioned Proust socially and aesthetically). In October 1912, he writes to the publisher Eugène Fasquelle, "I would like to be honest from the outset in warning you that the work in question is what used to be called an *indecent* one, much more indecent than what is usually published" [Je voudrais très honnêtement vous avertir d'avance que l'ouvrage en question est ce qu'on appelait autrefois un ouvrage *indécent* et beaucoup plus indécent même que ce qu'on a l'habitude de publier].[45] How many books would one have to choose to ignore or forget in order truly to believe in the great indecency of Proust's book, or in its bold innovations regarding the representation of same-sex sexuality?

As we have seen, Proust is quite exercised in particular by what he experiences as the indecency of the word *tante*, a word he has a great longing to use, a longing matched by an enormous hesitation. In one of the drafts for *Sodom and Gomorrah*, Proust cites the passage in which Balzac uses the word, and comments:

Balzac, whose audacity I wish I was able to imitate, uses [says crudely] the only term that would be suitable for me. . . . This term would be particularly appropriate in my book where those characters to whom it would be applied, being nearly all of them older, and most of them part of high society, are often to be seen socializing in exclusive circles, where, slightly ridiculous and magnificently dressed, they natter on. *Les tantes!* Just in that word that carries skirts along with it you see their solemnity and their elaborate outfits, you see the tufts of feathers and the particular warblings characteristic of their particular species. "But the sensibilities of the French reader must be respected," and so, not being Balzac, I must be content to use invert.

[Balzac, avec une audace que je voudrais bien pouvoir imiter, emploie [dit plus crûment] le seul terme qui me conviendrait . . . Ce terme conviendrait particulièrement, dans tout mon ouvrage, où les personnages auxquels il s'appliquerait, étant presque tous vieux, et presque tous mondains, ils seraient dans les réunions mondaines où ils papotent, magnifiquement habillés et ridiculisés. Les tantes! on voit leur solennité et toute leur toilette rien que dans ce mot qui porte jupes, on voit dans une réunion mondaine leur aigrette et leur ramage de volatiles d'un genre différent. «Mais le lecteur français veut être respecté» et n'étant pas Balzac je suis obligé de me contenter d'inverti.][46]

What is the source of this compulsion to say *inverti* instead of *tante*? We might think that if Proust dare not use the word, it's not only because he is not Balzac. It is also because he is not Montesquiou and not Lorrain. For in fact Lorrain's la Mélie uses the word *tante* exactly in the sense that interests Proust: as a way of chastising or caricaturing upper-crust men. Here again we see how important the indexical value of linguistic register can be: if Lorrain used the word in his novel and had it spoken by a character such as la Mélie, if Montesquiou used the word with careless nonchalance, this might well contribute to the reluctance of someone like Proust, wanting to be who he is, to make use of the word himself.

What indecency is for Proust is not what indecency is for everyone. He would perhaps like to believe that his sense of indecency is widely accepted. It was probably shared by many, but certainly not by everyone. It is a pragmatic kind of indecency, a social point of view Proust would hope to entail or to occasion or to further by means of his writing; but it is hardly something that can be presupposed. It is an index that points to a social position as well as to a particular conception of literature.

If Proust and Gide had a certain amount of disdain for Lorrain, he was nonetheless a strong presence in their world. Colette displays rather a friendship and even a loyalty to him.[47] As a final example of the usefulness of thinking about the indexical value of registers when one is trying to understand literary texts dealing with same-sex sexualities, and as evidence that Lorrain counts as a crucial part of Colette's context in the early 1900s, we could consider the virtuosic paragraphs that open her *Les Vrilles de la vigne* from 1908 (a text I will treat at greater length in chapter 3). In these paragraphs we see how carefully Colette is working with the word *vrille*, with its slang sense (la Mélie uses *vrille* specifically to refer to those upper-class women and courtesans whose sexual tourism brings them to places in which they might find working-class women to pick up) as well as with its polite botanical one ("tendril"), in order to create a mixed effect of registers. We can see how she allows the word to resonate with its slang sense, but in a hushed way, so that it is only slightly compromised. Simultaneously, thanks to the foregrounding of its polite meaning, it works to achieve a certain *discretion* or *reticence* in its reference to loves between women—loves it manages to evoke with pleasure in the first person, at the same time as it avoids the obligation to name them or to admit to them explicitly. It is a brilliant and innovative pragmatic performance:

Imperious, clinging, the tendrils [vrilles] of a bitter vine shackled me in my springtime while I slept a happy sleep, without misgivings. But with a frightened lunge I broke all those twisted threads that were already imbedded in my flesh, and I fled . . . When the torpor of a new night of honey weighed on my eyelids, I feared the tendrils [vrilles] of the vine and I uttered a loud lament that revealed my voice to me.

All alone, after a wakeful night, I now observe the morose and voluptuous morning star rise before me . . . And to keep from falling again into a happy sleep, in the treacherous springtime when blossoms the gnarled vine, I listen to the sound of my voice. Sometimes I feverishly cry out what one customarily suppresses or whispers very low—then my voice dies down to a murmur, because I dare not go on . . .

I want to tell, tell, tell everything I know, all my thoughts, all my surmises, everything that enchants or hurts or astounds me; but always, toward the dawn of this resonant night, a wise cool hand is laid across my mouth and my cry, which had been passionately raised, subsides into moderate verbiage, the loquacity of the child who talks aloud for reassurance and the return of sleep . . .

I no longer enjoy a happy sleep, but I no longer fear the tendrils [vrilles] of the vine.

[Cassantes, tenaces, les vrilles d'une vigne amère m'avaient liée, tandis que dans mon printemps je dormais d'un somme heureux et sans défiance. Mais j'ai rompu, d'un sursaut effrayé, tous ces fils tors qui déjà tenaient à ma chair, et j'ai fui . . . Quand la torpeur d'une nouvelle nuit de miel a pesé sur mes paupières, j'ai craint les vrilles de la vigne et j'ai jeté tout haut une plainte qui m'a révélé ma voix! . . .

Toute seule éveillée dans la nuit, je regarde à présent monter devant moi l'astre voluptueux et morose . . . Pour me défendre de retomber dans l'heureux sommeil, dans le printemps menteur où fleurit la vigne crochue, j'écoute le son de ma voix . . . Parfois, je crie fiévreusement ce qu'on a coutume de taire, ce qui se chuchote très bas—puis ma voix languit jusqu'au murmure parce que je n'ose poursuivre . . .

Je voudrais dire, dire, dire tout ce que je sais, tout ce que je pense, tout ce que je devine, tout ce qui m'enchante et me blesse et m'étonne; mais il y a toujours, vers l'aube de cette nuit sonore, une sage main fraiche qui se pose sur ma bouche . . . Et mon cri, qui s'exaltait, redescend au verbiage modéré, à la volubilité de l'enfant qui parle haut pour se rassurer et s'étourdir . . .

Je ne connais plus le somme heureux, mais je ne crains plus les vrilles de la vigne.][48]

Colette's poetic "Je voudrais dire, dire, dire tout ce que je sais" is to an extent an earlier iteration of Proust's "Vous pouvez tout raconter . . . mais à condition de ne jamais dire: *Je.*" Her interest in the word *vrille* parallels that of Proust in *tante*. In terms of literary register, she deploys in this passage forms of discretion and indiscretion (as well as a stylistic virtuosity) reminiscent of Gide in *Fruits of the Earth* or *The Immortalist*. But for those readers in the know about the subcultural use of the word *vrille* (especially if they had been following the details of Colette's love life as reported in the Parisian press), there is a slight wink here in the direction of someone like Lorrain, as well as an homage to her lover of the moment, Mathilde de Morny. After all, Colette's sophisticated literary practice of discretion on the page is penned by someone whose contemporaneous public persona showed no hesitation regarding indiscretions of many kinds in other places. This is the subject of the next chapter.

three

Colette, the Moulin Rouge, and Les Vrilles

> Let me say at once that the question "What is it that's going on here?" is considerably suspect. Any event can be described in terms of a focus that includes a wide swath or a narrow one and—as a related but not identical matter—in terms of a focus that is close-up or distant. And no one has a theory as to what particular span and level will come to be the ones employed. To begin with, I must be allowed to proceed by picking my span and level arbitrarily, without special justification.—ERVING GOFFMAN, *Frame Analysis*

"I want to do as I please," cries Colette in *Les Vrilles de la vigne*. "I want to perform in pantomimes, even plays. I want to dance naked if a leotard bothers me or mars my figure." [Je veux faire ce que je veux. Je veux jouer la pantomime, même la comédie. Je veux danser nue, si le maillot me gêne et humilie ma plastique].[1] Colette's first person is not in this instance a direct one. Her speech is being reported—by her dog, Toby-Chien, to her cat, Kiki-la-Doucette. By the time Toby-Chien first reported this (the text in which it appears, "Toby-Chien parle," initially appeared in the magazine *La Vie Parisienne* on April 27, 1907) Colette was already performing pantomimes, having done so for the first time in February 1906, dressed as a faun. In March 1906 she played her first speaking role—cross-dressed as a man, an aristocrat, who picks up a loose woman in a bar and kisses her onstage. Reports say that some of the performances were booed—not because of the cross-dressing, which was common enough onstage, perhaps not even because of the kiss between the two women (probably not that uncommon either), but rather because of the disapproval of some people in the audience that someone of Colette's standing, someone who had up to this point moved in polite society, had chosen to take up a disreputable career in the theater.[2] Colette's costumes for her pantomimes in these years could be quite scanty, and some press commentators noted that Colette was gaining a following among a certain group of women, "le tout Mytilène," as it was sometimes referred to: high-society women with a sexual interest in other women. As for nudity onstage, that would come in the pantomime *La Chair*, in which Colette first appeared in November 1907. In *La Chair*, her partner at one point rips her clothing and reveals one of her breasts.

Colette recounts the moment where this gesture was decided upon in another article for *La Vie Parisienne* (published on January 4, 1908) that also makes its way into her book *Les Vrilles de la vigne*. Here appearing nude is not presented as part of a quest for liberation from the conventions imposed on women's bodies, but is rather understood as a purely commercial gesture imposed by a theater administration aiming to produce a sensation. The relevant scene in Colette's text is narrated in the third person. An actress named Mme. Loquette has just arrived at a dress rehearsal with a costume that is specially designed to be ripped open to reveal a bit of shoulder and a bit of leg. Seeing the effect tried out in rehearsal, the director and the producer find it insufficiently dramatic. (The actress merely wants the rehearsal to be over so that she can grab a sandwich):

The men approach the leading lady. Studied silence. With the indifference of a filly that is up for sale she allows their gaze to traverse her bared shoulders, her leg as it is revealed by the ripped tunic . . .

The owner ponders, mouths odd noises, and grumbles, "Of course, of course . . . There isn't . . . There isn't enough . . . enough nudity, right there!"

The indifferent filly shivers as if she has been stung by a horsefly.

"Not enough nudity! How much do you want?"

"Hmm! I want . . . well, I don't know. It's the right effect, but it's not startling enough, not naked enough, I insist! Here, this bit of chiffon about your throat . . . It's not right, it's ridiculous, it's too restrictive . . . Something's missing . . ."

Inspired, the owner takes three steps back, extends his arm and, with a voice like a balloonist leaving the earth behind, cries:

"Let us see a breast!"

[Les hommes se rapprochent de la principale interprète. Silence studieux. Elle laisse, plus indifférente qu'une pouliche à vendre, errer leurs regards sur ses épaules découvertes, sur la jambe visible hors de la tunique fendue . . .

Le patron cherche, clappe des lèvres, ronchonne:

«Évidemment, évidemment . . . Ce n'est pas . . . Ce n'est pas assez . . . pas assez nu, là!»

La pouliche indifférente tressaille comme piquée par un taon.

«Pas assez nu! qu'est-ce qu'il vous faut?

—Eh! il me faut . . . je ne sais pas, moi. L'effet est bon, mais pas assez éclatant, pas assez nu, je maintiens le mot! Tenez, cette mousseline sur la gorge . . . C'est déplacé, c'est ridicule, c'est engonçant . . . Il me faudrait . . .»

Inspiré, le patron recule de trois pas, étend le bras, et, d'une voix d'aéronaute quittant la terre:

«Lâchez un sein!» crie-t-il. (1:1053)]

The tone here is notably different from that in "Toby-Chien parle," where Colette cried out for the sake of her own freedom to do as she chose. Here we find a woman performer trapped in a culture of sensationalism, subjected to the economic pressures of the world of competing music halls, fully aware of how a well-known woman's body can be exploited economically (an exploitation that Loquette/Colette seems to force herself to put up with out of some kind of professionalism).

A year and a half later, again in *La Vie Parisienne*, on August 14, 1909, Colette publishes "Une Lettre," a text that purports to be a letter to her (imaginary) friend Valentine. They had last seen each other at the beginning of the summer. Valentine, a well-to-do woman about town, was just about to head off to various exclusive resorts for the duration of the summer season, whereas Colette, a struggling artist, a woman trying to make a living, was about to head off on another theatrical tour including a revival of *La Chair*. Valentine, a great believer in social propriety, even if a devoted enough friend of Colette's to continue seeing her after she had lost all her social standing by taking up a stage career, expressed disapproval of this plan. In the letter, Colette reminds her friend of the scene that took place between them the last time they met:

You had asked me what I was doing this summer and I'd answered, "Well . . . first of all I'm going to do 'Flesh' in Marseille." To which you said, "Again!"

Me: "What do you mean 'again'?"

You: "That horrid thing again!"

Me: "It's not horrid, it's a 'sensational mime-drama'!"

You: "It's perfectly horrid! Isn't that the one where your dress is torn off and you appear . . ."

Me: "Undressed. Precisely."

You: "And it doesn't matter to you?"

Me: "What do you mean, 'it'?"

You: "To show yourself off in public in an outfit, in a costume . . . well . . . it's beyond me! When I think that you stand there, in front of the whole world . . . oh . . .!"

Seized by an irresistible shudder of modesty, you covered your face with your hands and your whole body cringed, so that your dress, clinging to you, outlined you for an instant worse than naked . . . each and every detail of your graceful body appeared to me so clearly beneath the crepe de Chine that it made me uncomfortable.

But there you were, already uncovering your incensed eyes.

"I have never ever seen, what can I call it? . . . recklessness like yours, Colette!"

To which I responded, with witless rudeness, "My dear, you bore me. You're neither my mother nor my husband; therefore . . ."

[Vous m'aviez demandé «ce que je faisais cet été» et je vous avais répondu: «Mais . . . je vais d'abord jouer *la Chair* à Marseille.» Là-dessus, vous: «Encore!»

MOI.—Quoi «encore»?

VOUS.—Encore cette horreur!

MOI.—C'est pas une horreur, c'est un «sensationnel mimodrame.»

VOUS.—Une horreur, parfaitement! C'est bien là-dedans, n'est-ce pas? qu'on vous arrache votre robe et que vous apparaissez . . .

MOI.—Sans robe, parfaitement.

VOUS.—Et ça ne vous fait rien?

MOI.—Ça, quoi?

VOUS.—De vous montrer au public dans une tenue, dans un costume . . . enfin . . . Ça me passe! Quand je songe que vous restez là, devant tout le monde . . . oh! . . .

Saisie d'un frisson irrésistible de pudeur, vous avez voilé votre visage de vos mains réunies, avec un tel recul du corps que votre robe, collée à vous, vous dessina un instant pire que nue . . . tous les détails de votre gracieux corps m'apparurent si nets, sous la crêpe de Chine, que j'en fus gênée . . .

Mais déjà vous dévoiliez vous yeux courroucés:

—Je n'ai jamais vu de . . . d'inconscience pareille à la vôtre, Colette!

A quoi, je répondis, avec une grossièreté sans esprit:

—Mon enfant, vous me barbez. Vous n'êtes ni ma mère, ni mon mari; par conséquent . . .][3]

Here is yet another perspective, that of a jaded performer attuned to economic pressures, returning to a pantomime that is known to be a moneymaker, annoyed by the conventionality of her friend (for whom money is no issue), annoyed that her friend seems unconscious of the fact that her elegant and expensive dress is revealing in its own way, and even perhaps troubled by her reaction to the graceful body of her privileged friend.

Colette's relation to nudity onstage, to her own nudity, to her theatrical career, and to her public celebrity is framed differently in each of these texts.[4] Her relation to these questions seems perhaps to evolve over time; her own self-figuration shifts with each presentation. We might say that each presentation challenges the way she figures in the others. This is typical of Colette's writing of these years: her relations to certain topics having to do with sexuality, with celebrity, with the female body onstage, with the bodies of other women, with a woman's economic condition, are constantly being refigured, being assigned to a particular first-person figuration rather than assumed in any definitive way. Colette will thereby be able to reveal how attitudes toward or assumptions of same-sex sexualities are part of a project of impersonation—a project of taking up a person. Moreover, she shows a keen awareness of how the success of an impersonation involves not only the abilities of the person trying to carry it off, but also the frame (or the frames) established for the impersonation, as well as the sometimes contentious relations between the person enacting the impersonation, that person's interlocutors, audience, critics, and so on.

During the years in question in this chapter (roughly 1905–10), Colette lives or acts out a great deal of her life in public, so to speak, but there are many Colettes and many publics, and there is much negotiation not only between the different figures Colette provides for herself but also between each of those figures and its public or publics. The complexity of Colette's writing and of her construction of her public self in these years is reflected in the ongoing negotiation between these sequential figurations of her self, and also in the negotiations between her selves and the divergent publics to which they seem addressed. Her canniness in these negotiations between selves and between self and public has to do with an unfailing awareness that many different contexts can be brought to bear on any act of public figuration or representation—making it mean in different ways, making it available to different publics in different ways. If you work at it carefully, you can make the multiple contexts to which you refer interfere with each other or overlap each other in remarkable ways. Colette during these years proves to be a master of the art of making contexts interfere.[5]

> Everyone who reads *La Vie Parisienne*, man or woman, will want to own the new book by Colette Willy.
>
> The delicious, tender, and innocently perverse talent of the confidant of the *Claudine* novels, of the mistress of Toby-Chien, of the heroine of *The Retreat from Love*, has, in *The Tendrils of the Vine*, created a new masterpiece that everyone will want to read and that everyone will be talking about.
>
> —Advertisement for *Les Vrilles de la vigne* in *La Vie Parisienne* of November 7, 1908

Colette's *Les Vrilles de la vigne* (The Tendrils of the Vine) first appeared in book form in November 1908, assembling a group of eighteen short texts she had published separately in a number of different magazines in the years since 1905. The eighteen texts present a variety of personas, many of which speak in the first person. I would like to situate the work of figuration that went into the first persons of these texts in the context of Colette's own public life at this time, in the context of various discourses on same-sex sexuality circulating at the time, and in the context of other discourse that overlapped with them. *Les Vrilles de la vigne*—"the book all of Paris is talking about," according to one advertisement from early 1909—was published by *La Vie Parisienne*, the weekly magazine in which many of the texts making up the book originally appeared, and which also had a small book-publishing enterprise attached to it. Colette had begun contributing regularly to the magazine in 1907. (Her first column for the magazine was in fact "Toby-Chien parle" in April of that year.) She made only a few small changes to the texts when she assembled them into a book, adding a few words, paragraphs, and sentences here and there, but as we shall see later in this chapter, those small changes were occasionally quite significant.

Colette's fame as a Parisian personality and as a writer was something she and her husband Willy had been carefully cultivating since the beginning of the century.[6] The year 1907 was crucial in the development of that public personality as well as in her development as a writer and as an actress. Perhaps her most notorious stage appearance would be in January 1907 at the Moulin Rouge (three months before Toby-Chien would speak to us of his mistress's ambitions). By that time, Colette and her husband Willy were in fact living separately, although still collaborating in a number of ways.[7] Those who had failed to read about the separation in the papers that regularly covered the doings of Colette, Willy, and their intimates were informed of it in the "Avertissement" that opened the first of Colette's novels to appear under the name Colette Willy, *La Retraite sentimentale* (The Retreat from Love), published by the Mercure de France in February 1907, a month after the incident at the Moulin Rouge. (*La Retraite sentimentale* is the conclusion of the Claudine series, the other volumes of which had appeared under the name of Willy. Colette had already signed two other books—not novels—with the name Colette Willy: in 1904 and 1905 she published *Dialogues de bêtes* and *Sept dialogues de bêtes*, the opening installments in the ongoing series of imaginary conversations between her dog, Toby-Chien, and her cat, Kiki-la-Doucette.) In this same period, she also began an affair with a well-known French aristocrat, Mathilde de Morny (known familiarly as Missy, or, to some friends, as Uncle Max). This was a development of which various newspapers also took note. It was with Missy that Colette would appear onstage at the Moulin Rouge in January 1907 in the pantomime *Rêve d'Égypte*. Willy and his new love interest, Meg Villars, would be in the audience.[8]

The Moulin Rouge had opened in Montmartre in 1889.[9] It might be thought of as one of the emblematic institutions of the French Third Republic—a music hall that from the day it had opened succeeded in drawing through its doors not only "Tout-Paris" (the Parisian "A list" of notable aristocrats, the richest members of the bourgeoisie, courtesans, celebrated actresses and actors, and occasionally artists and writers who had achieved the appropriate forms of celebrity), but also the artists and popular crowd associated with the Montmartre neighborhood in which it was located. The events of January 3, 1907, involving Colette and Missy belong to many histories: to the history of the Third Republic music hall in general and of the Moulin Rouge in particular; to the history of French aristocratic culture after the fall of the Second Empire; to the history of Tout-Paris and how (and of whom) it came to be composed in the Third Republic; to the sexual culture of Tout-Paris during those years, in particular the courtesan culture to which famous courtesans such as Liane de Pougy and Emilienne d'Alençon belonged;[10] to the history of Third Republic relations between the press and the state, between the press and the aristocracy, between the press and popular sexual cultures, between the press and the celebrated personalities of Tout-Paris, and between the press and the theater; to the history of French images of Egypt; to the history of the use by same-sex sexual cultures of figures from the ancient world; to the history of French nationalism; to the history of French discourses on race. Finally, there is the history of Colette's evolving public personality and her evolving body of literary work to be considered. Colette had an amazing practical sense of the possibility of situating her actions at the crossroads of many of these multiple histories. Her ability to play with contexts in such subtle ways depends on this practical sense of hers. Reconstructing some of the contextual play in which she indulged will help us appreciate the multifaceted nature of the event that the performance of *Rêve d'Égypte* turned out to be. The contexts to be found surrounding that event will in turn help us to an understanding of Colette's own writerly play with contexts as she composes the texts that become *Les Vrilles de la vigne*.

Rêve d'Égypte

On Thursday, January 3, 1907, the following headline could be found on page four of the Parisian daily *Le Matin*: "The Emperor's Niece Onstage in a Music-Hall—The Marquise de Morny and Colette Willy Open Today at the Moulin Rouge."[11] Note that it is Missy's impending appearance that is deemed most newsworthy. That she is appearing with Colette is an important second piece of information. Similar headlines (along with their accompanying stories) could be found in a good number of the Parisian dailies on or around that Thursday. The article in *Le Matin* begins as follows:

> The news spread through Paris like wildfire. The Marquise de Morny, niece of the emperor and ex-wife of the Marquis de Belbeuf, opens tonight at the Moulin-Rouge, along with Mme Colette Willy, in a pantomime titled *Dream of Egypt*, whose story is by the Marquise, and whose music is by a gentleman who must remain anonymous. Only a few performances will take place at the Moulin-Rouge and they promise to be quite the spectacle. The entire Faubourg Saint Germain is up in arms. Both the Marquise and the Moulin-Rouge have been strongly encouraged to give up on this project, but to no avail.

Dream of Egypt offered its spectators a scene in which an Egyptologist (played by Missy), having discovered a method for reviving mummies, successfully applies that method to one particular mummy, played by Colette. As *Le Journal* would put it on the same day, Colette was to play not "one of those nasty mummies who have been inside their sarcophagus for thousands of years" but rather "a nice little mummy who in the end comes back to life." And when she does, she gives a kiss to the Egyptologist who had revived her.

The second of the two paragraphs in *Le Matin* that day went as follows:

> *Dream of Egypt* is a very precise evocation of the customs of ancient Egypt. It is based on documents from the Louvre Museum consulted by Colette Willy. We have heard that this will be a pantomime of high quality. The notoriety of the marquise de Morny is such that anyone who is anyone in Paris will flock to the Moulin Rouge, but *Dream of Egypt* will not simply be, as one might imagine, a source of scandal; it will be a work of art arousing intense emotions.

We see the distribution of roles here: Colette is meant to provide some kind of intellectual and aesthetic integrity to the production, whereas the appearance of Missy is meant to draw the crowds. Now, when reading the journalistic accounts surrounding the performance at the Moulin Rouge on January 3 and the scandal it provoked, it is necessary to keep in mind to what extent Colette, Willy, and Missy were tied into journalistic circles and their corresponding networks of friendship and of professional association and rivalry.[12] No reporting about them can be thought of as objective; much of it is clearly a form of orchestrated publicity. Everyone seems aware of Missy's role in attracting attention to the production, and this is a key component in the publicity leading up to the evening. And clearly no one who was susceptible to outrage at the idea of Mathilde de Morny appearing onstage was going to be moved by *Le Matin*'s arguments as to the artistic merits and the exacting research (regarding which we might ourselves be forgiven for entertaining a few doubts) associated with *Rêve d'Égypte*.

It seems almost de rigueur in the Parisian press to rehearse Missy's genealogy when discussing the events at the Moulin Rouge on January 3, 1907. This is because for many in the audience at the Moulin Rouge that evening, as well as for those who wrote the stories in the press publicizing the event, the source of the scandal created by Colette and Missy's appearance that evening seems not so much to have been the fact that Colette and Missy, a couple of women openly living together, performed a pantomime in which they kissed onstage while one of them was dressed as a man. In many newspaper accounts, these facts were, when referred to, treated as rather incidental. (Later accounts of the evening will often assume the "lesbian" kiss to have been the focus of the scandal that evening, but in making that assumption they rely on an association between scandal and public displays of lesbianism that is characteristic of a later cultural moment or of a different cultural space and ignores the way scandal was structured in French aristocratic circles and in Parisian music halls in 1906–7.) Rather, the scandal and the efforts to disrupt the performance came about because of the outrage felt by certain people in aristocratic circles at the idea that someone of Missy's social position would sully her name by appearing onstage in a public music hall. This is not to say that for some of the members of the public the fact that the two women kissing were known to form a couple could not become a convenient aggravating factor. Colette and Missy were insulted from the audience that evening in sexual terms: "A bas les gousses!" [Down with the dykes!] was one of the cries heard at the theater.[13] But that was only part of the story. Le Journal of January 4, 1907, reports a different cry from the public, which was taken up as soon as Missy appeared onstage: "Jouera pas" [She won't perform], referring in the third-person singular to the marquise. Multiple frames are necessary to come to grips with all the different questions of *enactability* Colette and Missy raised in this performance.

Colette and Missy's relationship had been public knowledge (that is, had been referred to in major newspapers) for at least a few months before the performance at the Moulin Rouge. In November 1906, Colette seems more or less to have moved in with Missy; at the same time Willy set up house with a young woman called Meg Villars. The *Cri de Paris*[14] calls these new living arrangements to the attention of its readers in late November 1906, provoking a letter from Colette dated November 25, which the *Cri* publishes on December 2:

> I read the items in your newspaper with pleasure, and lately you have spoiled me! It is a shame that you titled one of your wittiest "As a Family"! By so doing you made it seem as if Willy, who is my friend, the marquise and myself, and that calm and gentle dancer Willy calls Meg, all belonged to some sordid phalanstery. . . . You thereby caused at least three of us a certain amount of sorrow. Please do not unite in, dare I say it, such an intimate fashion in the minds of your readers two couples who have ar-

ranged their lives in what seems to me the most normal way possible: according to their pleasure.

The openness regarding the sexual nonconformity of these couples was part of the publicity strategy of Willy as a writer of louche novels and of Colette as a person launching a career not only as a writer but as a woman of the stage—pantomime, dancer, and actress—willing to break with conventional standards of propriety as she made (or in order to make) a name for herself. As we see here, Colette had no hesitations about referring to the fact that she and Missy formed a couple in an open letter to the editor.

In the same month in which that letter was written, on the front page of *Le Journal* on Saturday, November 17, 1906, there is an article with the title "The Former Marquise de Belbeuf Performs a Pantomime." The article is illustrated with an image of a languorous Colette standing in front and leaning back against the shoulder of the cross-dressed marquise. The caption to the image reads: "The marquise (dressed as a man) and Colette Willy, from a snapshot taken by M. Anthony during a rehearsal of *The Gypsy Girl*."[15]

Le Journal's article on November 17 again appears to be as much advertising as information. It begins: "Everyone in Paris is talking about it: 'Have you heard? The ex-marquise Belbeuf is going to appear in a pantomime with Colette Willy!' The news was as intriguing as it was unexpected; I decided to find out if it was true, and so, yesterday, I paid a visit to the marquise." The article continues, with the author (Fernand Hauser) suggesting (disingenuously) to his readers that the publicity he aimed to provide was unwelcome: "As I waited in the hallway to be received, I overheard loud exclamations from Colette Willy herself. 'He wants to see the marquise? He wants to publish a portrait of her? Tell him to get lost!' " The journalist is brought before Colette, who declares to him: "What is it to you if the marquise appears onstage with me? It's for a private audience; it's no business of the newspapers."

At this point, the journalist tells us, someone else enters the room: "A man dressed in black velours and holding a palette came in. The man is, in fact, the marquise dressed for her role in *The Gypsy Girl* by Paul Franck and Edouard Mathé, a role she will be playing today." The marquise, too, insists that her performance does not concern the general public: "I will be performing tomorrow at the Cercle des Arts et de la Mode, of which I am a member. . . . We amuse ourselves as best we can. But why inform your readers of this? I really cannot permit." But here Willy comes in and interrupts, insisting that there is no refusing a journalist from *Le Journal*. The marquise gives way and answers a few questions, while insisting on the private nature of her performances:

> "I wanted to amuse a certain number of my friends," she tells me, "by appearing in a pantomime with Colette Willy, but it will go no further than that. I am appearing as an amateur, I am not being paid . . . and I appear under the pseudonym of Yssim."
>
> "You have no intention of appearing in front of the general public?"
>
> She hesitates, and then says, "I wouldn't dream of it . . ."
>
> "Write that down," Colette Willy insists, dwelling on each syllable. "She would not dream of it."

The journalist stays to watch a rehearsal, and concludes that the marquise isn't half bad as a performer.

This article, clearly written with the full complicity of Colette, Missy, and Willy, makes no secret of the liaison between Missy and Colette. It more or less assumes such information already to be public knowledge, and foregrounds instead the question of the appropriateness of Missy performing in public, or the difference between performing in public and performing in private, the importance for her honor of not being paid and of using the pseudonym even though it is a perfectly transparent one. The article is clearly preparing the way for an impending public appearance by the marquise and Colette—creating a bit of sensational anticipation.

On January 2, 1907, the day before the performance at the Moulin Rouge, *Le Journal* returns to the topic of the marquise's theatrical aspirations, signaling the impending performance under its rubric "Théâtres et Concerts" on page 6. It notes that the marquise's family has begun to make its displeasure felt at the idea she would appear in a public theater and recounts an interview with Colette that touches on this question:

> One of our colleagues was saying to her yesterday that the family would never permit this! What about society, its customs and prejudices?
>
> Colette was outraged.
>
> "We will see about that indeed!" she replied. "The marquise is free to choose her own course of action, and she will make her debut with me on January 3, I promise you, onstage at the Moulin Rouge. Even if it sparks a revolution. She will not be swayed by threats or imprecations. She loves the theater and will be a part of it, and that's all there is to it."

Colette will not be moved. Neither cabals nor failure frighten her. She adds:

"Yes, we will go on despite all the noise and all the ill-wishers united against us. My goodness, it would simply be too bizarre if the fact of belonging to the French nobility meant a woman could not do what she wanted. The marquise is prepared to brave any storm, and you can tell all these people they are wasting their breath and their ink."

This is the Colette of "Toby-Chien parle." She offers a framing of the event in terms of a woman's right to public expression and in terms of a critique of aristocratic attitudes toward the dishonor associated with the stage, yet it is clear that the advertising campaign that has been calling attention to the impending event has in fact been playing on the sense that Missy's appearance on a public stage (under a pseudonym, but having signed a contract including economic remuneration) would be a form of social transgression worthy of media attention, and would therefore draw an audience.

The day after the premiere, on January 4, now on the front page, in an article accompanied by an illustration of Colette and Missy during a rehearsal at the Moulin Rouge, *Le Journal* comments that "the scandal was greater than anyone expected." The house was full of both supporters and detractors. *Le Journal* describes what happened when Missy came onstage: "Throughout the entire performance shouts alternated with whistles being blown. Small benches, orange peels, cigarettes, matchboxes, even vegetables rained down on part of the stage—thrown by women and aimed both at the marquise de Morny and at Colette Willy. Yet even so the entire pantomime was performed." Many of the journalistic accounts of the evening will comment on the fortitude of the two performers, something that apparently earned them the respect even of some of their enemies. (After the curtain came down on the pantomime, there were further disturbances in the audience, with some of the public taking the occasion to insult Willy, who was present, by calling him a *cocu*, a cuckold—cuckolded apparently by the marquise. A certain amount of physical violence seems to have followed.) *Le Journal* then goes on to recall for the readers the reason for the scandal: "Our readers know that Madame the Marquise de Morny, former wife of the Marquis de Belbeuf, is the niece of Napoléon III. She has already on several occasions, in the company of Colette Willy, performed pantomimes at private parties." That is, this highly placed aristocrat was— in the eyes of her peers—transgressing the boundaries of acceptable behavior by appearing onstage in a music hall in a performance open to the general public.

On the front page of *Gil Blas* on January 4, 1907, there is a short article with the headline: "The Family Tree of Mme. de Morny." It is a kind of primer in how the aristocracy of the time must have thought about lineage, providing its readers a good many details regarding Missy's family, suggesting that within aristocratic circles knowledge about illegitimate as well as legitimate parentage circulates freely, and that one is responsible in one's behavior to protect the honor of the name of one's illegitimate as well as one's legitimate forebears: "Everyone knows she is the niece of Napoléon III. What is less well known is that she is the great granddaughter of Louis XV and, at the same time, the great granddaughter of Talleyrand." There follow several paragraphs covering the particular chain of adulterous affairs that justifies these assertions regarding her ancestry. The article concludes by noting that Missy is firmly tied into the most ancient network of European royalty as well as popes.

In a commentary (again on the front page) in this same paper on January 5, a certain Pierre Mortier would comment: "One has to say that one is a bit uncomfortable seeing a vice that has, since the time of Sappho, lost most of its beauty being glorified publicly onstage; above all it is scandalous that the priest—I dare not say the priestess—of this painful and noisy rite is the daughter of a great statesman and the niece of the last emperor of the French." A bit later in his column, Mortier continued:

> She bears a name that is not simply her own. . . . If she really had a taste for theater, which I may, despite all the respect I owe her, be allowed to doubt, she could renounce her title. . . . But it is surely the case that Yssim is only paid fifteen hundred francs a night to perform in a silly pantomime because she is the duchess of Morny. Yet it is not for her simply to profit from her name. She has obligations to it as well. It is only natural that there should be people to remind her of this fact.

Mortier thus mentions mostly in passing the "sapphic" side of the scandal, focusing mainly on the scandal surrounding Missy's putative damage to her family name.

Missy would respond to Mortier in a letter that *Gil Blas* published on the front page on January 6 and that imperiously ignores all mention of her "vice," addressing solely the question of her obligations to the name she bears:

When I signed a contract with the Moulin Rouge, I formally demanded to perform only under the pseudonym of Yssim.

So it is entirely against my will and in an exaggerated attempt at publicity that the administration of the Moulin Rouge used my family coat of arms on its posters. Indeed, they hid these posters from me until the day they were put up.

This explains, without of course justifying it, the protests made by the public, who saw a challenge on my part, whereas it was my intention only to perform calmly in a small pantomime no better or worse than any other.

One might be excused for not believing a word she says, or for imagining that Mortier's article and her reply were as scripted as the pre-publicity for the pantomime in *Le Journal*. In any case, we note the extent to which they contextualize this event as having to do with that particular duty to a name it is the prerogative only of aristocrats to perform or fail to perform. (Colette's reputation may suffer. Her name belongs to a different symbolic economy.)

We know that Missy did not hesitate to display signs of her sexuality in public. In her letter to *Gil Blas* she leaves it unaddressed, as if it were an insignificant question, and devotes herself to the question of aristocratic duty, a duty she states she had fulfilled by using a pseudonym—even though the real name behind that pseudonym had been published in many newspapers in the days leading up to the January 3 performance. In journalistic exchanges such as this, one distinguishes with difficulty between what is intended as a public statement of intent or opinion or a defense of someone's honor, and what is merely a contribution to the ongoing stream of publicity surrounding an event whose sensationalism has been carefully orchestrated. *Gil Blas* was not, after all, the most serious of newspapers. Founded in 1879 as a publication with literary pretensions, it had quickly, under the influence of writers such as Catulle Mendès and Guy de Maupassant, fallen into the category of what Pierre Albert calls "les feuilles grivoises"—the saucy papers.[16] Unsurprisingly, it would be precisely in papers that tended toward the feuille grivoise category that the sexuality of the two women would be most explicitly invoked, with the clear intent to increase the sensationalism surrounding the event, as well as the circulation of the paper. (*Gil Blas*, for instance, had made a point in the past of following in some detail the twists and turns of Liane de Pougy's various sexual exploits, including her affairs with women.)[17] Yet even among the different representatives of this particular kind of journalism—of which we will consider a few more examples in a moment—it was not obvious *how* the sexuality of the two women would be invoked in relation to the issue of Missy's appearance onstage—scandalous enough in its own right. In their own participation in the campaign to sensationalize the evening, Colette and Missy—whatever they imagined themselves doing onstage by performing the kiss in question—concentrated exclusively on the question of Missy's status and her right to appear onstage, leaving to others the job of evoking their sexuality in print. Contexts interfere here in interesting ways, both productive and unproductive as far as the careers of Colette, Missy, and Willy are concerned.

It is not my intention to assert that the act of two women who were known to be living together kissing in an amorous fashion onstage didn't matter. But it mattered differently to different people, and it mattered more or less to different people. It is a question of context. Clearly even those to whom it mattered less could take advantage of the sexual background to the performance in order to intensify the vehemence of their protest against Missy's appearance. For instance, some of the vegetables that were being thrown onto the stage that night at the Moulin Rouge were cloves of garlic. This is because the word for "garlic clove" is *gousse*, which is also a slang term for lesbian.[18] The audience came well prepared, but while they thought ahead far enough to bring garlic, it is nonetheless probably true that their idea was in the first instance to protest the simple fact of Missy being onstage.

The presence of garlic cloves among the missiles is not referred to directly in the account of the evening given in *Le Journal* or other newspapers. Yet even if certain newspaper accounts did not report the specific detail of the garlic, or of the crowd yelling "A bas les gousses," this is not to say that the Parisian press had any problem referring to the sexual relation between the women, or that it showed much censoriousness regarding such relations.[19] Indeed, as we shall see, Parisian dailies as well as weekly magazines had for several decades represented aspects of certain female same-sex sexual cultures with reasonable regularity. Consider in this regard the way Colette and Missy are presented in an interview published on the front page of *L'Intransigeant* on January 5.[20] Note in particular the way Colette and Missy refer to one of the hostile women in the audience, who had apparently prepared a stack of cushions to throw at the two performers. The interviewer (who signs his article Flem) strikes a droll tone, beginning by chastising the *audience* at the performance for the violence that it directed at two performers who were, after all, women. Here is how Flem sets the scene of his interview: "The vestibule at number 2 rue Georges-Ville, where Mme. de Morny lives, is filled with flowers: expressions of sympathy. I find the two debutantes fresh out of bed. The marquise is in a dressing gown. Colette, as pretty as an angel with her wide eyes, is in a pink peignoir." Recently risen from their bed, immediately distinguished by the journalist as to their different gender roles, the two performers seize the occasion to criticize the violence of the people who attacked them. They attest to the fact that they had been forewarned of the storm that was brewing, but had been unable to think of any precautions they might have taken. They then comment specifically on two of the people in the audience:

> THE MARQUISE—Prince M . . . had rented a row of boxes. As for the woman throwing cushions and cigarettes, that was Mlle. X . . . , who is always to be found in the Bois, and who is always loudly telling people off: it's a mania of hers. She never rides side-saddle . . .
>
> COLETTE—(laughing) Nor do I . . .
>
> THE MARQUISE—She's always astride her horse, dressed as a man.
>
> COLETTE—She even has a nickname: the *panther.*

Colette and Missy go on to inform the interviewer that they do not intend to be intimidated and plan to continue performing for the whole scheduled run. The police (doubtless pressured by influential members of Missy's family and their friends) had other ideas, and let it be known that they would shut down the Moulin Rouge if Missy appeared onstage again. The music hall's administration replaced her with Georges Wague and renamed the pantomime *Songe d'Orient* (Oriental Dream). The audience on the evening of January 4, on being told of the changes, apparently protested the absence of the marquise nearly as violently as the audience the previous evening had protested her presence, showing once again that different contexts can give different meanings to the same gesture.

The prince M . . . Missy refers to is probably Prince Murat, an important member of the Bonapartist aristocracy and of the Jockey Club. As for the woman throwing the cushions (who appears in a number of different accounts of the evening, being named Mlle. Noilhan in an article in *Gil Blas* on January 4), it seems clear that she moved in the same circles as Colette and Missy, that she cross-dressed and refused to ride side-saddle, and that she had a reputation (borne out by her cushion throwing as well as by her tendency to assault people verbally at the drop of a hat) for not respecting usual standards of feminine decorum. Yet despite what might seem like characteristics that would incline her toward sympathy for Missy and Colette's action were it to be thought of primarily as an assertion of an alternative sexuality, she too found grounds to object vociferously to Missy's appearance onstage. Let us look at another account of the evening at the Moulin Rouge in which the Panther figures prominently, described in a way that will help us expand a bit further our sense of the social and discursive contexts of the evening at the Moulin Rouge.

La Vie Parisienne, another feuille grivoise and the weekly magazine to which Colette would begin making regular contributions later in 1907, had its own peculiar way of describing the scene at the Moulin Rouge on January 3. Its issue dated January 12, 1907, includes an article titled "The Opening Night of 'Lysistrata.'" This article purports to be the account by "Scribe de Lydie" of the tumultuous first performance of Aristophanes's *Lysistrata* in Athens in 412 BCE. We are informed that many famous courtesans were present. The thinly disguised names provided in the article leave no doubt that the courtesans being referred to are, among others, Liane de Pougy and Caroline Otéro, members of Paris-Mytilène known for their affairs with both women and men, friends of both Colette and Missy. The account of the evening provided by *La Vie Parisienne* suggests that there were two main aspects to the scandal of this performance. The first is that one of the performers is a niece of Alcibiades:

> In the center, in the area reserved for knights, a menacing group of Alcibiades's partisans was crowded together. It was well known that on that very day a niece of the famous exile was going to profane his name onstage. It was the first time that a woman performed publicly in this way, taking part in the Theater. And it would be the last time. For the Athenians, even though they had renounced Alcibiades's government and forced him to take refuge in Sparta, nonetheless remained respectful of his person and of the tradition represented by it. They could hardly suffer to see a descendant of this illustrious race don the mask of a histrion. So they joined forces with the small clan of people still faithful to Alcibiades in order to protest against this display and to insult the guilty party, calling her "leech's gullet" [gosier de sangsue], "*olisbos*," and "wild cucumber" [concombre sauvage].

Alcibiades stands in for Napoléon III, whose honor would somehow suffer were his niece to act onstage in public. Acting onstage is an insult to the race, *race* being used in this context to distinguish the ruling elite from more demotic subjects. The offence against Alcibiades's honor produces the series of odd insults recorded in the article. *Olisbos* is the Greek word for "dildo"; orientalist travel narratives had reported for centuries that women in seraglios were served only cucumbers that had already been cut into pieces to prevent them being used as sex toys; it is probably safe to assume that "gosier de sangsue" makes some kind of reference to sexual relations between women as well.[21]

La Vie Parisienne is thus, like other sources, clear about the fact that the insults regarding Missy's sexuality were used primarily to reprimand her for what *Gil Blas*, in an article on January 4, uses the word *déchéance* to designate: a shameful slight to honor, a fall from social grace. The magazine is also clear that the reprimand was coming from a particular social group (a certain set of aristocrats) who themselves seemed a ready-made target for ridicule.[22] The article describes in some detail the scene in which Alcibiades's niece administers an oath to Calonicia, whose role is being played by "a young hermaphroditic slave said to be of Egyptian birth because of the almond shape of her eyes." The slave has recently been bought by Alcibiade's niece.[23] The oath administered during the play is cited in full in the article, and is lifted more or less verbatim from *Lysistrata* itself (lines 215–45). Calonice is made by Lysistrata to place her hands on a cup and swear never to be welcoming to a husband, however passionate his advances may be, to dress provocatively around the house, yet never to give way to a man's desire, to remain cold in his arms in all circumstances.

The article notes that this oath appears not to have been to the audience's liking: "There was a huge ruckus. A young woman, daughter of one of the great agitators who wished to chase all the metics out of Athens, threw amphoras at the stage, where they shattered noisily."[24] Now *Gil Blas* had referred to Mlle. Noilhan, the cross-dressing cushion thrower also known as the Panther, as the daughter of a former "secretary general of the Patrie Française." In *La Vie Parisienne* she is the daughter of someone who actively pursued the deportation of metics, resident aliens, from Athens. This mysterious cushion-throwing woman—and the fact that she catches the eyes of a number of journalists who describe her in very specific ways—give us an occasion to pause to wonder about the ways in which various nationalistic and racialized discourses in the France of 1907 help frame the performance Colette and Missy gave at the Moulin Rouge.

I present all of these journalistic materials partly as a way of demonstrating the wide range of discursive and cultural contexts relevant to Colette's writing and to her public personality, and as a way of revealing the conflicting contexts through which one might understand that personality and those writings. It should also by now be clear how difficult it is to imagine a single frame that would encompass an event such as the one at the Moulin Rouge on the evening of January 3, 1907—which in itself may not actually be a *single* event. "It is obvious," Goffman points out, "that in most 'situations' many different things are happening simultaneously—things that are likely to have begun at different moments and may terminate dissynchronously. To ask the question 'What is *it* that's going on here?' biases matters in the direction of unitary exposition and simplicity."[25] Thus I am here asking a set of nested questions: What is it that's going on at the Moulin Rouge on January 3, 1907? (As if there is any one, single thing going on.) What is it that different people, different groups in the audience think is going on? What is it that is going on in French culture at the time that causes this event to be construed as it is construed? And then, what is it that Colette is doing in her career as a public person and in her writing in the years around this one evening, and how does this one evening fit into those years? How might those years provide a frame for this one evening?

The figure of Mlle. Noilhan, the Panther, helps us envision a number of other contexts that might count as frames for the event at the Moulin Rouge—frames that intersect with and complicate other already overlapping frames such as that of Missy's aristocratic derogation, Colette's orchestration of her growing celebrity as an actress, or that of the choice of Missy and Colette either to seek out or to accept certain forms of publicity regarding their intimate relationship. *Gil Blas* has told us that the Panther's father was an official in the Ligue de la Patrie Française. A right-wing nationalist organization founded in 1899, the Ligue was quite successful at attracting members and making a name for itself in the first few years of its existence; it was a kind of forerunner to the *Action Française*. Well before 1907 it had mostly run out of steam, having been in trouble since at least late 1904 due to a scandal surrounding one of its leaders, Gabriel Syveton, who died in mysterious circumstances shortly before he was scheduled to make an important appearance in court.[26] Not only *Gil Blas*, but also *La Vie Parisienne* uses Mlle. Noilhan's connection to this organization through her father as a means of identifying and positioning her, having picked her out as one of the important spectators at the Moulin Rouge on the evening of January 3. *La Vie Parisienne* went even further: what they refer to as her father's interest in keeping Athens for the Athenians is part of a general emphasis on political and racial differences that runs throughout the article.[27] The scribe recording the events in Athens is from Lydia (the locus of Athens's own imagined decadent oriental other). Alcibiades has been exiled from Athens to Sparta; his niece in Athens is nonetheless still expected to respect the purity and honor of his house. She violates this not only by appearing onstage, but by doing so with a slave (and a hermaphroditic one at that) the shape of whose eyes causes her to be taken for an Egyptian. The way Mlle. Noilhan and her father are referred to in *La Vie Parisienne* along with the general tenor of the article suggest that we might do well to think about Egypt and about nationalist discourses on race as part of the context for what happens at Colette and Missy's performance at the Moulin Rouge.[28]

Thinking, as we are, about overlapping contexts for the events at this performance, about contexts that perhaps confuse rather than clarify each other, we might then wonder how different varieties of French nationalism map onto different social universes of that moment, to that of the Napoleonic aristocracy, for instance.[29] What was the ground of the alliance at the Moulin Rouge between Mlle. Noilhan on the one hand (hardly an aristocrat) and Prince Murat and the members of the Jockey Club on the other in opposition to Missy and Colette? Would favorable or unfavorable attitudes toward alternative sexual cultures and the people who belonged to them unite or divide nationalists, aristocrats, and nationalist aristocrats? How do the political affiliations of various organs of the press in regards to the nationalist movement interact with the way those organs do or do not cover the goings-on in various sexual cultures? How do various segments of the literary cultural universe relate to nationalist culture, aristocratic culture, and/or same-sex sexual cultures? How do issues of nationalism and of sexuality cause divides within each of these cultural sets? How might nationalist beliefs or same-sex sexual practices cause certain affiliations to break down and new ones to form?

Keeping these kinds of questions in mind, there are a few other things that might be said about Mlle. Noilhan herself and the circles in which she moved. It was apparently Missy who, well before the evening at the Moulin Rouge, had sponsored Colette and Willy so that they could join the high society club, the Cercle des arts et de la mode.[30] This was a club at which one gambled; there was also a private theater in which Colette and Missy appeared in some of their first pantomime performances before moving on to more public performance spaces. The Cercle was a place of some excess, and the description of it in Francis and Gontier's biography of Missy suggests that the excesses included instances of the most flagrant kinds of colonial arrogance: "Black children dressed in bedizzened uniforms with baggy breaches carried messages, and young Arab women took charge of the cloakroom and of fanning the ladies. Slavery had long been abolished, but it was still common practice to bring back young girls from North Africa for a lady's service or as a present. General X. gave one to Liane de Pougy. These Arab girls had no legal status; no one claimed them; no one defended them."[31] Missy's biographers indicate that a particular set of women with a sexual interest in other women also frequented the Cercle, that this group was in fact a club unto itself, in which the women had nicknames: "Elisabeth de Clermont-Tonnerre is Elation, Mme. Fabre-Luce is the Sultana. The group of Harmonies, Ideals, and Perfection would grow to include the Tigress, the Lioness, and the Panther. Later would come a princess Almond (Lucie Delarue-Mardrus), and a Vagabond who was Colette" (233). While Francis and Gontier do not indicate their sources for this information (indeed, their effort to document their sources throughout their biography of Missy is frustratingly minimal), the information they provide suggests the orientalist imaginary operant in this subculture and implies that our Panther might have been a part of it.

Pichois and Brunet inform us in their biography of Colette that an article profiling the Panther, along with her photograph, appeared in *Fantasio: Magazine Gai* (as grivois a magazine as one could imagine) on January 1, 1908, a year after the scandal at the Moulin Rouge.[32] *Fantasio's* article, while it is accompanied by a photograph of the Panther, makes a point of never providing her family name. It does, however, mention the evening at the Moulin Rouge as typical of the violent reactions (*horions*) for which the Panther is well known: "On another evening, at the Moulin Rouge, she was part of a noisy protest against a marquise who was making her debut. 'Why?' 'Because of the dishonor she was bringing to her name.' The Panther too has a name, one famous in the political annals of recent times. But she doesn't make a public display of it. She is simply the Panther." As for the Panther's personality and sexuality, the article notes that she is famous for her claws. "To be mean," she comments, "is for me a voluptuous pleasure." As for love, she says, "my soul is virginal," although lately she seems to have taken up with a Yankee sportsman. But she has only ever cried once, and it was for a horse: "For her great passion is horses. And yes, she rides like a man in the privacy of the Bois." The article is signed: Leopard.[33]

Fantasio's article indicates that the Panther cultivated a reputation as a newsworthy eccentric celebrity. It surrounds her with what we might call a simulacrum of discretion. It indicates fairly clearly the nonnormative nature of her sexuality. Like other articles we have seen that mention her, it situates her sociopolitically in relation to her father. (Not that French right-wing nationalist discourse of the time was anything other than conservative and normative in the gender roles it claimed were appropriate for women.) It indicates that whatever proximity the Panther might have to Missy in terms of a shared sexual culture, her disapproval of what happened at the Moulin Rouge has to do with questions of aristocratic family honor, questions that provoked strong emotions in this nonaristocratic nationalist.[34]

Colette and Willy were themselves not known for anticonformism or innovation in their properly political opinions. Judith Thurman tells us in her biography of Colette of a dinner party on the day in December 1905 on which the prime minister Emile Combes signed the legislation that separated church and state in France. At that dinner, Colette and Willy could be heard expressing opposition to the reforms. As Thurman puts it, Colette "saw no contradiction, and never would, between supporting conservative positions and living her life in revolt against them."[35] A similar lack of fit obviously applies in the cases of both Missy and the Panther as well: for each of them an assertive sexual nonconformity would seem to cohabit easily with right-wing aristocratic attitudes or with nationalist political leanings.[36] Indeed, what seems interesting in the case of the Panther is the way several journalistic accounts of the Moulin Rouge incident make a point of taking note of her specific intervention; they note her vociferous opposition to Missy's appearance onstage; they associate her via her father with the right-wing nationalist political movement; sometimes they point in one way or another to her gender or sexual nonconformity (in which she resembles both Missy, and, in her way of riding a horse, Colette); and they find nothing particularly surprising or contradictory in such a profile—all this in spite of the well-worn conservative positions on the feminine and maternal role that characterize the rhetoric of organizations such as the Ligue de la Patrie Française. In the Panther, then, we see an aristocratic racial set of attitudes being reshaped by a nonaristocrat to nationalist ends, and we see these attitudes used (commodified for public consumption, we might say) in a skirmish between three sexually nonconforming women—all three of whom were clearly aware that one of the things at stake is the celebrity each of them is striving to cultivate.

The Question of Pathologization

There is, in the press surrounding what happened at the Moulin Rouge, in its ways of covering both Missy and the Panther, a notable absence of the kind of remarks that could be taken as gender policing or as a pathologization of masculine women or of women sexually interested in other women. Such women were familiar figures on the cultural scene in question. The relative absence of pathologizing discourse in this body of journalism is worth dwelling on for a moment. We are, most of us, more than familiar with the version of the history of sexuality of nineteenth-century Europe laid out in Foucault's *The History of Sexuality, Volume 1*, in particular with the notion that the dominant late-nineteenth-century discourse on homosexuality was one tied up in the "perversion-heredity-degenerescence system": "Psychiatry, to be sure, but also jurisprudence, legal medicine, agencies of social control, the surveillance of dangerous or endangered children, all functioned for a long time on the basis of 'degenerescence' and the heredity-perversion system. An entire social practice, which took the exasperated but coherent form of a state-directed racism, furnished this technology of sex with a formidable power and far-reaching consequences."[37] Psychiatry, the legal system, the medical system, but apparently not the world of journalism, nor the world of the music hall or popular culture. Why is there so little of this kind of discourse in newspaper accounts of Colette, Missy, and the Panther at the Moulin Rouge? There are certainly expressions of opprobrium, for instance that by Gaston Calmette, editor of *Le Figaro*, whose comments appeared on *Le Figaro*'s front page on January 4, 1907:

> The scandal lies not in the vehement protests of a disgusted public, but in the paradoxical exhibition to which it was subjected. If certain people do not understand that their all too special forms of association should not be offered up for public admiration, then it is good that Paris remind them of this, even if it is by the brutal means of whistles. . . .
>
> Paris, always indulgent for so many weaknesses, demands at the least that

exhibitions of this kind be brief and discreet, and that the vehicle of the display be gracefully ornamented. Otherwise Paris may decide to police its own reputation, and it is right to do so. Let us hope that the lesson has been well learned.

In the first sentence of this passage, Calmette seems frustrated by the tendency, in many opinions expressed in the press and privately, to assign the blame for the scandal to an audience that should have behaved more politely toward the women onstage. The rest of his comments say nothing particularly derogatory about relations between women, except that they should be kept somewhat private. Indeed Calmette seems to indicate that he would be unsurprised and even unoffended by stage representations of this "all too special form of association" as long as they were kept brief and discreet and were aesthetically appealing.

If Calmette says nothing here that would associate him with a medicalized and pathologizing discourse about these kinds of relations, with a discourse of degeneracy, it is certainly not because that discourse was unavailable to him. There is, in fact, one stunning example of it around the time of the Moulin Rouge scandal: a portrait of Missy published in *Fantasio* on December 15, 1906. I will return to that particular exceptional article in a moment. But I would like first to demonstrate that if it is exceptional, if a pathologizing discourse directed at Colette or at Missy is notably absent in January 1907, this is not because it had not been directed at Missy previously. A look back to the 1880s and 1890s will reveal continuities and ruptures in the way journalists wrote about the sexual culture of women involved with other women.

Lorrain and Mendès on Missy and Her Friends

While *L'Écho de Paris* had, by 1907, become a staid newspaper affiliated with right-wing nationalists, in the 1890s it was as gossipy and as trashy as the best of them. Jean Lorrain contributed to it regularly, including a series of portraits of women called "Une Femme par jour" (A Woman a Day). On August 25, 1890, he published a piece belonging to that series titled "Celle qui s'ennuie" (The Bored One). "This duke's daughter, this bored royalty, has dreamed of everything, tried everything, dared everything and everywhere," he tells us.

> As for famous, that she most certainly is, all over Europe alas! . . . Her name means a stopover at Lesbos, and to be a friend of hers, male or female, is to

compromise your reputation for ever! Need one add that she is a marquise with nothing to fill up her time. The marquise! She has been the model for prickly and cruel novels by Catulle Mendès and Rachilde. . . . Her doings have filled the newspaper columns for the last ten years.[38]

The novels Lorrain refers to here are Rachilde's *La Marquise de Sade* (1887) and Mendès's *Méphistophéla* (1890). Missy's biographers describe how little difficulty readers of these novels would have had in recognizing the increasingly famous young Mathilde de Morny as a model for both novels' protagonists.[39] When Missy is in question in the late 1880s and 1890s, tropes of perversion, pathologization, and degeneracy come easily to the pens of writers such as Lorrain, Mendès, and Rachilde—drugs, infanticide, sadism, satanism, anything is fair game.[40] Lorrain, in *L'Écho de Paris* of December 28, 1891, published "Autour de ces dames" (Around Those Women), a story about the earlier days of a certain "Mizy, who has since become Mephistofela," who in that earlier moment was not yet "the deranged morphine addict" that she had since become. In the story this Mizy exposes the newborn child of a girl-friend of hers to the elements, and the child dies. The final line of the story is "Amazons only get rid of male children." The state would take both Lorrain and *L'Écho de Paris* to court for *outrage aux bonnes moeurs* (offenses against public decency) following the publication of this article, and Lorrain and the newspaper would each be fined 3,000 francs.[41] Lorrain would write to a friend, "I am sentenced to a fine of 3,000 francs for offence to public morality. . . . No more writing about lezzies!" [Défense de parler désormais de gougnotage!].[42] The lawyer for the newspaper would cast the trial as a "battle between magistrates and artists" and would note that the state's attorneys had prepared a dossier regarding the newspaper's "tendencies." In that dossier could be found a number of articles from the second half of 1891 by other contributors to *L'Écho de Paris*, such as Catulle Mendès and Henry Bauër. All these articles took up lesbianism in various ways.

There were many cases in the 1880s and 1890s in which newspapers, especially the ones noted for their *grivoiserie*, were taken to court for offending public decency. *Le Courrier Français*, for instance, vociferous in its defense of its right to include images of bare-breasted women in its pages, would be in and out of court often in these years. In an article on February 7, 1892, *Le Courrier Français* expresses its solidarity with Lorrain and *L'Écho de Paris* and also informs us of the court's opinion as to what was unacceptable about the publication of Lorrain's article:

"There are certain subjects that should not be discussed in newspapers, whose affordable price makes them available to anyone."[43] The lawyer for *L'Écho de Paris* insisted that since "this vice," "le vice lesbien," is talked about everywhere in French literature and French society, there is no reason it should not be in the newspaper as well. In any case, he adds, everyone knows the story Lorrain recounted is a true one, and besides, didn't Balzac write *The Girl with the Golden Eyes*?[44]

A law guaranteeing extensive freedom of the press was passed for the first time in France during the Third Republic, in 1881. Even that law included an exception to the press's freedom in the case of *outrage aux bonnes moeurs*, and the law itself would be much debated and occasionally rendered more restrictive in the years following its adoption.[45] Whatever occasional setbacks there would be (as in this case against Lorrain), certain sectors of the French press would not give up writing about women's sexual interest in other women over the next few decades, and the writing would not always be as full of condemnation as in the case of Lorrain's article, "Around Those Women." An interesting example would be the articles by Catulle Mendès apparently included in one of the dossiers prepared by the state for Lorrain's trial. Mendès may have been cruel and pathologizing in his treatment of Missy in his novel *Méphistophéla*, but in some of the columns he wrote for his series "The Serious Life" in *L'Écho de Paris*, he took a different tack.

One of the "echos" on the front page of *L'Écho de Paris* for Sunday, October 11, 1891, reads as follows: "Seen in the Bois recently, in a victoria led by fine horses, Émilienne d'Alençon, who was carrying in her arms a superb doll, an enormous and lifelike child. It seems there will be a big celebration for its baptism. Liane de Pougy and the baroness Gratty will be the godmothers of the 'Little Duchess.' That is what Émilienne's doll is called." Émilienne d'Alençon was, like Liane de Pougy, one of the most visible and successful courtesans of the period 1890–1910. Like Liane de Pougy and Caroline Otéro, she occasionally appeared onstage in Parisian music halls. The three together were known as "les trois grâces," and their doings were closely followed in the press, including, as here, their affairs with other women.[46] This echo, probably written by Mendès, prepares the ground for the installment in his "Serious Life" series that appeared on October 28, 1891, under the title "The Dolls." The article discusses the recent appearance of dolls in women's carriages in the Bois de Boulogne and in women's boxes at the theater. It has nothing to do, Mendès insists, with a certain "abominable sin" of which he has been known to accuse various women, nothing to do with "abnormal desires." Nonetheless it is a strange custom to which these dolls are linked:

> Such a lovely custom! When finally, between two young women, their mutual tenderness has survived many trials, when nothing has been able to break it, not jealousy, not rivalry over the beauty of outfits at some ball, when, without any lessening of delight, a certain number of months have passed—let's say seven months—or nine, it is more often nine—then, oh innocent imitation!, one of the lady friends gives the other a doll in which is embodied, sort of (for after all the doll is not really alive!) their ideal of mutual sweetness. Then, after the confinement is over—for she who gives the doll pretends to be fatigued by the effort—there are charming parties. First of all the baptism. Out of the names of the two ladies, a single name is forged.

Insisting again on the purity and chastity of the women involved in these strange rituals, Mendès concludes his column by saying about two specific women he knows who apparently allowed him to participate in their doll-associated rites, "As far as I am concerned, what I would wish for two such adorable and pure young ladies, who did not refuse to include me in the mysteries of their ideal hymen, would be that later one could say of them: they loved each other and lived chastely together and had many dolls!"

These pairs of feminine women lovers are rendered in prose that, however the register varies from moment to moment, never indulges in the pathologizing rhetoric we find in *Méphistophéla*. In any case, this particular women's subculture is for Mendès an endless source of copy. He creates a trio of recurring characters in his columns (including "The Dolls") named Jo, Lo, and Zo. Mendès assures his readers that Jo, Lo, and Zo never engage in any vicious sexual practices, but he advances this claim as part of a ploy that permits him to write endlessly about the details of the cultural universe in which such practices do indeed exist. This becomes exceedingly clear in the installment of "The Serious Life" for December 23, 1891, titled "The Pink Mass and the Black Mass." Mendès begins the article by summoning Jo, Lo, and Zo to an accounting. Are they responsible for the perversion of contemporary sexual morals of Parisian women? Would it be because of them, he wonders, that Alfred de Vigny's prophecy will come true? He is referring to a few lines from Vigny's poem, "La Colère de Samson," the same lines that Proust will make famous thirty or so years later by using them as an epigraph to his *Sodom and Gomorrah*. Mendès cites them here (misquoting them significantly):

La femme aura Sodome et l'homme aura Gomorrhe,
Et se jetant de loin un regard irrité
Les deux sexes mourront chacun de son côté.[47]

[Woman will have Sodom and Man Gomorrah
And from afar they will cast irritated glances at the other
And the two sexes will die, each apart from the other.]

Lo claims in response that "we simulated exquisitely a desire that was never ours." The three of them then go on to assert that in any case, were they ever to have indulged in same-sex sexual behaviors, they would have been doing nothing but imitating what they learned elsewhere. They were not the source of the corruption. To which Mendès replies: "It is nonetheless true that you do me little honor in the world, and were I to regret having imagined you I would be within my rights. True, you were only imitators, not initiators! But what matter? You would have done better not to fashion yourself on those models. The sins of others do not make you any more innocent." Lo, Jo, and Zo insist that were Mendès to go back and read everything he has ever written about them, he would discover that he has never put them in a truly, undeniably sexual situation with another woman: "You will not find a single line in which one of our smiles slipped unconsciously, definitively, into a clear kiss. In reality you are a singularly moral storyteller!"

The formula instantiated here is something Mendès was obviously ready to reuse endlessly.[48] We can see to what an extent his journalism and that of Lorrain (and the others who included the culture, scandals, and activities of women sexually interested in other women on their beat)[49] might also be considered to have as their subject what it is possible to represent in a newspaper (or in a novel), what it is possible to imply, and what approach to the use of proper names or other identifying features allows one to skirt a charge of defamation (all of this most particularly in relation to same-sex sexuality among women). In particular we can see that the journalistic world (or this segment of it) sets itself up against the "moralistic" universe of the courts, claiming that both artistic freedom and the freedom of the press justify its wish to be able to represent or to report on the same-sex sexual cultures of the world around it. Thus part of the history of the representation of same-sex sexualities for this period in France is interwoven with the history of the struggles between the press and the state, between the newspapers and the courts. (Colette and Missy are obviously still participating in this struggle in 1907.)

We might note that Mendès carefully mentions Liane de Pougy and Emilienne d'Alençon by name only in a separate item—the echo I mentioned—printed two weeks before his long article developing the theme of the dolls. It almost seems as if, by mentioning them in an unsigned echo as opposed to a signed article, he wanted to ensure he could if necessary deny in court that he had ever claimed the two women were themselves involved in any kind of nonnormative sexual practice. Such insurance policies were not always deemed necessary in the years ahead. Names would sometimes be given with impunity in the pages of newspapers (and sometimes without meaning to cause scandal and without causing it). We might also note a contrast between the way feminine women such as Pougy and Alençon are treated by writers such as Mendès and Lorrain and the way Missy is treated. Unlike the masculine woman, the feminine woman who shows a sexual interest in other women might be scolded, but she is nonetheless still considered charming. This particular discursive distinction is a durable one, and it brings us back to the period of 1906–7, from which we have been digressing.[50] For in the space of several weeks in November and December 1906, *Fantasio* published separate profiles of Colette, Liane de Pougy, and Missy, and the contrast between these profiles is instructive.

The profiles of Colette and Liane de Pougy both appear in the November 1, 1906, issue of *Fantasio*. Liane de Pougy has apparently just undergone a short hospital stay: "Praise be to Venus and Adonis! It was a false alarm. . . . Paris has not lost this ornament; Lesbos still retains this smile." The wide range of Pougy's sexual conquests is on full display, with no attempt at disguise: "Many are those who have passed through her life: the smitten American girl who covers her in flowers and inhales her perfume looking for the source of her attraction, the curious bourgeois woman, longing after the unknown, suspecting mysterious things, special love potions, forgetting her veil when she leaves . . . and all the rest, bored and worn-out great ladies, having already tried every form of pleasure, now requiring the abnormal."[51] Pougy seems, in a certain way, immune from criticism. Such was the way the celebrity of the courtesan functioned—placing her outside the system of usual moral expectations, and thereby creating the possibility for open, even normalized, references to same-sex sexual relations in the pages of large-circulation magazines and newspapers.

With Colette it is a different story. She cultivates the signs of her femininity, and the press is perfectly willing to help her with this, but she is open for criticism because she abandons her place in polite society to take up a career on the stage. It is apparently not only the stage that poses a challenge to normative bourgeois femininity, but a literary career as well. The profile in *Fantasio* thus also mentions how women defeminize themselves by becoming writers. Colette, the profile's author admits, has found a clever way around this: "We must note immediately that Mme. Colette Willy has written certain 'Animal Dialogues' that are, in their own way, masterpieces. And among all the women of letters of whom in these years of Our Lord we are obliged to notice the nearly daily prodigious blossoming, I believe there is not a single one who has been able to demonstrate a sensibility so strangely personal as that of the historiographer of Kiki-la-Doucette and Toby-Chien." Indeed, the publication of *Dialogues des bêtes* and the press coverage of that book served as occasions for friendly critics to insist heartily on Colette's difference from other women writers, on the "truly feminine" nature of her writing. Colette was no *bas-bleu*. A typical expression of the association between her femininity and her writing about her cat and dog can be found in a letter from Francis Jammes to Colette dated April 25, 1906: "You are endowed with the most delicate of feminine natures. You bring to the easy promulgation of your book a remarkably seductive form of discretion, an exquisite modesty. . . . One thus finds, between the public life you put on display and your actual personality, some kind of impermeable barrier."[52] Colette would convince Jammes to write a preface to the 1905 edition of her *Dialogues*, and in that preface, too, he would insist on her femininity:

> Mme. Colette Willy is a living, breathing woman, a woman *in every way*, one who has dared to be natural and who resembles much more a quiet village bride than a perverse woman writer. . . . Toby-Chien and Kiki-la-Doucette understand that their mistress is someone who could not harm a sugar cube or a mouse, a woman who, for our pleasure, walks a tightrope that she has woven from flower-made words that she never bruises, words with which she perfumes us. She sings—with the voice of a pure French stream—that song of sad tenderness that enlivens the hearts of animals.[53]

Animals, the landscape, and a slightly pagan and peasant relation to nature, a relation that is more natural than perverse—these are the elements out of which Colette's profile as a feminine writer are carefully assembled. If this profile applies to Colette's career as a writer, there remains nonetheless her scandalous stage career to deal with. The *Fantasio* article suggests, for instance, that a woman writer has no place onstage if she wants to be taken seriously, and it closes with a light jab at Colette for not respecting and safeguarding the honor of her literary talents: "And so, when she returns home, having gained the public's applause for *The Gypsy Girl*, surely she hears Toby-Chien and her cat Kiki-la-Doucette, who also whisper: 'What a shame! It's fine, as far as it goes, to perform pantomimes, and we hear you do it quite well. But there are others who would do just as well, whereas no other woman . . . could write the dialogues in which you celebrate us.' "[54] Damned if you do, damned if you don't, it might seem. The subtle and not-so-subtle forms of symbolic violence Colette had to deal with in these years as she pursued a stage career and a literary one are unremitting—as are her strategies for defending against those forms of violence.

Of course, the "correct" literary establishment (of which we might think of Gide as a representative) would prefer to avoid having anything whatsoever to do with Colette—or with Tout-Paris in general. For certain representatives of Gide's serious corner of the literary field, Colette's vaunted "femininity" would instead be coded as frivolity. *Fantasio* notes: "In fact, if the literature written by Mme. Colette Willy seems not to be taken seriously by her fellow women writers, it is because Mme. Willy has never seemed to take seriously either her fellow women writers or literature." The kind of serious literary ambition which a certain school of critics suggested defeminized women and which would have been taken in those other, more "serious" circles as the sign of mature literary ambition, was a form of ambition Colette claimed to eschew by writing about dogs and cats and by allowing her profile to appear in *Fantasio*.[55]

Finally, there is *Fantasio*'s portrait of Missy, which appeared on December 15, 1906. Francis and Gontier, in their biography of Missy, have suggested that this wicked piece of journalism (it is signed with the pseudonym "Le Vitrioleur") was written by Willy as he passed through a jealous phase during his evolving separation from Colette. They speculate that Willy was unpleasantly surprised by the ease with which Missy and Colette were attaining celebrity as a Parisian couple as well as by their success at negotiating on their own a contract with the Moulin Rouge for their pantomime performances.[56] Whatever the truth about the authorship of the article, it is particularly interesting to find it in the pages of a magazine that had just published a reasonably favorable profile of Colette and a celebratory article on the beauty and the varied loves of Liane de Pougy. The article on Missy resurrects all the pathologizing tropes found in representations of her from the 1880s and

1890s by Rachilde, Lorrain, and Mendès. It makes reference to many of the rumors that have floated around Paris regarding various more or less sordid details in her past. It even portrays her as a kind of tourist attraction:

> The specialty guides who show rich foreigners the secret curiosities and the corruptions of Paris never fail to point out (perhaps it is in the Allée des Acacias, or in certain bars or gambling joints), and never fail to explain with words you can well imagine, this unsexed being with a face of soft, bloated plaster, with the staring gaze of someone addicted to ether and to nocturnal hunting, whose lips seem dead and who is invariably found wearing a jockey's hat, tightly wrapped in a black vest, sometimes with a poodle in tow, sometimes a theater girl.

The vitriol of the piece is curiously accompanied by a comical carica- ture of Missy by Sem, one of the premier caricaturists of the time, who had drawn Colette (and Willy) several times in the preceding years, and who would soon do a well-known poster of Colette advertising her theater tours. The caption to Sem's caricature of Missy, "A sensational upcoming debut at a café-concert: La Marquise à la Mayolaise," associ- ates her with the popular singer Félix Mayol, known for his gender- bending performances. Sem's caricature and its caption (comical as much as derogatory) provides publicity for the upcoming performances by Missy and Colette by situating them within a "same-sex friendly" current (an extremely broad one) in French popular culture of the time.[57] Along with the caricature of Missy by Sem, the *Fantasio* piece presents three photographs, two of which include Colette. The photo- graphs are not at all derogatory in and of themselves, but are rather images where the couple seems to have cooperated with and posed for the photographer.

The text of the article is another matter. It starts off with a quite complicated and snide remark: "La Marquise Missy chasse de race." The remark is based on the French proverb "bon chien chasse de race" —a good dog has hunting in its blood. The expression is most fre- quently used to suggest that this or that aspect of someone's conduct is inborn, inbred, "in the blood." What is in Missy's blood, according to the article, is the tendency to pursue a life of pleasure. The article makes reference (as we have seen many articles about Missy do) to her geneal- ogy, and in particular to her grandmother, Queen Hortense, and her father, the Duke de Morny. Hortense was the unwilling wife of Napo- léon's brother, Louis Napoléon, which made her briefly the queen of

Holland. Her son, the Duke de Morny, was an illegitimate child whose father was the Count de Flahaut, one of Napoléon's generals. The Duke de Morny's birth was apparently a clandestine affair, kept secret from Hortense's family. Thus what the author of the *Fantasio* article says runs in Missy's blood is her grandmother's "passionate, romantic, and inconstant soul," which caused her to make of her life "a hunt for pleasure." The same trait was apparent in her father, the Duke de Morny, who, the article says, was as handy at pleasure seeking as at affairs of state, nearly rivaling Don Juan in the number of his conquests. Yet, if this trait was passed on to Missy, it was apparently affected by that part of her youth spent in Saint Petersburg, "where neurosis and vices are brewed and where the deranged and impulsive type is found in great numbers," with the result that Missy was led to "scorn the law of the sexes." The blood has thus turned sour, one might say, with the result that Missy is "*déclassée*, fallen as low as possible," and, the article claims, has been shut out of all noble houses. Her decision to appear onstage in a café concert merely confirms the diagnosis of degeneration.[58]

I will return in a moment to the article's use of the word *race*, for it helps us to understand the importance of a number of different but intersecting discourses on race in providing one of the many contexts for what happened at the Moulin Rouge. But I would like to dwell for a little while on the paradoxical nature of *Fantasio*'s piece on Missy. Missy would quite justifiably sue the magazine for defamation following its publication, yet it's clear that there was some kind of close relation between the magazine and the social set to which Colette and Missy belonged. And, whatever the defamatory quality of the article, it nonetheless provided publicity, photographs, and a caricature by an artist who grasped something about the cultural significance of what Missy and Colette were up to.[59] Colette would herself show no hostility to the magazine in the years ahead, contributing an article to *Fantasio* in April 1909 ("Impressions de danse") that made implicit but quite legible reference to her ongoing relation with Missy, and would contribute further articles in 1910, 1911, and 1912. It should also be noted that *Fantasio* regularly included stories about alternative sexual cultures, in Paris as well as elsewhere. In January 1908, they published an excerpt from a forthcoming book on homosexuality in Germany.[60] In July 1909, they published an article, "A Club for Women Who Live as Men," also describing an aspect of German sexual culture. In May 1909 and June 1909 they published a pair of articles surveying the queer bar scene in Montmartre. These articles were all traversed by a kind of

La Marquise

La marquise Missy chasse de race.
Sa grand'mère — de la main gauche — fut reine
un instant dans le pays qui lui ressemblait le moins,
composa des romances ingénues, prodigua à la briser,
une âme passionnée, romanesque et inconstante, d'aventure en vaenture, fit de la vie une partie de joie.

Son père renouvela presque les exploits du légendaire
séducteur des mille et trois, ne connut, dit-on, jamais
de cruelles, mena de front les affaires de l'État et le
plaisir.

Fleur tardive et un
peu délaissée, elle se
forma et s'épanouit
dans l'exil contre les
genoux d'une indulgente et frivole douairière qui ne pensait
qu'à la parer, qu'à
l'admirer, qu'à sourire de ses réflexions
d'enfant terrible.

Cette société de
Saint-Pétersbourg où
de même qu'en quelque nouvelle Byzance,
fermentent les névroses
et les vices, abondent
les impaisifs et les détraquées, l'induisit-elle
dès que s'éveillèrent
son cerveau et ses sens,
à mépriser la loi des
sexes.

Ou bien, comme elle
le prétendit naguère
dans une heure d'amertume, de lâches
violences, de criminelles tentatives d'un
familier de la maison,
qui aurait dû être des
premiers à la respecter,
saturèrent-elles sans
retour de dégoût et
de révolte contre le
Mâle sa chair et son
cœur ?

Point obscur.

Il y a tantôt vingt-cinq ans, — cela ne
nous rajeunit pas,
comme dirait Alfred
Capus, — alors que
les deux Faubourgs ne s'étaient pas encore mis à
l'unisson pour la renier et la jeter hors du monde, et
que son mari, — philosophe libertin du dernier bateau
ou pauvre amoureux désemparé qui fait la part du feu,
qui ferme volontairement les yeux, couvrait la marchandise, — on l'eût volontiers comparée à Diane chas-

seresse, ou à une héroïne de Barbey d'Aurévilly. Son
teint lilial aux transparences d'hostie, ses yeux fascinateurs aux reflets d'aigues-marines, son profil de jeune
Dieu que nimbaient de courtes bouclettes de la teinte
du tabac d'Orient, ses lèvres au retroussis dédaigneux
sur quoi elle semblait avoir écrasé tout un bâton de
fard, et où flottait un pâle sourire désenchanté, son
torse souple et élancé qui se libérait du corset, auraient ; la aussitôt à Helleu et à La Gandara, les portraitistes reconnus des
Dames de Perversion
et de Beauté.

Elle avait l'air de
traîner un boulet d'une
écrasante lourdeur, de
se mourir d'ennui, riait
à peine, fanfaronne de
vice qui cherche à
s'illusionner soi-même
plutôt que vicieuse.

Si les uns lui jetaient la pierre, d'autres étaient tentés de
la plaindre, de la consoler, de la soigner,
doucement et charitablement, comme on
soigne les neurasthéniques.

Il lui plaisait de
mêler du sentiment à
des essais de corruption. Les billets qu'elle
écrivait à ses disciples
préférées avaient un
parfum de XVIIIe siècle, égalaient par leurs
élans de désir, par
leur irrésistible chaleur, par leurs émouvantes prières les meilleures lettres de Mademoiselle Aïssé au
chevalier d'Aydie.

Elle ordonnait à
merveille un souper de
tête-à-tête ou une petite débauche, pratiquait les exercices de
grâce et de force, et,
pour en donner la
preuve, avait installé
un trapèze devant le

Un prochain et sensationnel début au café-concert :
La Marquise à la Mayolaise.

lit bas et large de la chambre à aimer, dans chacune de
ses garçonnières.

De mauvaises langues lui attribuèrent, probablement
à tort, les goûts cruels du divin marquis, narrèrent par
la ville une histoire diabolique qui aurait pu avoir pour
titre comme je ne sais plus quel mélo de l'Ambigu :

« La fille du Garde-Chasse »
et qui faillit très mal
tourner.

Un volume, du reste, ne
suffirait pas pour contenir
les anecdotes pimentées et
les traits barbelés qui ont
couru et qui courent sur
l'androgyne.

Plusieurs sont d'une ex-
traordinaire saveur, et entre toutes, celle où une
divette se tira d'affaires
par la plus réfrigérante des
répliques, celle aussi qui
se termina par une culbute
devant un vieux général
tunisien.

Commérages lointains!
Missy n'est aujourd'hui
que l'ombre d'elle-même,
qu'une manière de fan-
tôme qui a quelque chose
d'apeurant et de lamen-
table.

Les cicérones spéciaux
qui révèlent aux riches
étrangers les curiosités
secrètes et les tares de
Paris ne manquent pas
de leur montrer dans
l'allée des Acacias, dans
certains bars et certains
tripots avec des commen-

La marquise de Belbeuf en costume masculin

faires que vous devinez
cette désexuée au visage
de plâtre mou qui se
boursoufle, au regard fixe
d'éthéromane et de nycta-
lope, aux lèvres mortes et
qui est invariablement
coiffée d'un chapeau d'en-
traîneur et sanglée dans
un veston de drap noir,
qui remorque avec elle tantôt un caniche, tantôt une
théâtreuse.

Déclassée, tombée au
troisième dessous, n'ayant
plus pour continuer la fête
qu'un majorat ébréché,
elle finira soit par se
réfugier dans la paix d'un
Carmel, soit par tenir à
Monte-Carlo ou à Passy
quelque table d'hôte de
femmes, soit par échouer
dans la petite voiture
qui brouette les vieux messieurs à goûts spéciaux.

En attendant, elle se
met à jouer la pantomime
en compagnie d'une sienne
amie, déjà fameuse et de-
main elle débutera au Café-
Concert.

Pauvre Missy!

LE VITRIOLEUR.

Colette Willy et la Marquise

Pantomime au Théâtre   Pantomime à la Ville

The first and second pages of *Fantasio's*
December 15, 1906, article on Missy.
*From the collections of Green Library,
Stanford University.*

discourse of voyeurism and by occasional elements drawn from the pathologizing discourse typical of medical writings.[61] *Fantasio* is a regular participant in the effort visible in a certain segment of the journalistic universe of the time to maintain its freedom to represent a wide range of sexual culture. Yet clearly it feels no obligation to sustain with any consistency any particular kind of discourse, friendly or unfriendly, on those cultures.

Yet I would recall once again that the phobic and pathologizing discursive elements in *Fantasio*'s December 1906 piece on Missy are relatively exceptional in the press around the time of the Moulin Rouge event. Given that writers could be phobic about Missy (and had been in the past), the question remains why the press is not more so. Part of the answer would seem to be that much of the specific public addressed by this journalism found same-sex relations (at least between women) somewhat ordinary. For this public, the interest in the unrest at the Moulin Rouge would seem to have had more to do with the particular celebrities involved and with the antics of certain members of the aristocracy in the audience who were insisting on asserting certain kinds of privileges that everyone knew were fading into irrelevancy. Perhaps it did not occur to most journalists writing about the event that their reading public would be interested in what must have seemed like old-fashioned, nineteenth-century derogatory discourses about the sexual life of the marquise. (Which is not to say that what seemed old-fashioned to a sexually sophisticated Parisian public in 1906 and 1907 would remain so forever. Particular publics belong to particular times. Things that are old-fashioned around 1907 might well become extremely fashionable again, say, in the mid-1930s.)

One never knows if the public that a newspaper *imagines* in the way it presents what it decides is news in fact corresponds to an *actual* reading public with all of the attitudes, prejudices, and cultural beliefs ascribed to it by the newspaper. Still it is not hard to reconstruct patterns of interest in the kind of readership projected by newspapers such as *Le Journal*, *Le Matin*, *Gil Blas*, and so on at the time of the Moulin Rouge hullabaloo. Those imagined readers were thought to be interested in and perhaps slightly cynical about the attitudes of the aristocracy toward its own honor; they were interested in the behavior of certain eccentric public personalities, including those associated with various political tendencies of the time; they were familiar with and not necessarily hostile to certain kinds of sexual relations between women—especially when those relations involved actresses, courtesans, literary figures, aristocrats, and so on. This public was familiar with distinctions (not always well-formulated ones) between different kinds of sexual attraction and relations between women, distinguishing, say, between feminine women who included sexual relations with other women among their relations with men and the seemingly exclusive preference of masculine women such as Missy for other women. (Remember that *La Vie Parisienne* cites Lysistrata having Calonice take a solemn oath to remain forever cold to men, as if, without the oath, she might tend to do otherwise.)[62]

One might say that certain segments of the journalistic world cooperate with the world of the music hall—particularly with those music halls such as the Moulin Rouge that are home to popular entertainment and yet also home to glamour—to set up a kind of oppositional space: oppositional to the discourses of doctors, lawyers, and politicians whose efforts at social control and social policing go on in other locations and who sometimes try with greater or lesser success to interfere with the world of journalism or the world of the music hall.[63] Such an oppositional space—friendly in its own way to alternative sexualities—is unlikely to fit neatly with other kinds of political opposition, such as that between left and right. (The left in France, for instance, harbors a long-lived current of hostility to nonnormative and nontraditional forms of sexual expression.) If I say that this is a *space* of opposition, that is to indicate that while within it one can (sometimes) speak, act, and enjoy a kind of oppositionality that may not be durably attached to oneself. Leaving that space—the next morning, or later in life—there is no guarantee that the oppositionality remains a part of you. (This is, of course, as true for Colette as for anyone else.) And we should add that this oppositional space is perfectly permeable to any number of elements of dominant discourse—although those elements may undergo surprising resignifications as they enter this space. Let us consider, in this light, the way racialized and orientalist discourses come to be present at the performance of *Rêve d'Égypte* at the Moulin Rouge. As we do so, we might keep in mind some observations by Lisa Lowe:

> To allegorize the meaning of the representation of the Orient as if it were exclusively and always an expression of European colonialism is to analyze the relation between text and context in terms of a homology, a determination of meaning such that every signifier must have one signified and every narrative one interpretation. Such a totalizing logic represses the heterologic possibilities that texts are not simple reproductions of context—indeed that

context is plural, unfixed, unrepresentable—and that orientalism may well be an apparatus through which a variety of concerns with difference are figured.[64]

Race/Egypt

The canny and mean-spirited invocation of race in the first sentence of the article in *Fantasio* on Missy ("Missy chasse de race") references, conjoins, and confuses a whole set of meanings attached to that word. *Race*, when applied to animals, simply means "bloodline"; animals said to be *de race* are thoroughbreds. *Race* was also an important term within aristocratic ideology, related to the preservation of the aristocracy as a caste. This ideology is clearly still operative and present in many minds at the time of the Moulin Rouge incident. It is implicitly referenced in every article that touches on Missy's genealogy, on the fact that her ancestors—whether legitimate or illegitimate in terms of wedlock—are stunningly legitimate in terms of appurtenance to the aristocracy. *Race* is, in a related but nonaristocratic usage, common in nationalist discourse of the period, which readily speaks of French people, and "the essential qualities of their race," qualities that would distinguish them from Germans and English people.[65] Finally, of course, *race* is an important term within the discourse of degeneracy, a discourse of blood gone bad.

In his lectures at the Collège de France in 1976–77, published under the title *"Society Must Be Defended,"* Michel Foucault describes the historical confrontation between several discourses on race, in particular the discourse that allows the aristocracy to distinguish itself from the rest of the French populace, and the discourse that promulgates ideas of degeneracy and deviance:

> The theme of the binary society which is divided into two races or two groups with different languages, laws, and so on will be replaced by that of a society that is, in contrast, biologically monist. Its only problem is this: it is threatened by a certain number of heterogeneous elements which are not essential to it, which do not divide the social body, or the living body of society, into two parts, and which are in a sense accidental. Hence the idea that foreigners have infiltrated this society, the theme of the deviants who are this society's by-products.

Foucault also suggests that these two competing discourses correspond to two different visions of the state: "The State is no longer an instrument that one race uses against another: the State is, and must be, the protector of the integrity, the superiority, and the purity of the race."[66] If the police, thanks to the pressure put on them by Missy's relations, gave the Moulin Rouge a choice between being shut down or refusing Missy access to the stage, that is some indication that in certain circumstances in 1907, the state could still serve to help the aristocracy preserve its self-image and its political importance by controlling the actions of one of its own members. Colette's antiaristocratic insistence that "it would simply be too bizarre if the fact of belonging to the French nobility meant a woman could not do what she wanted" does not prevail. In this case, for the state, Missy is a marquise first and a woman second; the police enforce a (racial) distinction between aristocrats and the rest of French society.

The state is no one thing; its various agencies often have no singular agenda. In other circumstances, agents of the French state will treat Missy not as a marquise but as a woman, or perhaps more as one of those "heterogeneous elements" of which Foucault speaks, foreign to the social body. Consider what happens when Missy sues *Fantasio* for defamation after it publishes its profile of her in December 1906. She only barely prevails. In its issue of April 15, 1907, *Fantasio* happily publishes the text of the judicial decision against it. The correctional court in question grudgingly admitted that, because she was a woman, Missy should not have been attacked as viciously as *Fantasio* did: "If it must be recognized that the Marquise de Morny had laid herself open to the harshest of criticisms, given that these criticisms were addressed to a woman, they should not have been given the particular form they took in the article in question." It admits that *Fantasio* had portrayed her "as prone to all vices and forms of debauchery," and that therefore she is entitled to damages. Yet, instead of the 15,000 francs in damages Missy had requested, the court orders her to be paid only 25, and gives a very specific reason: because the nature of her relations with Colette had been rendered public by the letter that Colette herself sent to the *Cri de Paris* and that was published on December 2, 1906. "These payments for damages cannot be as large as she requests given the letter of Colette W . . . dated November 25, 1906, appearing in the issue of the *Cri de Paris* of December 2, in which she shamelessly puts her lifestyle on display."[67] The reasoning would seem to be that Missy is entitled to legal protection as a woman, but only to a small amount, because Colette has admitted publicly that the two women are living together. According to the court's logic, by openly living together Colette and Missy alienate themselves from their status *as* women, just as they alienate themselves from the social body itself along with the legal protections that normally accrue or adhere to female members of that body.

Foucault speaks of the "mobility" and the "polyvalence" of the elements of a given discourse; he speaks of discourse as "a tactical instrument" that, once put into place, can be used "in various different strategies." It's a question not of ideology, he says, but of discursive tactics.[68] His observations are useful for understanding the racialized discourses that swirl around Missy and Colette and around the performance of *Rêve d'Égypte* at the Moulin Rouge. There is no particular coherence to the way the elements of those discourses are put together, nor to the way people in different social locations take them up. What is clear is the extent to which differently racialized visions of the world were present in the minds of various actors, and the extent to which a fascination with race was part of the draw of the event.

In *Race and the Education of Desire*, Ann Laura Stoler recalls for us Eugen Weber's point in *Peasants into Frenchmen* that the French at this historical moment had a racialized understanding of many prominent social divisions: "Quoting a mid-nineteenth-century Parisian traveller in rural Burgundy who opines that 'you don't need to go to America to see savages,' Weber argues that the theme of the French peasant as the 'hardly civilized,' rural savage 'of another race' was axiomatic in a discourse that 'sometimes compared them unfavorably with other colonized peoples in North Africa and the New World.' "[69] Colette, of course, was from Burgundy and extremely attached to that fact, as well as to her regional accent, one she retained to the end of her life. She would herself sometimes write in a way that used a racialized understanding of regional French identities, in particular of her identity in contrast to Missy's. It also seems clear that there was a public perception of her own body as racialized in a number of ways, referenced in the fact that *La Vie Parisienne*, in its reformulation of the events of the evening at the Moulin Rouge, transforms her from an Egyptian mummy into "a young hermaphroditic slave said to be of Egyptian birth because of the almond shape of her eyes."

Francis and Gontier in their biography of Missy at one point refer to Colette at the time of her involvement with Missy as "this person with no roots and whose black blood was a secret for no one" (249). Colette herself made several pointed references to a mixed-race heritage at about the time of the Moulin Rouge incident—in a 1905 letter to Francis Jammes, for instance, where she mentions "a black stain in my blood."[70] Francis and Gontier also cite copy that can be found in a newspaper in Nice reporting on one of her acting visits to that town: "Colette Willy . . . indelibly Burgundian given her accent; but if you dig a little bit—not even that deeply—you will find ancestors of a singularly dark complexion."[71] It seems reasonable to assert that to some extent or other information suggesting a particular racial past for Colette circulated as a form of publicity about her, and that this information would have served to make her appearance onstage with Missy (not to mention her relation with her) all the more charged in the public's eye. (National differences and regional differences, often implicitly racialized, as well as a racialized colonialist discourse, seem to have been generic commonplaces in the entertainments music halls provided throughout this period.)[72]

All of this then serves finally to call our attention to the subject matter of the pantomime Colette and Missy performed, which more often than not is merely mentioned in passing in accounts of the evening.[73] In *Rêve d'Égypte*, an Egyptologist has apparently brought a mummy home from Egypt and is experimenting with ways of resuscitating it. He seems to be sexually drawn to the revived mummy, enacting a kiss that not only involves two female performers but also enacts the union of two "races." There were many different dreams of Egypt circulating within French culture in 1907. Here I will catalogue only those few of them that impinge most clearly on the evening in question.

Napoléon, of course, occupied Egypt from 1798 to 1801. Even though most of Napoléon's later imperial activities would have Europe as their arena, it is worth noting that there is a close link between Egypt and the myth of the Napoleonic Empire, a myth to which Missy is also linked by her ancestry.[74] Prosper Enfantin and a group of Saint-Simonians spent from 1833 to 1836 in Egypt with the idea of establishing some spiritual bond between East and West. The East was often figured as feminine by the Saint-Simonians, and the West as masculine. Missy and Colette's kiss enacts this bond. Ferdinand de Lesseps was a French vice-consul in Alexandria at the time Enfantin was there and would come to spearhead the effort to build the Suez Canal (something the Saint-Simonians dreamed of as a kind of material instantiation of a union between East and West), a project that lasted from 1859 to 1869 using local labor and financed by an international corporation involving many French stockholders. Toward the end of the nineteenth century, French colonialists would have the ambition of extending French colonial possessions from the west coast of Africa to the east. As part of that project, an expedition commanded by

Jean-Baptiste Marchand set out from Gabon in July of 1896, reaching Fachoda in July of 1898. Fachoda, now called Kodok, is on the upper Nile in present-day Sudan. Marchand claimed the region for France. A British general, Kitchener, arrived in the area a few months later and demanded that the French leave. The British were seeking a controlling colonial influence over Egypt and the Sudan. The confrontation generated an international diplomatic incident that lasted until November 1898, when France gave way, and Marchand left the territory. The French government had apparently decided that sustaining an alliance with Great Britain (against Germany) was more important than certain colonial ambitions in eastern Africa. The government's decision would be roundly denounced by right-wing nationalist groups, including the Ligue de la Patrie Française, whose Syveton was willing to blame Marchand's disgrace on the infamous "metics" he saw controlling French foreign policy.[75]

Out of the endless literary representations of Egypt, both ancient and modern, I will limit myself to recalling one text with an evident relation to the events at the Moulin Rouge, Pierre Louÿs's novel *Aphrodite* (1896). This novel deals both with love between women and with ancient Egypt. It and other of Louÿs's texts were known to the turn-of-the-century French reading public as titillating, vaguely perverse reading material protected by some kind of supposedly high-literary aura. Colette's teenage Claudine, in *Claudine at School*, is proud to brag to the school inspector that she has read *Aphrodite*, knowing that it marks her as sexually precocious. *Aphrodite* itself, with its subtitle *Moeurs antiques* (Ancient Customs), is filled with representations of all kinds of illicit sexuality, including relations between women. Set in ancient Alexandria, it shows a further fascination with many forms of racial and ethnic differences that someone might imagine serving to eroticize various kinds of bodies in that ancient metropolis, bodies that might be recognized as Syrian, Asian, Egyptian, Galilean, and so on. *Aphrodite* is one of those ambiguous texts that served both to offer up representations of sexual relations between women to a prurient male readership and to offer examples for women who loved other women to take up and reuse in their imagination of themselves.[76] It will serve here simply as evidence that ancient Egypt (as well as modern Egypt) figured prominently in a lesbian imaginary around the time that Colette and Missy performed *Rêve d'Égypte* at the Moulin Rouge.

The space around the performance of *Rêve d'Égypte* was thus a heavily charged one in many ways, an intersection of many kinds of social forces and many discourses, a space rich in signifying patterns, some of them potentially contradictory. Missy's Napoleonic lineage, nationalist displeasure at France's retreat from Fachoda, Missy's well-known sexual preference for women, a long-standing culture of sexual relations between women within the upper echelons of French society, the tendency to find both in the ancient world and in North Africa resources for imagining alternative sexual cultures, Missy's blue blood, Colette's cultivation of her own exoticism and rumors about her mixed race, a growing French feminist movement concerned with the rights of women to earn their own money, the birth of a French nationalist movement concerned with the Frenchness of French people and with the perpetuation of traditional gender roles, the culture of courtesans with their varied and quite public kinds of sexual interests, the culture of music halls and the place of music halls within popular culture, the particular cultural profile of the Moulin Rouge—all of these factors and more contribute to the contexts of the performance of *Rêve d'Egypte* in January 1907. They contribute to making the performance into a kind of experimental event in which someone (say Colette or Missy or even audience members such as the Panther, Liane de Pougy, Willy, and Meg Villars) could present a self and see how it would be received, how it would fit in or stand out, whether it would be tolerated, whether it still held up, whether they would be allowed to take it on, whether they could sustain doing so, and so on.

What links Colette's *writing* at this time with what she is doing in her public life and as a performer is her experimentation with context and with figures of self. She moves in lesbian circles, is openly coupled with another woman, appears with her onstage in a way calculated to attract publicity and scandal, and writes a series of first-person texts, some about Parisian same-sex culture and some about her relationship with Missy. Remarkably, she does all of this in a series of first-person figurations that arguably never assume a same-sex sexual identity even as they enact same-sex intimacies. Her first-person texts implicitly reflect on the *context* of the assumption of the first person, revealing the first person to be an interactive production rather than an assertion of identity. (We might also say that, whatever her differences from Gide, they were both looking in this first decade of the century for new forms of expressions, new generic possibilities, seeking out a road between apologia and satire, between confession and the assignation of perversion.)

Colette's first-person writings of these years (including those she collects in *Les Vrilles de la vigne* and a number of others that she writes and publishes in the year following the publication of *Vrilles*)[77] are experiments in the literary constructions of a self within a particular social and discursive context—the same context that I have just outlined for the performance at the Moulin Rouge. Rather than creating any particular, singular first-person voice in *Les Vrilles*, Colette creates a field of first-person voices. She thereby manages to call attention to issues like gender, sexuality, social class, race, nationality, and so on, and to the way these social structures shape first-person writing. Through the creation of this field of first-person voices she is able to portray a certain set of social tensions (the same tensions we find in place that evening at the Moulin Rouge) that impinge upon the assumption of the first person in a variety of contexts. Thus in the reading of *Les Vrilles* and associated texts that I offer here, I will be worrying less about the deictic quality of the first-person pronoun, per se, and less about the variations that can be rung regarding the relation between the referent of the pronoun and the genre of the text (autobiography, fictional autobiography, first-person fiction, autofiction, and so on). Rather I will be thinking about the first person as a figure produced within a given interactive context—about the act of figuring a first person as an intervention in a context, as work within a context. I am also interested in inquiring into what the various aspects of that figure could be said to index within the social order that surrounds the particular interactive context, and what role the context plays in the production of the figure.

Colette Chez Palmyre

Both individually and as an ensemble, the first-person figures Colette produces in *Les Vrilles de la vigne* reveal fault lines within various discourses that structure the social field; they play upon crucial tensions within that field, and they bridge certain heteronomous spaces within the field as well.

The Moulin Rouge is in the eighteenth arrondissement of Paris, on the Boulevard de Clichy near the Place Blanche. One of the more prominent queer bars in Montmartre in 1907, Chez Palmyre, was located in the ninth arrondissement at 5 Place Blanche—more or less across the street from the Moulin Rouge. But the spatial proximity of the Moulin Rouge and Chez Palmyre perhaps does not fully reflect the social distance that existed between them. Louis Chevalier recounts how the famous courtesan Caroline Otéro was once taken in for questioning by the police after being found in a low-class gambling joint frequented by suspicious men and women and located near the Place Clichy (another stone's throw from the Moulin Rouge). She was obliged to claim she had taken shelter there from a sudden rainstorm, indicating how much caution one sometimes had to exercise regarding precisely which Montmartre establishments one was seen to frequent.[78]

There is plenty of evidence that Colette and Missy frequented Chez Palmyre together, and from that evidence and other sources we can learn a good deal about what kind of an establishment it was. For instance, the gossip column ("Les On-dit") of *La Vie Parisienne* for April 27, 1907—the first issue in which we find a contribution by Colette—contains a description of an unnamed "cramped bar, but one whose bright sign attracts clients from afar": "It's quite a nice bar. Every night Otéro dances and puts on a number together with Bobette. Don't be alarmed. This is not the Otéro who, the Otéro that, the well-known Otéro. Otéro is a man very well shaven, dark skinned, missing some teeth, Spanish. Bobette is a young, blond-haired man, made up clumsily, and he has been well shaven as well." *La Vie Parisienne* goes on to say that the bar in question appears to be a place in which young folk of both sexes from the popular classes might be available to be picked up by elegant folk of either sex. As for why elegant folk would go there, it was because everyone famous did: journalists, actresses, actors, professional gossips, and even government officials. A 1908 letter from Colette to Charles Saglio, the editor of *La Vie Parisienne*, for instance, upbraids him for failing to show up for a dinner engagement he had with Colette and Missy at Chez Palmyre. Colette is especially vexed, because the proprietress (who is called Palmyre) had arranged specially for Bobette to be there to sing for them.[79] Other notorious aristocrats who frequented the bar include Jacques d'Adelswärd-Fersen. Judith Thurman cites an unpublished letter from Missy to Colette written around this time, while Colette was off touring with a theater company. The letter recounts an evening at Chez Palmyre during which Fersen gets drunk, gets slapped by Palmyre herself, throws a glass of wine at her, and is then thrown out of the bar by the regulars. He apparently then denounced the bar to the police as a hangout for dykes and queers, an obvious fact his own presence there merely served to confirm.[80]

Colette and Missy not only frequented Chez Palmyre, they were assimilated into its popular culture, just as Otéro had been. When, in May 1909, *Fantasio* publishes a prurient exposé on Montmartre's queer culture, "The Sentimental Heresy," it includes a description of a visit to Chez Palmyre (renamed Almire in the article) and provides a list of the performers there. Along with Otéro and Bobette (who, we are told, is the main attraction of the joint and also a *"cinaedus* or *pathicus*, who knows which"[81]) we find three other names among the bar's leading lights: La Marquise, Colette, and Lucienne. One assumes, then, that by 1909 Colette and Missy are famous enough within popular queer culture to be assumable as drag personalities by popular performers. We can also deduce from "The Sentimental Heresy" that queer performers in these popular circles took a lively interest in queer-inflected events in other, more elevated, social locations. Lucienne, for instance, is well known for the song she sings about the English painter Bulton, who was arrested in his Parisian atelier one night in March 1904 along with eighteen other men involved in what appears to have been a gay wedding banquet and orgy. The police were able to observe the proceedings through a skylight in order to pick exactly the right moment at which to intervene to arrest the participants. Apparently thanks to the police observations, many details about the orgy circulated among people in the know. Lucienne's song makes particularly humorous reference to the uses to which a variety of edibles from the banquet were put.[82]

When Colette herself writes about Chez Palmyre, she portrays it as a place she frequented, but on her own. She also changes its name to Le Sémiramis Bar. That name change in itself is interesting, another indication of the ways in which queer culture of the time reveled in references to the ancient world. Palmyra was an ancient city in Syria famous for its warrior queen Zenobia, who would unsuccessfully defend her city against the Romans. Colette makes a transference back in time a good number of centuries to rename the bar after the legendary queen of Babylon, Sémiramis. If the owner of Chez Palmyre is called Palmyre, of course the owner of the Sémiramis Bar will be called Sémiramis: "I go to a bar kept by Sémiramis, appropriately named—Sémiramis, warrior queen, helmeted in bronze, armed with the meat cleaver, who speaks a colorful language to her crowed of long-haired young lads and short-haired girls" [J'entre chez Sémiramis la bien nommée, Sémiramis reine guerrière, casquée de bronze, armée du coutelas à viande, qui parle une langue colorée à son peuple de jeunes hommes à longs cheveux et de jeunes femmes à cheveux courts].[83] The narrator of Proust's *Recherche* is famous for being able to find himself in the most queerly compromising situations without himself ever being compromised. "Le Sémiramis Bar" thematizes the question of compromising behavior or of compromising locales from the start, but also manages to avoid clarifying whether the first person in the text is in fact in any way compromised by the sexuality associated with the locale in question. That we find Colette claiming no affiliation to the other patrons of Chez Palmyre when she was well known for having kissed her girlfriend onstage in a theater just across the way provides some indication of the craft with which she wields the first person here.

Interlocution is key in *Les Vrilles de la vigne* and its related texts. The interlocutor for Colette's first person in "Le Sémiramis Bar" is Valentine, familiar to readers of three texts in *Les Vrilles*: "Belles-de-jour" (Morning Glories), "De quoi est-ce qu'on a l'air?" (What Would They Think of Us?), and "Une Guérison" (A Cure). (Valentine also appears in "Une Lettre," published in *La Vie Parisienne* in August 1909.) She is a tall and extremely blond high-society woman with very white skin, usually overly elegantly dressed, hair carefully done, with a penchant for extravagant hats. She has a rich husband and an artist as a lover. She moves with a chic set, and her movements are noted in the society columns. By way of the figure of Valentine, Colette takes up the loss of social status she experienced when she began her theatrical career. Valentine usually comes over to see Colette at teatime, as in the following passage from "De quoi est-ce qu'on a l'air," and it is made clear that she is one of the few high society women who have kept up their acquaintance with Colette following her breakup with Willy and the advent of her stage career:

> I appreciate the fact that she confides in me, that she comes back at the risk of compromising her position as a woman with a husband and a lover, for coming back here to see me with an affectionate persistence which verges on heroism. (*CSC* 84)

> [Je lui sais gré de se confier à moi, de revenir, au risque de compromettre sa position correcte de femme qui a un mari et un amant, de revenir chez moi avec un entêtement affectueux qui frise l'héroisme. (1:1021)]

She mentions to Valentine that she was recently snubbed by a woman next to whom she was seated at a concert, a woman to whom she used to speak socially: "I was making her uncomfortable. She doesn't know me anymore, since a certain separation and division of property changed me so much. She trembled every time I batted an eyelash, for fear I might kiss her" (*CSC* 80) [Je lui donnais chaud. Elle ne me connaît plus, depuis qu'une séparation de corps et de biens m'a tant changée. Elle tremblait, chaque fois que je bougeais un cil, que je l'embrassasse . . . (1:1017)].

One of the aspects of Colette that Valentine seems to appreciate is that Colette's gaze is not like the gaze of other women. Colette describes Valentine as:

> My friend the gourmand, who faithfully comes to have her tea with me because I indulge her little idiosyncrasies, because I listen to her chatter, because I never agree with her about anything . . . She can relax with me; she is quick to tell me, in a tone of gratitude, that I'm not really flirtatious, and I don't scrutinize her hat or her dress with an aggressive, female eye. (CSC 75)

> [Mon amie si gourmande, qui vient goûter assidûment chez moi, parce que je choie ses petites manies, parce que je l'écoute bavarder, parce que je ne suis jamais de son avis . . . Avec moi elle se repose; elle me dit volontiers, sur un ton de gratitude, que je ne suis guère coquette, et je n'épluche point son chapeau ni sa robe, d'un oeil agressif et féminin . . . (1:1009)]

Valentine seems to defend Colette in the presence of other society women and seems also to envy Colette some of the liberties she can allow herself because she now lives "on the fringes of society" (CSC 83) [en marge de la société (1:1020)]. Colette constructs in these pages involving Valentine the figure of two women friends fascinated by each other, fascinated, she makes clear, even perhaps attracted by, the other's femininity—two femininities that resemble each other so little. (Recall the passage from "Une Lettre" cited at the beginning of this chapter, in which Colette admits to being disturbed by the way that Valentine's summer dress reveals the contours of her body. Note as well the interesting ambiguity in Valentine's ready and grateful comment that Colette isn't really flirtatious or coquettish, meaning in part, one assumes, that there can be an ease in their own friendship because they won't be flirting with the same men, but also suggesting the possibility that some undefined kind of intimacy can arise between the two women because of that very ease.)

Valentine may be fascinated by Colette, her forms of femininity and her freedom, she may be loyal in her friendship, but she still finds ways of expressing her disapproval of some of Colette's activities:

> When I am off involved in my pantomime or my acting, my friend Valentine disappears from my life, discreet, alarmed, modest. This is her polite way of showing her disapproval of my sort of existence. I'm not offended by it. I tell myself that she has a husband in automobiles, a society-painter

lover, a salon, weekly teas, and twice-monthly dinners. Can you just see me, performing *Flesh* or *The Faun* at one of Valentine's soirees or dancing *The Blue Serpent* for her guests? I put up with it. I wait. I know that my more respectable friend will come back, sweet and embarrassed, one of these days. A little or a lot, she cares about me and proves it to me, and that is enough to make me indebted to her. (CSC 86)

[Durant mes stages de pantomime ou de comédie, mon amie Valentine disparaît de ma vie, discrète, effarée, pudique. C'est sa façon courtoise de blâmer mon genre d'existence. Je ne m'en offusque pas. Je me dis qu'elle a un mari dans les automobiles, un amant peintre mondain, un salon, des thés hebdomadaires et des dîners bi-mensuels. Vous ne me voyez guère, n'est-ce pas, jouant *La Chair* ou *Le Faune* en soirée chez Valentine, ou dansant le *Serpent bleu* devant ses invités? . . . Je me fais une raison. J'attends. Je sais que mon amie convenable reviendra, gentille, embarrassée, un de ces jours . . . Peu ou beaucoup, elle tient à moi et me le prouve, et c'est assez pour que je sois son obligée. (1:1024)]

Valentine provides the context in which a number of questions, a number of social predicaments, can find expression, and not always in what Colette and Valentine might say to each other, but in the terms of the interaction itself, an interaction shaped by the fact that Colette has compromised herself in certain ways, and that Valentine remains her friend despite social pressure to do otherwise. What is the social fate of a woman in polite bourgeois society who leaves her husband and takes up a theatrical career? The parameters of the interaction between Valentine and Colette allow a certain kind of first-person figure for Colette to emerge—interestingly, it is one that could still be *further* compromised. That is, even if this person has already been ostracized from certain parts of polite society and has dealt with that situation as best she can, and even if she insists that she cares not a bit about the possibility of further compromising herself, nonetheless that whole question of the process of, the effects of, and the ongoing potential for being compromised forms the context for the interaction between these two feminine figures.

It seems no accident, then, that Colette's description of Chez Palmyre in her article "Le Sémiramis Bar" is given in the context of a conversation with Valentine. Valentine—however grateful she may be for the moments she is able to spend in the unconventional Colette's company and away from the heavily constrained social environments in which she spends most of her life—remains extremely concerned that certain conventions be respected, even by Colette. "Le Sémiramis Bar" opens as Colette awaits the arrival of Valentine, who has written to let her know she is coming over to scold her for something. News travels fast in Paris, and Valentine has heard that "you dined at the Sémiramis bar day before yesterday" [vous avez encore dîné au Sémiramis-bar avant hier]. Colette does not try to defend herself:

"That's true. But so what?"

"So what? That's all. Isn't it enough for you?"

"Yes, it's enough, since I dine there two or three times a week. One eats well there." . . .

"Why, you unhappy creature, that is a place . . . a place . . ."

"With a bad reputation. Heavens, yes." . . .

"Really, my poor dear, it looks as though you wanted to make your friends' task of defending you impossible."

"Who has imposed that task on you? I certainly didn't."

"I mean, well, that . . . you know I'm very fond of you. What would you have me say when someone comes to tell me you were dining at the Sémiramis?"

"Tell them the plain truth—that it's none of your business." (CSC 51)

[—C'est vrai. Et alors?

—Et alors? C'est tout. Ça ne vous suffit pas?

—Si, ça me suffit, puisque j'y dîne deux ou trois fois par semaine. On y mange bien. . . .

—Mais, malheureuse que vous êtes, c'est un endroit . . . un endroit . . .

—Mal famé. Mon Dieu oui. . . .

—On dirait vraiment, ma pauvre amie, que vous voulez rendre impossible à vos amis la tâche de vous défendre . . .

—Qui vous l'impose, cette tâche? Pas moi, toujours?

—Je veux dire, enfin, que . . . vous savez que je vous aime beaucoup. Qu'est-ce que vous voulez que je réponde, quand on vient me dire que vous dînez chez Sémiramis?

—Répondez, en toute vérité, que ça ne vous regarde pas.]

Valentine insists that even though it may be none of her business, still Colette needs to admit that there is a difference between being someone who has been to such a bar once, and someone who is "a habitual customer, a regular" [une habituée, une abonnée de l'endroit]. Colette has been observed there "all alone in your corner, with your newspaper and your dog, and all those people who speak to you, those odd little men in weird jackets, who wear rings and have bracelets on their ankles" (CSC 52) [toute seule dans votre coin, entre votre journal et votre chienne, et tous ces gens qui vous disent bonjour, cet petits messieurs en veston à jupe, qui ont des bagues, et des bracelets à la cheville]. Moreover, Valentine has heard that late at night the bar can become rowdy in a way that is truly shocking.

Colette claims that she is never there late at night, admits that she has heard from Sémiramis many stories of the shocking late-night goings on, and then provides Valentine with a description of Sémiramis, and of various scenes she has seen at the bar. She takes the time to explain in some detail why she likes being there. Having gone on for several long paragraphs in this vein, she is interrupted by Valentine, who comments:

> "Yes, yes, that's all very nice. When you want to exonerate yourself from something you dress it up as literature and you tell yourself, 'If I talk very fast and insert some fancy words, I can pull the wool over Valentine's eyes!' It's easier than telling me to go to the devil, isn't it?" (CSC 540)

> [—Tout ça, tout ça, c'est très joli. Quand vous voulez vous disculper de quelque chose, vous habillez ça avec de la littérature, et vous vous dites: «En parlant un peu vite, et en mettant de jolis mots, Valentine n'y verra que du feu!» C'est plus facile que de m'envoyer promener, hein?]

Colette seems to be using this interaction with Valentine to insist on the possibility of her frequenting a queer bar without being obliged in any way to assume she will subsequently (in this conversation with her friend, for instance) be required to confess to or to assume any sexual identity. Valentine's comment here about Colette's intent in dressing something up as literature is particularly interesting, for it calls to our attention some of the many challenges dealt with in Colette's writing in the period immediately following the Moulin Rouge incident. How is it possible for her simultaneously to pursue a claim to literary authority as a woman writer, to pursue a career on the stage that includes a few key appearances with the scandalous and aristocratic Missy, to bare her breast on the stage in *La Chair*, and appear in scanty costumes in other contexts and yet retain a social identity that is somehow not that of just some dancer in the music hall or some scandalous stage celebrity, but that of a serious author? How is it possible for her to participate in, even to affiliate with, certain aspects of popular queer culture without compromising her literary career, or her affiliation with bourgeois literary culture? How is it possible to write for a publication such as *La Vie Parisienne* and to be taken seriously as a writer? How is it possible to represent Chez Palmyre in an acceptably literary way? Indeed, what is a serious literary representation of such a place?

Colette's way of affiliating with queer popular culture in "Le Sémiramis-Bar" and in "Gitanette" (another text set in the same bar and published in *La Vie Parisienne* roughly five weeks later) is to establish herself as a friendly and accepted *observer* of that culture, one who takes pleasure in what she sees there and reports on it in subtly crafted prose:

> Now I will dare to inform you that while dining at Sémiramis's bar I enjoy watching the girls dancing together, they waltz well. They're not paid for this, but dance for pleasure between the cabbage soup and the beef stew. . . . They waltz like the denizens of cheap dance halls, lewdly, sensuously, with that delicious inclination of a tall sail of a yacht . . . I can't help it! I really find that prettier than any ballet. (*CSC* 55)

> [J'ose à présent vous dire que je prends plaisir, en dînant, à regarder danser chez Sémiramis des femmes enlacées, qui valsent bien. Elles ne sont pas payées pour cela, et dansent pour leur plaisir, entre la potée aux choux et le boeuf bourguignonne. . . . . Elles valsent en habituées des bals de barrière, crapuleusement, voluptueusement, avec cette inclinaison délicieuse d'une haute voile de yacht . . . Que voulez-vous? Je trouve cela plus joli qu'un ballet.]

The illustration that accompanied "Le Sémiramis-Bar" in *La Vie Parisienne* takes up this moment, portraying three different couples of women, one of them dancing "lewdly." Is that Colette at the table in the back with Toby-Chien and another patron? The article ends with Valentine seemingly seduced by Colette's description of the dancing; she takes her leave from Colette, pausing to wonder if it wouldn't be possible for her to dress down some evening and join Colette for dinner at the bar without her husband ever finding out.

"Gitanette" pursues a similar rhetorical strategy. Valentine is no longer needed as an excuse to broach the subject of the bar. Colette once again dines in sympathy with, but not exactly in the same category as, the popular queer clientele surrounding her. A young woman, Gitanette, joins her for a chat, and after a moment Colette recognizes her as a dancer who, together with her partner Rita, was assigned the dressing room next door to hers during one of Colette's music hall gigs:

LE JOURNAL DE COLETTE

LE SÉMIRAMIS-BAR

The illustration from Colette's
"Le Sémiramis-Bar" in *La Vie Parisienne*.
*From the collections of Doe Library, University
of California, Berkeley.*

They danced neither well nor badly, and their story was the same as any other "dance number." You know it already, or perhaps you don't: they are young, supple, poor as a church mouse, and they've had their fill of women's bars and of the theater lobbies, so they save up their pennies in order to pay the weekly fee of a dance master who puts together a number for you, and of the costume maker . . . And if they are very, very lucky, they begin to perform around Paris, the provinces, and abroad.

[Elles ne dansaient ni mal, ni bien, et leur histoire était celle d'un tas de «numéros de danse». Vous savez—ou vous ne savez pas—ce que c'est: on est jeunes, souples, on est purées comme Crécy lui-même, dégoûtées du bar à femmes et du promenoir, alors on ramasse tous ses pauvres sous pour payer, tant par semaine, le maître de ballet qui vous règle un numéro, et le costumier . . . Et si on a beaucoup, beaucoup de chance, on commence à faire les établissements de Paris, de la province et de l'étranger.]

Here, as in "Le Sémiramis Bar," we notice Colette's knowledge of, interest in, and even attraction to the couples of women she meets in the music halls and the Sémiramis bar, her awareness of many details regarding the culture in which these women move.

Gitanette tells Colette the story of the end of her relationship with Rita: how happy they were together at the moment they were working alongside Colette, how they moved on to a big review at the Empyrée, where Gitanette became uneasy about all the competition among the women, and where Rita would meet Lucie Desrosiers, for whom she would eventually leave Gitanette—still miserable two years later. Colette is deeply moved by the story:

In spite of myself, I took her hand and squeezed it:
"My dear child, I feel so badly for you!"
Slightly surprised, she looks up at me with her beautiful, sincere, and tearless eyes and says:
"Go on, don't feel too badly. It sounds funny but I guess I wouldn't know what to do if I didn't feel bad. I couldn't do without it. It's what keeps me company."

[Malgré moi, j'ai pris sa main que je serre:
—Ma pauvre enfant, comme je vous plains!
Un peu surprise, elle lève sur moi ses beaux yeux sincères et sans larmes:
—Ne me plaignez pas trop, allez. C'est drôle à dire, mais . . . je ne saurais quoi faire si je ne souffrais pas. Je ne pourrais plus m'en passer. Ça me tient compagnie.][84]

Colette is writing here in the tradition of Jean Lorrain, bringing popular queer culture to the attention of a bourgeois readership, and doing so in a sympathetic way. (Lorrain, of course, was sometimes sympathetic, sometimes less so, when he did this.) It seems also worth pointing out that just as Colette simultaneously established an affiliation with and a distance from Valentine, she does the same with Gitanette. In both cases, part of what constitutes Colette's distinction from her interlocutors is her literary identity. That is to say that Colette is making the implicit claim that her experiences in Montmartre take much of their value from the fact that they are literary experiences—that they are one of the causes of her literary production.

Francis Carco, whose 1914 novel *Jésus-la-Caille* places him in the same literary current as Lorrain and Colette, made much the same kind of argument about his varied experiences in Montmartre:

> Montmartre was splitting at the seams with these individuals who seemed to belong to no known sex, whose only care was pleasure, and who—in certain ways, and within certain limits which, believe me, I never felt tempted to exceed—corresponded to my secret nature, to my obscure leanings. And so later I could say, "Jésus-la-Caille c'est moi." . . . It was less a question of telling the story of a certain kind of behavior than of giving way to the consequences of that behavior, as if in the throes of a kind of altered state in which my consciousness remained intact and yet which was also a kind of hallucination.

> [Montmartre regorgeait de ces individus ne ressortisant à aucun sexe déterminé, qui n'aimaient que le plaisir et qui, par de certains côtés, et jusqu'à des limites que je n'ai jamais, qu'on veuille bien me croire, éprouvé la tentation de franchir, correspondaient à ma nature secrète, à mes obscurs penchants. J'ai donc pu dire plus tard: «Jésus-la-Caille c'est moi . . .» . . . Il s'agissait moins de retracer des moeurs déterminées que d'en subir les conséquences, en proie à une sorte d'état second où ma conscience demeurât entière et qui tenait pourtant de l'hallucination.][85]

It is worth taking seriously Carco's (and also, I think, Colette's) claim to a kind of altered consciousness, or a search for an experience of such a consciousness by way of their exploration of a sexual culture to which they claim no determined belonging—indeed, to which they determinedly claim not to belong. In spite of not belonging, and of pointing out in various ways that they do not fully belong, there are consequences to pursuing the experiences in question, and those consequences are claimed as part of what goes into becoming a literary figure. They include being ostracized from polite society, not being reviewed, and so on.

Rachilde confirms this quasi-sacred status to which Colette and Carco are laying claim, and upon which they build their early literary enterprise. Often when she writes about Colette or Colette's books in these years, Rachilde resorts to a rhetoric of a kind of sacred paganism.[86] She notes in her review of *Les Vrilles de la vigne* that almost no one dared admit to admiring Colette's *La Retraite sentimentale* (published only a month after the Moulin Rouge incident), because of the scandal surrounding Colette at that moment. Yet it was a grotesque error, a failure, Rachilde implies, for critics not to recognize and celebrate the prophetic nature of Colette's voice in that book. She opens her review of *Les Vrilles de la vigne* as follows: "This nocturnal song, the voice of the terrifying mysteries of the earth and its waters, the cry of the dense forests, the final gasps of plants and animals who die for love, is a song forever accursed [*maudit*] for the deep impression it makes. Where, then, are the lovers of pure art (for true art is always pure) who have recognized the true place that Colette Willy should occupy among writers?" Rachilde, in advocating for Colette's literary status, implicitly invokes the tradition of the *poètes maudits* (Baudelaire, Rimbaud, Verlaine), and their status as sacred outcasts. She also relates this to a claim for the essential Frenchness of Colette's art. Colette is "a wild and perfect young songster, a special being—and set apart because of it—as marvelously French an artist as there could be in the French race, and worthy of recognition without any useless gestures of modesty."[87] Rachilde would appear to be arguing for the particular and essential Frenchness involved in a literary exploration of sexual subjects sometimes viewed as shameful, and for the consecrated status of someone with sufficient talent who is able to brave that imposition of shame. (Rachilde's comments help us to appreciate that however much Colette may have offended the reigning French nationalist sensibilities of her moment—by her use of stock lesbian tropes involving Egypt and the Orient, by her same-sex relations with a member of the French aristocracy, by her theatrical career, her failure to be a good mother, whatever —it is nonetheless very clear that her literary ambition was in itself in some ways inherently nationalist: to be an important *French* woman writer.)

What is notable about the authorial space that Colette constructs for herself in these years, and that Rachilde recognizes and describes, is her way of enacting a version of what Carco points to in writing that "it was less a question of telling the story of a certain kind of behavior than of giving way to the consequences of that behavior, as if in the throes of a kind of altered state in which my consciousness remained intact and yet which was also a kind of hallucination." That is, Colette is able to frequent queer bars, to be in a relationship with Missy, to assume in public the consequences of being in that relationship, to create literature from within the experience of that relationship, and yet to refuse to be determined by that relationship, to refuse to assume any kind of sexual identity that might be associated with it. Her ways of doing all of this in *Les Vrilles* and the texts surrounding it are multiple.

In this regard, we might note that Colette's relationship with Valentine and the visits to the Sémiramis bar they discuss seem to happen in a universe separate from her relationship with Missy. How could the figure she creates in Valentine ignore or be untroubled by Missy, especially given that Missy and Colette's relationship was such a big part of Colette's public profile in these years, and given that Missy is such a strong presence within certain of the texts making up *Les Vrilles* and some of those that follow it? Missy's absence is also quite notable in a text like "Gitanette," where Colette sympathizes with a woman devastated by the loss of her girlfriend while giving no indication that she and Missy frequented together the bar in which the conversation is taking place. What might it mean that Missy is never present in the relation with Valentine or in the texts on the Sémiramis Bar, even though it is a bar Colette frequented with her? What textual strategies dictate her presence in certain contexts and her absence in others? To frame the question another way, when Colette was clearly writing about her relationship with Missy in many of these texts, when that information was public knowledge, what does it mean that this information, so crucial to the context of *Les Vrilles* as a whole, seems to be of no import to Valentine (perhaps she is unaware of it), as concerned as she is for her friend Colette's respectability? That these questions suggest themselves is evidence of the work Colette is doing with multiple contexts—with creating a field of first-person voices through which to negotiate different social tensions—pursuing in the same space, but not exactly in the same voice or the same first person, her relation with Missy, her social trajectory as actress and writer, her interest in but separation from queer culture, her literary ambitions, the various aspects of her social identity, and so on. The complexities of interfering contexts lie at the heart of *Les Vrilles de la vigne*.

VRILLE, s. f.

Femme qui, dans un ménage lesbien, n'a de plaisir qu'à être l'élément actif.

(Voir *Gouine*.)

GOUINE, s. f.

Femme qui s'adonne à l'amour lesbien, mais qui n'a de plaisir qu'à jouer un rôle passif. C'est le contraire de la *vrille* (voir ce mot.)

[VRILLE, feminine noun. A woman who, in a lesbian couple only takes pleasure in the active role. (See *Gouine*.)

GOUINE, feminine noun. A woman given to lesbian love, but who only takes pleasure in playing the passive role. The opposite of a *vrille* (see under that word.)]

—LACASSAGNE, *L'Argot du "Milieu"*

The first half of the opening text of *Les Vrilles de la vigne*, which also bears the title "Les Vrilles de la vigne," was originally published in *Le Mercure musical* in May 1905. It is a fable that explains how the nightingale learned to sing at night. One spring night, the bird had settled down to sleep on a grapevine and awoke the next morning bound up in the new growth of the vine. Escaping the tendrils (*vrilles*) of the vine only after much struggle, the nightingale vowed never to sleep away the night again during the growing season of the vines. The song he sang to keep himself awake was a warning not to sleep while the vines grew, but in the singing, it became more than a warning; it became a song for its own sake, transcending any particular message by way of its aesthetic beauty.

As it was published in 1905, "Les Vrilles de la vigne" could sensibly be read as a parable of someone awaking from a style of life that, while comfortable, was also oppressive and inhibiting, and of how that awakening led to an artistic vocation that, while taking the difficult moment of awakening as its initial point of departure and subject, transforms it with art into something greater. At some undetermined moment before publishing the book *Les Vrilles de la vigne* in 1908, Colette added four more paragraphs to her parable, in which a first person takes up the story of the nightingale and applies it to herself.[88] (I cited these four paragraphs at the end of chapter 2.) In these closing paragraphs the woman speaking in the first person tells of having broken her bonds

("Imperious, clinging, the tendrils of a bitter vine shackled me" [Cassantes, tenaces, les vrilles d'une vigne amère m'avaient liée]) and having fled the comfortable yet stifling situation in which she awoke to find herself. Shortly thereafter, she finds herself caught up in another sweet night that she worries may only inhibit her once again: "When the torpor of a new night of honey weighed on my eyelids, I feared the tendrils of the vine and I uttered a loud lament that revealed my voice to me" [Quand la torpeur d'une nouvelle nuit de miel a pesé sur mes paupières, j'ai craint les vrilles de la vigne et j'ai jeté tout haut une plainte qui m'a révélé ma voix!]. She both resists and is drawn to this new nocturnal pleasure, one which reveals a path that her inspiration, her voice, can follow:

> I want to tell, tell, tell everything I know, all my thoughts, all my surmises, everything that enchants or hurts or astounds me; but always, toward the dawn of this resonant night, a wise cool hand is laid across my mouth and my cry, which had been passionately raised, subsides into moderate verbiage, the loquacity of the child who talks aloud for reassurance and the return of sleep . . .
>
> I no longer enjoy a happy sleep, but I no longer fear the tendrils of the vine. (*CSC* 101)

> [Je voudrais dire, dire, dire tout ce que je sais, tout ce que je pense, tout ce que je devine, tout ce qui m'enchante et me blesse et m'étonne; mais il y a toujours vers l'aube de cette nuit sonore, une sage main fraîche qui se pose sur ma bouche . . . Et mon cri, qui s'exaltait, redescend au verbiage modéré, à la volubilité de l'enfant qui parle haut pour se rassurer et s'étourdir . . .
>
> Je ne connais plus le somme heureux, mais je ne crains plus les vrilles de la vigne. (1:961)]

The wise cool hand in question would seem to be both a source of pleasure and a call to discretion.

In the 1908 edition of *Les Vrilles de la vigne*, the three texts that followed "Les Vrilles de la vigne" were "Nuit blanche," "Jour gris," and "Le dernier feu" (Sleepless Night, Gray Day, The Last Fire). They all bore the dedication "Pour M . . ." and all recounted scenes of Colette's life with Missy in the home they shared at Le Crotoy in Picardy, on the coast of the English Channel. "Nuit blanche" is in some ways the best known of these texts because its final sentence, thanks to the feminine form of one past participle, leaves no doubt as to the fact that it is describing two women in bed together, one of whom is pleasuring the other.[89] "You will accord me sensuous pleasure, bent [the French participle is in feminine form] over me, eyes filled with a maternal anxiety, you who seek in your impassioned loved one the child you never had" (CSC 93) [Tu me donneras la volupté, penchée sur moi, les yeux pleins d'une anxiété maternelle, toi qui cherches, à travers ton amie passionnée, l'enfant que tu n'as pas eu (1:972)]. Much ink has been spilled over Colette's way of interpreting Missy's desire as a version of failed maternity.[90] More germane here is to note how that final sentence instantiates the complicated process of simultaneous affiliation and disaffiliation (I diagnose you and the causes of *your* sexuality, which is not mine even though we share in this sexual act) that characterizes the relation of the first and second persons in the opening texts of *Les Vrilles de la vigne*. (It is perhaps not so different from the way that first person of "Le Sémiramis-Bar" and "Gitanette" both affiliates with and keeps her distance from the other patrons of the bar.) The first paragraph of "Nuit blanche" also invokes this tactic:

> In our house there is only one bed, too big for you, a little narrow for us both. It is chaste, white, completely exposed; no drapery veils its honest candor in the light of day. People who come to see us survey it calmly and do not avert their gaze in a complicitous manner, for it is marked, in the middle, with but one soft valley, like the bed of a young girl who sleeps alone. (CSC 91)

> [Il n'y a dans notre maison qu'un lit, trop large pour toi, un peu étroit pour nous deux. Il est chaste, tout blanc, tout nu; aucune draperie ne voile, en plein jour, son honnête candeur. Ceux qui viennent nous voir le regardent tranquillement, et ne détournent pas les yeux d'un air complice, car il est marqué, au milieu, d'un seul vallon moelleux, comme le lit d'une jeune fille qui dort seule. (1:969)]

It is "our" house, but somehow the bed, the only one in the house, implicates the two people in nothing. Only one person seems to sleep in it, so visitors need not acknowledge that two women sleep together there—even when they know full well that two women do. Acknowledged and unacknowledged, affiliated and unaffiliated, calm and candidly out in the open while also full of deniability, avowed and disavowed—together, the bed and the visitors to the house enact the pragmatic rhetorical relation to the sexuality of two women together that structures representation in *Les Vrilles de la vigne* more generally.

If the passage about the bed in "Nuit blanche" encapsulates the first person's and her friends' frank acknowledgment of her same-sex relation, the public assumption of that acknowledgment, and the crafty relation to a kind of discretion that is almost a form of disavowal and differentiation, so does Colette's use of the word *vrille* in the second half of the first text of the volume, "Les Vrilles de la vigne." In the first half of that text (about the nightingale), written in 1905 or so, Colette doesn't seem to be drawing much on the slang usage of that word, although the following passage from *Claudine Married* (1902), coming at the moment when Claudine and Rézi are on the verge of beginning a sexual affair, suggests that Colette was already capable of working subtly with the full resonance of the word:

> "Nowhere else in the world, Claudine, are the women as pretty as they are in Paris! . . . It's in Paris that you see the most fascinating faces whose beauty is waning—women of forty, frantically made-up and tight-laced, who have kept their delicate noses and eyes like a young girl's. Women who let themselves be stared at with a mixture of pleasure and bitterness."
>
> A woman who thinks and talks like that is not a fool. That day, I seized hold of her pointed fingers that were tracing tendrils of vines to illustrate what she was saying, as if to thank her for having charming thoughts.[91]

> [«Nulle part, Claudine, les femmes ne sont jolies comme à Paris! . . . C'est à Paris que se voient les plus attachantes figures de beauté finissante, des femmes de quarante ans, maquillées et serrées avec rage, qui ont conservé leur nez fin, leurs yeux de jeune fille, et qui se laissent regarder avec plaisir et amertume . . .»
>
> Ce n'est pas une niaise qui pense et parle ainsi. Ce jour-là, j'ai serré ses doigts pointus qui dessinaient ses paroles en vrilles de vigne, comme pour la remercier de penser joliment. (1:441–42)]

Clearly, in 1908, when the later paragraphs of "Les Vrilles de la vigne" were added, her association with the queer culture of Montmartre was such that anyone familiar with that culture's vocabulary could easily have perceived the way she was playing with the word's multiple meanings. Indeed, her ways of linking "Les Vrilles de la vigne" to "Nuit blanche" and "Jour gris" (the following two texts in the volume) make this clear. For the "wise cool hand" of "Les Vrilles" becomes the "amorous" hands of the lover in "Nuit blanche" and the "magician's" hands of the same lover in "Jour gris" (1:972, 974; CSC 93, 95). The penultimate sentence in "Nuit blanche" reads:

For I know quite well that you will then tighten your arms about me and that, if the cradling of your arms is not enough to soothe me, your kiss will become more *clinging*, your hands more amorous, and that you will accord me the sensual satisfaction that is the surcease of love, like a sovereign exorcism that will drive out of me the demons of fever, anger, restlessness.

[Car je sais bien qu'alors tu resserreras ton étreinte, et que, si le bercement de tes bras ne suffit pas à me calmer, ton baiser se fera plus *tenace*, tes mains plus amoureuses, et que tu m'accorderas la volupté comme un secours, comme l'exorcisme souverain qui chasse de moi les démons de la fièvre, de la colère, de l'inquiétude. (1:972; csc 93, my emphasis)]

If we remember that the vrilles de la vigne are "imperious, *clinging*" [cassantes, *tenaces*] (csc 101; 1:960, my emphasis) we can see here how the lover of "Nuit blanche" has become the vrille—tenacious with her kisses and wrapping her lover in a tight embrace that brings pleasure and peace. Colette clearly but discretely uses popular lingo for referring to same-sex relations between women, linking her lover to the role of the vrille, a vrille that now brings pleasure rather than fear.[92]

Yet if Missy is a vrille, it does not necessarily follow that Colette is a gouine, for one of the other effects of that final sentence of "Nuit blanche," with its diagnosis of Missy's "maternal anxiety," is to mark a separation, a disaffiliation between the two people involved, a difference that determines the form of the sexual relation between the two women (indeed, a difference that makes the relation possible) while apparently illuminating the sexual identity of only the second person, not the first.[93] (Colette's condescending diagnosis of Missy's desire resembles Mendès's way of presenting the relation of Emilienne d'Alençon to her doll, the thoughtless condescension of the reproductively privileged to those individuals or couples whom they assume—correctly or incorrectly—to have eschewed reproduction irrevocably.)

As for the first person of these texts, that person's eroticism runs along any number of axes, including that of gender, but also those of region or ethnicity or class. It may well be that these other axes prove just as fundamental to the sexual relation as the one having to do with the partner's sex. In gendered terms, the first person will inevitably be the one within the embrace, "my head on your breast" [la tête sur ta poitrine] (csc 99; 1:980); she will be the one who receives the lover's gifts:

You gave me the cream in the small jug of milk . . . You gave me the bread with the most golden crust . . . You threw over my shoulders a light mantle when a cloud longer than usual slowly passed, toward the end of the day, when I shivered.

[Tu m'as donné la crème du petit pot du lait. . . . Tu m'as donné le pain le plus doré. . . . Tu as jeté sur mes épaules une mante légère, quand un nuage plus long, vers la fin du jour, a passé ralenti, et que j'ai frissonné. (*CSC* 93; 1:971)]

But gender difference alone is not sufficient to capture the erotic structuring of the relation. Consider the description of the odor of their ambiguous bed:

It is a perfume that astounds, that one inhales attentively, in an effort to distinguish the blond essence of your favorite tobacco, the even blonder aroma of your extraordinarily light skin, and the scent of burnt sandalwood that I give off. (*CSC* 91)

[C'est un parfum compliqué qui surprend, qu'on respire attentivement, avec le souci d'y démêler l'âme blonde de ton tabac favori, l'arôme plus blond de ta peau si claire, et ce santal brûlé qui s'exhale de moi. (1:969)]

Missy's hair color, the smell of the tobacco she uses, and her skin all involve blondness of varying degress. It is as if there were blondness in her very soul, just as in Colette's soul one would find the odor of sandalwood, a tree native to India. The appeal of this perfume lies both in the particular mixture of which it is made and in the possibility of distinguishing between its different components. We find here the same recourse to exoticism, the same confrontation of the masculine French and the feminine exotic, that was figured in the pairing of the Egyptologist and the mummy in *Rêve d'Égypte*. But here, in *Les Vrilles de la vigne*, it is conflated with or condensed onto the difference that undergirds all the texts dedicated "Pour M . . . ," which is the difference between Burgundy and Picardy, between South and North, between dark and light, between forest and sea, between Colette the diasporic object of affection, and Missy the jealous local liege:

How pale you are and with such big eyes! What did I say to you? I don't know anymore . . . I was speaking, I was speaking about my country, in order to forget the sea and the wind . . . And here you are pale, with jealous eyes . . . You call me back to you, you can feel how far away I am . . . I must retrace my steps, I must once more tear up, out of my land, all my roots, which bleed . . .

Here I am! Once again I belong to you. I wanted only to forget the wind and the sea. I spoke in a dream . . . What did I say to you? Don't believe it! No doubt I told you of a country of wonders, where the savor of the air intoxicates? . . . Don't believe it! Don't go there: you would search for it in vain . . .

Take me back! I've come back. (*CSC* 96)

[Comme te voilà pâle et les yeux grands! Que t'ai-je dit? Je ne sais plus . . . je parlais, je parlais de mon pays, pour oublier la mer et le vent . . . Te voilà pâle, avec des yeux jaloux . . . Tu me rappelles à toi, tu me sens si lointaine . . . Il faut que je refasse le chemin, il faut qu'une fois encore j'arrache, de mon pays, toutes mes racines qui saignent . . .

Me voici! de nouveau je t'appartiens. Je ne voulais qu'oublier le vent et la mer. J'ai parlé en songe . . . Que t'ai-je dit? Ne le crois pas! Je t'ai parlé sans doute d'un pays de merveilles, où la saveur de l'air enivre? . . . Ne le crois pas! N'y vas pas: tu chercherais en vain. . . .

Reprends-moi! me voici revenue. (1:975)]

What is remarkable about Colette's writing in *Les Vrilles de la vigne*, just as in her construction of her public image as actress, writer, and public personality, is her ability to invoke simultaneously or in quick succession so many contexts—discursive, political, social, and literary— contexts that are so multifarious and sometimes even so contradictory that noticing one you almost necessarily lose a grip on the others. There is the context of long-standing beliefs about ethnic or regional differences within France and the place of those differences within French literary and social history; the discursive and political context of racial differences rendered salient by France's colonial history; the con- text of evolving social roles for women from different backgrounds; the multiple contexts (from high culture to popular culture and back again) in which sexual relations between women took form and came to representation and the use of reference to the ancient world and to the Orient in those representations; the context of a literary vocation that involves a nearly sacred commitment to socially marginal experiences and their representations; the context of evolving conventions for the representation of the female body onstage; the context of a relation to the writing of literature that can be construed as in some way feminine. Colette braids together strands from all of these contexts in her literary production. Is the relationship with Missy that between a vrille and a gousse, or is it the typically French relation between someone blond and someone dark-haired, or someone from Burgundy and someone from Normandy, or is it the relation between a colonial explorer and a colonized subject, or is it the relationship between a masculine woman and a woman who is just curious? When we expand the frame to consider the volume as a whole (taking in as well some of Colette's other writings of the same moment), we come up against the question why the relation between Missy and Colette is so central to the first few texts of *Les Vrilles*, only to be carefully ignored in the texts about Valentine or about the Sémiramis Bar (texts that nonetheless take up the question of relations between women in their own ways) or in the later texts in *Les Vrilles* that take place on the Channel coast.

In short, we might say that there are so many contexts that give *Les Vrilles de la vigne* its meaning, that justify the way it is assembled—bringing this or that aspect of the book as a whole into focus or providing clarity to this or that aspect of a given part of the book, while perhaps obscuring other aspects—that no context (and therefore no particular figuration of the first person) ends up being definitive. We might do worse than to think that the success of Colette's artistry in this book is to work with context so deftly, to work so carefully with the way text points to context in order to take on meaning, that we can no longer stop at any one context to fix the social, sexual, personal, or ideological contours of the first person we are faced with. If for the second half of the opening text, "Les Vrilles de la vigne," and for most of the few pages making up "Nuit blanche" it might seem like the context of a vrille/gousse relationship could ground the meaning of the text, Colette's first person perhaps seeming ready to settle inside a gousse identity, it has to be said that, beginning with the final sentence of "Nuit blanche" (the one that uses the unequivocal feminine past participle avowing the sexual relationship between the women, but also the one that offers a distancing diagnosis of Missy as a nearly simultaneous form of disavowal) this context and this identity begin to dissolve in the face of other identities and contexts; it will never come back into focus.[94]

Spring on the Riviera

Or almost never. The final text in the first edition of *Les Vrilles de la vigne* is called "Printemps de la Riviera," and its dedication reads: "Pour Renée Vivien." Willy and Colette had stayed at Vivien's villa near Nice during Mardi Gras week in 1906, and the opening section of "Printemps" recounts a carnival ball attended by Colette in the company of a number of women. (Chronologically speaking, then, this final text in the volume moves back to describe events that happened months before the beginning of Colette's relationship with Missy, before the moment of "Nuit blanche," for instance.) Colette and Willy were both at this time already part of the circle often referred to as Paris-Lesbos, and a good many figures from Paris-Lesbos (including, obviously, Renée Vivien, their host) were on the Riviera at this time. Among those mentioned in Colette's text, we find Liane de Pougy, Caroline Otéro, and Emilienne d'Alençon. "Il y a tant de belles dames," remarks Colette at one point. "There are so many beautiful women." At another moment she describes herself dancing with one of them:

> Playing my role as an avid Pierrot, I sweep up in my arms a gracious, svelte, supple, mauve, blond domino who carelessly tramples his train of satin and soft muslin, and we turn and we turn, carried, pressed, pushed, until we come to one of the black islands standing upright in the storm . . . What a surprise! The island moves, it brings us to a stop with a courteous but unyielding arm, and its well-known voice of the common sergeant tells us, "Stand apart if you please, ladies! There's to be no ladies dancing with the other ladies here, only decent behavior allowed (sic)!

> [Et j'enlace, en Pierrot empressé, un gracieux domino mauve, svelte, souple, blond, qui piétine, insoucieux, sa traîne de satin et de mousseline molle, et nous tournons, nous tournons, portés, pressés, poussés, jusqu'à l'un des îlots noirs debout parmi la tempête . . . Ô surprise! l'îlot s'émeut, nous arrête d'un bras courtois mais inflexible, et sa bonne voix de sergot bourru nous dit: «Séparez-vous, s'il vous plaît, mesdames! C'est défendu ici que les dames elles valsent entre elles, rapport aux convenances (sic)!» (1:1061)]

Colette is able in this text, just as in "Nuit blanche," to play with past participles. Two women in costume are carried along, squeezed, and pushed this way and that with the past participles appropriate to a couple that includes at least one man (*portés, pressés, poussés*, and not *portées, pressées, poussées*). Colette's prose here in fact genders both herself and her partner as masculine, and this same-gendered couple happily moves around the carnival with their associated past participles allowing them this same-sex dalliance for a brief moment. Until, that is, they come up against an agent of the law, who reminds them, among other things, of the error in the gender of their shared participle. For indeed they are a same-sex couple—but they were using a participle of the wrong desinence. And, in any case, at this dance women don't dance together, no matter whether the couple they form be same-gendered or cross-gendered.

Colette expresses her surprise and annoyance at the call to order by invoking her friend Jean Lorrain: "O Nice, o carnival of Nice! My friend Jean Lorrain painted you with the most tempting of vices, but what calumnies he inflicted on you!" [Ô Nice, ô carnaval de Nice! toi que mon ami Jean Lorrain fardait des vices les plus tentants, comme on t'a calomnié!]. She knows, of course, as is clear from her own choice of companions in Nice, her own interest in pretty women, and her brief foray into the masculine-gendered category while dancing with one of them at the ball, that Lorrain's version of the varied sexual cultures present in Nice (at carnival time and others) is as much a part of the reality of life on the Riviera as is the policeman's reaction. It is just a question of context. And having thus fleetingly recalled for us her interest in women, her masculine side, her feminine side, and the ways they both may or may not inflect her interest in women, Colette then allows the context of this final text to shift a few more times, moving away from balls and casinos and their disappointments and into the natural world of the French Riviera, which she now reveals she dislikes, comparing it, in the final paragraphs of her book, to the countryside in Burgundy:

You handsome but mendacious Midi. I would give all your roses, all your light, all your fruit for a single February afternoon, neither warm nor cold, when, in the land I love, the bluish snow slowly melts in the shadows of the hedges, uncovering one by one the stiff stalks of young wheat, moving in their greenness . . . A shining blackbird, perched on a thorn that is still black, gurgles his melody, pouring out notes that are round and limpid—and the perfume of the liberated earth, along with the sure aroma that rises from the carpet of dead leaves that have been steeping for four months, kneaded by the frost and the rain, fills my heart with the bitter and incomparable happiness of spring . . .

[Joli Midi menteur, je donnerais toutes tes roses, toute ta lumière, tous tes fruits—pour un tiède et frais après-midi de février où, dans le pays que j'aime, la neige bleuâtre fond lentement à l'ombre des haies et découvre, brin à brin, le jeune blé raide, d'un vert émouvant . . . Sur l'épine encore

noire, un merle verni glouglouté mélodieusement, égoutte des notes limpides et rondes—et le parfum de la terre délivrée, l'arome sûr qui monte du
tapis de feuilles mortes macérées quatre mois, triturées par le gel et la pluie,
emplissent mon coeur de l'amer et incomparable bonheur printanier . . .
(1:1063)]

So ends the 1908 edition of *Les Vrilles de la vigne*, with one of those
brilliant literary performances for which Colette became famous, a
melodious and lyrical evocation of a precise and sensual relation to a
particular landscape, a kind of feminine writing, we might be tempted
to say. The book is thus carefully framed: it begins with a nightingale
singing in a vineyard in the spring, and ends with a blackbird singing in
a wheatfield in a different spring, but nonetheless thereby recalling the
opening vegetal and aviary motif of a vine, its vrilles, and their prisoner.
The vegetal motif was displayed graphically on the book's front and
back cover, as well as on its table of contents, and on the title page for
each individual chapter—sometimes creating a visual effect it would be
tempting to call lesbian in its own right. Other kinds of vrilles, as we
have seen, move about in the casinos of the Riviera, in narrow beds in
Picardy, in the music halls of Paris and the Sémiramis Bar in Montmartre. Colette seems, dancing with another woman in Nice near the
end of the volume, to recall (or foreshadow) the relationship with Missy
delineated in the volume's opening texts. Yet when the closing paragraphs of the volume reinvoke the nightingale in the mythic vineyard
by way of the blackbird in the wheat field in Burgundy, the word vrille
itself is absent. Colette seems to arrange matters so that in closing the
human vrille is de-emphasized in favor of a more general reference to
the turning of the seasons. Yet even if those human vrilles do not get the
final word, it turns out that Colette (by the way she has insistently called
our attention to frames that shift, overlap, and interfere with each other
as meaning is constructed) has probably given them some claim, as
good a claim as anyone else's, to providing the volume with its context.

Colette's play with a first person in some close but unspecified relation to same-sex sexualities and to the cultures that sustain them—in a
pantomime such as *Dream of Egypt*, in "Le Sémiramis-Bar" and in *Les
Vrilles de la vigne*—reveals with astonishing clarity the complications of
the evolving relation between literary practices of the first person and
the ascription or assumption of a same-sex sexual identity. Like Gide,
Colette uses the first person obsessively and craftily. They establish,
each in their own way, a metapragmatics of its usage—of its literary

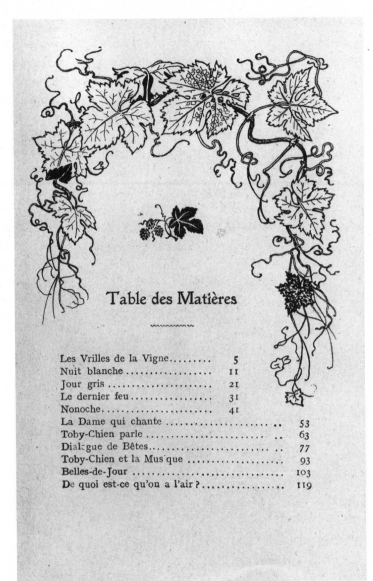

Table des Matières

The first page of the table of contents
from the 1908 edition of *Les Vrilles de la
vigne. Author's copy.*

usage—constantly pointing to the fact that literary first persons are figural, and thereby revealing, of course, that all first persons are figural —produced out of the need to assume a countenance, to keep face, to save face, within whatever social situation one finds oneself and at the same time out of a desire to bring to literary expression forms of experience that can be avowed only with difficulty. As figures, the first persons they create quickly become artifacts, entering into the world of impersonality and intersubjectivity. "We need to know," Maurice Merleau-Ponty asserts in *Phenomenology of Perception*, "how an object in space can become the eloquent relic of an existence; how, conversely, an intention, a thought or a project can detach themselves from the personal subject and become visible outside that subject in the shape of a body, and in the milieu that subject constructs" (348–49). Or, we might add, in the first person, or in the practice of the first person, that individual offers and then leaves behind for others (Beauvoir, Leduc, Duras) to take up.

four

Gide and Posterity

Of the three main literary figures preoccupying me in these pages
(Colette, Gide, Proust), only Gide undertakes the project of constructing a literary first person in which to speak not only *about*, but also
unequivocally *for* and *as* someone sexually drawn to people of the same
sex. Colette, as we have just seen, by way of a dizzying set of rapidly
shifting contexts, manages to situate herself nearly simultaneously inside of, outside of, alongside, aslant the sexual cultures and identities of
women together. Proust, we will see in the following two chapters,
works, like Colette, with context—producing in his novel a narrator
who provides a more or less friendly context in which to watch the
cross-cutting relations between same-sex sexual cultures and other social formations.

Yet Gide is fully aware that a too facile, too sentimental, too easily
confessional assumption of a first person in relation to same-sex sexuality will carry no aesthetic weight. Recall the terms of his reaction to
Rachilde's review of *The Immoralist*, where he endeavored to articulate
an aesthetic project that could be construed neither as satire nor as
apologia. He can neither be so separate from his first person as to be
seen as treating that figure and its practices satirically, nor so closely
attached to that first person that what he does is merely to ask for
recognition for himself. His project is thus simultaneously that of treating a particular subject matter and that of developing a literarily sophisticated way of treating it.

We can see in Gide's journal entry for July 12, 1910, an expression of
his desire to be on the cutting edge:

> Feeling of the indispensable. I have never had it more strongly, since I wrote
> *André Walter*, than now that I am writing *Corydon*. The fear that someone

else might get ahead of me; it seems to me that the subject is floating in the air; I am amazed that no one reaches out to seize it before me. . . . I knew a similar fear at the moment of *Les Nourritures*. (1:226)

[Sentiment de l'indispensable. Je ne l'ai jamais eu plus fort, depuis que j'écrivis *André Walter*, qu'à présent pour *Corydon*. L'appréhension qu'un autre me devance; il me semble que le sujet flotte dans l'air; je m'étonne qu'aucun ne fasse geste de le cueillir avant moi. . . . J'ai connu pareille appréhension au moment des *Nourritures*. (644)]

Gide's desire is to be at the forefront of what is *aesthetically* innovative as well as what is most daring in terms of subject matter. But the daringness in terms of subject matter and the aesthetic sophistication are, as we see indicated here in his use of the word *indispensable*, to be supported by a claim for the social and moral utility of the work he intends to produce.

Gide and his circle often read their works in progress aloud to each other. We could think of this practice in a number of ways. It involved, of course, a process of vocalization, the assumption of a voice, the testing out—especially in the reading of first-person narratives or dialogues such as *Corydon*—of the credibility, the sustainability, the particular effect of a given first-person figure. In Gide's case, as he struggled to find his own way of treating male same-sex sexuality with a certain degree of explicitness, it was also a question of assembling an appropriate group of friends to whom a given text could be read. Some of the works he produced in these years—*La Porte étroite* (*Strait Is the Gate*), *Isabelle*, or *La Symphonie pastorale*—could be read to any of his friends and to his wife. The drafts of *Corydon*, certain sections of *Les Caves du Vatican*, *Les Faux-Monnayeurs*, and *Si le grain ne meurt* required more caution. The decision actually to publish *Corydon* and *Si le grain ne meurt* meant offering for the first time in public what had previously been texts for a privileged few.[1]

Among those few to whom Gide could for many years read anything was Henri Ghéon—his companion not only in literary matters, but on many sexual exploits in Paris or elsewhere in France or abroad. They would have a parting of ways after World War I, the traumatic experience of which would transform Ghéon into a devout Catholic and an ardent nationalist. In 1917, he would write to Gide:

Alas! What common ground remains for us, given that I have decided never again to write a line that is not useful to someone, to see in pure literature nothing but a pitiful last recourse. . . . To think that I had begun writing a book with the intent of rallying people to the cause of my sin! Seen from a distance it seems not so much odious as ridiculous. Henceforth I wish only to stir men according to a common measure, the common good.

[Hélas! sur quel terrain te rejoindrais-je, moi qui suis décidé à n'écrire plus une ligne qui ne soit utile à quelqu'un, à ne me résigner à la littérature pure que comme un pis-aller pitoyable. . . . Dire que j'avais commencé d'écrire un livre pour rallier le monde à la cause de mon péché! Quand on voit ça de loin, ça nous paraît moins odieux que ridicule. Je ne veux plus désormais émouvoir les hommes que selon la règle commune et pour le bien commun.][2]

Ghéon has here tactically rearranged all the terms in which Gide was striving to conceive of his simultaneously aesthetic and moral project of producing literature about same-sex sexuality. Ghéon assigns such a project to the "purely" literary, something with no social or moral utility, and shudders with horror at the idea that he had worked so hard and so long on a novel, tentatively titled *L'Adolescent*, that conformed to Gide's preferred way of thinking about things: a writing project on same-sex sexuality that thought of itself as simultaneously aesthetically and morally daring *and* socially useful.

Ghéon worked on *L'Adolescent* as Gide worked on *La Porte étroite*, which does not broach the subject of same-sex sexuality. Gide offered Ghéon advice on both plot and structure. Hearing Ghéon read from his novel provoked Gide into frenzies of composition for new works more explicit in content—*Corydon* and *Les Caves du Vatican* in particular.[3] In August 1914, at the front with a Red Cross ambulance team, Ghéon wrote a will in which he named Gide and a few other friends literary executors and left to them the decision as to what among his manuscripts should be published—including, perhaps, his unfinished novel. In March 1919, Ghéon destroyed all but ninety-six pages of the manuscript of the novel, writing on the bottom of the last remaining page, "Today, March 21, 1919, the rest of this book was burned as shameful and bad. Glory be to God."[4]

One of the key figures in Gide's imagined audience for *Corydon* and his other writings on same-sex sexuality had thereby moved into another camp, joining those actively discouraging Gide not only from publishing certain things he was writing, but even from writing them.

Imagining a first person involves imagining an audience for that first person. Ghéon's conversion could be thought of as a challenge to at least one of Gide's many first-person figures. Gide was not so dependent on Ghéon that this shift mattered that much in the end. He had had the sense to anchor his first person(s) not only in his relation to his various circles of friends and to his public, but also to the future. In this chapter, I turn to Gide's relation not only to his contemporary readers (such as Ghéon) but also to the posterity he imagined for himself as he worked to create and sustain a certain public first person (that of a celebrated literary figure who writes about sexual relations between men) and also the particular first person of his 1926 memoirs, *Si le grain ne meurt*.

In a passage from *Les Nouvelles Nourritures* that Gide apparently composed during the early 1920s, he presents a figure of posterity:

You who will come when I no longer hear the noises of the earth and my lips no longer drink of its dew—you who will perhaps read me later—it is for you that I write these pages; for you are perhaps not astonished enough with living; you do not properly admire this stunning miracle that is your life. It seems to me sometimes that you will drink with my thirst, and that what inclines you toward this other being whom you caress is already my own desire.

[Toi qui viendras lorsque je n'entendrai plus les bruits de la terre et que mes lèvres ne boiront plus sa rosée—toi qui, plus tard, peut-être me liras—c'est pour toi que j'écris ces pages; car tu ne t'étonnes peut-être pas assez de vivre; tu n'admires pas comme il faudrait ce miracle étourdissant qu'est ta vie. Il me semble parfois que c'est avec ma soif que tu vas boire, et que ce qui te penche sur cet autre être que tu caresses, c'est déjà mon propre désir.][5]

This decision to represent oneself as writing with an aim to being read posthumously by the arguably young and male figure, who takes time out from caressing his arguably young and male friend in order to cast his eyes over Gide's words, represents an intriguing moment in Gide's way of figuring posterity to himself. Compare, for instance, what he says in his journal entry of December 22, 1918, about the loss of his letters to his wife, Madeleine: "Certain days, certain nights especially, I feel crushed by regret for those annihilated letters. It was in them above all that I hoped to survive" [Certains jours, certaines nuits surtout, je me sens broyé par le regret de ces lettres anéanties. C'est en elles surtout que j'espérais survivre" (1080)].[6] Gide's wife Madeleine burned her correspondence with her husband in 1918 upon learning that Gide was taking an extended trip to Cambridge with the young Marc Allégret, to whom he had formed a deep and abiding attachment. André and Madeleine had married in 1895. André evidently considered the marriage (apparently never consummated) a profound spiritual commitment that did not preclude sexual adventures elsewhere—mostly with other men. His sexual adventures were generally brief encounters; the liaison with Marc was much more serious, and Madeleine, faced with this new departure of Gide's, apparently reread the entire correspondence and then burned it.[7] Like many, though not all, writers, Gide experiments obsessively with figures of posterity as part of the project of figuring himself. The years encompassing the writing of the two passages I have just cited are years in which Gide's diverse representations of posterity come into acute conflict, and his journal entries for the last months of 1918, as he mourns the loss of his letters to Madeleine, are rich in traces of that conflict.

If the imagined future reader of Gide's correspondence with his wife seems hardly likely to be the same reader he imagines as he composes *Les Nouvelles Nourritures* (and if his first person is correspondingly different), it is not as if there is a clean change of regime from one image of posterity to the next. The rhythm according to which one or the other assumes primacy at any given moment is complex; it is a conflictual rhythm that is apparent in Gide's literary output from the very beginning of his career. Consider, for instance, the following passage from Gide's *Journal*, dated November 24, 1918:

> To her alone would I write with abandon.
>
> Not a cloud, never the least disturbance between us. *Possibly there was never a more beautiful correspondence*—for it does not suffice to say that my best was to be found there, but hers as well, for I never wrote for myself alone. Ah! Next to those letters, of what value are my *Porte étroite*, my *Nourritures*, fragile sparks escaped from an immense hearth.
>
> At least now nothing prevents me any longer from publishing in my lifetime both *Corydon* and the Memoirs.

> [A elle seule j'écrivais avec abandon.
>
> Pas un nuage, jamais le moindre souffle entre nous. *Peut-être n'y eut-il jamais plus belle correspondance*—car il ne suffit pas de dire que le meilleur de moi s'y trouvait, mais d'elle également, car je n'écrivais jamais pour moi-

même. Ah! que valent près de cela ma *Porte étroite*, mes *Nourritures*, étin-celles fragiles échappées d'un immense foyer.

Du moins à présent rien ne me retient plus de publier durant ma vie et *Corydon* et les Mémoires. (1077)][8]

The abrupt switch from the despairing, melodramatic rhetoric around the loss of his letters to his wife, to the flatter, almost cold statement of the last sentence, "at least now nothing prevents me," catches the ear, indicating some kind of split in his voice, some kind of rhythmic to and fro between different figures of self. (It seems that one of the ways Gide tried to mend the split was by reading *Corydon* out loud to his wife, but the reading appears not to have had the desired effect.)[9] The "any longer" of Gide's "nothing prevents me any longer" lets us know that the difficult negotiation between the different versions of posterity as well as between the different voices that correspond to those differing versions has been long ongoing. Likewise the question of what to do with his treatise on male love, *Corydon*, and his memoirs, *Si le grain ne meurt*, has been in the air for a long time.

Corydon had already been privately published at this point. And Gide was thinking of the same course for *Si le grain ne meurt*, a fair amount of which he had already finished composing. Indeed, it is worth noting that Gide's discovery that his wife had burnt his letters happened be-cause he asked her for access to the correspondence to verify a date for his memoirs. As he mourns the loss of the correspondence, he spends his time putting the final touches on *Si le grain ne meurt*, and, still hesitant whether he'll send the manuscript to his publisher or not, he nonetheless makes sure he keeps an extra copy of his own, perhaps for posterity's sake:

> I am busy going over and polishing the draft of my *Memoirs* so as to keep a complete text if I give a copy to Verbecke [his publisher]. I am not very satisfied with this rereading: the sentences are soft. It is too conscious, too careful, too literary.

> [Je m'occupe à revoir et mettre au point le brouillon de mes *Mémoires*, de manière à garder un texte complet si j'en confie un à Verbecke. Je ne suis pas très satisfait de cette relecture: les phrases sont molles; cela est trop conscient, trop surveillé, trop littéraire. (1079)][10]

Si le grain ne meurt—how to write it, what to do with it—seems to represent for Gide a new relation to posterity (conceivably a new relation to literature itself), as well as a new practice of the first person. All of these considerations (of style, of literature, whether or not to publish, what relation to posterity to hope for) become related, as we shall see in what follows, to a concern with the odd question of how most appropriately to say what Gide will refer to as "everything" [tout dire]—where "everything" means not exactly everything, but, more specifically, how to tell of sex between men. Gide's dealings with his friend and fellow writer Roger Martin du Gard are an optimal place for observing the interrelation of Gide's concerns about explicitness, its relation to style, genre, and to his person, and about his general relation to literature and "literary posterity."

Martin du Gard's association in Gide's mind with these questions is indicated clearly enough in his mischievous way of inscribing his friend into the very text of his memoirs. At the end of the first part of *Si le grain ne meurt*, Gide writes:

> Roger Martin du Gard, to whom I have shown these Memoirs, finds fault with me for never saying enough in them, and for leaving the reader unsatisfied. And yet I have meant all along to say everything. But in making confidences, there is a limit which cannot be overstepped without artifice, without strain; and what I aim at above all is to be natural. (232)

> [Roger Martin du Gard, à qui je donne à lire ces Mémoires, leur reproche de ne jamais dire assez, et de laisser le lecteur sur sa soif. Mon intention pourtant a toujours été de tout dire. Mais il est un degré dans la confidence que l'on ne peut dépasser sans artifice, sans se forcer; et je cherche surtout le naturel. (280)]

Gide thus turns Martin du Gard into a voice encouraging him on his new experimental path, seconding Gide's efforts to renovate his literary profile, to pursue a kind of avant-garde openness about his sexuality. And indeed, reading Martin du Gard's October 7, 1920, letter to Gide, one is inclined to think that Gide, in *Si le grain ne meurt*, has understated Martin du Gard's position:

> The more I think of your memoirs the less I am satisfied with them. I have read three hundred pages, and I have yet to have encountered you. . . . Now is the time to open fully the secret door, to enter there, and to take us with you, in a stream of light. . . . *What child were you, for yourself, in your solitude?* What sort of affection did you have for those around you? What dreams of the future? What precise and successive troubles assailed you from age

twelve to age sixteen? And afterward? How was your literary vocation born? What were your childhood vanities, your infatuations, your particular weaknesses? Your curiosities? Your initiations? Your nocturnal reveries? And on awakening, what remained of them that you then combined with your waking life?[11]

"Now is the time to open fully the secret door . . . and to take us with you," announces Gide's seemingly daring friend, demanding precision in a way that, despite a flimsy veil of seemingly sociologically informed curiosity ("from age twelve to age sixteen"), seems rather more prurient. Further, as we shall see, Martin du Gard's "us" is not particularly inclusive, and the temporality of "now is the time" is not as based in the "present" as it might at first seem. Or rather, it turns out to be the present of posterity. In Martin du Gard's journal entry from the previous day, October 6, he says of his conversation with Gide (he both wrote to him and spoke in person with him about this), "I made him recognize that he had here the opportunity to write *the immortal book about his true interior life*, and that it was necessary not to shy away from any secret, but to descend to the absolute depths, to the most troubled abyss, and to unfold the truth in its integrity. Such was the price of the work's beauty."[12] Martin du Gard thus understands his advice to increase the explicitness of the text as crucial to Gide's literary posterity— conceived, we shall see, in a way that Gide cannily chooses not to accept. He further characterizes his advice as *aesthetic* advice—advice to reach for the beauty lying in a radical practice of confessional writing— and it seems worth trying to comprehend how, for both Gide and Martin du Gard, there were important questions of aesthetics residing both in the choice to portray sex between men (where one of the men is the author) in some detail, and in finding the appropriate style, genre, and publication strategy through which to do so.

But to return to Martin du Gard's "now is the time" for a moment: in point of fact, Martin du Gard, for all his eagerness to give advice, and happiness at being one of the people Gide asked to read his manuscripts or to hear them read, also claims not to have wanted Gide to publish his memoirs. We might therefore surmise that he would be unhappy to be mentioned in the published version of *Si le grain ne meurt* as a person asking for more explicitness. And indeed he wrote a reply to Gide's invocation of his name, which he inserted into his own copy of *Si le grain ne meurt*, imagining, correctly, that it would find its way to posterity's eyes:

I don't deny having encouraged André Gide, with all of my affection, to write his life's confession, nor do I deny having pushed him to stay as close as possible to the truth, to multiply authentic details, no matter how uninhibited; in a word, *to say everything*. But, on the other hand, no one was more opposed than I to the *publication* of these memoirs; and I persist in thinking that they should not have appeared in the author's lifetime (nor even soon after his death).

I even believe that my indiscreet insistence on this point was not unrelated to Gide's long hesitation, for, after having 6,000 copies of a first edition printed, and after ordering and then canceling their delivery to bookstores twenty times, he kept this stock for nearly two years in his cellar (from 1921 to 1923), before resolving to put it into circulation.[13]

Martin du Gard's qualifications encourage us to consider how the version of posterity by which one chooses to be guided is crucial to the shaping of one's literary career. What would the shape of Gide's literary career have been had he chosen to leave *Si le grain ne meurt* in his basement, awaiting posthumous publication? One is reminded of a comment Gide makes in *Si le grain ne meurt*, regarding his mother's attempt to dissuade him from bringing Athman to Paris: "It has not often happened to me to renounce a thing on which I have set my heart; a postponement is the utmost that obstacles wring from me" (294) [Il ne m'est pas arrivé souvent de renoncer. Un délai, c'est tout ce qu'obtient de moi la traverse (355)]. The statement works fairly well as a version of Gide's publication strategies as well, and it is clear that his delays were in fact never so long as to jeopardize the establishment and maintenance of the particular literary profile he came to imagine for himself. (Martin du Gard's delays were quite a bit longer, and to telling effect.)

Quite early on in their friendship, Gide shows a full awareness of the significance of Martin du Gard's differing relation to posterity. Consider the following interesting reflections from Gide's journal entry for October 5, 1920, just after the conversation with Martin du Gard regarding the desirable level of explicitness for *Si le grain ne meurt*.

He informs me of his deep disappointment: I have side-stepped my subject; from fear, modesty, anxiety about the public, I have dared to say nothing really intimate and only succeeded in raising questions . . . [These reflections would disturb me more if I did not begin to comprehend that it is in the character of M du G always to dream of a chimerical beyond, yet in such a way that any realization of it would leave him unaffected. One of the most curious characters that I have ever encountered.]

Since I have been here, received from him a long, excellent letter in which he goes over all the points our conversation had touched upon. Yet I feel that I have related of my childhood everything of which I have any recollection and as indiscreetly as possible. It would be artificial to put more shadow, more secret, more deviation into it. (2:257)

[Il me fait part de sa déception profonde: j'ai escamoté mon sujet; crainte, pudeur, souci du public, je n'ai rien osé dire de vraiment intime, ni réussi qu'à soulever des interrogations . . . [Ces réflexions m'ébranleraient plus si je ne commençais à comprendre qu'il est dans le caractère de M du G de rêver toujours un au-delà chimérique, de sorte que toute réalisation le laissera loin du compte. Un des plus curieux caractères que j'aie rencontrés.]

Depuis que je suis ici, reçu de lui une longue, excellente lettre où il revient sur tous les points que notre conversation avait touchés. J'ai pourtant conscience d'avoir raconté de mon enfance tout ce dont j'avais gardé souvenance et le plus indiscrètement possible. Il y aurait artifice à y mettre plus d'ombre, plus de secret, plus de détour. (1110–11)][14]

The variant sentences from the manuscript that I have included in brackets in this citation show Gide already having understood that posterity functions for Martin du Gard in a way inappropriate to Gide's intentions regarding his public persona. Martin du Gard's call to explicitness is enabled by his belief in a posterior moment at which that explicitness carries no price—but therefore, Gide must realize, also no gain. Also interesting in this passage is Gide's careful effort to calculate the appropriate level of explicitness for his memoirs: "Yet I feel that I have related of my childhood everything of which I have any recollection and as indiscreetly as possible." One might well take the first claim of the sentence (to have recounted everything he remembers) with a grain of salt. The second claim is more interesting: to have been as indiscreet as "possible"—where "possible" clearly doesn't mean "as indiscreetly as *anyone else* might have done." As the whole interaction with Martin du Gard makes clear, the calculus as to what is possible, how much of a risk one can take in the field of indiscretion, is a complex one involving questions of style, reputation, literary and social prestige, as well as any number of interrelated personal and psychological struggles.

Martin du Gard's intense desire for more confession is not to Gide's taste; it is not in accord with the particular practices of the first person he is developing so carefully. This would seem to be the point behind

Gide's remark that "it would be artificial to put more shadow, more secret, more deviation" into his account of his childhood. Perhaps Gide is hearing in Martin du Gard's call for more information about "your curiosities," "your particular weaknesses," "your initiations," or "your nocturnal reveries" a request for some additional overly gothic, melodramatic, or apologetic material. Perhaps Gide has the sense that to add more information would distort his style, ruin his carefully calculated position vis-à-vis reticence. Martin du Gard seems to play a useful role for Gide by embodying an *arrière-garde* to Gide's avant-garde. He is one of the many forces within Gide's contemporary literary field to serve as an important counterexample in terms of both stylistic choices and strategic literary positioning. We might almost say that he (unwittingly?) helps Gide to experience his own more productive, more successful relation to posterity.

Here, considering Gide's relation to Martin du Gard, we could turn again to some of the insights from Pierre Bourdieu's essay "L'Illusion biographique" that were so useful in thinking about Gide and Colette in chapter 2. Remember Bourdieu's point that

> To try to understand a life as a unique and self-sufficient series of successive events without any connection other than their association with a "subject" whose consistency is undoubtedly only that of a proper name is just as absurd as attempting to make sense of a subway ride without taking into account the structure of the system, that is to say, the matrix of objective relations among the different stations. Biographical events take shape as so many placements and displacements in social space, that is, more precisely, in the different and successive states of the structure governing the distribution of different kinds of capital which are at stake in the given field.[15]

We can insist again here on the relational aspect of each event that contributes to the shaping of a literary career. Examining the relationship between Gide and Martin du Gard helps us to perceive the structure of the social space in which Gide is making complicated decisions about what it means to be an openly homosexual (or is it pederastic?) literary figure. To be openly homosexual is (for Gide) a relational act in which the complex interplay between the literary field, Gide's place within it, and that field's place within the larger social field is crucial. Why Gide, at that moment, in that way?

Watching how Gide establishes a different relation to "posterity" than that of many of his contemporaries (such as Martin du Gard) is one way of perceiving how he innovates within the literary field. A relation to "posterity" is not solely a psychological fantasy. It is a complicated historically and socially sedimented structure that helps form a particular practice of literature. That practice will involve many literary choices, choices having to do with style, genre, plot, publication strategies, establishments of archives, and so on.

Consider in this light some "aesthetic" (though clearly not *just* aesthetic) advice that Martin du Gard offered Gide in a letter of December 16, 1921, about narrative choices and choices of characterization in Gide's *Les Faux-Monnayeurs*:

> The more I think about it the more I would want to remove from this work, which truly seems destined to become something great, any unnecessary occasion for personal scandal. I suspect that at times you have too much courage, a useless temerity. Do not be angry if I tell you that, all things considered, I do not see what the character of Édouard gains from a too clear exposition of his private inclinations. (I even find myself wondering this morning if it truly is more profitable than harmful to make a novelist of him, and if this is not a means, and a most dangerous one, to reintroduce the "subjective" into a work that would otherwise do quite well without it.) I would prefer, should you insist on Édouard having those inclinations, that his life remain mysterious, and that the reader have *as many* reasons for doubting as for believing things about it.[16]

Martin du Gard's Édouard sounds a bit more like the protagonist Michel of the earlier *The Immoralist* than like the character Gide actually created for this later book. One can begin to appreciate how complicated and multivalent Martin du Gard's "aesthetic" obsessions with novelistic "objectivity" or "subjectivity" must in fact have been, and how his own thinking about the first person had not kept up with Gide's practice.

Gide's intensely abstracting reflection on what it means to use the first person in literature, combined with the sense of a social mission driving him to publish his texts dealing with same-sex sexualities, provides him with a different relation to posterity than that of Martin du Gard, and, concomitantly, with a different trajectory through the literary field of his time. Influencing Gide's actions and decisions, we have seen, are not only his background, and the various kinds of literary and social capital he is aiming to accumulate or has accumulated, but also his perception of the choices being made by his competitors and predecessors. To cite Bourdieu again, "This means that one may only understand a trajectory . . . on condition of having first constructed the successive states of the field in which it unfolds, the ensemble of objective relations that have tied the given agent—at least in a certain number of pertinent states—to the ensemble of other agents engaged in the same field and confronted with the same space of possibilities."[17] Martin du Gard is clearly one important interlocutor for Gide, in relation to whom Gide imagines what is possible for him, what risks are appropriate. Let us note here some of the other figures to whom Gide has a relation in this regard—sometimes, even if they are more distant from Gide's daily life, a more consequential relation than the one with Martin du Gard, perhaps also because of their greater literary or intellectual weight: Wilde, Proust, Freud, and Dostoyevsky.[18]

As regards Dostoyevsky, whose presence in this list might seem at first glance the least self-evident, consider a journal entry of Martin du Gard's from March 11, 1922, just as Gide apparently makes the decision to forsake Martin du Gard's advice and bring the copies of *Si le grain ne meurt* up out of the basement:

> Gide has told me that he feels the need to publish as soon as possible *Corydon* (a dialogue on homosexuality) and *Si le grain ne meurt* . . . , the complete confession of the first thirty years of his life.
>
> I am in a state of desperation over it. I am certain that nothing can damage the full flowering of his maturity more than this useless scandal, whose wound he will feel intensely, and which will create around him a new atmosphere of suspicion, of indignation, and of contemptuous slander. This will merely serve to arm his enemies, who are legion, more strongly and to drive from him the two-thirds of his current friends who accept a situation that is dissimulated, discreet, but who will have to take a position once Gide has cynically declared to the public the nature of his private life.
>
> He claims that he feels a compelling need to escape from the thick cloud of lies that has suffocated him since childhood.
>
> In reality, he is above all the victim of a Russian intoxication. It is Dostoyevsky who eggs him on. He has now spent several months engaged with Dostoyevsky in order to prepare his lectures and his book on Dostoyevsky. And he has been infected. He feels the need to make public confession.[19]

This telling passage shows Martin du Gard not only misunderstanding once again Gide's relation to "confession," but also miscalculating the possibilities of the literary field, and of Gide's position in it. Yet we can also see Martin du Gard's clear sense that what is under consideration here is a strategic decision about a literary career. His use of the word *cynically* is quite telling in this regard ("once Gide has cynically declared to the public"): it does imply, after all, that what one might otherwise have taken as Gide's confessional *impulse* is hardly impulsive, that it is rather carefully timed, as if Gide has known how to wait sufficiently long to put his friends into an awkward position, knowing that at present they would have too much to lose in turning away from him.

Martin du Gard persists in imagining that Gide, through this timely or untimely publication, will damage both his social and literary position and his relation to posterity. That is, without appropriate management of the aesthetic effort to "say everything" (discretion, dissimulation), an author risks his or her professional relationships as well as the remainder of her or his career ("the full flowering of his maturity"), and, consequently, a chance at literary posterity. Gide's calculation would appear to be different: that his relation to posterity now depends on the putting at risk of certain relations with his contemporaries. Yet that risk, as Martin du Gard's "cynically" clearly suggests, is one that Gide has managed carefully. His closest literary friends already have copies of both *Corydon* and *Si le grain ne meurt*. The very ethos of his group of friends and associates at the *Nouvelle Revue Française*,[20] the friendships and professional relations that constitute that group, and the credibility and literary prestige that it has accumulated since its establishment all serve to limit Gide's risk.

Gide's "Russian intoxication," portrayed by Martin du Gard as a dangerous attraction to certain forms of self-revelation and confession, could just as profitably be seen as part and parcel of the aesthetic and literary preoccupations that he shares with his associates. His preoccupation with Dostoyevsky intermingles in a complex way the aesthetic and literary concerns of the NRF group with his own morally and aesthetically conceived project of sexual self-revelation; through this intermingling, Gide's work on Dostoyevsky may well contribute to his effort to legitimize a variety of tasks in which he is engaged: "explicit" (if complicatedly voiced) self-representation (*Si le grain ne meurt*), complexly figured public advocacy of a certain kind of male same-sex sexual relations (*Corydon*), and the insertion of more and more openly non-heterosexual characters and themes into the French novel (*Les Faux-Monnayeurs*).[21] Martin du Gard was not yet closely attached to the NRF group in 1913–14 when the groundwork for this productive confusion of agendas was laid within that group. In March 1914, the NRF published the third installment of Gide's *Les Caves du Vatican*, which included a paragraph of homoerotically inclined reminiscences on the part of its protagonist, Lafcadio Wluiki. Paul Claudel, an NRF contributor, read the paragraph with consternation and wrote to Gide demanding a confession whether Gide shared Lafcadio's inclinations, and also demanding suppression of the offending paragraph. Claudel suggested to Gide that if he eliminated the paragraph in question from future versions of the novel, people would gradually forget that he had ever written it. In the end, Claudel would obtain something like a confession from Gide, though perhaps not as repentant as he would have liked. Regarding the excision of the passage, here is how Auguste Anglès recounts Gide's response: "As for the invitation to suppress out of 'prudence' the incriminating sentence—really a paragraph,—he regretted not being able to give in there. The 'reassuring' prophecy,— 'little by little one will forget,'—appeared 'shameful' to him: 'No, do not demand from me either cover-up or compromise; or it is I who will have less esteem for you.' "[22] That his clumsy invocation of an appropriately cleansed relation to the future was strategically the least adroit tactic Claudel could have chosen seems clear from the tone of Gide's response.

Interesting for our purposes is the strategic positioning of the offending paragraph from *Les Caves du Vatican* within the novel. It comes just before one of the plot's most crucial moments—indeed, one of its most Dostoyevskian moments: Lafcadio, Gide's most Dostoyevskian character, is about to kill, for no apparent reason, the person with whom he is sharing a train compartment. When Anglès is analyzing the preoccupations in the NRF group with the form of the novel in the years surrounding the publication of Gide's *Caves du Vatican* (1913–14), he describes the group as "at the confluence of the waters of the Russian novel and of the English novel," and notes that Gide in particular "strove to capture and unite in his *Caves du Vatican* the two currents of *Tom Jones* and the *Brothers Karamazov*."[23] A reading of Anglès's account of the writings in which various members of the NRF group grapple with the form of the novel reveals many parallels between those formulations and Gide's ideas in his lectures on Dostoyevsky from nearly a decade later.[24] As Gide has it in those lectures,

> In the work of Dostoyevsky . . . children abound; moreover, it is worth noting that most of his characters, and some of the most important, are creatures who are still young, hardly formed. . . . He is particularly attached to disconcerting cases, to people who rise up as challenges to accepted morality and psychology.

[Dans l'oeuvre de Dostoïevsky . . . les enfants abondent; même il est à remarquer que la plupart de ses personnages, et des plus importants, sont des êtres encore jeunes, à peine formés. . . . Il s'attache particulièrement aux cas déconcertants, à ceux qui se dressent comme des défis, en face de la morale et la psychologie admises].[25]

Anglès points to Jacques Copeau's reasons for preferring H. G. Wells's *Ann Veronica* to the novelistic production of a typical French writer like Paul Bourget: "Copeau dedicates himself to justifying an adolescence that breaks with conformity. But it is not by chance that an ethos complicit with youth orients its adherents toward a particular type and tone of novel. The novel runs the risk of calcifying in a 'learned and sterile thesis,' or it risks drying out 'on the steppes of theory': but here [in *Ann Veronica*], we have here a book that is 'human, spontaneous, direct and probing' without being 'systematic or premeditated.' "[26] The terms of the discussion as to the nature of the novel are both aesthetic and generational, Bourget being cast in the role of the old generation. For the NRF writers, the project in question is a renovation of the French novel as it was being practiced by people like Bourget, and to this end they fashion themselves as an avant-garde whose favored topics include the kinds of indeterminacy they see particularly well instantiated in adolescence. They claim to find friendly examples of similar novelistic practices and priorities in the contemporary English novel, and profound precursors in the Russian novel.

Gide, in his lectures, contrasts Dostoyevsky to Balzac and ends up finding in favor of Dostoyevsky's method for constructing characters (one Gide was clearly working with in both *Les Caves du Vatican* and *Les Faux-Monnayeurs*):

> I would also say that not only the characters of the *Comédie humaine*, but those of the real comedy that we live as well, form themselves—that all of us French, such as we are, we, too, form ourselves—after a Balzacian ideal. The inconsistencies of our nature, should there indeed be any, appear embarrassing, ridiculous, to us. We deny them. . . . What does Dostoyevsky present us with in this regard? Characters who, without any concern about remaining consistent, yield obligingly to all of the contradictions, all of the negations of which their own nature is capable. It seems as if that is precisely what interests Dostoyevsky the most: inconsistency. Far from hiding it, he continually makes it stand out; he illuminates it.

[Aussi bien dirai-je que, non seulement les personnages de sa *Comédie humaine*, mais ceux aussi de la comédie réelle que nous vivons, se dessinent —que nous tous Français, tant que nous sommes, nous nous dessinons nous-mêmes—selon un idéal balzacien. Les inconséquences de notre nature, si tant est qu'il y en ait, nous apparaissent gênantes, ridicules. Nous les renions. . . . En regard de cela, que nous présente Dostoïevski? Des personnages qui, sans aucun souci de demeurer conséquents avec eux-mêmes, cèdent complaisamment à toutes les contradictions, toutes les négations dont leur nature propre est capable. Il semble que ce soit là ce qui intéresse le plus Dostoïevsky: l'inconséquence. Bien loin de la cacher, il la fait sans cesse ressortir; il l'éclaire.][27]

Proust will also think of both Balzac and Dostoyevsky when he reads *Les Caves du Vatican*. In one letter to Gide, he writes, in praise it seems, of the portrayal of Lafcadio, and in particular of his sexuality: "But in the creation of Cadio, no one has been objective with that much perversity since Balzac and *Splendeurs et misères*. All the more so, it seems to me, since Balzac was aided in inventing Lucien de Rubempré, by a certain personal vulgarity."[28] In a letter a month or so later, Proust speculates (with arch wickedness) whether Gide would not be taken as a mere imitator of Dostoyevsky in his way of portraying Lafcadio's criminality, but then decides that Gide need not fear the comparison; his originality is secure, for Dostoyevsky would never have given one of his ambiguous criminals Lafcadio's seductiveness and "immorality" (34). Proust's speculations, whatever invidious competitive undercurrents they may contain, reveal the imbrication both he and Gide perceived, relied on, sought to legitimate, between their aesthetic projects and their portrayals of same-sex sexuality. That is, both Proust and Gide saw their struggles to bring representation of same-sex sexualities into the novel as a crucial part of their claim to be doing something new with the novel and with literature more generally. They both saw Balzac as a precursor to work both with and against in this regard. They both thought of Dostoyevsky as an important figure in establishing the novel's claim to work with anomalous social outsiders. Their claims on literary posterity, their claims to be working within and to be advancing the tradition of the European novel rely in part on their innovative use of sexuality as they combined lessons learned from both Balzac and Dostoyevsky. Reciprocally, they intend their aesthetic success to legitimize their representation of that sexuality.

As Gide and Proust would have it, then, the sexual and the aesthetic advances they were striving for should be thought of as inextricably intertwined. *Les Caves du Vatican* is evidently one of the better, more prestigious examples that the NRF group has of the kind of avant-garde or renovated French novel it is trying to encourage.[29] The protagonist is an adolescent in revolt, and one whose characterization reveals a novelistic concern with "inconsistency" [*inconséquence*]. The passage that includes reflections on his sexually adventurous past and leads up to his rather Dostoyevskian crime is a key element in the work the novel does with this notion of inconsistency.[30] Gide would, of course, claim that his novel was not an illustration of the aesthetic theories of his associates at the NRF. Jacques Rivière, who had (in his essay "Le Roman d'aventure," published in the NRF in May, June, and July 1913) written the most coherent statement of the group on their hopes for the novel, would find *Les Caves du Vatican* "imperfect," and its subject matter unsufficiently mastered.[31] Even so, it is clear that an aesthetic interest in Dostoyevsky and the psychology of his characters, a preoccupation with novels about rebellious adolescents, and an effort to transform the French novel are all in the air at the NRF, and that in combination they create a set of circumstances in which Gide successfully publishes a novel whose "pederastic" passages catch many eyes, threaten a number of friendships, and yet ultimately constitute a step along a career path Gide will feel able to pursue even further in the years ahead.

We have seen Roger Martin du Gard refer to part of Gide's pursuit of this literary cutting edge as "cynical." How cynical or how impulsive are the calculations that lead Gide to decide to publish *Corydon* and *Si le grain ne meurt*? Martin du Gard's vocabulary in the passage cited earlier reveals his own indecisiveness in this regard: on the one hand, Gide is making certain careerist decisions "cynically," on the other hand, "it is Dostoyevsky who eggs him on . . . he's been infected." Consider the same indecisiveness reflected in two passages from Martin du Gard's journal entry three days later:

Why throw off the mask at this very moment? Above all because the times are changing; the books of Proust, the movement of ideas in Germany and in Italy where one claims freedom for love, the theories of Freud will all bring about very quickly a moment when one will regard sexual deviance with a completely different eye; there will no longer be anything courageous about throwing off the mask.

There is more than simply courage in him, and desire for truth; there is more than merely a desire for mortification and opprobrium. There is also the ambition to perform a gesture that he finds noble, and the hope that this sincere gesture, disinterested, courageous, will secure for him, in the eyes of certain others, *in the eyes of posterity*, a particular veneration, a renewal of grandeur, of influence.[32]

The ethical and temporal quandaries, the quandaries about sincerity, that arise out of these passages are all linked to the odd structure of the relation to posterity. Figures of posterity are often shared fantasies, social forces. Up to this point, I have suggested that Gide and Martin du Gard relate to posterity differently, and that this difference provides one measure of the ongoing difference both in their reputations and in their literary practices. While I will be detailing a bit further their differences in what follows, it is also worth insisting that, from a slightly more removed perspective, their relation to a particular set of practices of posterity is part of their *shared* literary ethos—one which dates and socially positions both of them.

Consider for a brief moment a figure of posterity provided in Jean Schlumberger's *Madeleine et André Gide*. Schlumberger wrote this book to defend his memory of Madeleine Gide against the image Gide provided of her in *Et nunc manet in te*.[33] Schlumberger justifies his project by reference to a certain posterity: a truer image of Madeleine Gide should be made available for the future. Yet if the book is undertaken out of devotion to Madeleine, at the very end of it, Schlumberger sabotages his own undertaking. In its last several pages, Schlumberger turns from his task of rescuing Madeleine, and, orthodox man of letters of his moment that he is, provides us with a wonderfully clear, wonderfully banal personification of "posterity" itself. (In Schlumberger's original French, his anaphoric use of "elle" to refer to posterity, and his way of personifying it, creates a strong sense of it as a female presence.)

> Posterity cares little for what occurred in the hearts of those who are now dead. It is interested in those of their works that remain vital. The question posterity will pose will be the following: Did this love serve Gide's oeuvre or did it rein it in?
>
> Posterity will place side by side all of the passages where Gide interrogates himself on this point.

> [La posterité se soucie peu de ce qui s'est passé dans le coeur des défunts; ce qui l'intéresse, c'est leurs oeuvres demeurées vivantes. La question qu'elle posera sera celle-ci: Cet amour a-t-il servi l'oeuvre de Gide ou l'a-t-il bridée?

Elle mettra côte à côte tous les passages où il s'est interrogé sur ce point.][34]

Whatever the innate value Schlumberger saw in Madeleine Gide's particularity, it is effaced in this imagined scene of future literary scholarship, in which it is the value of Gide's literary work that is at stake. Having imagined here how some scholar in the future will be spending his or her time, Schlumberger then ends his book being of some help to that scholar, looking for a few pages at passages where André Gide tries to answer what is imagined to be posterity's question. As Schlumberger presents it, Gide more or less decides that his work did indeed benefit from Madeleine's influence. Schlumberger seems not to have noticed the cruel irony in his book: through his own devotion to this cult of *literary* posterity, he has sabotaged his own project of rescuing the figure of Madeleine from André's final picture of her in *Et nunc manet in te.* That his impulsive devotion to Madeleine should be thus deflected indicates how powerful this fantasy of literary posterity was among those in Gide's circle. For obviously a first step toward revaluing her would have been to avoid giving way to this particular (and particularly literary) fantasy.

Gide, Martin du Gard, and Schlumberger were all deeply engaged in a set of practices that constitute a cult around this literary-critical figure of posterity (a cult that includes attending carefully to one's correspondence with one's literary friends, attending to the preservation of the letters from those correspondences, devoting oneself as well to the writing of journals, taking care with regard to testamentary dispositions of archives, obeying intensely felt obligations to write down memories of literary friends, developing a variety of publication strategies for posthumous material, and so on). Martin du Gard is quite clear about this in a telling passage from his memoir of Gide, *Notes sur André Gide,* one more offering on the altar of this figure of posterity:

> If posterity should scent in all this introspection a certain skewing of reality, it may well come to be over-suspicious of everything he says about himself (and which, for the most part, is exceptionally truthful and clear-sighted). *Future literary historians*, reading at a distance, unable to tell the difference between what is indulgence, what is flirtatiousness, and what is true, may simply, regrettably, choose to believe the venomous accounts of those who misunderstood or slandered Gide; and they may reject out of hand the image he has created for them and put in its place something different, a myth, which will be even less accurate.[35]

What would it mean if one could only write with this scholarly agent of posterity in mind, if what one wrote, how one wrote, even how one conceived of one's identity as a writer, conceived of one's career, all had to pass inspection by this agent? How does this imagining of what literature is (and will remain) affect what can be said in print (or in private manuscripts) about sexuality?

Consider Martin du Gard's 1931 play, *Un Taciturne* (A Taciturne Man), about a repressed homosexual man's discovery of his sexuality (and his subsequent suicide), or the story he published in the same year, *Confidence africaine* (African Secret), about incest. These texts can help us to understand how, given the literary and sexual ideologies of a particular moment, different position-taking can produce not only different reputations, different careers, different ways of thinking about the meaning of writing, different presentations of self, but also different aesthetic choices reflecting the "school" in which one undertakes to write. Martin du Gard's dated allegiances to "naturalist" subject matter and "naturalist" ideas about heredity and degeneration are telling in this regard, as is the place that "objectivity" held in his literary ideology. It is because of his need for "objectivity," for instance, that he begins *Confidence africaine* with the death of the child, Michele, born of the incest that the rest of the story will recount. When Gide wrote to Martin du Gard that Dorothy Bussy had criticized this way of beginning the story, Martin du Gard wrote an angry letter in reply:

> Perhaps we see here, exactly here, the secret weakness of your life and your work, the profound cause that will diminish its future impact. You admit—"you," Gide, with Mme. Bussy behind you—that had you had the idea to write this story, your primary *intention* would have been, not to aim for verisimilitude, simply to tell the story, but to try to trip up received morality. . . . By these involuntary admissions, one notes, Gide, that when you write you are really not a disinterested artist, but an advocate, camouflaged with great art and cleverness. . . .
>
> My goodness, my dear friends, Michele has tuberculosis, she's sickly, inbred [un sang-bleu], delicate and fragile, condemned to rickets and to death, *because that's the way nature is*—however much you'd rather (for the sake of your partisan impulses) find proofs to the contrary. You always show this pathological *preference* for the calf with five legs [le veau à cinq pattes].[36]

Gide responds as a naturalist: "You speak of consanguinity as someone who has never bred animals, and who has only a superficial grasp of the matter" (1:459). Martin du Gard in turn insists on both the aesthetic and the scientific necessity of what he portrays in his story, on the link between objectivity and verisimilitude:

> I can give the example, from my own family, of several marriages between cousins that produced terrible results, both physically and intellectually. And I have other examples in mind too, involving hunting dogs. . . . Of course the child of a Leandro and an Amalia could, exceptionally, thanks to the particular vigor of those two participants, have been a robust child. But I have no right to choose this exceptional outcome, *precisely* because such a choice would imply, or seem to imply, an intention to make a case, an ulterior motive. . . . Therefore I, the writer, represent things as they generally are, because I hold verisimilitude to be an essential part of my "aesthetics." (1:462–63)

How could we capture the relation between this "aesthetics" and sexuality, the way that a sexual ideology helps produce an aesthetic program? How should we understand the role that Martin du Gard's friendship with Gide—yet also his care not to be too closely associated with Gide—was playing in the elaboration of this aesthetic and the works that embodied it? Especially when, in the same letter, Martin du Gard, speaking of *Un Taciturne*, insists on the necessity (once again an "aesthetic" one) of the suicide of his protagonist: "The suicide of my central character, on suddenly discovering that his feelings lie outside the boundaries of traditional sexuality, will perhaps seem to you . . . a 'concession' to conventional morality. In my eyes, and in the design of my play, this suicide is simply *the logical act for a given character to perform in a particular situation*. If it is *psychologically realistic* nothing else matters to me" (1:463, emphasis original). What shall we understand from this pretension to objective verisimilitude, one ostensibly neutral in ideological terms? At least we might appreciate that such a pretension depends on a mutually constitutive relation between an ideology of literary practice, a set of ideas about the literary import of sexuality, and a certain cult of posterity. In responding to his friend, Gide lightly deflates Martin du Gard's claims to disinterestedness: "You have a great tendency to look only at fields where your calf with four legs can safely pasture. I freely admit that on my land grow plants that particular calf could not graze on. You fail to persuade me that I should begin to focus on cultivating plants for fodder" (1:468).

Let us characterize specifically the practical insight Gide had that some others lacked: Schlumberger and Martin du Gard anachronistically depend on future people to conform to their ideas about posterity and still to be invested in the critical and literary procedures that these men practice, encourage, and foresee being continued. Gide, more practically, it seems, gambles that many things shift with time, that what is courageous and innovative—and of critical interest—today may not be so tomorrow. So, all the while indulging in the same archival practices that to a large extent constitute the cult of posterity current in his circle, Gide nonetheless publishes texts like *Si le grain ne meurt* shortly after having written them, whereas others would have left them to be published posthumously if at all. If the ghostly figure of posterity for this group often seems to be that strange future literary archivist whose attitude toward illicit forms of sexual expression is unclear but seems likely to be disapproving (or to be dismissive of such expression as irrelevant to literary value), the archivist, in Gide's case, has a strong competitor in the figure of the young man entwined with his lover, some kind of general reader, it would seem, who calls Gide to immediate publication and validates Gide's sense that the literary value his contemporaries might withhold may well accrue in the future to works published then and there that represent the forms of sexuality that interest him.

Consider Gide reading Martin du Gard's own childhood memoir. Martin du Gard had offered him a few chapters in exchange for *Si le grain ne meurt*, and Gide notes in his *Journal* (in a passage from October 3, 1920, that was first published only in the 1996 edition of Gide's *Journal*):

> Read last night, in bed, the pages of reminiscences that Roger Martin du Gard had delivered to me that very morning. They interested me more than he could have believed and seemed excellent to me. I do not see how *Si le grain ne meurt* is any better, except perhaps for the strangeness of my case if it in fact is more strange. But my story is not better, nor more honest, nor more emotional. The abominable agitation that he describes persuades me once again that nothing can be more desirable in the life of a child than the love of an older boy who instructs him and initiates him.

> [Lu hier soir, dans mon lit, les pages de souvenirs que Roger Martin du Gard m'avait remises le matin même. Elles m'ont intéressé plus qu'il ne pouvait croire et m'ont paru excellentes. Je ne vois pas en quoi *Si le grain ne meurt* l'emporte sur elles, sinon peut-être par l'étrangeté de mon cas si tant est qu'il soit plus étrange. Mais mon récit n'est pas meilleur, ni plus honnête, ni plus ému. Le trouble abominable qu'il décrit me persuade une fois

de plus que rien ne peut être plus souhaitable pour un enfant que l'amour d'un aîné qui l'instruise et qui l'initie. (1110)]

The sentence "I do not see how *Si le grain ne meurt* is any better, except perhaps for the strangeness of my case if it in fact is more strange" catches the eye. Is Gide suggesting that the only factor that makes *Si le grain ne meurt* more compelling than Martin du Gard's memoirs—or at least the chapters in question here—is that Gide is portraying a child developing a set of same-sex erotic practices and that Martin du Gard does not portray this? As for the words "if it in fact is more strange," they had the effect of ensuring that, a decade and a half after the passage was written in 1920, it would become an enormous bone of contention between the two friends. At first glance, Gide is apparently merely wondering if there is anything that greatly differentiates the childhood troubles that were the forerunners of his same-sex sexuality from the childhood troubles that were the forerunners of Martin du Gard's own sexuality. But Martin du Gard will apparently have a more paranoid reading of the phrase, imagining it to suggest that there was not much difference between Gide's sexuality (childhood or adult) and his.

Gide writes to Martin du Gard on July 5, 1934, about the journal passage from October 3, 1920, which is ready to go to press as part of volume 9 of Gide's *Oeuvres complètes*. He asks if Martin du Gard would prefer to be identified by the initial *X*, or if he'd prefer the passage be cut altogether. This provokes a lively correspondence, not all of which Martin du Gard allowed to be published. The following passage, at least, he let past his censor. It is from a letter of July 12, 1934:

> If tomorrow I were to burn this chapter of my "Souvenirs d'enfance" and nothing was left of it except what is in your *Journal*, the impression would remain that my childhood was troubled by sexual disorders *analogous to your own*; and that I wrote (later destroyed) a confession concerning *homosexual* tendencies. But, as you well know, this is a flagrant imprecision, since, in these memories of a troubled childhood, it is only a matter of the distur- bance provoked by the revelation of the phenomena of *procreation*! . . . The idea did not come to you to write: "M. du G. has written some memoirs of childhood in which he relates such and such kind of sexual disturbance. And, *even though the sources of his agitation were very different from and even almost the opposite of my own*, I note, *in spite of that*, that they confirm me in my conviction that the initiation of an older homosexual is of benefit, etc., etc." If all of the documents about our era were to disappear and there were

to remain only your testimony, the future historian would conclude: "Gide lived in a curious time when all of the calves were born with five feet."[37]

Note the persistence of this odd fantasy of the future historian, of figures of posterity in the archives, of destruction and misreading. Note in particular how the fantasy of a misinformed posterity occurs in tandem with concerns about being thought to have shared Gide's sexual inclination. Martin du Gard took out a further insurance policy regarding posterity's relation to this episode: the editor of the 1996 edition of Gide's *Journal* (which restores unpublished passages and reveals the names behind the initials) provides the text of a "rectification" that Martin du Gard wrote, dated November 29, 1951, nine or so months after Gide's death, and inserted into the manuscript of Gide's *Journal* at the place of the unpublished 1920 entry, so that whenever that manuscript came into the hands of an editor interested in publishing it in its entirety, as Martin du Gard knew it would, his reservations might also become part of the published record. Martin du Gard's rectification seems to show him becoming an ever more inexact reader of the original entry from 1920:

> The way in which Gide, a victim of his private obsessions, insists on the "strangeness" of my "case" [Martin du Gard's misreading is quite astonishing]; the complacent comparison he makes between my banal adventure and his first sexual stirrings, as he analyses them in *Si le grain ne meurt . . .* , allow one to suppose quite another thing from what my story contains.
>
> My two chapters of *Mémoirs* are still in my archives; and the exactness of what I advance today will be easy to verify.
>
> However, as I have taken steps so that my papers should remain sealed for at least thirty years after my death, and as the unpublished material from Gide's *Journal* will very likely be known well before this delay is over, it seemed to me useful to append the present rectification to the *Carnet* of 1920.[38]

In point of fact, Martin du Gard's childhood memoirs (published in the first volume of his *Journal*) beat Gide's *inédits* to posthumous publication by about four years.

To summarize: an entry in Gide's journal from 1920 about a text Martin du Gard wrote for his friends and for posterity is the subject of an exchange in 1934. Gide excises the disputed passage from his published *Journal*. But the passage and the threat it represents remain active in Martin du Gard's mind for several decades, provoking him in 1951 to concoct a carefully placed rectification and affecting the publication strategy he lays out in his will for various posthumous texts of his own.[39]

Posterity is closely tied to sexual revelation for these writers, just as it is tied to a certain set of literary practices, and a certain understanding of the kind of institution literature is and the kinds of work that support that institution. Indeed, part of what distinguishes this group of writers and their place in this moment in literary and social history is their relation to what they imagine posterity to be. Linked to their image of posterity is an entire set of practices and beliefs concerning the private or public nature of sexual experience, and also a set of practices and beliefs that for them anchor the very institution of literature in which they see themselves participating. The figure of posterity determines where and when various first-person figures can be assumed—in writing and in person. Gide's innovations are to violate the standard practices of his group regarding the conditions for the assumption of a first person in relation to same-sex sexuality, conditions that were in some way controlled or even dictated by the posterity they imagined.

It is interesting, in this light, to read of Martin du Gard's consternation, in 1947, upon reading in *Les Temps modernes* the essays that would become Sartre's *Qu'est-ce que la littérature?* (What Is Literature?). One of those essays was called "Pour qui écrit-on?" (For whom does one write?) Sartre's answer was definitely not "posterity." Martin du Gard's consternation results from a fear that a new generation has somehow rejected and will no longer practice literature according to his generation's conception of it and of its forms of value. In his introduction to the correspondence between Gide and Martin du Gard, Jean Delay cites a letter from Martin du Gard to Maria van Rysselberghe on this subject: "Sartre's manifesto did me in. . . . [It gave me] the impression that a tombstone, icy and heavy, implacable, definitive, had just fallen on everything that had been furnishing us some reason to continue living and exercising our wills."[40] He takes a more philosophical tone in his letter to Gide on the subject, praising Sartre's essay as being full of startling new insights, and instructive as to the difference between the generations. He speaks of being *dépassé* (outdated) and even claims there might be an advantage to that position: "These are the products of a different climate; but they are not degenerate products. Very instructive for us! . . . The sole consolation of decrepitude is that it is not incompatible with an increase in lucidity." Gide replies in a similar vein: "We are 'outdated' (I take up your word) by those who follow; just as they will be outdated by those who will come later. It is painful to remark that the stocks with which one built up a portfolio, those we had considered sure things, are no longer traded; it is painful for oneself and one's work no longer to have anything to offer except historical interest" (2:376–78). Gide's economic metaphor—his literary values being compared to the safest, surest of investments—seems oddly appropriate in the context of Sartre's criticism of those who rely too easily on "eternal" values. On the very first page of "Pour qui écrit-on?" he writes: "It is dangerously easy to speak too quickly of eternal values: eternal values are seriously lacking in substance."[41] Of course, Gide was not of merely historical interest to Sartre. He was an important precursor to be dealt with. In "Pour qui écrit-on?" Sartre deals with Gide by assigning him to a particular socioeconomic class, thereby choosing to ignore the import of Gide's writing on sexuality. For Sartre in this text, Gide provides an example of how a writer necessarily imagines and therefore necessarily writes for a certain class of readers. Writing of the reader implicitly addressed by Gide's *Fruits of the Earth* (*Les Nourritures terrestres*), Sartre is at his invidious best:

Thus do all works of genius contain in themselves an image of the reader to whom they are addressed. I could, having read *Les Nourritures terrestres*, paint a portrait of Nathanaël [the person to whom that book of Gide's is addressed]: as for the alienation that he is invited to overcome, I see that it has to do with the family, the fine properties that he possesses or will possess through inheritance, the utilitarian project, a received moralism, a narrow theism; I also see that he possesses a certain culture, as well as leisure time. After all, it would be absurd to propose Ménalque [the exemplar of nonconformity offered to Nathanaël] as an example to a manual laborer, or to someone unemployed, or a black from the United States. I know that he is menaced by no exterior peril. . . . The unique danger that he runs is that of being the victim of his own milieu. Thus he is white, Aryan, rich, the beneficiary of a great bourgeois family that still lives in a relatively stable and comfortable epoch, in which the ideology of the property-owning class has scarcely begun to recede. He is precisely the Daniel de Fontanin [a character in Roger Martin du Gard's *Les Thibault* who reads *Les Nourritures terrestres* at an important point in the novel] whom Martin du Gard presented to us later as an enthusiastic admirer of André Gide. (92)

The terms of Sartre's class analysis seem hard to deny. One might see him as posterity's revenge on Gide, Martin du Gard and their circle, with their particular understanding of the institutions that make up the literary world and assign value within it. (Their understanding and belief, of course, are still operant in many scholarly circles.) But Sartre here reveals an almost thoughtlessly narrow idea of who might find profit, solace, or inspiration in reading about a person from a different social position than their own who nevertheless struggles with alienation they might recognize. In the case of Gide, it would seem reasonable to take more seriously the future reader that Gide imagined in a sexual embrace with his friend in the "Toi qui viendra" ("You who will come") passage with which I began. That is to say that it is not without effect, not without considerable and enduring success, that Gide allowed his literary career to be inflected by the figure of posterity represented by that *toi*, not without effect on what he ended up writing, not without effect on his readership. (Similarly, it is not without consequence that Martin du Gard was never effectively able to envision and write for another posterity than the dominant one in his group.) In fact, Gide immediately had, and has always had since, readers—certainly sometimes hostile and vengeful—whose allegiances have been primarily to a queer posterity, Sartre sometimes among them. They would include such French writers as Marcel Proust, Marguerite Yourcenar, Jean Genet, Roland Barthes, Christiane Rochefort, Hervé Guibert, and many others.[42] In short, pace Sartre, they would fit no easy profile. If Sartre gives voice to a certain revenge of "posterity" on Gide and his friends, it might equally be said that the motley group that makes up Gide's readers represents a certain revenge (sexuality's this time) on Sartre.

five

Proust's Queer Metalepses

Quoi!

Two young men stand on the threshold of an all-male brothel, unable to bring themselves to enter. Unable to decide, perhaps, if they can trust each other's complicity enough to risk the adventure together. "Quoi! Après tout on s'en fiche?" [Well! After all, what do we care?], says one of the young men, over and over, apparently addressing some aspect of their situation at the threshold. The "quoi" itself is given an exclamation point rather than a question mark. It seems unable to be clearly interrogative; perhaps it's more of a simple sound—expressive of the need for there not to be silence, or of the need to perpetuate the possibility of entering. And then there is the half-interrogative sentence: "Après tout on s'en fiche?" After all, what does it matter? What does it matter whether or not we go in? What does it matter what happens if we do go in? What does it matter if you are not as good a friend as I think you are? What do I know about what matters to you or to me? What does it matter that I can't quite articulate in your presence or to you my desire to have sex with a man? This scene from *Le Temps retrouvé* seems somehow paradigmatic of the difficulty of queer sexual expression in Proust's novel.

The narrator of the *Recherche* apparently understands as much and launches into an intriguing analysis of what is going on:

"Well! After all, what do we care?" But though no doubt he meant by this that after all they did not care about the consequences, it is probable that he cared rather more than he implied, for the remark was not followed by any movement to cross the threshold but by a further glance at his companion, followed by the same smile and the same "After all, what do we care?" And in this "After all, what do we care?" I saw a perfect example of that portentous language, so unlike the language we habitually speak, in which emotion deflects what we had intended to say and causes to emerge in its place an entirely different phrase, issued from an unknown lake wherein dwell these expressions alien to our thoughts which by virtue of that very fact reveal them.

[«Quoi! Après tout on s'en fiche?» Mais il avait beau vouloir dire par là qu'après tout on se fichait des conséquences, il est probable qu'il ne s'en fichait pas tant que cela car cette parole n'était suivie d'aucun mouvement pour entrer mais d'un nouveau regard vers l'autre, suivi du même sourire et du même *après tout on s'en fiche*. C'était, ce *après tout on s'en fiche*, un exemplaire entre mille de ce magnifique langage, si différent de celui que nous parlons d'habitude, et où l'émotion fait dévier ce que nous voulions dire et épanouir à la place une phrase tout autre, émergée d'un lac inconnu où vivent ces expressions sans rapport avec la pensée et qui par cela même la révèlent. (4:401)][1]

"Is there a better definition of the unconscious?" asks Gérard Genette, after citing that last sentence, from the words "that portentous language" to the end (thereby leaving out the context of the effort to engage in queer sex). He juxtaposes it to a definition of the unconscious that Freud gave, and decides in Proust's favor. Freud (as cited by Genette) said, "The speaker decides not to put it [the repressed intention] into words, and after that the slip of the tongue occurs: after that, that is to say, the purpose which has been forced back is put into words against the speaker's will, either by altering the expression of the intention which he has permitted, or by mingling with it, or by actually taking its place." Proust's definition is preferred because it seems "more rigorous perhaps in its very ambiguity."[2]

But in the scene at the brothel, there does not in fact seem to be that much distance between what the man finds himself saying and what he might actually have meant to say. These two fellows are actually at the door of the male brothel, so they already seem fairly compromised or committed. (As indeed, it would appear the narrator is, given that he is on the other side of the threshold!) They've come this far together. They might as well go in. It doesn't seem the sentence in question contains any lapsus per se, nor does it really seem to be an "entirely different phrase" of the kind Proust's narrator refers to. Whatever their ambiguity, the young man's words seem perfectly capable of meaning what they are supposed to mean. And whatever they meant, the narrator notes in a parenthetical remark a paragraph later that the two did finally put an end to the moments of hesitation filled by the repetition of that phrase: "the two Russians had decided to penetrate [into the building]—'After all, what do we care?'" (193, 4:402). When the narrator cites that phrase for the fifth and final time, the men have comported themselves as if they understood and accepted the most immediate, superficial meaning of the phrase: "What does it matter, who cares, if we go in here and have sex with some other men?" That is, after all, probably what they came for, however much difficulty we might imagine they had expressing that desire to each other, coming up with a pair of first persons who could decide to make the trip to the brothel together—who could even admit that they knew of the brothel.

More than the sentence, then, it is perhaps the scene itself—quite an incidental one, we might think—that emerges from the unknown lake the narrator has described to reveal something crucially important all the while seeming purely incidental. Standing on the outside of that same queer threshold, the two young men are nonetheless queered by their position. Standing on the inside of the queer threshold, the narrator has no such worries. Outside, they stutter, unable to get out of the rut of "Quoi! Après tout on s'en fiche?" Inside, the narrator does not seem to have the same impediment. What kind of fragmentation does it take to speak queerly?

While Genette does not mention the context of the narrator's definition of the unconscious (that it takes place across the threshold of an all-male brothel), he does, in the final pages of the same essay, "Proust and Indirect Language," make some interesting observations about how same-sex sexuality finds its way into speech:

The *Recherche du temps perdu* . . . cannot but appear . . . as an immense text, at once allusive, metonymic, synecdochic, (metaphoric, of course) and disavowing, of involuntary avowal, in which are revealed, but by concealment and disguise in innumerable transformations, a small number of simple statements concerning its author, his origins, his ambitions, his morals [*mœurs*: also habits], everything he shares secretly with Bloch, with Legrandin, with Charlus, and of which he has carefully exempted his hero, the colorless, yet idealized image of himself. We know with what perhaps naive severity André Gide judged such trickery; to which Proust replied that one can say anything so long as one does not say "I." By "can," of course, Proust meant "has the right"; but perhaps the verb should be given a stronger meaning: perhaps there is no truthful language, in literature as elsewhere, outside indirect language. (284)

This is a slippery paragraph. On the one hand Genette seems to suggest that there are a few "simple" things that one might say about Proust and his mœurs. That he, like Charlus and Legrandin, was homosexual, for instance. Then, that it was the figural work done on "simple" statements such as "I am homosexual" that produced the complex narrative structures of the *Recherche*.[3] But if Proust is to be rescued from Gide's implied accusation of cowardly cheating, Genette suggests in the final sentence I've cited, it is by understanding that there may be no simple, direct, veridical statement that can be made *outside* of literature, or at least outside of figurality, about Proust and his sexuality. Genette concludes his essay: "It is the conflict between language and truth that *produces*, as we have seen, indirect language; and indirect language is, above all, writing—the work [c'est l'écriture—c'est l'œuvre]" (286). Proust's writing, his work, has to do with the struggle between sexuality and truth that happens in figural language, has to do with the figurality of sexuality itself, of its assumption in discourse, Genette implies. Perhaps, we might add, Proust's novel investigates the work of the figuration of a first person in which one could speak of or even engage in same-sex sexual relations. Indirection, impersonation, and abstraction fill the space between the author's first person and his work.

Suppose we feel an inclination to drag Genette's insights a bit further out of his formalist framework, into a different critical vein. We might then juxtapose his observations with something Foucault said, in a conversation about Raymond Roussel:

Between cryptography and sexuality as a secret there is certainly a direct relationship. Let's take three examples: Of Cocteau, people said, "It's not surprising that he flaunts his sexuality, his inclinations and his sexual choices with such ostentation since he is a homosexual." Fine. Of Proust they said, "It's not surprising that he simultaneously hides and reveals his sexuality, that he lets it appear clearly while also so assiduously concealing himself in his work, since he is a homosexual." And it could also be said about Roussel, "It's not surprising that he hides it completely since his is a homosexual." In other words, of the three possible modes of behavior—hiding it entirely, hiding it while revealing it, or flaunting it—all can appear as a result of sexuality, of which I would certainly say that it is a way of living. It's a choice in relation to what one is as a sexual being and also as a writer. It's the choice made in the relationship between the style of sexual life and the work. One might think of saying, "Because he is homosexual, he hid his sexuality in his work, or else it's because he hid his sexuality in his life that he also hid it in his work." It would be better, I believe, to try to understand that someone who is a writer is not simply doing his work in his books, in what he publishes, but that his major work is, in the end, himself in the process of writing his books. The private life of an individual, his sexual choices, and his work are interrelated not because his work translates his sexual life, but because the work includes the whole life as well as the text. The work is more than the work: the subject who is writing is part of the work. [La vie privée d'un individu, ses choix sexuels et son œuvre sont liés entre eux, non pas parce que l'œuvre traduit la vie sexuelle, mais parce qu'elle comprend la vie aussi bien que le texte. L'œuvre est plus que l'œuvre: le sujet qui écrit fait partie de l'œuvre.][4]

As opposed to imagining that there are or were "a few simple statements," statements anyone might easily have understood, about the author and his habits that were used to produce or to provoke the work of figuration that became Proust's novel, we might better imagine that such statements, however simple they might seem to us many years later, were actually rather difficult to construct and enunciate. As I noted in my introduction, the words that would be chosen in order to make them were under dispute and far from self-evident; the availability of interlocutors to understand them in the same way that you understood them was not a foregone conclusion; the very social protocols that would enable a scene of communication involving them were far from widely established. What it means to be a person who can say certain things remains to be established. (This seems rather to be the point of the scene that is taking place across the threshold of the brothel.) We get a better sense of this from Foucault's description of the way that Proust, Cocteau, and Roussel form a set of possible strategies for constructing an oeuvre that includes not only what and how one writes, but also what and how one lives, figures of the self—all of these constructions requiring creative energy. From this point of view, we might consider that the scene of the two men at the threshold of the male brothel who struggle to state and to pursue their desire while being observed by a narrator who is already in the brothel (but only by happenstance) need not exactly be about something being repressed and therefore translated into figural language unbeknownst to any or all of the parties. Perhaps the queer work in the *Recherche* has to do with a particular method of finding and assigning, of figuring, a voice, and not necessarily a singular one. There is in the *Recherche* a peculiar politics of sharing what wishes to be spoken among various speakers—some of whom seem to play only the most incidental roles. Let us consider the construction of a few scenes in which speech is shared out and examine how that sharing is done.

"Perhaps Even You and I Belong to Some Narrative"

I will approach my subject again from a slightly different angle, but using a similar proceeding. I take my inspiration from another part of Genette's formalist account of the *Recherche*, his famous study *Narrative Discourse: An Essay in Method*, and launch from there into a not-quite-so-formalist account of the place of sexuality in the *Recherche*. One of the many figures Genette calls to our attention is what he names *narrative metalepsis*. By that term he designates moments when there is a "transgressive" invasion of the diegesis (the spatiotemporal universe designated by a narration) by something that should be extradiegetic, something that should by rights exist only outside the narrated universe. Genette provides the example of a story by Cortázar in which a man is murdered by a character from the novel he is reading. Other examples Genette offers include Genet's theater in those moments when it demonstrates what it learned from Pirandello about actors who can simultaneously be actors and characters, and Robbe-Grillet's novels, which easily skip from level to level, "characters escaped from a painting, a book, a press clipping, a photograph, a dream, a memory, a fantasy, etc." Genette continues:

> All these games, by the intensity of their effects, demonstrate the importance of the boundary they tax their ingenuity to overstep, in defiance of verisimilitude—a boundary *that is precisely the narrating (or the performance) itself*: a shifting but sacred frontier between two worlds, the world in which one tells, the world of which one tells. Whence the uneasiness Borges so well put his finger on: "Such inversions suggest that if the characters in a story can be readers or spectators, then we, their readers or spectators, can be fictitious." The most troubling thing about metalepsis indeed lies in this unacceptable and insistent hypothesis, that the extradiegetic is perhaps always diegetic, and that the narrator and his narratees—you and I—perhaps belong to some narrative.[5]

Genette gives no examples of Proust using transgressive metalepsis the way Cortázar or Robbe-Grillet or Genet would. Instead, the presentation of metalepsis opens onto his fascinating discussion of the shift in form of the narration between Proust's early draft of a novel *Jean Santeuil* and the *Recherche* itself. *Jean Santeuil* is narrated by a person who meets someone else who is writing a book about the adventures of yet someone else named Jean Santeuil. Eventually, the narrator of *Jean Santeuil* lays his hands on the manuscript and reproduces it for his readers. One might think that the move to the *Recherche* is thus one of simplification: the shedding of a series of frames around an awkwardly embedded autobiographical narrative. Genette understands this to be an unsatisfactory way of looking at things:

> Most obviously significant in this turn-around is the late, and deliberate, assumption of the *form* of direct autobiography, which we must immediately connect to the apparently contradictory fact that the narrative content of the *Recherche* is less directly autobiographical than the narrative content of *Santeuil*—as if Proust first had had to conquer a certain adhesion to himself, had to detach himself from himself, in order to win the right to say "I," or more precisely the right to have this hero who is neither completely himself nor completely someone else say "I." So the conquest of the *I* here is not a return to and attendance on himself, not a settling into the comfort of "subjectivity," but perhaps exactly the opposite: the difficult experience of relating to oneself with (slight) distance and off-centering—a relationship wonderfully symbolized by that barely suggested, seemingly accidental semihomonymy of the narrator-hero and the signatory. (249)

This is a nice characterization of what I have been referring to throughout these chapters as the abstraction of the first person. The "je" of the *Recherche* is a figure, a procedure, a technique, more than a subjectivity, Genette is arguing, and this explains certain of the aspects of the novel that might seem like incoherencies if one imagines the "je" simply to be a subjectivity:

> Now into a narrative in autobiographical form there has to be integrated a whole social chronicle that often goes beyond the field of the hero's direct knowledge and sometimes, as is the case with *Un amour de Swann*, does not easily enter even the narrator's knowledge. . . .
>
> So he [Proust] needs both an "omniscient" narrator capable of dominating a moral experience which is now *objectivized* and an autodiegetic narrator capable of personally taking up, authenticating, and illuminating by his

own commentary the spiritual experience which gives all the rest its ultimate meaning and which, for its part, remains the hero's privilege. Whence that paradoxical—and to some people scandalous—situation of a "first-person" narrating that is nevertheless occasionally omniscient. Here again —without wanting to, perhaps unknowingly, and for reasons that result from the profound (and profoundly contradictory) nature of its purpose— the *Recherche* attacks the best-established convention of novelistic narrating by cracking not only its traditional "forms," but also—a more hidden and thus more decisive loosening—the very "logic" of its discourse. (250–52)

But perhaps the *Recherche* has its own logic, one that has something to do with an effort not only to say or show things that are difficult to say or show, but also to think abstractly about the process through which such difficulties are dealt with and sometimes overcome through a variety of strategies of self-figuration or impersonation.

Genette has sometimes been criticized for not being daring enough in his description of what is sometimes the rather wild figurality of the "je" of the *Recherche*.[6] I am interested here in one particular way in which we might extend his insight in new directions, finding another way of tapping into the potential of the figure of metalepsis to help us read the *Recherche*. For Genette, the narrator of the *Recherche* has a "monopoly" on what he calls the "ideological function" of the narrative—didactic commentary, explicatory and justificatory discourses, and so on. Genette notes that often ideological novelists (Dostoyevsky, Tolstoy, Mann, Broch, Malraux) assign to this or that character some part of the task of commentary or didactic discourse. "Nothing of the sort takes place in Proust, who, other than Marcel, has given himself no 'spokesman.' A Swann, a Saint-Loup, a Charlus, despite all their intelligence, are objects of observation, not organs of truth or even genuine interlocutors . . . their errors, their absurdities, their failures and fallings-off are more instructive than their opinions" (258). In this observation, Genette may be mistaken. He has, of course, written brilliantly about Swann's role as a precursor for Marcel and the odd diegetic status of *Un Amour de Swann* (241–43). Yet it may well be worth considering that other characters are not so excluded from that position from which to offer commentary or explicatory discourse as Genette asserts. Not only Swann but also Charlus might legitimately lay claim to it on occasion. I propose to consider this possibility in some detail by watching a certain bit of Proustian text move from a letter he wrote in 1908 into the voice of the narrator of *Contre Sainte-Beuve* and then into the voice of Charlus in the *Recherche* itself.[7]

Vulgar Characters: Proust with Balzac and Wilde

Here is one thing Oscar Wilde, writing in 1886 as a critic, had to say about Balzac and his character Lucien de Rubempré: "A steady course of Balzac reduces our living friends to shadows and our acquaintances to the shadows of shades; who would care to go out to an evening party to meet Tomkins, the friend of one's boyhood, when one can sit at home with Lucien de Rubempré? It is pleasanter to have the entrée to Balzac's society than to receive cards from all the duchesses of Mayfair."[8] It might not be too farfetched to think of Wilde here identifying in an offhand way a particular readerly practice of queer self-definition: the construction—through relations to authors and their characters—of a countersocial realm, an alternate sociality in which an intensely affective same-sex relation to the fictional Lucien de Rubempré is more significant than one's day-to-day connection to the nonfictional Tomkins. Proust, as we are about to see, crafts a relation to this same countersocial realm, one including Wilde, Balzac, and certain of their characters.

Like Proust, Wilde was happy to take material written in one context and reuse it, voicing it differently in subsequent contexts. Thus, the material on Balzac, in particular the witticism about Lucien de Rubempré, will find itself recycled into the dialogue titled "The Decay of Lying" (first published in 1889). The queerness of that particular dialogue is signaled long before the handsome Lucien de Rubempré is ever mentioned. The two interlocutors within the dialogue are named Cyril and Vivian, and Cyril opens the dialogue by exhorting his friend: "My dear Vivian, don't coop yourself up all day in the library. It is a perfectly lovely afternoon. The air is exquisite. There is a mist upon the woods, like the purple bloom upon the plum. Let us go and lie on the grass and smoke cigarettes and enjoy Nature."[9] Vivian is not feeling cooperative. His hostility to nature, which according to him should only be a pendant to art, rises to such heights that he is moved to declare, in even more extreme terms than in Wilde's own review of Balzac: "A steady course of Balzac reduces our living friends to shadows, and our acquaintances to the shadows of shades. His characters have a kind of fervent fiery-coloured existence. They dominate us and defy skepticism. One of the greatest tragedies of my life is the death of Lucien de Rubempré. It is a grief from which I have never been able to completely rid myself. It haunts me in my moments of pleasure. I remember it when I laugh" (976). If there is present here a certain comic excess that had not yet found its way into the earlier review, that excess also creates room for a note of seriousness. Or perhaps more accurately, that excess, together with the underlining of the queer subtext, might give a pointedly social edge to the laughter. For when Vivian observes that he is haunted by his grief over Lucien's death even in his moments of pleasure, it is easy enough to understand those pleasures to be queer and that haunting to stand for an awareness of the social costs sometimes attendant on those pleasures.

Wilde's book *Intentions* (1891), in which "The Decay of Lying" was reprinted, was published in a French translation in 1905, and the passage concerning Balzac and Lucien caught Proust's eye. A reaction to it can be found in his correspondence; a reworking of that reaction can be found in *Contre Sainte-Beuve* (*Against Sainte-Beuve*); a reworking of the *Contre Sainte-Beuve* passage can be found in *Sodom and Gomorrah*. In each of these reworkings, the reaction to Wilde will be voiced differently, and I would like to call attention to this question of voicing. In the first two versions of Proust's reaction to this passage from Wilde, Wilde will be named. In the final instance, in *Sodom and Gomorrah*, when the reaction is voiced through Charlus, Charlus will not name Wilde but will say instead, "And the death of Lucien! I forget who the man of taste was who, when he was asked what event in his life had grieved him most, replied: 'The death of Lucien de Rubempré in *Splendeurs et Misères*'" (611) [Et la mort de Lucien! je ne me rappelle plus quel homme de goût avait eu cette réponse, à qui lui demandait quel événement l'avait le plus affligé dans sa vie: «La mort de Lucien de Rubempré dans *Splendeurs et misères*» (3:437–38)]. In the notes to the most recent Pléiade edition of the *Recherche*, the editor (Antoine Compagnon) informs us, a bit inaccurately, that "the 'man of taste' was Oscar Wilde." But then he clarifies: "In «The Decay of Lying», a dialogue published in *Intentions* in 1891, Vivian, obviously a spokesman for the author, says: 'One of the greatest tragedies of my life is the death of Lucien de Rubempré.' . . . By way of the example of Wilde, Proust criticizes what he elsewhere names idolatry, the confusing of art and life, in which one treats art as the true life and lives life as if it were a work of art" (3:1588). Why could Proust's character Charlus not be referring to Wilde's character Vivian? This is a moment full of those metaleptic possibilities that dog the practice of "realist" fiction. Can fictional characters move from the works of one author to another? Can we invite fictional characters into our real world just as authors introduce names of real people into their fictional worlds? Does it make sense to suggest, as Compagnon does, that Proust is referring to Wilde when one of his characters refers ambiguously to someone who is probably either Vivian or Wilde? Can Wilde be said to have said Vivian's words (which we assume Wilde wrote)? What is more challenging to read in Wilde (as he revoices material from his article into the dialogue) and in Proust (as he reforms material from previous enterprises and puts it into the mouths of various characters) is their similar abstracting investigation of the figurality of the instance of vocalization. In particular, their investigation of that figurality is a crucial part of their investigation of practices of queer self-definition and queer sociality. For Wilde and for Proust the enactment of queerness is also a practice of figurality—it involves putting forth a particular figure of self, often in an instance of first-person vocalization. But the enactment of queerness also involves the establishment of a queer context as well as of queer content. To use the terminology of an earlier chapter, a queer interaction not only involves the creation of a sustainable queer first person, it also requires that queerness (a social positioning produced in relation to the set of possibilities known to exist within the larger social context in which the interaction takes place) be indexed by the interaction—either referentially or nonreferentially. Mourning Lucien indexes queerness. In the case of Vivian and Cyril, for instance, to imagine that Vivian speaks *for* Wilde, speaks his queerly coded thoughts, is to miss the point that in "The Decay of Lying" Wilde is primarily purveying a *context* for queer speech (the subject positions, the cultural repertory, the very possibility, the illocutionary context in which to speak as queer), a queerness thus entailed by the given instance of speech itself (the utterance) more than by the matter of what is said (the statement).[10]

Compagnon is not alone in collapsing Vivian into Wilde; Proust does so as well. It happens in the intriguing letter he wrote in 1908 to his friend Robert Dreyfus in which the Wilde passage is first mentioned.[11] This letter is written in the same month as the famous one to Louis d'Albufera, in which Proust offers a list of the projects he has under way:

a study of the nobility
a novel of Paris
an essay on Sainte-Beuve and Flaubert

an essay on Women

an essay on Pederasty

   (not easy to publish)

[une étude sur la noblesse

un roman parisien

un essai sur Sainte-Beuve et Flaubert

un essai sur les Femmes

un essai sur la Pédérastie

   (pas facile à publier)][12]

Only a few days after composing that list, Proust is describing for Dreyfus a writing project on which Dreyfus has apparently frowned. Proust is now wondering whether to write up the project of which Dreyfus disapproves as an article or as a piece of fiction: "I intended to ask you if you thought the forbidden article would be as inoffensive . . . in the *Mercure* or in another journal as in a volume. But, in the meantime, my plan has become more precise. It will be, rather, a short story so there will be time to consult you again" [J'avais l'intention de te demander si tu trouvais que l'article défendu serait aussi inoffensif . . . au *Mercure* ou dans une autre Revue qu'en volume. Mais dans l'intervalle mon projet se précise. Ce sera plutôt une nouvelle et alors il y aura le temps de te reconsulter]. Dreyfus, in thinking back to the occasion of the letter, offered the following clarification:

I believe I remember very vaguely that during the course of my recent visit Proust had spoken to me of a plan for an article which I had not encouraged, doubtless wrongly. Perhaps it was related (I have sometimes wondered in rereading this letter) to his plan, still mysterious, to explore the accursed regions upon which he was later to raise the edifice of his great work.

[Je crois très vaguement me souvenir qu'au cours de ma récente visite, Proust m'avait parlé d'un projet d'article que je n'avais pas encouragé, sans doute à tort. Peut-être cela se rapportait-il (je me le suis parfois demandé en relisant la lettre) à son dessein, encore mystérieux, de fouiller les régions maudites sur lesquelles il devait ensuite édifier sa grande œuvre].[13]

Given this context, it seems especially intriguing that Proust should here choose to confuse Wilde with one of his characters. Here is the relevant passage from Proust's letter:

But the same reason that makes me think that the importance and the suprasensible reality of art prevent certain anecdotal novels, however pleasant they may be, from altogether meriting, perhaps, the rank you seem to assign them . . . this same reason does not allow me to make the realization of a dream of art depend upon reasons which are themselves also anecdotal and too much drawn from life not to participate in its contingency and irreality—which, moreover, presented thusly seems not false but banal and deserving of some sharp slap from irritated existence (like Oscar Wilde saying that the greatest grief he had known was the death of Lucien de Rubempré in Balzac, and learning a little afterwards, in his trial, that there are griefs more real). But you know that this banal aestheticism could never be my aesthetic philosophy.

[Mais la même raison qui me fait penser que l'importance et la réalité suprasensible de l'art empêchent certains romans anecdotiques, si agréables qu'ils soient, de mériter peut-être tout à fait le rang où tu sembles les placer . . . cette même raison ne me permet pas de faire dépendre la réalisation d'un rêve d'art, de raisons elles aussi anecdotiques et trop tirées de la vie pour ne pas participer à sa contingence et à son irréalité. Ce qui d'ailleurs présenté ainsi à l'air non pas faux mais banal et mériter quelque soufflet cuisant de l'existence irritée (comme Oscar Wilde disant que le plus grand chagrin qu'il avait eu c'était la mort de Lucien de Rubempré dans Balzac, et apprenant peu après par son procès qu'il est des chagrins plus réels).

Mais tu sais que cet esthétisme banal ne saurait être ma philosophie esthétique. (8:123)][14]

The "banal aestheticism" Proust disdains here seems at first glance to involve confusing the contingent material of day-to-day life (the stuff of anecdotes) with the project of a serious work of art (the attainment of a suprasensible reality in which contingency no longer prevails). Proust can accuse Wilde of this banal aestheticism only by confusing him with his character Vivian. This is an odd situation: the accusation of banal aestheticism Proust levels at Wilde is possible only because of Proust's conflation of Wilde with Vivian, and yet it is occasioned by Wilde's (or Vivian's) putative willingness to confuse Lucien de Rubempré with a real person. As in the previous chapter, we can see here how Proust's choice of example reveals the mutually implicating relation between representational questions regarding sexual matters, aesthetic ideology and practice, and the assumption and maintenance of a particular first person both in relation to sexuality and in relation to aesthetic practice.

Proust's fascination by this problematic confusion of real and fictional characters seems to have to do with Wilde, with Balzac, with queer sexuality, and with contexts for queer speech. As further evidence of this, we could note another part of the passage in *Sodom and Gomorrah* concerning Charlus's fascination with Balzac. Charlus is not only, like Wilde and Wilde's characters, fascinated by Lucien de Rubempré, but also by the Princess de Cadignan. Charlus believes Albertine to be dressed in an outfit resembling one worn by the Princess:

> Albertine, who was interested in this mute language of clothes, questioned M. de Charlus about the Princess de Cadignan. "Oh! it's such a delightful story," said the Baron in a dreamy tone. "I know the little garden in which Diane de Cadignan used to stroll with Mme d'Espard. It belongs to one of my cousins." (619)

> [Albertine, qu'intéressait ce muet langage des robes, questionna M. de Charlus sur la princesse de Cadignan. «Oh! c'est une nouvelle exquise, dit le baron d'un ton rêveur. Je connais le petit jardin où Diane de Cadignan se promena avec Mme d'Espard. C'est celui d'une de mes cousines.» (3:442)]

Here Proust plays for comic effect with what is increasingly seeming to be a queer cognitive disorder—the confusion of orders of reality and representation. Charlus is making the same error of which Proust had accused Wilde—and indicating something about himself as he does so.

Given this textual genealogy that moves from Balzac to Wilde to Proust, we might consider that the terms of Proust's "critique" of Wilde and his aesthetic errors might not be something to be taken with absolute seriousness. Speaking or writing about Wilde is, after all, the *occasion* out of which a particular practice of speech about same-sex sexuality can be allowed to arise. Proust's constant references to Balzac's vulgarity (another permutation of the kind of accusation he directs at Wilde) are, as we shall see, particularly interesting when considered in this light.[15]

Thus the different moments in which Proust returns to write and rewrite this material concerning the Balzac/Wilde conjuncture are perhaps not so much occasions to say *something in particular* about appropriate aesthetic experience or literary practice as they are occasions to produce and observe a scene of queer sexual *and* aesthetic culture in interaction. Consider how the same accusation of *banal aestheticism* leveled against Wilde by Proust in his correspondence can be directed against Balzac by the narrator of *Contre Sainte-Beuve*. In Balzac's case, the word used is *vulgarity*. Balzac *as a person* is, in general, vulgar: "So great was the vulgarity of his feelings that life was unable to raise him up" [La vulgarité de ses sentiments est si grande que la vie n'a pu l'élever].[16] Yet perhaps this personal vulgarity allows Balzac to approach certain subjects (queer sexuality, for instance)[17] that a less vulgar person wouldn't touch: "But this same vulgarity, you see, may be the source from which some of his portraits derive their vigour" (58) [Mais, vois-tu, cette vulgarité même est peut-être la cause de la force de certaines de ses peintures (231)]. The downside of the vulgarity is rather Wildean; it causes a confusion between life and art: "in his writing we savour pleasures scarcely any different from those afforded us by life" (61) [nous goûtons souvent dans sa littérature des plaisirs à peine différents de ce que nous donne la vie (238)]. This Wildean vulgarity sometimes has another consequence, Proust's Vivianian fallacy, we might call it: characters are sometimes not sufficiently differentiated in voice from their author, which makes them seem contingent rather than necessary:

> Lucien sounds too much like Balzac and ceases to be a real person, different from all the others. Which happens now and again, for one reason or another, in spite of the prodigious variety among Balzac's characters and their identity with themselves. (83)

> [Lucien parle trop comme Balzac et il cesse d'être une personne réelle, différente de toutes les autres. Ce qui, malgré la prodigieuse diversité entre eux et identité avec eux-mêmes des personnages de Balzac, arrive tout de même quelquefois pour une cause ou une autre. (241)]

But maybe not for any old reason. Balzac's relation to Lucien seems for Proust a founding moment in the tradition of novelists writing about same-sex sexuality, and so the relation of Balzac to Lucien, like the relation of Wilde to Lucien, becomes both a figure for the novelistic representation of same-sex sexuality and an occasion for repeated attempts at voicing queer literary speech. Consider, for instance, the forms of ambivalence to Balzac voiced in a passage (a bit of which I already cited in the previous chapter) from a letter Proust wrote to Gide as he was reading *Les Caves du Vatican*:

> But in the creation of Cadio, no one has been objective with that much perversity since Balzac and *Splendeurs et misères*. All the more so, it seems to

me, since Balzac was aided in inventing Lucien de Rubempré by a certain personal vulgarity. There is a particular "grain to the skin" in Lucien's words which has an enchanting naturalness about it, but which one also finds in Balzac and even in his correspondence. Whereas you, creating Lafcadio!

[Mais dans la création de Cadio, personne ne fut objectif avec autant de perversité depuis Balzac et *Splendeurs et Misères*. Encore, je pense, que Balzac était aidé, pour inventer Lucien de Rubempré, par une certaine vulgarité personelle. Il y a un certain «grain de peau», dans les propos de Lucien, dont le naturel nous enchante, mais qu'on retrouve chez Balzac et même dans sa correspondance. Tandis que vous, pour créer Cadio!]¹⁸

This "vulgarité personelle," this "grain de peau," moves, in what seems for Proust to be a failure of objectivity, from Balzac's own speech in his correspondence directly into the speech of his character Lucien. This is apparently evidence of a failure in novelistic artistry, a failure to have fully objectified one's own speech and a failure at establishing the necessity of the speech of one's characters. Yet plenty of things, when Wilde and Balzac are being spoken about, move more or less directly from Proust's own correspondence into the voice of the narrator of *Contre Sainte-Beuve*, or into the voice of the narrator of the *Recherche*, or into the voice of the character Charlus. Perhaps all this material suggests that queer textual practices in Proust have precisely to do with certain kinds of objectivity being in crisis, with a contingent need claiming a right to expression, with a nearly intentional metaleptic failure to respect distinctions between the real world and literary characters, a failure that produces borrowings and sharings among characters as well as between real people and characters. While this may cause a breakdown of one way of imagining a "rigorous" attention to novelistic artistry, it may well produce another kind of rigor. This failure in "objectivity" may be what produces a kind of reflection on the functioning of a first person— both in literature and in social interactions—a first person dealing with the forms of its own figurality, the pragmatics of its relation to same-sex sexuality and speech about it in various contexts, including that of a first-person novel.

In this light, consider the following lengthy passage from *Contre Sainte-Beuve*, which in fact begins as an observation about the success of Balzac's "objectivity," his ability to individuate the speech of his characters, but then quickly swerves to other subjects:

Balzac having preserved a style that in some respects was unorganized, one might imagine he did not seek to objectify the language of his characters. . . . But quite the reverse. . . . Even in his asides Lucien de Rubempré has just that vulgar jollity, that whiff of uncultivated youth, that will appeal to Vautrin. . . . In fact, Vautrin was not alone in loving Lucien de Rubempré. In his earlier days . . . Oscar Wilde, who was later to learn from life, alas, that there are keener sorrows than those we get from books, said: "The greatest sadness of my life? The death of Lucien de Rubempré in *Splendeurs et misères des courtisanes.*" There is something peculiarly dramatic moreover about this predilection and compassion in Oscar Wilde, at the height of his success, for Lucien de Rubempré's death. He felt compassionate, no doubt, because he saw it, like all readers, from Vautrin's point of view, which is also Balzac's point of view. From which point of view, moreover, he was a peculiarly choice and elect reader to adopt this point of view more completely than most readers. But one cannot help reflecting that a few years later he was himself to be Lucien de Rubempré. The end of Lucien de Rubempré in the Conciergerie, when he has seen his brilliant career in the world come crashing down after it has been proved he had been living on intimate terms with a convict, was merely the anticipation—as yet unknown to Wilde, it is true—of exactly what was to happen to Wilde. (64–65)

[Balzac, ayant gardé par certains côtés un style inorganisé, on pourrait croire qu'il n'a pas cherché à objectiver le langage de ses personnages. . . . Or c'est tout le contraire. . . . Lucien de Rubempré, même dans ses apartés, a juste la gaîté vulgaire, le relent de jeunesse inculte qui doit plaire à Vautrin. . . . Et de fait, Vautrin n'a pas été seul à aimer Lucien de Rubempré. Oscar Wilde, à qui la vie devait hélas apprendre plus tard qu'il est de plus poignantes douleurs que celles que nous donnent les livres, disait dans sa première époque . . .: «Le plus grand chagrin de ma vie? La mort de Lucien de Rubempré dans *Splendeurs et Misères des Courtisanes.*» Il y a d'ailleurs quelque chose de particulièrement dramatique dans cette prédilection et cet attendrissement d'Oscar Wilde, au temps de sa vie brillante, pour la mort de Lucien de Rubempré. Sans doute, il s'attendrissait sur elle, comme tous les lecteurs, en se plaçant au point de vue de Vautrin, qui est le point de vue de Balzac. Et à ce point de vue d'ailleurs, il était un lecteur particulièrement choisi et élu pour adopter ce point de vue plus complètement que la plupart des lecteurs. Mais on ne peut s'empêcher de penser que, quelques années plus tard, il devait être Lucien de Rubempré lui-même. Et la fin de Lucien de Rubempré à la Conciergerie, voyant toute sa brillante existence mondaine écroulée sur la preuve qui est faite qu'il vivait

dans l'intimité d'un forçat, n'était que l'anticipation—inconnue encore de
Wilde, il est vrai—de ce qui devait précisément arriver à Wilde. (255–57)

Let's just note a few things about this rich passage in its relation to the
previous one. Balzac resembles both Lucien (in his manner of speech)
and Vautrin (in his love for Lucien); the vulgarity of Lucien's speech
seems to be understood as truly objectified in one passage from Proust
but is tied personally to Balzac in the other. That speech is a source of
appeal to Vautrin and to Wilde, who share Balzac's point of view in this
regard.[19] It will be the revelation of Lucien's social vulgarity—as evi-
denced in his intimate relation to Vautrin—that will cause his downfall.
Finally, let's note the startling version of the Vivianian fallacy with
which this passage ends: the attraction of the brilliant Wilde to the sexy
Lucien is a form of unrigorous aesthetic behavior, yet "one cannot
help" but remark the appropriateness of the identification of the imprisoned Wilde with the imprisoned Lucien. The height of queer metaleptic vulgarity, one might say.

There is, in Proust, an elaborate and deeply contradictory set of
protocols to ensure not only that same-sex sexuality is represented in
the novel, but also that speech contexts that are themselves queer both
can be produced in and by the novel and can also be subject to the
novel's commentary. Same-sex sexuality is brought into discourse by
way of a complicated set of figural detours that include impersonation
and the creation of speech contexts in which different first-person
figurations are assumed and even, we might say, tested. Proust's indebt-
edness to Balzac and to Wilde lies in the fact that they provide both the
occasion for vulgar talk (which turns out to be talk about same-sex
sexuality), and the figures, the ghosts, even, through which to do the
talking. Of Charlus's relation to Balzac's *Les Secrets de la Princesse de
Cadignan* (the Princess was worried, like Charlus, that her sexual secrets
might be revealed to the wrong person at the wrong moment), the
Proustian narrator observes in *Sodom and Gomorrah*:

> And now that he had suddenly begun to identify his own situation with
> that described by Balzac, he took refuge, as it were, in the story, and for the
> calamity which was perhaps in store for him and which certainly he feared,
> he had the consolation of finding in his own anxiety what Swann and also
> Saint-Loup would have called something "very Balzacian." (623)

> [Et maintenant que depuis un instant il confondait sa situation avec celle
> décrite par Balzac, il se réfugiait en quelque sorte dans la nouvelle, et à

l'infortune qui le menaçait peut-être, et ne laissait pas en tous cas de l'effrayer, il avait cette consolation de trouver dans sa propre anxiété ce que Swann et aussi Saint-Loup eussent appelé quelque chose de «très balzacien». (3:445)]

Here Charlus is described as trapped in a dream world similar to the one in which Proust in his 1908 letter placed Wilde, waiting for the cruel slap of reality to awaken him. That slap, of course, would be a social enforcement indicating that a certain sexuality—or a certain assumption of that sexuality, or a representation of it, or a certain use of the first person in relation to it—was being disallowed. It might be the police raiding the brothel. The sharing out of queer speech in the *Recherche* is an aesthetic, preemptive act of defense against any such violence.

When the police do come knocking at the brothel, there might be some question whether and how they will distinguish between someone like the narrator, who just happens to be there, the two men hesitating about crossing the threshold, the proprietor, his employees, and their clients. And indeed the police did, late in the evening of January 11, 1918, raid the brothel run by Albert Le Cuziat (Proust's model for Jupien) and found Le Cuziat in a room on the ground floor of the establishment, drinking champagne with "three individuals who looked like pederasts." One of the three, the police report informs us, was "Proust, Marcel, 46 years old, independently wealthy, 102, boulevard Haussmann." The two other men were soldiers on medical leave. The police also found several pairs of men in more compromising positions in other rooms. Most of the couples consisted of soldiers on leave who were in the company of minors (seventeen, eighteen, and nineteen years old). In February, Le Cuziat's establishment was declared off-limits for soldiers. In March he was sentenced to four months of prison and a fine of 200 francs for corruption of minors and for serving alcohol after hours. Only in January 1919, after the intervention of several high-placed figures, would the army's restrictions on Le Cuziat's establishment be removed.[20]

One last observation on the way things are voiced in the *Recherche* as opposed to in *Contre Sainte-Beuve*. The first person of *Contre Sainte-Beuve* (speaking, we recall, to his mother) has no trouble himself being deeply moved by the same scene that moved Oscar Wilde and will move Charlus:

But finest without question is the wonderful passage where the two travellers pass before the ruins of Rastignac's chateau. This I call the "Tristesse d'Olympio" of Homosexuality: "He wanted to visit it all again, the pond next to the spring." We know that at the Pension Vauquer, in *Le Père Goriot*, Vautrin formed, to no purpose, the same plan of domination over Rastignac as he now has over Lucien de Rubempré. (66)

[Mais le plus beau sans conteste est le merveilleux passage où les deux voyageurs passent devant les ruines du château de Rastignac. J'appelle cela la Tristesse d'Olympio de l'Homosexualité: *Il voulut tout revoir, l'étang près de la source.* On sait que Vautrin, à la pension Vauquer, dans *Le Père Goriot*, a formé le même dessein de domination qu'il a maintenant sur Lucien de Rubempré (258).]

In the *Recherche* itself, it is not the narrator but Charlus who voices a version of this aesthetic praise of Balzac. Charlus implies that Swann shared his point of view, as it was Swann who suggested that Balzac had done for men who love other men what Hugo, in his poem "Tristesse d'Olympio," had done for men who love women: "It's so beautiful— the scene where Carlos Herrera [Vautrin's pseudonym] asks the name of the château he is driving past, and it turns out to be Rastignac, the home of the young man he used to love; and then the abbé falling into a reverie which Swann once called, and very aptly, the *Tristesse d'Olympio* of pederasty" (611) [C'est si beau, le moment où Carlos Herrera de- mande le nom du château devant lequel passe sa calèche: c'est Rastig- nac, la demeure du jeune homme qu'il a aimé autrefois. Et l'abbé alors de tomber dans une rêverie que Swann appelait, ce qui était bien spir- ituel, la *Tristesse d'Olympio* de la pédérastie (3:437)]. Who gets to say "pederasty" here and allow it to involve an aesthetically crafted sense of emotional depth and beauty? Is it Charlus or Swann or the narrator or Proust? What does the assumption of this first person entail? The very fact that Charlus utters the word *pédérastie* in public is greatly amusing to a number of his listeners within the novel, as their whole goal in the conversation in question had been to manage to direct it toward "homosexuality," so that Charlus will find himself taking up the subject, speaking as if they don't know what they know about him:

> At the word borrowed from the Greek with which M. de Charlus, in speaking of Balzac, had followed his allusion to *Tristesse d'Olympio* in con- nexion with *Splendeurs et Misères*, Ski, Brichot and Cottard had glanced at one another with a smile perhaps not so much ironical as tinged with that satisfaction which people at a dinner-party would show who had suc- ceeded in making Dreyfus talk about his own case, or the Empress Eugénie about her reign. (615–16)

[Au mot tiré du grec dont M. de Charlus, parlant de Balzac, avait fait suivre l'allusion à la *Tristesse d'Olympio* dans *Splendeurs et misères*, Ski, Brichot et Cottard s'étaient regardés avec un sourire peut-être moins ironique qu'empreint de la satisfaction qu'auraient des dîneurs qui réussiraient à faire parler Dreyfus de sa propre affaire, ou l'impératrice de son règne. (3:440)]

But what kind of a context does the narrator himself (as opposed to Ski, Brichot, and Cottard) offer Charlus?

I noted earlier Genette's assertion that the "je" of the *Recherche* has a monopoly on the spokesperson function of narration: "A Swann, a Saint-Loup, a Charlus, despite all their intelligence, are objects of observation, not organs of truth or even genuine interlocutors."[21] It may sometimes appear that the narrator wants this to be the case, yet everything about the way observations move from character to character as text moves from letters to *Contre Sainte-Beuve* to the *Recherche* itself suggests that the situation is more complicated.[22] Let's allow Jupien, too, the manager of the brothel where we began, to become for a moment an important spokesperson for the novel and its projects. He is (in the novel's final volume) speaking to the narrator about his role as manager of that brothel (the brothel, we might say, in a queer metalepsis of our own, in which Proust once found himself being questioned by the police following a raid on the establishment):

Besides, I may as well admit to you . . . that I have very few scruples about making money in this way. The actual thing that is done here is—I can no longer conceal the fact from you—something that I like, it is the flavor of my life. Well, is it forbidden to receive payment for things that one does not regard as wickedness? (205)

[D'ailleurs, vous avouerais-je . . . que je n'ai pas un grand scrupule à avoir ce genre de gains? La chose elle-même qu'on fait ici, je ne peux plus vous cacher que je l'aime, qu'elle est le goût de ma vie. Or, est-il défendu de recevoir un salaire pour des choses qu'on ne juge pas coupables? (4:410)]

Charlus's interlocutors attempt to trick him into speaking of "his" sexuality in a way that would reveal that he is in some way unable to fully assume that sexuality in his own first person. The narrator observes their game. The material the novel uses, regarding Balzac and Wilde and the aesthetics of voice and character in the novel, is material Proust voiced a number of different ways in different contexts—experiments, we might say, in the figuration of a first person in relation to same-sex sexuality, all of this caught up in an ongoing reflection regarding the construction of a first-person novel. The brothel scene is just such a literary experiment. It is finally in the context of a conversation between Jupien and the narrator at the end of that scene that a first person is finally found that can speak with reasonable freedom about "the flavor of my life." A great deal of effort (not all of it aesthetic) clearly went into finding and figuring such a first person (one able to speak freely in the friendly context the narrator provides). Surely part of that effort was meant to allow this particular first person to act at least for a moment as a spokesperson for the novel.

six

Sodom and Gomorrah

Proust's Narrator's First Person

("I say *me* to you," said Swann to me, "because it's the Prince who is speaking to me, you understand?")

[(Je vous dis *me*, me dit Swann, parce que c'est le prince qui me parle, vous comprenez?)]
—MARCEL PROUST, *Sodom and Gomorrah*

The Social Stuff of Impersonation

The playful snippet of prose I offer as an epigraph demonstrates Proust's interest in the linguistic problem of impersonation. Proust's novel regularly shows people (in particular, but not only, the narrator) manipulating the signifiers of the first person and also the terms of its enactment. In the *Recherche*, Proust analyzes processes of self-presentation with great attention, intricately linking various predicaments associated with those processes to his investigations of both social mobility and sexuality. It is during the party given by the Princess de Guermantes (recounted in the first chapter of the second part of *Sodom and Gomorrah*) that Swann impersonates the Prince in a conversation with the narrator.[1] Earlier in the evening, the narrator had caught a glimpse of Swann among the members of the crowd at the party and was on the point of making his way over to him when Swann was whisked away by the Prince for a private conversation: "In order, some people said, 'to show him the door'" (75) [mais me dirent certaines personnes, «afin de le mettre à la porte» (3:56)]. If Swann were to be shown the door, it would be because his openly pro-Dreyfus sentiments would have clashed too strongly with what everyone assumes are the strongly anti-Dreyfus sentiments of his hosts.[2] What transpired during Swann's conversation with the Prince is apparently much gossiped about throughout the entire evening, and the narrator makes many thwarted attempts to find Swann and engage him in a conversation on that subject. Finally, having overcome various obstacles, having found a quiet place in which he will not feel distracted by the conversation of Charlus, who is trying to seduce a handsome young aristocrat, the narrator is able to give all his attention to Swann, who warms to the subject: "To come back to my conversation with the Prince, I shall tell one person only, and that person is going to be you" (140) [Venons à l'entretien avec le prince, je ne le raconterai qu'à une seule personne, et cette personne cela va être vous (3:102)].

It is during that recounting (for the narrator's ears only), a recounting to be interrupted several more times, that Swann reveals that the Prince has confessed to him that both he and the Princess are closeted supporters of the Dreyfus cause, having recently (and without either of them telling the other) been separately converted from their previous anti-Dreyfus position. They learned of each other's conversions through an indiscretion on the part of their priest:

> "At last we're alone," he said. "I quite forget where I was. Oh yes, I had just told you, hadn't I, that the Prince asked the abbé Poiré if he could say his mass next day for Dreyfus. 'No, the abbé informed me' ("I say *me* to you," said Swann to me, "because it's the Prince who is speaking, you understand?"), 'for I have another mass that I've been asked to say for him tomorrow as well.—What, I said to him, is there another Catholic as well as myself who is convinced of his innocence? . . .' "(150)

> [«Enfin seuls, me dit-il; je ne sais plus où j'en suis. N'est-ce pas, je vous ai dit que le prince avait demandé à l'abbé Poiré s'il pourrait faire dire sa messe pour Dreyfus. " 'Non, me répondit l'abbé' " (je vous dis *me*, me dit Swann, parce que c'est le prince qui me parle, vous comprenez?) " 'car, j'ai une autre messe qu'on m'a chargé de dire également ce matin pour lui.— Comment, lui dis-je, il y a un autre catholique que moi qui est convaincu de son innocence? . . .' "» (3:109)]

The punctuation is complex, written traces of the verbal and gestural work of impersonation. The priest's and the Duke's first person are nested inside Swann's. Thanks to a set of parentheses, the narrator manages to nestle his own first person simultaneously inside and outside Swann's. This is an excellent example of the narrator's stance through-out the novel—his pretense of being separate from the social world in which the text of the novel nonetheless insists on embedding him. It is also an example of the role played throughout the novel by impersona-tion—the more or less successful manipulation of the indicators of the first (and other) persons—in the construction and maintenance of our social selves, in the enunciation of the statements that simultaneously reveal and advance (presuppose and entail) claims for our own social position. *Sodom and Gomorrah I*, along with the sections of the novel that immediately precede and follow it (including this scene at the Princess's party), is an excellent moment for observing this crucial strand of the novel's analytic project at work. As Swann's confidence to the narrator reveals—a confidence in which he breaks a confidence the Prince has made to him and tells of the Prince telling of a priest break-ing a confidence the Princess had made to him, all of these confidences being broken by the narrator in presenting the whole conversation to us—patterns of discretion and indiscretion are at the heart of this mo-ment in the novel. Manipulating such patterns correctly (knowing who can say what to whom and how and when, knowing what *you* or *I* can say at any given moment and finding the appropriate way to say it) is one way of belonging to—participating correctly in—a particular social group. Social climber that he is, the narrator (like the novel) is fasci-nated by these intensely social, palpable yet immaterial patterns. He and the novel attend to them—their form, their function, their causes and effects, their every nuance—as they would attend to a complex work of art. One might say that these socially circulating patterns of speech are the raw materials available for crafting or figuring a first person in different circumstances. Various compositional aspects of the novel al-low it to reveal the ways in which the first person of the narrator, like the first person of any of its other characters, is shaped from this very stuff. What is a given first person made of? What is the narrator's first person made of? How is it pieced together out of enunciations that gain it a place in a social universe? The turning point of *Sodom and Gomorrah I* is a fine moment to look at in order to grasp how the composition of the novel reveals its interest in the processes of enunciation and figura-tion through which first persons come to be.

Sodom and Gomorrah I, the part of the *Recherche* that caused so much talk
in Parisian literary circles when it was published in May 1921 at the end
of the volume that also contained *Le Côté de Guermantes II*, begins with
a sort of temporal hiccup:

> The reader will remember that, well before going that day (the day on
> which the Princesse de Guermantes's reception was to be held) to pay the
> Duke and Duchess the visit I have just described, I had kept watch for their
> return and in the course of my vigil had made a discovery which concerned
> M. de Charlus in particular but was in itself so important that I have until
> now, until the moment when I could give it the prominence and treat it
> with the fullness that it demanded, postponed giving an account of it. (1)

> [On sait que bien avant d'aller ce jour-là (le jour où avait lieu la soirée de la
> princesse de Guermantes) rendre au duc et à la duchesse la visite que je
> viens de raconter, j'avais épié leur retour et fait, pendant la durée de mon
> guet, une découverte, concernant particulièrement M. de Charlus, mais si
> importante en elle-même que j'ai jusqu'ici, jusqu'au moment de pouvoir
> lui donner la place et l'étendue voulues, différé de la rapporter. (3:3)]

What, specifically, about the prominent placement of this discovery are we
meant to notice? What is the role of the novel's composition at this point?

The sentence just cited refers back to a moment near the end of *Le
Côté de Guermantes II* (a passage that would have been in the same
volume for Proust's first readers, although it is in a separate volume for
most of today's readers) when the narrator has just received an invitation to the evening party to be given by the Princess de Guermantes.
Sufficiently unsure of his own social standing to entertain doubts regarding the invitation's authenticity, he is hoping to be able to ask either
the Duke or the Duchess de Guermantes, with whom he is already
acquainted (and who live in the same building as his family), to verify
the authenticity of the invitation. The Duke and Duchess have been
away vacationing in Cannes, but as luck would have it, on the very
morning of the party the narrator learns of their return. Alas, he also
learns that they have already left the house for the morning. Demands
on his time apparently being few, he decides to occupy himself with
watching the entryway to the building so he will know first-hand of the
moment of their return:

Now this wait on the staircase was to have for me consequences so considerable, and to reveal to me so important a landscape, no longer Turneresque but moral, that it is preferable to postpone the account of it for a little while by interposing first that of my visit to the Guermantes when I knew that they had come home. (786)

[Or cette attente sur l'escalier devait avoir pour moi des conséquences si considérables et me découvrir un paysage non plus turnérien mais moral si important, qu'il est préférable d'en retarder le récit de quelques instants, en le faisant précéder d'abord par celui de la visite que je fis aux Guermantes dès que j'appris qu'ils étaient rentrés. (2:861)]

Le Côté de Guermantes moves directly on at this point to the account of the narrator's visit to the Guermantes with no further mention of what he has discovered while sitting on the stairs, the discovery he saves for later, at the beginning of *Sodom and Gomorrah I*. A number of aspects of this displacement and the way the novel highlights it for us provide insight into the particular predicaments of the narrator's first person.

The *Recherche* is famous for the temporal twists and turns in its manner of arranging and recounting the past, and Gérard Genette's *Narrative Discourse* has provided one of the most thorough formal accounts of this aspect of Proust's novel, along with an elaborate terminology with which to describe, among the various formal aspects of the *Recherche*, those he labels its "anachronies."[3] The specific terms that apply to the situation at hand would be an "ellipsis" of the particular moment skipped over toward the end of *Le Côté de Guermantes II*, so that the opening of *Sodom and Gomorrah I* becomes a brief "internal homodiegetic analepsis" (51), a movement backward to fill in the stretch of time that had been skipped over. Genette in fact comments about the hiccup in question that it "is obviously motivated by the narrator's desire to have done with the properly worldly aspect of the 'Guermantes way' before approaching what he calls the 'moral landscape' of Sodom and Gomorrah" (72). It's not clear to me, first of all, that the *narrator's* "desire" should ever be taken as sufficient motivation for a decision regarding the formal construction of the novel. Second, whatever the narrator may say or desire, there is, pace Genette, no obvious shift at this point in the novel from "worldly" aspects to "moral" ones, from social analysis to an analysis of sexuality. For instance, in *Sodom and Gomorrah II* the novel returns—during the scene at the Princess's party—to its previous concerns with the "worldly." Further, toward the end of the earlier volume, *Le Côté de Guermantes II*, we find a bizarre, comic, and emotionally tumultuous seduction scene between Charlus and the narrator, a sexualized reading of which (as we shall see shortly) is provided retrospectively by a few sentences in *Sodom and Gomorrah I*. The novel makes no clear division between its concern with social analysis and the issue of sexuality; it assumes no separation, analytic or thematic, between the two topics. To the contrary, it suggests particularly strongly, by the way it is composed, that the two cannot be understood in isolation.

There is a general interpretative question here, and the novel calls it to our attention by way of the opening gambit of *Sodom and Gomorrah I*: How is a reader to understand and render meaningful the way certain passages are woven into the novel, where they are placed, how they are approached, how they are framed? As it happens, to understand these structural questions is, for a reading of Proust, at least as important as dwelling on what transpires in any given passage. Why, we might ask, in this specific case, was the recounting of the observed sexual encounter between Charlus and Jupien delayed so as to take place just before the long scene at the Princess de Guermante's party that opens *Sodom and Gomorrah II*? We find an answer to this question not so much by distinguishing between the "wordly" and the "moral" aspects of the novel as by showing their interrelation, by situating the novel's analysis of sexuality within its larger set of sociological interests.

As we know from the list Proust sent to Louis d'Albufera in 1908 (cited in the preceding chapter), Proust was in that year, as he came to imagine what his novel would be, thinking of composing an essay on pederasty as well as a novel about Paris and a study of the nobility. In early 1909 he drafted a set of reflections, along with a title "La Race des tantes" (The Race of Aunties—or Fairies), which together constitute an early version of many of the narrator's general reflections on inverts that occur in the course of *Sodom and Gomorrah I*.[4] "La Race des tantes" was, in its original state, a set of reflections arising from the narrator's observation of the face of the sleeping M. de Guercy (an early avatar of Charlus). In the published novel, those general reflections follow upon the narrative account offered by the narrator of his discovery of Charlus's sexuality, an account, to be precise, of himself spying on Charlus and Jupien having sex. In Proust's notebooks from 1909 we can also find a draft of an encounter between the Marquess de Guercy (or Gurcy, or later Fleurus) and a florist named Borniche, an early version of the encounter between Charlus and Jupien.[5] Originally, there was no link between the two men's meeting (which did not yet include a sexual encounter) and the essayistic reflections on inversion provoked by the vision of Guercy's sleeping face. As Antoine Compagnon notes in his helpful commentary in the Pléiade edition of *Sodom and Gomorrah*, it is hard to know exactly when in the gestation of the novel Proust decided to bring these two elements together, the essayistic (or, we might say, the pseudo-sociological digression) and the narrative, just as it is hard to know where in the novel's progression the sexual encounter (with or without the essayistic reflections) would end up being placed. Speaking of the state of affairs in 1912, shortly before the first volume of the *Recherche* was published, Compagnon notes: "As of 1912, the context of the meeting between Charlus and Jupien remains unknown, as does its novelistic function, for "La Race des tantes" was introduced by the vision of the sleeping M. de Gurcy . . . Charlus's meeting with Jupien . . . would make for a more dramatic opening onto the world of inversion, but if it had no connection with the essay, where would it have been placed?" (3:1220). Compagnon makes the case that it is around 1916, the date at which a clean manuscript of *Sodom and Gomorrah* is produced, that Proust first situates the meeting of Charlus and Jupien between the visit to the Duchess in the afternoon and the party at the Princess's that evening. Even so, Proust would still do a great deal of revising between 1916 and 1921 and 1922, when the two parts of *Sodom and Gomorrah* would finally be published, and many of his latest revisions bear importantly on the way in which *Sodom and Gomorrah I* is textually linked both to what precedes it in the final scenes of *Le Côté de Guermantes II* and to what follows it in the opening scene of *Sodom and Gomorrah II*. I wish to call attention to the function of these compositional links in revealing the narrator's labor of constructing and maintaining a first person with social ambitions and with a strong relation to same-sex sexuality.

Compagnon notes one of the major directions of the revisions that took place between 1916 and 1921:

In the manuscript, Charlus is the only representative of the accursed race which, after 1916, would become all-encompassing: Vaugoubert appears on one of the pieces of paper attached to the manuscript; a notation in notebook 62 goes so far as to suggest a youthful liaison between him and Norpois. The liaison between Nissim Bertrand and the employee of the Grand-Hôtel, Charlus's rendez-vous with a footman, his correspondence with Aimé—all of this appears together on one long attachment to the manuscript. The Duke de Châtellerault is invented even later still, as is the liaison between the Prince de Guermantes and Morel. (3:1249–50)

Châtellerault figures most prominently in the opening pages of *Sodom and Gomorrah II*, but in one of the latest revisions to *Sodom and Gomorrah I* (a revision made sometime between late 1919 and 1921), a specific mention of him is added, a compositional link between the two sections of *Sodom and Gomorrah II*. The reasons for this link are worth speculating about.[6]

Indeed, most of the pages in *Sodom and Gomorrah I* in which the narrator reports a conversation he overhears between Charlus and Jupien after they have finished having sex (pages that contain the earlier reference to Châtellerault) are among the late additions to the text. These pages also contain a reference by Charlus to the narrator, a reference that refers *back* to the highly charged confrontation between the two of them toward the end of *Le Côté de Guermantes II*. This link, too, I wish to dwell on a bit, along with two other moments in the text: the description of the narrator crossing the courtyard in order to spy upon Charlus and Jupien having sex (also one of the latest additions to the text), and the revelation, in *Sodom and Gomorrah II*, that the narrator, even before the afternoon in which he sees Charlus and Jupien having sex, had, in a particularly testy moment, claimed to his parents that Charlus had propositioned him in an inappropriate way. In short, I am interested in the ways Proust, once he had decided how to link together the narration of a sexual act between two men with a somewhat Balzacian digression on inversion drafted in 1909, and once he had decided where to position those passages in the novel, then worked to incorporate them, to weave them in, to attach them to what came before and after, giving them a context and making them the context for the text around them.

Consider the following passage from *Sodom and Gomorrah I*, added in early 1921 to the typescript that Proust was revising.[7] Charlus and Jupien have gone into Jupien's shop and closed the door behind them. Our ever-curious narrator recalls that there is a vacant shop for rent in the same building next door to Jupien's. To get there and continue his spying, it would suffice, he tells us, to take the service staircase down from his family's apartment to the basement, traverse the basement until coming to the part of it corresponding to the vacant shop, and take the stairs up to the shop. Were he to do so, no one would be able to observe his movements. This is not, however, the course of action he chooses to follow:

This was the most prudent method. It was not the one that I adopted; instead, keeping close to the walls, I edged my way round the courtyard in the open, trying not to let myself be seen. If I was not, I owe it more, I am sure, to chance than to my own sagacity. And for the fact that I took so imprudent a course, when the way through the cellar was so safe, I can see three possible reasons, assuming that I had any reason at all. (10)

[C'était le moyen le plus prudent. Ce ne fut pas celui que j'adoptai, mais longeant les murs, je contournai à l'air libre la cour en tâchant de ne pas être vu. Si je ne le fus pas, je pense que je le dois plus au hasard qu'à ma sagesse. Et au fait que j'aie pris un parti si imprudent, quand le cheminement dans la cave était si sûr, je vois trois raisons possibles, à supposer qu'il y en ait une. (3:9)]

The three reasons the narrator then gives in trying to arrive at an understanding of the motivations for his own actions are intriguing in their own right. But rather than moving into a psychological analysis of the narrator's explanatory hypotheses for his own actions, we might just notice that he feels it appropriate to offer such hypotheses, thereby suggestively calling our attention to the opacity of his own psychology to his narrating self, an opacity that might seem less odd were it not the case that other characters' thought and motivations are sometimes all too transparent to him. Now the kinds of incoherence found in the patterns of limited knowledge versus omniscience in the narration of the *Recherche* are well known. Genette has discussed them in *Narrative Discourse* and summarized the general theoretical problem in his *Narrative Discourse Revisited*. Proust's narrator disobeys (with a fair amount of abandon) the conventions that usually correspond to what Genette has labeled homodiegetic and heterodiegetic narration:

> As for the homodiegetic narrator, he is obliged to justify ("How do you know that?") the information he gives about scenes from which "he" was absent as a character, about someone else's thoughts, etc., and any breach of that trust is a paralepsis. This is manifestly the situation for Bergotte's dying thoughts, which absolutely no one but Bergotte could know, and it is less distinctly the situation for many other people's thoughts, which there is little likelihood of Marcel's ever having come to know. We could therefore say that homodiegetic narrative, as a consequence of its "vocal" selection, submits a priori to a modal restriction, one that can be sidestepped only by an infraction, or a perceptible distortion.[8]

The narrator of Proust's novel sometimes does not know about himself, his motivations, and his actions, the kinds of things he appears to have no trouble knowing about many other people—such as Châtellerault, as we shall see shortly.

Of the narrator's description of his bizarre behavior crossing the courtyard and of his bizarre contortions in offering explanations for it, we should also simply note that they *are* bizarre, and that they thereby encourage us to wonder about the status, the "reliability," to use a standard term, of the narrator.[9] We might also note an important set of verbal echoes that occur barely a page later, in the short paragraph in which the narrator reflects on the foolishness of Charlus and Jupien in imagining that they had somehow successfully entered into a private space in which to have sex when they closed the door to Jupien's shop behind them:

> But when I was inside the shop, taking care not to let the wooden floor make the slightest creak, as I realised that the least sound in Jupien's shop could be heard from mine, I thought to myself how rash Jupien and M. de Charlus had been, and how luck had favoured them. (11)

> [Mais quand je fus dans la boutique, évitant de faire craquer le moins du monde le plancher, en me rendant compte que le plus léger bruit dans la boutique de Jupien s'entendait de la mienne, je songeai combien Jupien et M. de Charlus avaient été imprudents et combien la chance les avait servis. (3:10)]

Notable here is the shared imprudence of Jupien and Charlus in the shop and the narrator traversing the courtyard ("so imprudent a course"), as well as their shared luck at escaping observation ("I edged my way round the courtyard in the open, trying not to let myself be seen. If I was not, I owe it more, I am sure, to chance than to my own sagacity")—except that, of course, the narrator *has* seen Charlus and Jupien. (What the narrator knows—or so he would have us believe— apparently does not count socially, as if he, like an omniscient narrator, were not part of the social world that apparently includes all the un- known people who might have looked out their windows to see him sneaking around the courtyard, or who might have been shocked to see what Charlus and Jupien were getting up to.) We might then say that through its verbal patternings the text of the novel associates the narra- tor with Charlus and Jupien in a way the narrator himself does not explicitly acknowledge. We are left to make sense of an association that may be beyond the narrator's grasp.

Proust's novel makes a habit of giving us reasons to mistrust the narrator—who knows what he shouldn't and doesn't know what he should, who is constructed as a figure by the same language in which he attempts to figure those around him. That is, there are both psychological (representational) and formal reasons (and probably other kinds as well) for not taking the narrator at face value. The many reasons for being troubled by the narrative instance located in Proust's narrator always seem intensified when sexuality is being foregrounded in the novel. Here is the narrator standing in the shop next to Jupien's listening to the noises made by Jupien and Charlus as they have sex:

> I did not dare move. The Guermantes groom, taking advantage no doubt of his master's absence, had, as it happened, transferred to the shop in which I now stood a ladder which hitherto had been kept in the coach-house, and if I had climbed this I could have opened the fanlight above and heard as well as if I had been in Jupien's shop itself. But I was afraid of making a noise. Besides, it was unnecessary. . . . Finally, after about half an hour (during which time I had stealthily hoisted myself up my ladder so as to peep through the fanlight which I did not open), the Baron emerged and a conversation began. Jupien refused with insistence the money that M. de Charlus was trying to press upon him. (11–12)

> [Je n'osais bouger. Le palefrenier des Guermantes, profitant sans doute de leur absence, avait bien transféré dans la boutique où je me trouvais une échelle serrée jusque-là dans la remise. Et si j'y étais monté j'aurais pu ouvrir le vasistas et entendre comme si j'avais été chez Jupien même. Mais je craignais de faire du bruit. Du reste c'était inutile. . . . Enfin au bout d'une demi-heure environ (pendant laquelle je m'étais hissé à pas de loup sur mon échelle afin de voir par le vasistas que je n'ouvris pas), une conversation s'engagea. Jupien refusait avec force l'argent que M. de Charlus voulait lui donner. (3:10–11)]

Again, the narrator's luck (this time at finding the ladder present) is notable, as is his unreliability.[10] He could almost be said to be lying when he writes, "If I had climbed this I could have opened the fanlight above and heard," for it turns out he *does* climb the ladder, even if he doesn't open the window, because he can hear anyway. In any case he can, as it turns out, *see* the two men, and yet he represents for us nothing visual about their sex together (only the sounds of it) even though, as soon as the sex is over, he returns to a combined visual and aural account, telling us of movements he sees and words he hears:

Then M. de Charlus took one step outside the shop. "Why do you have your chin shaved like that," asked the other in a caressing tone. "It's so becoming, a nice beard." "Ugh! It's disgusting," the Baron replied. Meanwhile he still lingered on the threshold and plied Jupien with questions about the neighborhood. (12)

[Puis M. de Charlus fit un pas hors de la boutique. «Pourquoi avez-vous votre menton rasé comme cela, dit-il au baron d'un ton de câlinerie. C'est si beau une belle barbe!—Fi! c'est dégoutant», répondit le baron. Cependant il s'attardait encore sur le pas de la porte et demandait à Jupien des renseignements sur le quartier. (3:11)]

The ladder and the little window bear some thinking about. They are, on the one hand, the props of the instance of narration. They remind us of conventions regarding first-person narration. And yet the narrator is almost willing to lie about his use of props and about their necessity. They render plausible his access to visual information about the scene in question, and yet he pretends for a significant amount of time that he is too scared of making noise to use them, either to hear better or to see. He then admits shamelessly that he has used them, that he had been *watching* a scene he has just narrated as if he had only been *hearing* it.[11]

Here it is by means of the ladder on which the narrator stands in order to see what he at first claims only to hear that the novel calls attention to its own scaffolding, to the status of the narrator's knowledge, to the absence of similar ladders in other circumstances where the narrator probably "realistically" had as great a need for them. The ladder stands, we might say, at the crux of the first and third person vectors in the novel.[12]

Mario Lavagetto makes the argument, in *Chambre 43: Un Lapsus de Marcel Proust*, that the particularly uneasy relation of the first person to omniscience in Proust has to do with Proust's attitude toward sexuality, his decision to write a first-person novel in which confusion would intentionally be created as to the relation of the author to the narrator, in which there would be a palpable tension between a desire to represent homosexuality in the novel, and his desire to mask his own homosexuality:

In the *Recherche*, the narrator (call him an autodiegetic one if you wish) obstinately and painstakingly situates *I*, who is on two occasions named Marcel,—even if "*I* is not (or is not always) me"—*outside* the space of homosexuality. When he assigns him a role as spy or as spectator who, through windows, dividing walls, bull's eye windows, fanlights, manages to see the consummation of a homosexual relation without himself being seen, no scruple, no descriptive detail in the setting of the scene, no qualification is neglected in order to vouch for and justify the circumstances that allow for the testimony.[13]

Lavagetto takes great pleasure at the close of his book in revealing a misstep in what is for him Proust's careful strategy of self-protection, a misstep that occurs in the novel's final volume. Lavagetto points to a particular inconsistency that finds its way into the scenes in the male brothel found there. The narrator takes a room in the brothel (room 43) in order to rest and drink a glass of cassis. Charlus (in room 14b) is engaged in a sexual encounter the narrator will once again overhear and spy upon. Yet some pages later the narrator refers to Charlus's room as room 43, that is, as the room given to the narrator. This is, for Lavagetto, a "catastrophic" slip: "Proust's scheme falls to pieces. Marcel escapes from his control; for once *I* finds himself *inside* the homosexual scene and all the maneuvers by way of which his position had so rigorously been determined turn out to have been in vain" (119).

About Lavagetto's conclusion, Compagnon remarks that it's not obvious "whether it is a slip on the part of the narrator or of the author." He goes on: "In fact the only way in which the substitution of 43 for 14b might be interesting is if we could be sure that it was not a slip of Proust's but a clue the author intentionally placed for the reader, intending it to be taken as a slip on the part of the narrator."[14] Often discussions of the relation of the narrator and the author in Proust remain simple attempts to adjudicate to whom the first person refers at this or that moment, or to whom intentionality (conscious or unconscious) can be assigned, where the possibilities envisioned are either Proust or the narrator, and where sometimes the narrator is divided into different selves corresponding to different moments in the time span covered by the novel and its writing. Yet to imagine that such questions circumscribe the novel's interest in the functioning of the first person would be too limiting. There is, in the *Recherche*, a constant interest in the linguistic, social, and sociological functioning of the first person, the pragmatic and metapragmatic aspects of its invocation and assumption. To get at these other forms of interest in the first person requires closer attention to structural details in the novel. We have seen that the novel associates the narrator, Charlus, and Jupien by way of the different forms of imprudence and luck associated with their enactment of impulsive behaviors that would not normally bear public scrutiny. Charlus and Jupien are lucky, we might say, to have found this particular narrator and this particular novel: a novel whose narrator's motives are open to question, allowing us to ponder what he gains (and what the novel gains) by representing what he represents, and when, and how; a novel that in its very form (its hybrid use of first- and third-person conventions) asks us to notice the differing ways in which distinct sets of novelistic conventions permit events and acts that are meant not to be public to be represented, asks us to question how the narrator of the novel and the novel's own analytic projects are forged within these criss-crossing conventions, and how the narrator's social and representational ambitions and the novel's analysis of them and of him are all enabled by the novel's narrative form.

Speaking about the Eulenburg Affair Before It Happens

"My single concern is composition" [Je n'ai qu'un souci, qui est la composition], Proust wrote to Jacques Boulenger in November 1921, a month in which he was working on the final corrections to *Sodom and Gomorrah II*. He continues,

> But since I had the misfortune to begin my book with I and it hasn't been possible to change that, I am "subjective" *in aeternum*. Had I begun instead: "Roger Beauclerc, who lived in a house, etc.," I would have been classed as objective.

> [Mais comme j'ai eu le malheur de commencer mon livre par Je et que je ne pouvais plus changer, je suis «subjectif» *in aeternum*. J'aurais commencé à la place: «Roger Beauclerc occupant un pavillon, etc.», j'étais classé objectif.][15]

I am proposing that we consider what kinds of meaning might reside within what Proust here calls the "composition" of his novel, how that composition might help us think in objective terms about the novel's study of the assumption of a first person. Consider, for another moment, the narrator perched on top of his ladder. We are never specifically told when he comes down from there. It appears he stays long enough to hear and see the sexual act between Charlus and Jupien and then also to overhear their subsequent conversation. It might almost seem that the version of the 1909 essay "La Race des tantes" that Proust

incorporates at this juncture in the novel (just after the postcoital conversation of Charlus and Jupien) is presented to the reader as if it were
going through the narrator's mind as he sits on top of the ladder having
just watched Charlus and Jupien have sex, and having just listened to
them converse. What meaning is there in the fact that the novel is
composed in this way? Perhaps these aspects of the novel's composition
—the weaving together of the narrated sex scene with the digression on
"men-women" and the ways in which the scene and the essayistic
passage themselves are woven into the novel as a whole—are what will
allow us to pursue a querying of the more "objective" side of the novel:
who (what kind of a person) would think *that* (what the digression says)
about (as the narrator puts it) "what is sometimes, most ineptly, termed
homosexuality" (9) [ce qu'on appelle parfois fort mal l'homosexualité
(3:9)]? Who would say what the digression says in the way it says it, and
why? To whom is the digression addressed, and to what end? The
statement that "you can say anything as long as you never say: *I*" can
mean many things, but surely *one* of the things it means (one of the
ways it is instantiated in Proust's novel) is not that a novelist can't *use* the
first person, but that the first person has to be used objectively. The
conditions of its use in this or that context have to be part of what is at
stake. "I," thought about in this way, is never simply used so that "I" can
say what it means, meant, or will mean. Rather any "I" enacts statements whose social force or social meaning are also part of the novel's
subject: "I say *me* because . . ." The space of Proust's novel becomes a
space in which that which an "I" can say (and also what it *cannot* say)
echoes long enough for us to begin to appreciate the pragmatics and the
metapragmatics of the enunciation—the social structure in which it
occurs and intervenes, the social structure it enacts in the place of its
speaking, the social project it engages as it speaks, the social project that
grounds and enables the first person. This is what we might think of as
the sociological work of *voicing* in Proust's novel. In the previous chapter, in watching a passage on Oscar Wilde and Balzac move from one of
Proust's own letters to the drafts for *Contre Sainte-Beuve* and then into
the voice of Charlus in the *Recherche*, we had to take account of the
significance of the work of voicing and the work of context on the
meaning and effects of the passage in question. Just so do we have to
work to understand the shift in meaning of "La Race des tantes," a text
written in 1909, when it is finally woven into a novelistic composition a
number of years later.

Those 1909 comments find their appropriate place in the *Recherche* due to the compositional efforts of Proust apparently sometime around 1916; the work of linking the various parts of the text of *Sodom and Gomorrhe I* together and also to the surrounding volumes goes on until 1921. Within the novel's own chronology, the episode recounted in *Sodom and Gomorrah I* itself seems to take place sometime around the year 1900.[16] Critics have, of course, noted that while the internal chronology of the *Recherche* makes it seem probable that the events of *Sodom and Gomorrah I* and *II* happen in and around 1900, it is also the case that within those volumes characters make references to events that happen later. A salient example of this is Charlus's references in *Sodom and Gomorrah II*, while dining with Mme. Verdurin's other summer guests, to the Eulenburg Affair, which dates from 1907–8 (471, 3:338).

The Eulenburg Affair and the publicity surrounding it (which Proust credited with making the word *homosexualité* acceptable within the French language, a word he disliked because it sounded too German)[17] constitute an important moment in the history of the representation of male same-sex sexuality in Europe and of the shifting consequences of such representations. It has often been noted that the Eulenburg Affair was one of the key catalysts in the development of Proust's vision of the *Recherche*.[18] In recent commentary on the Eulenburg Affair, there is an understandable tendency to contextualize it and the trials to which it led in relation to other trials and scandals bearing on sex between men (Wilde in England in 1895, Adelswärd-Fersen in France in 1903, and so on).[19] They can all be claimed as evidence of an effort to repress same-sex sexuality and speech about it, an effort in some ways self-defeating. For even if those brought to trial did indeed suffer various forms of ignominy and punishment, such trials also invariably produced sufficient publicity about the sexual behaviors in question so as to seem counterproductive as part of an effort intended to quash discourse about and the practice of those sexualities.

Each of these trials also takes place in its own national context and can be understood as revealing quite *different* things about the way sex between men is situated and can be made use of within different national contexts. In the first of the trials in the Eulenburg Affair, just as in the first of the Wilde trials, someone accused of immoral sexual behavior (the Count von Moltke) accuses someone else of libel (the journalist Maximilian Harden). In a series of articles, Harden had implied that Moltke and Eulenburg—close friends of Kaiser Wilhelm and important figures in diplomatic and military circles—were involved in improper kinds of relations with other men. But, however similar this may sound to

Wilde's case (the first move in his legal trajectory was a failed libel trial against Alfred Douglas's father), there are many differences as well. For instance, Harden, the journalist who manufactured the Eulenburg scandal, while he had for many years been an enemy of Eulenburg's, had not always been hostile to men with a sexual interest in other men. As James D. Steakley notes, "Harden's mordent attacks on Eulenburg are particularly noteworthy because they signalled a complete about-face. In 1898, Harden had become the first German editor to support the campaign for homosexual emancipation led by Hirschfeld. . . . He claimed that the flood of hate mail he received during the Eulenburg Affair from homosexuals in all walks of life convinced him that this tolerance was entirely misplaced."[20] As in Wilde's case, there would be a series of trials in the Eulenburg Affair, and certain principals would go to jail. But even though the trials brought a lot of attention to a well-established same-sex sexual culture among German aristocrats, diplomats, and military figures, Harden's motivation for provoking the scandal had little to do with his feelings about the sexual practices of those involved. Rather, he objected to the foreign policy Eulenburg was working to further. It was apparently too Francophilic and not interested enough in pursuing projects related to Germany's own colonial ambitions. The breaking point for Harden was apparently the Algeciras Conference in 1906, which took place to mediate between competing French and German colonialist claims in Morocco. Harden suggested in print that because the French Ambassador Raymond Lecomte was a "friend" of Eulenburg's, the French ambassador had gained access ahead of time to information that allowed the French to come out of the mediation at Algeciras with things settled in their favor.[21] (The Algeciras Conference was also a key moment in the ongoing history of shifting European alliances in the early twentieth century. France, having retreated from Fachoda and conceded to England free reign in Egypt, was supported by England against Germany as regards Morocco.) Harden turned to what he knew about Eulenburg and Moltke's sexuality, and to what he knew publicity about that sexuality could achieve, in order to pursue political goals related to foreign policy.

What Proust might have learned from his careful attention to the Eulenburg Affair, then, was that a certain long-standing aristocratic same-sex sexual culture was no longer protected by aristocratic privilege. It was vulnerable to attack in newspapers and in courts of law. Certain rules of the game had changed. Certain contexts had shifted. Certain kinds of self-presentation were becoming untenable. New speaking positions from which new kinds of influence could be wielded had become available. Nonaristocratic social agents supporting nationalist projects, when they came up against the entrenched power of aristocrats in diplomatic circles, could use knowledge of same-sex sexual practices in aristocratic circles together with the institutions of the modern press to challenge the social standing and thereby the political programs of influential aristocrats.

Consider in this regard the moment in *Sodom and Gomorrah II* when Charlus, in an attempt to attach the musician Morel to him more tightly, invents a duel he says he is going to fight to protect Morel's reputation. In order to sustain his fiction, Charlus goes as far as to ask Cottard to be his second and is obliged then to thank him for this imaginary service:

> M. de Charlus, desirous of showing his gratitude to the Doctor, just as the Duke his brother might have straightened the collar of my father's greatcoat or rather as a duchess might put her arm around the waist of a plebeian lady, brought his chair close to the Doctor's, notwithstanding the distaste which the latter inspired in him. And, not only without any physical pleasure, but having first to overcome a physical repulsion—as a Guermantes, not as an invert—in taking leave of the Doctor he clasped his hand and caressed it for a moment with the kindly affection of a master stroking his horse's nose and giving it a lump of sugar. But Cottard, who had never allowed the Baron to see that he had so much as heard the vaguest rumours as to his morals, but nevertheless regarded him in his heart of hearts as belonging to the category of "abnormals" . . . imagined that this stroking of his hand was the immediate prelude to an act of rape for the accomplishment of which . . . he had been enticed into a trap and led by the Baron into this remote apartment where he was about to be forcibly outraged. (642)

> [M. de Charlus désireux de témoigner sa reconnaissance au docteur [Cottard], de la même façon que M. le duc son frère eût arrangé le col du paletot de mon père, comme une duchesse surtout eût tenu la taille à une plébéienne, approcha sa chaise tout près de celle du docteur, malgré le dégoût que celui-ci lui inspirait. Et non seulement sans plaisir physique, mais surmontant une répulsion physique, en Guermantes, non en inverti, pour dire adieu au docteur il lui prit la main et la lui caressa un moment avec une bonté de maître flattant le museau de son cheval et lui donnant du sucre. Mais Cottard qui n'avait jamais laissé voir au baron qu'il eût même entendu courir de vagues mauvais bruits sur ses moeurs, et ne l'en considérait pas

moins dans son for intérieur, comme faisant partie de la classe des «anor-
maux» . . . se figura que cette carresse de la main était le prélude immédiat
d'un viol pour l'accomplissement duquel il avait été . . . attiré dans un guet-
apens et conduit par le baron dans ce salon solitaire où il allait être pris de
force. (3:458–59)]

This passage reveals a number of things: that Charlus is completely
ensconced within a particular interpretive context for his behavior and is
impervious to the idea that his behavior might be interpreted in any
other light; similarly that Cottard, operating within a notably different
context, arrives at a competing interpretation of Charlus's behavior that
he also does not conceive of as open to challenge; that the narrator, as
usual, presents himself as the objective arbiter of the separate contexts—
to neither of which (the pathologizing bourgeois interpretive grid of
Cottard on the one hand and Charlus's condescending framework of
aristocratic privilege on the other) he apparently, in his objectivity, feels
any attachment; and yet, finally, that his stance of objectivity may well be
one that he cannot control. For as he seemingly incidentally notes ("just
as the Duke his brother might have straightened the collar of my father's
great-coat or rather as a duchess might put her arm around the waist of a
plebeian lady"), Charlus's behavior recalls to him in the first place the
kinds of condescending and probably irritating behavior, however polite
or well-intentioned, that the Duke (Charlus's brother) has shown toward the narrator's father. Or (that first thought set aside, but not fully
covered over by the following), perhaps it would—given Charlus's "inversion"—more appropriately recall the behavior of a condescending
Duchess. The narrator is thus on some level conscious of being marked,
like his father, as plebeian in his relations with the Guermantes, and
further—under the influence of this train of thought about social hierarchies—reveals a habit of mind in which he pathologizes Charlus ever so
slightly by means of reference to the "scientific" model of inversion. The
novel, in the way its sentences are composed, in the way one clause
follows and qualifies another, regularly reveals the reflexes that structure
the narrator's thinking, reflexes the narrator is sometimes aware of,
sometimes not, reflexes the narrator sometimes tries to compensate for
and neutralize in order to establish the objective-seeming speaking
position he so avidly covets.

Here the kinds of complex lessons that Proust could have learned
from the Eulenburg Affair seem especially clear. They have to do not so
much with sexuality per se, but rather with the intersection of a par-

ticular aristocratic sexual culture with an increasingly prevalent popular and bourgeois discourse *about* sexuality per se (about homosexuality more particularly). They have to do with shifting attitudes toward the aristocracy in general, with the cultural force of an increasingly powerful journalistic establishment, and with a varied set of political agendas harboring different ideas about nationalism. (This particular intersection of concerns would obviously not be configured in the same way, nor be producing the same effects, in France, in England, or in Germany.) Harden's actions in the Eulenburg Affair of course demonstrated the political utility and defamatory force of accusations of sexual relations between men. His actions were carefully planned to break down other forms of institutionalized privilege and thereby achieve specific political or social ends. They had the added consequences (just as the Wilde trials did) of producing public discourse about sex between men. As that discourse is produced, so are appropriate, tenable positions for taking up that discourse or that subject matter. What Proust does in *Sodom and Gomorrah* is portray, through the figure of his narrator, the struggles of a young bourgeois man—one with very specific aesthetic and social ambitions—to speak about sex between men: to take up a tenable position, to strike the right figure, to speak in an appropriate register, within the discursive parameters available in a particular Parisian social universe at a moment roughly corresponding to that of the Eulenburg Affair. Learning to talk to Charlus as well as to talk about him (and to and about other men interested in sex between men) forms part of his apprenticeship in self-presentation.

Sex with Charlus?

Proust's novel shows that one's manner of speaking publicly about same-sex sexuality is often of crucial importance in establishing the self one presents to society. This social fact is something the *Recherche* foregrounds compositionally, something it investigates in its own manner of weaving the first part of *Sodom and Gomorrah* together with the second and with the section of *Le Côté de Guermantes* that immediately precedes it. The threads of that weaving are particularly clear in the following passage, which occurs in *Sodom and Gomorrah II*, the narrator having safely arrived at the evening party being given by the Princess de Guermantes, and catching a glimpse of Charlus there:

I might well have asked M. de Charlus to introduce me to the Prince de Guermantes, but I feared (and with good reason) that he might be displeased with me. I had treated him in the most ungrateful fashion by letting his offers pass unheeded for the second time and by giving him no sign of life since the evening when he had so affectionately escorted me home. And yet I could not plead the excuse of having anticipated the scene which I had witnessed that very afternoon enacted by himself and Jupien. I suspected nothing of the sort. It is true that shortly before this, when my parents reproached me for my laziness and for not having taken the trouble to write a line to M. de Charlus, I had accused them of wanting me to accept a degrading proposal. But anger alone, and the desire to hit upon the expression that would be most offensive to them, had dictated this mendacious retort. In reality, I had imagined nothing sensual, nothing sentimental even, underlying the Baron's offers. I had said this to my parents out of pure fantasy. But sometimes the future is latent in us without our knowing it, and our supposedly lying words foreshadow an imminent reality. (53)[22]

[J'aurais bien demandé à M. de Charlus de me présenter au prince de Guermantes, mais je craignais (avec trop de raison) qu'il ne fût fâché contre moi. J'avais agi envers lui de la façon la plus ingrate en laissant pour la seconde fois tomber ses offres et en ne lui donnant pas signe de vie depuis le soir où il m'avait si affectueusement reconduit à la maison. Et pourtant je n'avais nullement comme excuse anticipée la scène que je venais de voir, cet après-midi même, se passer entre Jupien et lui. Je ne soupçonnais rien de pareil. Il est vrai que peu de temps auparavant, comme mes parents me reprochaient ma paresse et de n'avoir pas encore pris la peine d'écrire un mot à M. de Charlus, je leur avais violemment reproché de vouloir me faire accepter des propositions déshonnêtes. Mais seuls la colère, le désir de trouver la phrase qui pouvait leur être le plus désagréable m'avaient dicté cette réponse mensongère. En réalité, je n'avais rien imaginé de sensuel, ni même de sentimental, sous les offres du baron. J'avais dit cela à mes parents comme une folie pure. Mais quelquefois l'avenir habite en nous sans que nous le sachions, et nos paroles qui croient mentir dessinent une réalité prochaine. (3:40)]

It was toward the end of *Le Côté de Guermantes II* that the narrator, after dining with the Duke and Duchess de Guermantes, paid a late-night visit to Charlus at Charlus's own home. That visit includes a rather violent altercation between the narrator and Charlus in which the narrator, in a fit of rage, tramples Charlus's top hat. After their nerves have calmed down again, and their breathing returned to normal, Charlus offers to accompany the narrator home in his own carriage. The passage just cited recalls the odd behavior of the narrator as well as that of Charlus and implicitly poses a question as to how the narrator's already odd behavior around Charlus and his speech about him will be altered by his witnessing the sex scene recounted in *Sodom and Gomorrah I*. But in doing so, it adds an interesting bit of information: even before witnessing Charlus's encounter with Jupien, the narrator had felt some kind of ambivalent attraction and aversion for Charlus that spilled over into a cruel remark the narrator made to his parents with the aim of putting a halt to their efforts to push him in Charlus's direction. The narrator had been slow to offer any formal acknowledgment to Charlus in return for certain of his recent attentions, in particular his offers to serve as the narrator's guide in high society; the narrator's parents had reproached him for this failure in courtesy, and he had, in a fit of pique, justified himself to his parents by accusing Charlus of having sexual designs upon him. He tells us that he held no real belief in the truth of his accusation; it was "une folie pure," pure fantasy. But it was apparently well calculated to silence his parents. The narrator, we might say, is learning (a bit like Harden) to use sexual accusations to other ends, refusing to pursue the alliances his parents suggest to him in the manner they view as appropriate. He clearly has well under control certain insulting ways of speaking about men with sexual interests in other men, or of accusing other men of such interests. Perhaps the encounter he witnesses between Charlus and Jupien does something to call these ways of speaking into question.

There are those who have read the narrator of the *Recherche* as a closeted homosexual, one who slowly provides us with all the clues we need to discover his secret.[23] Certainly the narrator does not do much to sustain the verisimilitude of the *suddenness* of his discovery of Charlus's sexual attraction to other men. His remark to his parents, had it been included in the novel at the moment when it occurred (before he had spied upon Charlus and Jupien) would have rendered that verisimilitude all the more tenuous. Reporting the remark after the fact, at the point where he does, serves to call our attention to the effects speech about sexual relations between men can have in various contexts, as well as to the question of the strategic deployment of such speech. It encourages us to think about the whole of *Sodom and Gomorrah I* as further strategic speech of this kind by the narrator to the reader.

That the narrator tells us of his previous remarks at the moment he recounts his hesitancy about approaching Charlus in order to persuade him to introduce him to the host of the party is also not insignificant. The narrator may have decided he does not want Charlus as his primary guide to high society, but this is not to say he wants no relation to Charlus at all. Here, it appears he would at least welcome him as a friend to speak with in a party full of strangers, and as a source of introductions to other people at the party, including his host. Later episodes make it clear that the narrator carefully cultivates a friendship with Charlus. How is he then to speak of the sexuality of his friend, of its social effects, of its effects on the perception of the baron by those in his social circle and by others in the world, of its effects on the friendship he and the baron construct between them? By way of such questions we can begin to appreciate the complexity of the speaking position that is slowly being put together by and for the narrator in this section of the novel.

A number of other aspects of the scene of discovery in *Sodom and Gomorrah I* contribute to our understanding of the complexity of the narrator's newly found speaking position. While on his ladder in the neighboring room, he hears Charlus tell Jupien of the characteristics of his attraction to younger men:

> With what you might call "young gentlemen," for instance, I feel no desire for physical possession, but I am never satisfied until I have touched them, I don't mean physically, but touched a responsive chord. As soon as, instead of leaving my letters unanswered, a young man starts writing to me incessantly, when he is morally, as it were, at my disposal, I am assuaged, or at least I would be were I not immediately seized with an obsession for another. (15)

> [Pour les jeunes gens du monde par exemple, je ne désire aucune possession physique, mais je ne suis tranquille qu'une fois que je les ai touchés, je ne veux pas dire matériellement, mais touché leur corde sensible. Une fois qu'au lieu de laisser mes lettres sans réponse, un jeune homme ne cesse plus de m'écrire, qu'il est à ma disposition morale, je suis apaisé ou du moins je le serais, si je n'étais bientôt saisi par le souci d'un autre. (3:13)].

Charlus having made this general observation about "les jeunes gens du monde," about young gentlemen, it becomes clear in his subsequent remarks that he divides "jeunes gens" (young men) into a number of different groups. He proceeds to question Jupien regarding his knowledge of the young men "du monde," the "gentle" men who visit the

Guermantes. Jupien recalls one in particular, whom he describes in some detail. Charlus is unable to recognize the person Jupien is describing, but the narrator helpfully informs the reader that Jupien always confuses *brun* (brown-haired) with *blond*. Jupien's substitution of one word for the other in his description of the young man in question has confused Charlus but not the narrator, who says he recognizes the Duke de Châtellerault in Jupien's description. Following this exchange (interesting in its own right as an indicator of the significance of hair color, and in particular of blond hair, as a signifier of aristocracy) Charlus resumes his disquisition about his relation to gentlemen with the words, "Pour revenir aux jeunes gens qui ne sont pas du peuple" [To return to young men not of the lower orders]. Young men who might be "du peuple" (of the lower orders) clearly receive a different form of sexual attention from Charlus. But Charlus has also made a very slight distinction between those young men who are "du monde" (gentlemen—of whom the text's example is the Duke de Châtellerault) and those who "ne sont pas du peuple" (are not of the lower orders), of whom Charlus goes on to give his own specific example:

> At the present moment my head has been turned by a strange little chap, an intelligent little bourgeois fellow who shows with regard to myself a prodigious want of civility. He has absolutely no idea of the prodigious personage that I am, and of the microscopic animalcule that he is in comparison. But what does it matter, the little donkey may bray his head off before my august bishop's mantle. (16)

> [En ce moment j'ai la tête tournée par un étrange petit bonhomme, un intelligent petit bourgeois, qui montre à mon égard une incivilité prodigieuse. Il n'a aucunement la notion du prodigieux personnage que je suis et du microscopique vibrion qu'il figure. Après tout qu'importe, ce petit âne peut braire autant qu'il lui plaît devant ma robe auguste d'évêque. (3:14)]

Here there is another interruption, for Jupien is astonished by Charlus's self-designation as a bishop, requiring Charlus to explain that it is not in this instance a religious designation but a particular titular privilege that he possesses. Interruption aside, it is clear that Charlus is here referring to the narrator—even if the narrator does not directly acknowledge the fact. Not exactly, but almost, for Charlus continues:

> "Besides," he added, *less perhaps by way of conclusion than as a warning*, "this attraction that I feel towards young people who avoid me, from fear of

course, for only their natural respect stops their mouths from crying out to me that they love me, requires in them a superior social position. Even then their feigned indifference may produce nevertheless a directly opposite effect. Fatuously prolonged, it sickens me." (16, my emphasis)

[Du reste, ajouta-t-il *peut-être moins en manière de conclusion que d'avertissement*, cet attrait qu'exercent sur moi les jeunes personnes qui me fuient, par crainte bien entendu, car seul le respect leur ferme la bouche pour me crier qu'elles m'aiment, requiert-il d'elles un rang social éminent. Encore leur feinte indifférence peut-elle produire malgré cela l'effet directement contraire. Sottement prolongée elle m'écoeure. (3:14)]

For whom, we might wonder, does Charlus say this "less perhaps by way of conclusion than as a warning"? Why would Jupien need to be warned about the workings of, the typical evolution of, Charlus's erotic relations with "les jeunes gens qui ne sont pas du peuple"? If Charlus is warning anyone, surely it is the narrator hidden in the next room. Or perhaps we might imagine that in this instance the narrator, on his ladder, feels himself to be addressed by Charlus's words, reassured perhaps, that nothing sexual is required of him, flattered to be considered by Charlus among the eligible young men of the world, sensible to the warning that there is a danger in keeping his distance for too long, worried, perhaps, that he might be disadvantaged given that his "rang social" (as opposed to his elevation on the physical ladder on which he is sitting) is not as eminent or as elevated as that of his competition. In short these overheard remarks would appear to be a key moment in the ongoing negotiation of an appropriate relationship between the narrator and Charlus.

Toward the end of *Sodom and Gomorrah I*, the protocols of the relationship that seems to exist between the two men are emphasized yet again:

There were in fact certain persons whom it was sufficient for him to invite to his house, and to hold for an hour or two under the domination of his talk, for his desire, inflamed by some earlier encounter, to be assuaged. By a simple use of words the conjunction was effected, as simply as it can be among the infusoria. Sometimes, as had doubtless been the case with me on the evening on which I had been summoned by him after the Guermantes dinner-party, the relief was effected by a violent diatribe which the Baron flung in his visitor's face, just as certain flowers, by means of a hidden spring, spray from a distance the disconcerted but unconsciously collaborating insect. (39–40)

[Il y avait en effet certains êtres qu'il lui suffisait de faire venir chez lui, de tenir pendant quelques heures sous la domination de sa parole, pour que son désir, allumé dans quelque rencontre, fût apaisé. Par simples paroles la conjonction était faite aussi simplement qu'elle peut se produire chez les infusoires. Parfois, ainsi que cela lui était sans doute arrivé pour moi le soir où j'avais été mandé par lui après le dîner Guermantes, l'assouvissement avait lieu grâce à une violente semonce que le baron jetait à la figure du visiteur, comme certaines fleurs, grâce à un ressort, aspergent à distance l'insecte inconsciemment complice et décontenancé. (3:30)]

The implicit play between the words *semonce* (diatribe) and *semence* (sperm, seed) is hardly even needed for the narrator to make his point here. He acknowledges an encounter with Charlus (the one involving the destruction of Charlus's top hat) that was apparently sexual for one of the participants (Charlus) and may or may not have been so for the other (the narrator).[24] The encounter might conceivably be part and parcel of the sexual identity and practices of one of those involved and may or may not have anything to do with the sexual identity of the other.[25]

It is a peculiar speaking position we see being constructed for the narrator: that of a young bourgeois man apparently not given to male same-sex sexual practices, but not insensitive to the "beauty" of such practices ("tout m'y sembla empreint de beauté," he ends up saying of Charlus's encounter with Jupien, "everything about it seems marked with beauty" [3:29, 38]); that of a young bourgeois man as capable as anyone like him of giving way to insulting, defamatory responses and retorts about men sexually drawn to other men, but here apparently learning to call those responses and retorts into question, to strategize differently about their deployment; that of a young bourgeois man who is even willing on occasion to provide a friendly context for representations of and speech about male same-sex sexuality.[26] There is a complicated negotiation going on in the novel between the social positions represented by Charlus and by the narrator. One of the things at stake in that negotiation is the extent to which and the ends to which the narrator (and perhaps the novel) will, in his own social career, make use of the ambient ideological currents that carry a hostility to same-sex sexual relations and that provide paradigms for pathologizing and derogatory thinking about "inversion" and the like. This negotiation is part of what makes *Sodom and Gomorrah I* such an interesting compositional moment, for the textual material Proust produced in 1909's "La

Race des tantes" is evidently rife with the unfriendly ambient ideology of its time. It is in the work of weaving that earlier material into a particular moment in the novel, it is in the ways of associating the narrator with that early material and yet also making the moment at which the material is inserted into the novel a key turning point in the development of the narrator's friendship or alliance with Charlus, that the effects of the negotiation between the two men can be perceived. For it is in *Sodom and Gomorrah II* that the narrator and Charlus each learn to ally with the other in something it seems appropriate to call their ongoing friendship, one in which they will each come to understand it to be in their mutual interest to respect something about the social or sexual identities of the other party.

The negotiation between the social positions represented by Charlus and by the narrator is sketched in the novel in many ways, often in ways that pay no respect to the realist narrative conventions according to which the novel only sometimes seems to be written. Thus, in *Sodom and Gomorrah I*, we can take Charlus to be speaking to the narrator, informing him of a set of terms in this negotiation, as the narrator— apparently unbeknownst to Charlus—sits perched on his ladder in the next room; thus the narrator can confirm that he has absorbed this set of terms when he refers a few pages later to what he has come to see as the beauty of the encounter between Charlus and Jupien, and when he acknowledges without hostility that he himself has participated in what was for Charlus a sexual encounter, even if it may or may not have been one for the narrator.[27]

Châtellerault, the Narrator, and the Doorman

In the opening paragraphs of *Sodom and Gomorrah II*, the narrator and the blond-haired Duke de Châtellerault will arrive simultaneously at the door of the Princess de Guermantes. The seeming coincidence is part of the careful composition of this whole section of the novel I have been discussing here. In the coincidence we find the signs of the novel's interest in the way social and sexual interests intersect both in the negotiation of certain personal relations and in the construction of certain social trajectories. Jupien's description of Châtellerault and Charlus's description of the narrator as the "strange little chap" currently fascinating him happen in neighboring sentences in *Sodom and Gomorrah I*. Given their textual proximity there, it seems hardly surprising to find them bumping into each other again a few pages later, arriving at the evening party at exactly the same moment, and entering one on the heels of the other. In the paragraphs describing their entrance to the salon where the Princess's guests are being announced by her doorman, we find arranged in a mutually reinforcing pattern all of the diverse elements of the novel we have encountered so far: its formal play with the conventions of first-person narration; its practice of what Genette referred to as narrative polytonality; its ethnographic interest in the modalities of public sex between men; its social investigation of class relationships; and, in particular, its investigation of the narrator's own social trajectory and the way that trajectory is tied up with the speaking position the narrator assumes regarding sexual relations between men.

The doorman (or usher, as Proust's translators have it) is the key figure through whom all these elements are brought together.[28] Through him the novel is able to associate for us the diverse predicaments of Châtellerault and the narrator as they cross the threshold into the party. For it turns out that the doorman and Châtellerault had met a few days earlier while both were cruising for sex on the Champs-Elysées, and that they engaged in a brief dalliance:

> There was one person who, on that evening as on the previous evenings, had been thinking a great deal about the Duke de Châtellerault, without however suspecting who he was: this was the Princess de Guermantes's usher (styled at the time the "barker"). M. de Châtellerault, so far from being one of the Princess's intimate friends, although he was one of her cousins, had been invited to her house for the first time. . . . Now, a few days earlier, the Princess's usher had met in the Champs-Elysées a young man whom he had found charming but whose identity he had been unable to establish. Not that the young man had not shown himself as obliging as he had been generous. All the favours that the usher had supposed that he would have to bestow upon so young a gentleman, he had on the contrary received. But M. de Châtellerault was as cowardly as he was rash; he was all the more determined not to unveil his incognito since he did not know with whom he was dealing; his fear would have been far greater, although ill-founded, if he had known. He had confined himself to posing as an Englishman, and to all the passionate questions with which he was plied by the usher, desirous to meet again a person to whom he was indebted for so much pleasure and largesse, the Duke had merely replied, from one end of the Avenue Gabriel to the other: "I do not speak French." (46)

[Il y avait quelqu'un qui, ce soir-là comme les précédents, pensait beaucoup au duc de Châtellerault, sans soupçonner du reste qui il était: c'était l'huissier (qu'on appelait dans ce temps-là «l'aboyeur») de Mme de Guermantes. M. de Châtellerault, bien loin d'être un des intimes—comme il était l'un des cousins—de la princesse, était reçu dans son salon pour la première fois. . . . Or, quelques jours auparavant, l'huissier de la princesse avait rencontré dans les Champs-Élysées un jeune homme qu'il avait trouvé charmant mais dont il n'avait pu arriver à établir l'identité. Non que le jeune homme ne se fût montré aussi aimable que généreux. Toutes les faveurs que l'huissier s'était figuré avoir à accorder à un monsieur si jeune, il les avait au contraire reçues. Mais M. de Châtellerault était aussi froussard qu'imprudent; il était d'autant plus décidé à ne pas dévoiler son incognito qu'il ignorait à qui il avait à faire; il aurait eu une peur bien plus grande—quoique mal fondée—s'il l'avait su. Il s'était borné à se faire passer pour un Anglais, et à toutes les questions passionnées de l'huissier désireux de retrouver quelqu'un à qui il devait tant de plaisir et de largesses, le duc s'était borné à répondre, tout le long de l'avenue Gabriel: «*I do not speak french.*» (3:35)]

The first question to spring to mind might be, of course, *How could the narrator know all this?* Perhaps a better version of that question (for someone attuned to the novel's iconoclastic way of vacillating between the conventions of first- and third-person narration) would be, *Why does the narration suddenly choose at this point to borrow from the conventions of third-person narration?* Lavagetto has already insisted upon this moment's oddity: "This narrator . . . at the moment of the Princess de Guermantes's reception, is suddenly endowed with miraculous and mysterious gifts. The narrator is all at once able not only to guess at, but also to *see*—to read as in the pages of an open book—the deep emotion of a servant at the moment he announces the Duke de Châtellerault who, a few days earlier, had approached him on the Champs-Elysées."[29] Rather than following Lavagetto and thinking about this passage in terms of the narrator's habit of being suspiciously overinformed about a sexual culture in which he claims not to be a participant, we might step back and wonder what the novel achieves by doing whatever is necessary in order to be able to juxtapose the scene of the narrator's own passage past the doorman with that of Châtellerault's.

Clearly the narrator does, at this point, reveal a great deal of knowledge about the shared sexual culture in which Châtellerault and the doorman both move: the narrator knows the location of their cruising areas, knows that encounters there are often anonymous, that they sometimes (but not always) involve people from widely separated social milieus, often involve the exchange of money, often involve sexual acts in which the roles are distributed according to the age of the participants. The narrator also seems to know that in the case of the encounter between the Duke and the doorman, the distribution of roles was atypical. Money seems to have changed hands in their encounter, but not in the direction that the doorman would have expected. We might surmise that the doorman is used to paying younger men for the privilege of servicing them, whereas in this case he was paid by the generous Châtellerault, who also "amiably" and unexpectedly satisfied the doorman's physical desires.

It is easy to understand the unpleasant shock Châtellerault is about to receive as he notices the doorman, realizes who he is, and is forced to tell him what name to announce. It is both odd and noteworthy that the narrator should insist that his own predicament both does and does not resemble Châtellerault's. Still not sure he has truly been invited to the Princess's party as he faces the doorman in his turn, the narrator comments on the "function—terrible to me, although not in the same sense as to M. de Châtellerault—of this usher garbed in black like an executioner" [fonctions terribles pour moi—quoique d'une autre façon que pour M. de Châtellerault—de cet huissier habillé de noir comme un bourreau]:

> But from the first moment the usher had recognised him. In another instant he would know the identity of this stranger, which he had so ardently desired to learn. When he asked his "Englishman" of the other evening what name he was to announce, the usher was not merely stirred, he considered that he was being indiscreet, indelicate. He felt that he was about to reveal to the whole world (which would, however, suspect nothing) a secret which it was criminal of him to ferret out like this and to proclaim in public. Upon hearing the guest's reply: "Le Duc de Châtellerault," he was overcome with such pride that he remained for a moment speechless. The Duke looked at him, recognised him, saw himself ruined, while the servant, who had recovered his composure and was sufficiently versed in heraldry to complete for himself an appellation that was too modest, roared with a professional vehemence softened with intimate tenderness: "Son Altesse Monseigneur le Duc de Châtellerault!" But now it was my turn to be announced. . . . The usher asked me my name, and I gave it to him as mechanically as the condemned man allows himself to be

strapped to the block. At once he lifted his head majestically and, before I could beg him to announce me in a lowered tone so as to spare my own feelings if I were not invited and those of the Princess de Guermantes if I were, roared the disquieting syllables with a force capable of bringing down the roof. (49–50)

[Mais dès le premier instant l'huissier l'avait reconnu. Cette identité qu'il avait tant désiré d'apprendre, dans un instant il allait la connaître. En demandant à son «Anglais» de l'avant-veille quel nom il devait annoncer, l'huissier n'était pas seulement ému, il se jugeait indiscret, indélicat. Il lui semblait qu'il allait révéler à tout le monde (qui pourtant ne se doutait de rien) un secret qu'il était coupable de surprendre de la sorte et d'étaler publiquement. En entendant la réponse de l'invité: «Le duc de Châtellerault», il se sentit troublé d'un tel orgueil qu'il resta un instant muet. Le duc le regarda, le reconnut, se vit perdu, cependant que le domestique, qui s'était ressaisi et connaissait assez son armorial pour compléter de lui-même une appellation trop modeste, hurlait avec l'énergie professionnelle qui se veloutait d'une tendresse intime: «Son Altesse Monseigneur le duc de Châtellerault!» Mais c'était maintenant mon tour d'être annoncé. . . . L'huissier me demanda mon nom, je le lui dis aussi machinalement que le condamné à mort se laisse attacher au billot. Il leva aussitôt majestueusement la tête et, avant que j'eusse pu le prier de m'annoncer à mi-voix pour ménager mon amour-propre si je n'étais pas invité, et celui de la princesse de Guermantes si je l'étais, il hurla les syllabes inquiétantes avec une force capable d'ébranler la voûte de l'hôtel. (3:37–38)]

Châtellerault more or less disappears from the novel at this point. He seems to have played his role by becoming, along with the doorman, a subject for the narrator's ethnographic gaze, and then by providing a point of comparison for the narrator's own relation to the doorman.[30] The parallels his presence has enabled are numerous and fruitful to consider.

The narrator's and Châtellerault's names are both roared (*hurler*) with great force or energy. The unequal status between the narrator and the Princess, who may or may not have invited him, is paralleled by the unequal status between the doorman and the Duke. There is also a clear parallel between the doorman, obviously uninterested in taking any advantage of his prior acquaintance with Châtellerault or in spilling the beans about his sexual activities, and the narrator, who has already (but to what end?) told us about the encounter in great detail. There is another parallel between the doorman and the narrator, one that brings us back to the consideration of metalepsis from the previous chapter. For if the narrator has no non–meta- or paraleptic way of knowing the details of the sexual encounter between the doorman and the Duke, it is interesting to note that the doorman, who announces both to the reader and to the guests at the party Châtellerault's proper name (which, of course, the reader already knew), carefully announces the narrator's proper name *only to the guests*, leaving the reader uninformed as to the details of the "disquieting syllables" making up the narrator's name, about which the reader might thus suddenly realize at this point in the fourth volume of the novel he or she still has no information.[31]

The doorman, like the narrator's ladder, is thus a reminder of the novel's scaffolding, its construction, of the labor of its composition and of the analytic purpose behind that composition. In order to understand something of the analytic purpose behind this juxtaposition of the narrator and the doorman and of the narrator and Châtellerault, we could just imagine what the doorman *might* have said about each of them: "The Duke de Châtellerault, with whom I recently had a delightful dalliance in a public toilet on the Champs Élysées, in which he surprised me by offering me money and by providing me a certain pleasure, whereas I was expecting—given that he is handsomer and younger than I am—to pay him and to perform for him." And as for the narrator: "The narrator of this novel in which I am a character, and who seems so far throughout this novel to be making a secret of his proper name, yet who is worried that once I announce it he will be escorted away as an imposter—someone not really invited to this party that he is so eager to attend." These are things the doorman *might* have said, but probably would not, in the case of the information about Châtellerault, for such a violation of context would surely have cost him his position. Only the narrator could safely provide us with the information about the sexual encounter, and only by violating the conventions of first-person narration. And because the narrator does so, we learn not only of the sexual proclivities of these two men, but of the doorman's delicacy, his pleasure, his happiness, the tenderness he feels toward the Duke—matters of which Châtellerault himself seems unaware.

As for the narrator, perhaps only in the context of his encounter with the doorman, following on the heels of an *altesse* like Châtellerault, could his shame about his own name be so clearly revealed, shame he imagines might even extend to the princess should it be too publicly known that she has invited someone of his social standing to her party. Thanks to this moment in which the narrator's name is called out to the assembled party guests but not to us, we are reminded of the social aspect to the narrator's curious reluctance to be named, his vulnerability as he pursues a set of social ambitions for which his name, he apparently feels, is inadequate. In this way his tender, if misplaced, concern for the embarrassment the Princess might suffer were that name of his to be announced too loudly mimics the tenderness the doorman feels for Châtellerault—a vaguely mystified relation to a talismanic figure from an elevated social position. (We might note again here that sexuality in the novel is analyzed in the same way as any other social variable that contributes to hierarchies of distinction and also that the particularities of the relation of the narrator and the doorman to the talismanic value of aristocratic names and people is part of what distinguishes them—and their courses of action in regards to knowledge about other peoples' sexuality—from other kinds of social agents.) How does the novel enable itself and its narrator to talk in a way sometimes friendly, sometimes catty, about same-sex sexual relations? Is it the same first person who talks to the reader and who worries about whether the princess has actually invited him? Will he know how to talk once he's admitted to the party, and about what? Will he tell people there what he knows about Châtellerault and the doorman?

Clearly, the aspects of the analytic project of the *Recherche* that we find so complexly realized in this moment of the novel would seem only to be hindered by too great a respect for the routine conventions of first and third person narrations or for too great a respect for the integrity of the novel's own different narrative levels. (Proust's formal inventiveness often works in the service of his sociologically analytic bent.) Part of the goal of the novel is to think abstractly about the particular first person of the narrator as it constructs itself—to analyze the ongoing social project that is the construction of that first person, the kinds of things it can say, what it will mean by the kinds of things it can say, how it thinks it will be perceived because of the kinds of things it says. The first person in question continually finds ways to speak about same-sex sexuality, to overhear speech about it, to observe and report upon scenes of that sexuality's culture in action. Much of the time the narrator spends at the Princess's party will be taken up with constructing social maps of knowledge circulation regarding the sexual interest of certain male guests for other men and in learning the protocols by which this and other forms of "private" knowledge are hinted at or studiously ignored, do or do not circulate in words openly spoken, or in words spoken in corners and whispers.[32] Part of a project of learning to assimilate into a new social group is learning the patterns of discretion and indiscretion that function there, and the topics around which those patterns are formed. The narrator pursues these patterns with all the zeal he applies to the pursuit of aesthetic forms elsewhere in the novel.

The first-person narrator of the *Recherche* finds that within the social circles in which he hopes to move there is much to be gained *socially* in a relatively friendly relation to same-sex sexuality and to certain of the people who practice it. The narrator constructs this relation within a social context rich in ambient ideologies and discourses hostile to same-sex sexual practices, and while he sometimes takes on that hostility, those ideologies, and those discourses, he is never fully or enduringly aligned with them. We might even say that he implicitly argues for the advantages (both social and aesthetic perhaps) to be found in *not* taking up that hostile alignment. (In this, as in other ways, he holds himself distinct from other characters in the novel, notably Mme. Verdurin.)

But the first person whose crafting is part of the project of the *Recherche* is not necessarily a generalizable one. It is rather a very specific one, one that for particular reasons makes the decision that a certain degree of friendliness (in fact a fairly generous degree) toward men who engage in same-sex sexual relations could be to its own advantage. It is also a first person engaged in a novelistic project of revealing knowledge about those relations, about the social forms that give them shape, about the specific culture in which they elaborate themselves—and, inevitably, about the kind of person who would engage in such a project. Such a first person is tied for Proust to a specific time and place and to a particular social, aesthetic, and analytic agenda of becoming. The project of constructing a first person is, of course, never done. It is a form of cultural work that requires constant attention, constant revision, for both the person and the social field in which the person acts are changing. As Proust's novel consistently shows, it is not only the pronoun that makes a first person, it is also the discourse that pronoun takes up, the context in which it does so, and the social consequences and achievements that are possible in that context, with that discourse, for that person, speaking or writing to a given public.[33] "You can tell anything," Proust perhaps said to Gide, speaking about the same-sex sexualities that interested them, "but on condition that you never say: *I*." Proust's novel, it turns out, investigates rather something else: If I want to say *this* about same-sex sexualities, who am I? Who do I have to be to have people listen to me? And, of course, who will I become in the saying?

Epilogue

"As I was telling him what I would one day demonstrate about this subject, Proust broke in: 'But I do hope you won't speak about this saying "he," I beg of you!' To the contrary, I will, I told him; that is the only way I can speak of these things."

[«Comme je lui parlais de ce que je montrerais un jour là-dessus: "Mais j'espère bien que vous ne parlerez pas de cela en disant 'Il,' je vous en prie!" dit Proust. Mais si, au contraire, dis-je; je n'en puis parler que de cette manière.»]
— MARIA VAN RYSSELBERGHE, *Les Cahiers de la petite dame*

On August 19, 1921, Maria Van Rysselberghe reports, in the notebooks she kept of her daily interactions with him, what Gide told her about a conversation he had had earlier that year with Proust.[1] Between May 1921, when Gide noted in his journal that Proust objected to his use of the *first* person, and August, when Van Rysselberghe says he says Proust objected to the *third* person, what had changed? Did Gide's memory become confused? Did Van Rysselberghe get things wrong? Was Gide perhaps talking about two different conversations? On May 13, Gide brought Proust a copy of *Corydon* to read and had a discussion with him about *Si le grain ne meurt*, his memoirs, on which he was working steadily at the time. It was during the discussion of Gide's memoirs on May 13 that Proust was supposed to have objected to Gide's use of the first person. Sometime thereafter, still in May, Proust has read and returned the copy of *Corydon* and the two have another conversation in which Gide complains to Proust about Proust's portrayal of "uranists" in *Sodom and Gomorrah I*. Gide notes in his *Journal*:

But he shows himself to be very much concerned when I tell him that he seems to have wanted to stigmatize uranism; he protests; and eventually I understand that what we consider vile, an object of laughter or disgust, does not seem so repulsive to him. (2:267)

[Mais il se montre très affecté lorsque je lui dis qu'il semble avoir voulu stigmatiser l'uranisme; il proteste; et je comprends enfin que ce que nous trouvons ignoble, objet de rire ou de dégoût, ne lui paraît pas, à lui, si repoussant. (1126)]

When Gide reports to Maria Van Rysselberghe Proust's comment on Gide's third person, he is speaking about a conversation he had with Proust about *Sodom and Gomorrah*. It is in the course of that conversation that Proust expresses his indignation at the idea that anyone could believe he would ever want to stigmatize the people of whom he writes in that book. "What, I who have never loved any but those kinds of love!" [Comment, moi qui n'ai jamais aimé que ces amours-là!]. In Van Rysselberghe's notebook, Gide reports Proust's protest regarding his own intentions in *Sodom and Gomorrah* just before reporting Proust's comment on Gide's third person. Could the third-person comment then have been about *Corydon*, in a conversation in which Gide is offering that book as a counterexample to what Proust has done in *Sodom and Gomorrah*? Could Proust have objected to Gide's first person one week and his third person the next?

In any case, it's not clear exactly what Proust's expostulation about "il" would exactly have meant. Is it some kind of ethical objection to the distancing treatment of certain kinds of people who are spoken about only in the third person? In this case, the comment does not really address the complexities of *Corydon*, for it is a set of dialogues, an exchange between multiple first persons who speak about, for, against, and even as pederasts in different fashions. And even if Gide and Proust were speaking of Gide's novel *Les Faux-Monnayeurs*, Gide's narrative technique in that novel is too quirky to be treated simply as a narration in the third person.[2] Certainly *Corydon* is filled with theoretical discourse about pederasts who do not exactly speak for themselves in the first person (even if one of the two people speaking about them in the dialogues is an avowed pederast). But *Sodom and Gomorrah* too, in its digression on the type of the "man-woman," has the narrator speaking only about "him." Exactly what Proust said and meant by what he said (as opposed to what Gide or Van Rysselberghe report him having said and meant), we will never know. Yet clearly Gide and Proust were both deeply engaged not only with the subject matter in question, but also with the form in which it was to be presented, with the forms of address that come into play when the subject of same-sex sexuality is to be broached. Indeed, the formal choices were as crucial as, inseparable from, the subject matter.

It rankled Gide that *Sodom and Gomorrah* was published before *Corydon* and *Si le grain ne meurt*. "I cannot console myself that I did not publish *Corydon* ahead [of Proust]," Van Rysselberghe reports him telling her, "the question will have been badly posed in the public's mind, and still others will arrive to muck about with the subject. All of that comes on top of the fact of not being the first to take up the question, to which, I admit, I attach some importance" [Je ne me console pas de ne pas avoir publié *Corydon* avant; la question va être mal posée dans l'esprit du public, et d'autres encore viendront patauger dans la matière. Même mis à part le fait de n'être pas le premier à aborder la question, à quoi, je l'avoue, j'attache de l'importance] (95). Proust annoyed Gide for having gotten there "first" (however many previous literary treatments of the subject Gide has to ignore in order to imagine himself and Proust as the only pioneers here); he annoyed Gide by making an "invert" rather than a "pederast" the exemplary figure of "uranism." He annoyed Gide by his manner of writing: "Proust poisoned me sometimes, making me doubt myself; but I think that his manner reveals more avarice than richness: yes, the need to let nothing, nothing be lost, constantly adding things, as opposed to economy" [Proust m'empoisonnait parfois et me faisait douter de moi; mais je considère que sa manière révèle plus d'avarice que de richesse: oui, le besoin de ne rien, rien laisser perdre, l'addition constante, au lieu de l'épargne].[3] The economy that Gide strove for by way of his classical style has a lot to do with what we saw Lucie Delarue-Mardrus referring to as his "reticence," a kind of subtle discretion or indirection that marked in particular his practice of the first person. It was, for Gide, not just what Proust chose to portray about "uranism" that lacked dignity or refinement or discretion; Proust's vulgarity resulted from his (lengthy) manner of presentation—his endless excess and lack of economy, the missing *épargne* of classicism—as well as from the tastelessness (for Gide) of what he chose to represent.[4] Proust's first person did not have the proper relation to its subject, did not even quite find the correct subject to address.

In 1907 Gide may have found Colette and Missy shameless in their behavior at the Moulin Rouge; they may, in his eyes, have been doing a disservice to their peers by way of their representational activities. Gide may have been embarrassed to find he admired her novel *Chéri* when he read it in 1920.[5] By 1941 he finds himself easily enjoying her literary mastery; she is by this point someone of whose style he has to approve (if still a bit grudgingly):

> What flavor in her language, it's almost excessive. . . . Oh, how I like Colette's way of writing! What sureness of touch in her word choice! What a nice feeling for the nuance! And all that as if it were child's play, like La Fontaine, without seeming to pay attention, the exquisite result of a pains-taking elaboration.
>
> "I sat down rather glum before a piece of work undertaken without appetite and forsaken without decision." This "forsaken without decision" is a marvel of the intentional, discreet to the point of going unnoticed by the average reader, most likely, which delights me. (4:59–60)

> [Une langue savoureuse presque à l'excès . . . ah! combien me plaît la façon d'écrire de Colette! Quelle sûreté dans le choix des mots! Quel délicat sentiment de la nuance! Et tout cela comme en se jouant, à la La Fontaine, et sans avoir l'air d'y toucher, résultat d'une élaboration assidue, résultat exquis.
>
> «Je m'assis assez maussade devant un travail commencé sans appétit, délaissé sans décision.» Ce «délaissé sans décision» est une merveille d'inten-tion, discrète jusqu'à l'inaperçu pour le commun des lecteurs sans doute, qui me ravit.][6]

Gide here cites with approval a sentence he finds in Colette that he could have written himself, one that addresses problems of desire, in-tention, and responsibility in the case of a first person writing. He is reading at the time Colette's *Bella-Vista*, a set of four stories having to do with various kinds of sexual secrets, two of which involve a subtle and nuanced use of a first person narrator. Doubtless it is the symbiosis between her style, her subject matter, and her particular deployment of the first person that earns her Gide's approval.

Colette, in turn, had her own way of both approving and disapprov-ing of Proust's representational efforts in *Sodom and Gomorrah*, and her forms of disapproval in some way resemble Gide's. But the approval first. It comes in a letter to Proust that Colette wrote in July 1921, having just read the volume that included *Sodom and Gomorrah I*. "*No one in the world* has ever written pages like that on the invert," she exclaimed in her letter. "I swear that no one after you, other than you, could add anything to what you will have written" [*Personne au monde n'a écrit des pages comme celles-là sur l'inverti, personne! . . . Je jure que personne après vous, autre que vous, ne pourra rien ajouter à ce que vous aurez écrit*].[7] From the Claudine novels onward, when Colette wrote about what she first used the words "unisexual" or "unisexuality" to refer to and later "homosexual" and "homosexuality," she would usually show the men who fitted such words—and with whom obviously both she and her characters entertained quite friendly relations—as conforming to a model of inversion. They were often portrayed as exotic, delicate, touchy and bitter personalities to be treated with a certain amount of irony and, occasionally, disdain and condescension. Her approval of the representation of inverts provided by Proust's narrator in *Sodom and Gomorrah I* thus comes as no surprise. (Perhaps she was also drawn to the ambiguous stance assumed by his first person narrator in presenting this material.)

She would reflect again on Proust's treatment of the topic of same-sex sexuality a decade later, having by this time read the rest of the volumes in the *Recherche*. The passage in question appeared in her book *Ces plaisirs . . .* , which was first published in 1932:

Ever since Proust shed light on Sodom, we have had a feeling of respect for what he wrote, and would never dare, after him, to touch the subject of these hounded creatures, who are careful to blur their tracks and to propagate at every step their personal cloud, like the cuttlefish.

But—was he misled, or was he ignorant?—when he assembles a Gomorrah of inscrutable and depraved young girls, when he denounces an entente, a collectivity, a frenzy of bad angels, we are only diverted, indulgent, and a little bored, having lost the support of the dazzling light of truth that guides us through Sodom. This is because, with all due deference to the imagination or the error of Marcel Proust, there is no such thing as Gomorrah. Puberty, boarding school, solitude, prisons, aberrations, snobbishness—they are all seedbeds, but too shallow to engender and sustain a vice that could attract a great number or become an established thing that would gain the indispensable solidarity of its votaries. Intact, enormous, eternal, Sodom looks down from its heights upon its puny counterfeit.

[Depuis que Proust a éclairé Sodome, nous nous sentons respectueux de ce qu'il a écrit. Nous n'oserions plus, après lui, toucher à ces être pourchassés, soigneux de brouiller leur trace et de propager à chaque pas leur nuage individuel, comme fait la sépia.

Mais—fut-il abusé, fut-il ignorant?—quand il assemble une Gomorrhe d'insondables et vicieuses jeunes filles, dénonce une entente, une collectivité, une frénésie de mauvais anges, nous ne sommes plus que divertis, complaisants et un peu mous, ayant perdu le réconfort de la foudroyante vérité qui nous guidait à travers Sodome. C'est, n'en déplaise à l'imagination ou l'erreur de Marcel Proust, qu'il n'y a pas de Gomorrhe. Puberté, collèges, solitude, prisons, aberrations, snobisme . . . Maigres pépinières, insuffisantes à engendrer et avitailler un vice nombreux, bien assis, et sa solidarité indispensable. Intacte, énorme, éternelle, Sodome contemple de haut sa chétive contrefaçon.][8]

Colette's description of Proust's Gomorrah may or may not be accurate. In any case, the rhetorical stance she takes up in this passage is one we have seen many times in this book. She is, it seems, happy to let male practitioners of same-sex sexuality be "vicious," but she is not willing to understand female practitioners as being so. The details of the passage reveal that Colette relates "vice" to shame, aberrance, and sexual dissidence. But most crucially, she links it to *community* (une entente, une collectivité). The implication is that the men in question, because they are organized around their vice, inevitably form a community. Whereas Proust's error, she suggests, is in understanding there to be some collectivity of women who love other women. We have here a contentious and paradoxical performance of what Michael Silverstein has called an "identity event" or an "identity display." It is in fact both paradoxical and paradoxically normative. As a ritual performance of a certain kind, along with advancing a set of claims about the social world, it is also much concerned with figuring an appropriate first person in which to advance those claims.[9] As Silverstein notes about such events or displays:

> The key identity-relevant attributes of such cultural texts are not necessarily anything like represented "content" as such, but rather all the verbal and nonverbal signs that, displayed by and around the self, in effect wrap social personae, social spaces, moments in social-organizational time, even institutional forms, with "in-group" (versus "out-group," of course) status. Such occasions of display are performative; in and by wearing, singing, saying, eating such-and-such, an identifying quality of person, place, event, etc. comes into being—here and now—in a framework of categorization that is now made relevant to whatever is going on or can go on. (538)

Colette's display in *Ces plaisirs . . .* is normative in its represented content: she offers a set of terms for what love between women *should* be. But paradoxically, while she insists on dictating a shape to this identity, the shape she dictates would disallow any potential for community in the identity involved. She denies commonality to these women who she demonstrates have something in common:

> Yes, I want to speak with dignity, that is, with warmth, of what I call the noble season of feminine passion. . . . The noble season of those loves that are condemned by most people shows its nobility by disdaining any particular form of sexual or sensual pleasure, by refusing to reflect, to see things clearly, to organize a future. Where would they obtain the sense of a future, these two enamored women who, at every moment, demolish and deny it, who envisage neither beginning nor end nor change nor solitude, who breathe the air only *à deux*, and, arm in arm, walk only in perfect step with each other?

> [Oui, je voudrais parler dignement, c'est-à-dire avec feu, de ce que je nomme la saison noble d'une passion feminine. . . . La saison noble des amours que le commun condamne place sa noblesse dans son dédain de la volupté précise, dans le refus de réfléchir, de voir juste, et d'organiser l'avenir. Où prendraient-elles le sens de l'avenir, ces deux amis qui, à tout instant, le défont et le nient, qui n'envisagent ni commencement ni fin, ni changement, ni solitude, ne respirent l'air qu'à deux, ne vont, le bras sur le bras, que d'un pas bien accordé?][10]

Singularly ill-suited to any political activity, to any sense of commonality with others like them, to any desire to organize in any way, these women-loving women of Colette's also notably refuse to identify around or to have a preference for any particular sexual practice (or, one assumes, division of sexual roles). This passage, together with the previous one cited in which she directly addresses Proust's novel, shows Colette's critique of Proust to have a normative cast in a way we are familiar with from Gide's reactions to Proust. Proust, Colette suggests, provides the wrong *examples* of the identity in question. His sense of exemplarity is faulty. Women who imagine organizing a future, who imagine themselves having an enduring identity based on their present passion, women who associate with each other around particular sexual acts, are, it would seem, bad examples.

Colette differs from Gide (the advocate of pederasty who frowns on inverts) in that her preferred example of female same-sex sexuality is that of an identity that cannot be used programmatically, an identity that is somehow inadequate to providing a basis for a durable identitarian community. But Colette's very gesture—of describing an identity that functions as a social category, but not one to which a woman can durably belong, not one with any political potentiality, any future—is a ritualistic one that situates her socially. It is itself a socially familiar performance, repetitive in nature. Such ritual gestures structure a great deal of speech and literary writing about same-sex sexuality in France in the rest of the twentieth century. In some versions these rituals seem meant to assure that queer-identified people cannot speak for themselves. When a first person is found in which to speak for such people, that speech must somehow include a critique of the terms of their identity, their authenticity, the possibility of them speaking for themselves. It is, to return to the place where this epilogue began, a ritual that puts into place a particular relation between the first and the third person.[11] Colette's performance of this ritual is, of course, brilliantly filled with many forms of ambiguity:

How reluctant I am to examine clinically so fragile a creation as this, and one endangered from so many directions: a couple of women in love! The time is past when such a thing could arouse me in some way, but I still retain the necessary impartiality, a delicacy of vision of that which itself is truly delicate and poignant in its attempt, the union of two beings whose good-will is, at the outset, almost always complete. (115, translation modified)

[Qu'il me déplaît de palper froidement une création aussi fragile, et de tout menacée: un couple amoureux de femmes! Le temps de m'en émouvoir est passé; mais il me reste l'équité nécessaire, une vue délicate de ce qui est réellement délicat et poignant dans l'essai, l'union de deux êtres de qui, presque toujours, la bonne foi est au départ, entière. (103)]

If there is something of Gide in Colette's criticism of Proust, there is something of Proust's narrator in the construction of the first person we see here—simultaneously implicated in and disavowing of a sexual relation whose beauty and oddity are being offered to our vision.

"Never say *I*," Proust may have said, or perhaps he said he had some reservations about Gide saying "he" or "they," or perhaps both. But in the end, it was a troubled negotiation between the first and the third person in which Proust, Gide, and Colette found themselves engaged. They struggled not only over what would be said, how same-sex sexualities would be conceptualized and represented, and in what manner they would be treated, but also over who could say what needed to be said, who could be taken seriously in doing so. They did not arrive at the same solutions, but between and among them, we see coming into place the set of terms in which literary negotiations around this kind of speech, these acts of interpretation, would happen for at least the next several decades. (Even today similar negotiations often seem to be conducted in much the same terms, however much they may sometimes seem to have dated.) We could remember here Deleuze and Guattari suggesting in *A Thousand Plateaus* that "there is only individuation of the utterance, there is only subjectivation of the utterance to the extent that the impersonal and collective assemblage demands and determines it."[12] The works I have been examining here bear out Deleuze and Guattari's sense of the way certain books take on a role as impersonal sources of innovation, offering a kind of *agencement*, a space of crossings in which various kinds of collective agencies emerge into discourse, in which various kinds of discursive assemblages sometimes produce new places from which to speak about new things, in which new kinds of speech sometimes happen, sometimes manage to make themselves more widely available. "You can say anything," Proust reminded Gide, referring to same-sex sexualities, but only under certain conditions. We have been watching here the productive collision of those pragmatic conditions that shape speech and identity with a variety of aesthetic imperatives and with what we might call an impulse toward just representation—a representation that even in the first person takes on a kind of impersonality as it strives to find ways of giving some justice (by giving form) to what is.

Notes

Introduction: Referring to Same-Sex Sexualities in the First Person

1   For helpful commentary on the phrases *coming out* and *the closet*, see Chauncey, *Gay New York*. On the closet, he notes (about the North American context), "given the ubiquity of the term today and how central the metaphor of the closet is to the ways we think about gay history before the 1960s, it is bracing—and instructive—to note that it was never used by gay people themselves before then. Nowhere does it appear before the 1960s in the records of the gay movement or in the novels, diaries, or letters of gay men and lesbians" (6). Lawrence Schehr questions the utility of the notion of the closet for the study of certain authors (including Proust) in *The Shock of Men*, 20–27.

2   On the closet and coming out, see also Warner, *Publics and Counterpublics*. Warner comments pithily that the closet is "produced by the heteronormative assumptions of everyday talk. It feels private. But in an important sense it is publicly constructed. . . . It is this deformation of public and private that identity politics—and the performative ritual known as coming out—tries to transform" (52–53).

3   See, for example, Manalansan, *Global Divas*. The whole of Manalansan's project is relevant to this issue, but see in particular "Coming Out and Coming Over: Do Closets Travel?" (27–35).

4   Chambers, *Untimely Interventions*, 24–25. Or consider this helpful statement by Freadman: "Genres are kinds of cultural events—royal visits, for example, ceremonial parades, or trials or elections or sporting contests. They have certain regular and predictable features, and they are the occasion for a certain kind of experience. Some theorists would go on to say that each genre assigns a role to its participants, this including its audience. This being so, each

genre has something like a social or an ideological function, putting the public into its place and using it for its own ends. . . . Genre theory can illuminate the question I have asked: what is it to participate in a culture? It rarely if ever means being scripted by the rules of a single genre. When we step outside our script, it is not to discover a space of pure unscripted freedom. 'Outside' is a jumbled and chaotic space of other genres" ("When the King and Queen of England Came to Town").

5 Warner's *Publics and Counterpublics* is very suggestive on these questions. For instance: "There is no speech or performance addressed to a public that does not try to specify in advance, in countless highly condensed ways, the lifeworld of its circulation: not just through its discursive claims—of the kind that can be said to be oriented to understanding—but through the pragmatics of its speech genres, idioms, stylistic markers, address, temporality, mise-en-scène, citational field, interlocutory protocols, lexicon, and so on. Its circulatory fate is the realization of that world. Public discourse says not only 'Let a public exist' but 'Let it have this character, speak this way, see the world in this way.' It then goes in search of confirmation that such a public exists, with greater or lesser success—success being further attempts to cite, circulate, and realize the world understanding it articulates" (114).

6 Bourdieu, "Description and Prescription," 127.

7 See Halperin's incisive account of the word *homosexuality*, its slow spread into common usage, the meanings that came to adhere to it as it spread, and the social significance of its general adoption with those meanings in his entry "Homosexuality" in *Gay Histories and Cultures*, 45–55. For a meditation on the pitfalls of names and categories, and for a helpful rundown on the historical and anthropological literature on the subject, see Rupp, "Toward a Global History of Same-Sex Sexuality."

8 Gumperz and Cook-Gumperz, "Introduction: Language and the Communication of Social Identity," 1.

9 In another context, Marin has written about the relation between commentary and the discourse that attracts that commentary that "if interpretative commentary is an effect of the dialogic organization of discourse and, in the final instance of its enunciative structure, in inverse fashion, that commentary itself appropriates discourse by constituting it as a 'work,' as a 'book' and in the same moment manifests certain real or symbolic interests by way of that appropriation. The work is then an *effect* of commentary, just as commentary is an *effect* of discourse" (*Pascal et Port-Royal*, 31).

10 Proust, *Correspondance*, 20:187. *Sacer esto* is a Roman formula for a person who, by contravening a law, has renounced any legal protections on his or her life and who may therefore be killed with impunity. Yet Montesquiou seems rather to use the term as a synonym for sacerdocy—the function of a priest. *Sacer* could be thought of as one of those double-edged words, point-

ing both to a thing and to its opposite—the sacred and the taboo, the consecrated and the abject. Agamben's *Homo Sacer* reflects on this particular subject.

11   Gide, *If It Die . . .* , 232; *Si le grain ne meurt*, 280.

12   Other subjects of course take on a relation to this problematic throughout the century as well—for instance, female sexuality, forms of popular life and speech, abortion, prison culture, torture, racial oppression and violence, colonial oppression and violence, fascist and totalitarian violence—and twentieth-century French literature contains experiments in the first person related to all these subjects. Chambers's *Untimely Interventions* is a superb account of the figural work involved in referring to, indexing, or bringing to representation subjects or events others might rather not hear about. As for *tout dire* in relation to the first person, it is obviously not only a twentieth-century problem. Rousseau's ghost looms large for many people dealing with the issue. Remember the famous claim at the opening of the *Confessions*, "Je veux montrer à mes semblables un homme dans toute la vérité de la nature; et cet homme ce sera moi" [I wish to show to my fellow men a man in all the truth of his nature; and that man will be me].

13   Cited by Jansiti, *Violette Leduc*, 268.

14   See Jansiti's afterword to *Thérèse et Isabelle* for an account of the history of the text.

15   See Bourdieu, *The Rules of Art*.

16   See Borrillo, "Droit."

17   Foucault, "Folie, littérature, société," in *Dits et écrits*, 2:117.

18   Ibid., 117–18.

19   Proust, *Correspondance*, 20:187, 195: "«Gros dividendes» m'a fait tristement sourire, car je ne gagne rien avec mes livres." Compare Pierre Bourdieu in *The Rules of Art*: "The symbolic revolution through which artists free themselves from bourgeois demand by refusing to recognize any master except their art produces the effect of making the market disappear. In fact they could not triumph over the 'bourgeois' in the struggle for control of the meaning and function of artistic activity without at the same time eliminating the bourgeois as a potential customer. At the moment when they argue, with Flaubert, that 'a work of art . . . is beyond appraisal, has no commercial value, cannot be paid for,' that it is *without price*, that is to say, foreign to the ordinary logic of the ordinary economy, they discover that it is effectively *without commercial value*, that it has no market. The ambiguity of Flaubert's phrase, saying two things at once, leads to the uncovering of a sort of infernal mechanism, which is set up by artists and in which they find themselves caught: making a necessity of their virtue, they can always be suspected of making a virtue of necessity" (81).

20   See Thurman, *Secrets of the Flesh*, 129.

21   Here and elsewhere I will be citing in French from the 1996–97 two-

volume Pléiade edition of Gide's *Journal* (in this particular instance, *Journal I*, 547). This Pléiade edition prints many passages from the manuscripts of Gide's journals that were not included in previous published editions. The passage about Colette and Missy is one of those and thus is not to be found in the four-volume English translation of *The Journals of André Gide* that was made from an earlier edition.

22 Bourdieu's description of Flaubert's achievement of the "pure gaze" that assures the primacy of the place of *style* in his work resonates in interesting ways with Miller's reading of Jane Austen's style in *Jane Austen, or The Secret of Style*. For Miller, Austen's style is "the work of abstracting" (28). "Style flaunts its mastery," he writes at another point, "its ability to enter and then exit a character's state of mind at will, while always retaining, at whatever level of intimacy, the immunity of its impersonality" (66). Miller's analysis of *Persuasion* is particularly interesting in this context. That novel broached the "temptation of Austen Style to revert to the Person it had constituted itself against" (76).

23 Landy's erudite " 'Les Moi en Moi': The Proustian Self in Philosophical Perspective," a well-elaborated discussion of what a self might be in Proust, manages quite consistently to evade broaching the question of the functioning of the first person on a more abstract level in Proust's novel. Landy does comment at one point that "what involuntary memory gives to the future book is less its content than its *form*, if not its very condition of existence: a narrating instance sufficiently unified as to be able to say 'I' and to speak for a multiplicity of selves in past and present tenses" (102). The 'I' of the *Recherche* can thus stand for "a secret site of constancy" (105) in the self. It seems rather that what is remarkable about the "I" in Proust's novel is the attention paid to the potential and actual incoherence of its use, the project of revealing how the use of "I" as a figure for a person in the social world produces only the illusion of coherent reference. Indeed the novel's analytic force, the work it does on form and via form, arises to a great extent from the disturbances it introduces in our everyday understanding of the patterns of coherence in the use of the first person. Proust's influence within subsequent twentieth-century French literature is due to a great extent to his formal work in this area.

24 Salient examples of efforts to perpetuate this tradition would include essays by Butor such as "Le Roman comme recherche" ["The Novel as a Form of Research"] in *Répertoire I* and "L'Usage des pronoms personnels dans le roman" ["The Use of Personal Pronouns in the Novel"] in *Répertoire II*, or Sarraute's essays collected in *L'Ere du soupçon*. Wittig comments in "The Mark of Gender" that "personal pronouns are, if I may say so, the subject matter of each one of my books" (*The Straight Mind and Other Essays*, 82).

25 The typographical methods—quotation marks, italics, small capitals—

by which a writer indicates that he or she is, as a linguist would say, *mentioning* the first person pronoun rather than *using* it as a shifter also reveal that pronouns (even when they are being used as shifters) have symbolic functions as well as indexical ones. On indexicality and on the Peircean distinction between (and interrelation of) index, icon, and symbol, see Freadman, *The Machinery of Talk*, esp. 105–34.

26 Benveniste, *Problems in General Linguistics*, 230.

27 Ibid., 219–20.

28 See *Roland Barthes par Roland Barthes*, 168–72 (in English, 165–69). Lejeune's erudite and thorough work on the first person and autobiography also takes its inspiration from this intellectual tradition. Lejeune's body of work, with all of its interesting developments (from *Le Pacte autobiographique*, to *Je est un autre*, and then to *Moi aussi*, for example) is not one I turn to for inspiration here because, in thinking about the problem of the first person, he rarely looks in detail at the relation between literary texts and the various social contestations that form part of their context.

29 Duvert, *La Parole et la fiction*, 9.

30 Butor, "L'Usage des pronoms personnels dans le roman," 68. For a helpful article on the concept of apprenticeship in the first person, one that productively challenges Benveniste's definition of personal pronouns, see Urban, "The 'I' of Discourse."

31 See, on this topic, Banfield, "Where Epistemology, Style, and Grammar Meet Literary History," and, of course, her book *Unspeakable Sentences*.

32 Goffman, *Frame Analysis*, 523.

33 In a review of Colette's *Naissance du jour* (*Break of Day*), the critic André Billy wrote that Colette's novel "offers something extremely new and daring, without precedent, I think, in literature . . . it's that the heroine of the novel is none other than the author. . . . There is no transposition . . . it's the author in the flesh, in her house, with her friends bearing their real names." Colette would reply, "Dear friend, your clairvoyance sees everything: you have figured out that in this novel there is no novel." See Colette, *Lettres à ses pairs*, 270–71. For the most recent vigorous tongue-lashing of Proust critics for their methodological failings, see Landy, "Proust, His Narrator, and the Importance of the Distinction."

34 Proust, *The Captive*, 91; "Elle retrouvait la parole, elle disait: «Mon» ou «Mon chéri», suivis l'un ou l'autre de mon nom de baptême, ce qui, en donnant au narrateur le même prénom qu'à l'auteur de ce livre, eût fait l«Mon Marcel», «Mon chéri Marcel»" (*À la recherche du temps perdu*, 3:583). The sentence is remarkable for its strange intimation that the narrator might know the author—an odd metalepsis indeed—or, just as incomprehensibly, that the first person of the sentence might correspond neither to the author or the narrator. The sentence also functions most simply as a reminder that the

novel works abstractly on the first person and its functioning. There are other sentences like this in the *Recherche*. For evidence that such sentences have provided food for thought for later novelists interested in abstraction, see Lindon, "Le Lecteur impossible," a reflection on a few sentences from *The Captive*, including this one: "And yet, my dear Charles Swann, whom I used to know when I was still so young and you were nearing your grave, it is because he whom you must have regarded as a young idiot has made you the hero of one of his novels that people are beginning to speak of you again and that your name will perhaps live" (262). When Lindon himself would publish *literary* texts in *Minuit* in the 1970s, he did so under the name Mathieu David. For this critical article on Proust, he was Mathieu Lindon. In the list of contributors, his name was given as Mathieu David Lindon. The character who represents Mathieu Lindon in some of Hervé Guibert's novels is called David, perhaps providing evidence that Guibert too, whatever he may have said about his reading of Proust (or lack of it), was still, like Lindon, a bit caught up in his wake.

35 Cicourel, "The Acquisition of Social Structure," 62–63.

36 Goffman, *Frame Analysis*, 519.

37 Wittgenstein writes about the first person in both *The Blue Book* and *Philosophical Investigations*. Anscombe, writing on the first person after Wittgenstein, can come to sound like Beckett: "And, for example, an interpreter might repeat the 'I' of his principal in his translations. Herein resides the conceivability of the following: someone stands before me and says, 'Try to believe this: when I say "I," that does not mean this human being who is making noise. I am someone else who has borrowed this human being to speak through him' " ("The First Person," 33). One rapidly runs out of punctuation marks when it comes to writing about the first-person pronoun.

38 Shortly after Proust's death in November 1922, Walter Berry reminisced about conversations in which "we always came back to the subject of the novel, of the form of the novel, which was a preoccupation of his, a passionate interest—to the modern novel, which he claimed was becoming sclerotic, to the novel whose frontiers he did so much to expand. He would ask for details about English novels, and particularly about Henry James's way of writing—that is, the novel that is *seen*, entirely seen, by one of the characters, by *only* one of the characters, as, notably, in *What Maisie Knew*" ("Du Côté de Guermantes," 79).

39 Bourdieu, *The Weight of the World*, 625–26. Dubois, in *Pour Albertine*, analyzes *À la recherche du temps perdu* in these terms, noting that the novel can be read as "a patient process of self-objectivation . . . the effort an individual exerts on his or her self in order to figure out their place in the field of relations" (194–95).

40 Goffman, *Forms of Talk*, 147.

41 Bourdieu, *Outline of a Theory of Practice*, 26.

42 Mertz, "Beyond Symbolic Anthropology," 5, 6.

43 Ibid., 6.

44 Silverstein, "Shifters, Linguistic Categories, and Cultural Description," 32.

45 Ibid., 42, 53.

46 Silverstein, "Language and the Culture of Gender," 222.

47 Silverstein, "Indexical Order," 273.

48 Freadman and Macdonald, *What Is This Thing Called "Genre"?*, 46.

49 It is perhaps a bit unfair to include Paul Bourget in this list. With the exception of Rachilde, all these authors are little read and studied nowadays. In the early twentieth century, however, Bourget could justifiably have laid claim to a serious literary stature none of the others obtained.

50 Deleuze and Guattari, *A Thousand Plateaus: Capitalism and Schizophrenia*, 80, translation modified.

51 Deleuze, "Cinq propositions sur la psychanalyse," 383.

1 Gide, Bourget, and Proust Talking

1 Bourdieu, "Social Space and the Genesis of 'Classes,'" 239.

2 See the introduction to Lucey, *Gide's Bent*, 3–20, and Eribon, *Insult and the Making of the Gay Self*, 187–88 and 213–16.

3 Rachilde, "Les Romans," *Mercure de France*, July 1902, 184.

4 Indeed, the biographers of Mathilde de Morny charge Paul Bourget with exactly this: with having been one of the gay young men who avidly frequented Morny's salon in the 1880s but became straight around the time of the Wilde trial and subsequently remained so. See Francis and Gontier, *Mathilde de Morny*, 126.

5 The variants can be found in the notes to the Pléiade edition of Gide's *Journal I*, 1632. They are not available in the English translation.

6 Goodman, "On Likeness of Meaning," in *Problems and Projects*, 229.

7 On the particularities of nomenclature for female same-sex relations, see Albert, *Saphisme et décadence*, 69–82.

8 For more information on Raffalovich, see Rosario, *The Erotic Imagination*, 97–101.

9 The doctor from Lyon who edited the *Archives d'anthropologie criminelle*, Alexandre Lacassagne, exemplifies this overlapping. See the account of his life by Artières in his introduction to *Le Livre des vies coupables*, 26–35. Jean Lacassagne, son of Alexandre, followed in his father's footsteps in the practice of legal medicine, and also showed a literary interest in the subcultures with which he came into contact through his experience with criminals. He pub-

lished a very interesting slang dictionary, *L'Argot du "Milieu,"* in 1928 with a preface by Francis Carco.

10   Raffalovich, "*Les Hors Nature*, par Mme Rachilde"; Rachilde "Les Romans" *Mercure de France*, February 1905, 596; Raffalovich, "Les Groupes uranistes à Paris et à Berlin"; Régis, "Un Cas de perversion sexuelle à forme sadique"; Dr. Cazanove, "La Dépravation sexuelle chez les relégués à Saint-Jean-du-Moroni (Guyane française)." For Gide's interest in much of this material, see Pollard, *André Gide.*

11   There is also an entry under "Soupe (tremper la)" in Lacassagne and Devaux's *L'Argot du "Milieu"* that confirms the meaning of the expression given by Cazanove.

12   On Gide's social positioning in *Corydon*, see Eribon, *Insult and the Making of the Gay Self*, 215–30.

13   In a book coauthored with Catherine Z. Elgin, Goodman makes a helpful distinction between "truth" and "correctness" regarding systems of classification. A system of classification is "correct" when it is felt to "fit." See *Reconceptions in Philosophy and Other Arts and Sciences*, 155–59. See also the helpful article by Douglas, "Rightness of Categories."

14   In the preface to *Corydon* that he wrote in 1922 and published in 1924, Gide makes public reference to the distinctions he would like to put into place between, on the one hand, inversion, effeminacy, and sodomy, and, on the other, pederasty. He notes that his book is only concerned with "pederasty—in which no effeminacy is involved, for either party," but he also notes that one of the "great shortcomings" of his book is that it does not consider other forms of "homosexuality" ("inversion, effeminacy, sodomy"), which "turn out to be much more frequent than I previously supposed." See Gide, *Corydon*, 8–9 (in French), xx (in English). For a longer reading of *Corydon*, see Lucey, *Gide's Bent*, 68–94.

15   Goffman, "On Face-Work," 38–39.

16   Goffman, *Frame Analysis*, 551, 546.

17   Whereas, for example, in *Corydon* it is by creating the particular character of Corydon that he finds a means to express views such as the following: "In homosexuality, just as in heterosexuality, there are all shades and degrees, from Platonic love to lust, from self-denial to sadism, from radiant health to sullen sickliness, from simple expansiveness to all the refinements of vice. Inversion is only a small part of all this. Besides, between exclusive homosexuality and exclusive heterosexuality there is every intermediate shading. . . . Homosexuality, just like heterosexuality, has its degenerates, its vicious and sick practitioners; as a doctor, I have come across as many painful, distressing, or dubious cases as the rest of my colleagues. I shall spare my readers that experience; as I've already said, my book will deal with healthy uranism or, as you just put it yourself, with *normal pederasty*" (French, 30–32; English, 18–20).

18   Then again, perhaps Gide truly would have wanted to know more about Bourget and Régis's ways of placing "homosexuality" under the rubric of sadism or masochism—or perhaps such a turn in the conversation would have provided Gide with a chance to put forth a different figure who might have been able to offer a challenge to Bourget, Régis, and their worldview.

.   19   On Wharton, Fullerton, and James, see Erlich, *The Sexual Education of Edith Wharton*, 87, 124. On Wharton, Bourget, and Lee, see Dwight, *Edith Wharton: An Extraordinary Life*, 42, 44, 75.

20   In all of these passages, Justin O'Brien had translated the word *uraniste* as *homosexual* and *uranisme* as *homosexuality*. I have therefore modified his translation here. In his translation of *Ainsi soit-il*, he did translate *uranisme* as *uranism* (see note 21).

21   Near the end of his life, in *So Be It* (*Ainsi soit-il*), he writes, speaking of Charles du Bos, "He had no very definite idea about pederasty and needed explanations. The conversation was frightfully painful. Uranism was not the only thing that Charlie did not understand; the same could be said of life in general" (28) [Il ne se faisait pas sur la pédérastie une idée bien précise, avait besoin d'explications. L'entretien fut atrocement pénible. Ce n'est pas seulement à l'uranisme que Charlie ne comprenait rien; c'est à la vie (38)]. As a counterexample to the idea that Gide always uses *uranisme* in less public, less oppositional, more friendly situations, one might cite the moment in *Corydon* in which the homophobic narrator speaks of "the irritating question of uranism" (3) [l'irritante question de l'uranisme (15)]. The general point that *uranism* never entered common usage could be attested to by looking at the frequency of the different words used by the respondents to the questionnaire distributed by the journal *Les Marges* in 1926. The journal asked a selection of writers whether or not in their view "la préoccupation homosexuelle" had developed in postwar French literature, and whether or not the presence of "personnages invertis" [characters who are inverts] in literature could affect public morals. A rough count of the responses printed in the March 15, 1926, issue reveals the following: cognates of *homosexualité* appear 101 times; cognates of *pédérastie* appear 40 times; cognates of *inversion* appear 29 times; *vice* appears 21 times; *uraniste* appears twice, and the adjective *uranique* once; cognates of *lesbien* appear twice; *tante* and *tata* appear twice; *gousse, tapette, sodomie, tribades* appear once.

22   Obviously, given the infrequency of the word *uranist* among speakers of today, the patterns in Gide's usage of *uranist* versus *homosexual* that I am suggesting here had a similar degree of durability as the distinction he tried to make between *pédéraste* and *inverti*. If people like Gide and Proust speak in terms of *uranistes* and *uranisme*, this usage indicates their status as intellectuals as well as the fact that it is two gay men (so to speak) speaking among themselves. If *uraniste* and *uranisme* are words that have mostly fallen out of

use, this is partly because their use had always been limited—patrician, one might say. (The term itself was coined by Karl Heinrich Ulrichs from the speech of Pausanias in Plato's *Symposium* [180d to 185c] in which he links a pure love between men to the heavenly Uranian Aphrodite.)

23 Proust, *Correspondance*, 20:261–63.

24 Ibid., 20:270–73.

25 Van Rysselberghe, *Les Cahiers de la Petite Dame*, 98.

26 Goodman, *Ways of Worldmaking*, 8.

27 As Goodman himself notes elsewhere: "If statements of similarity, like counterfactual conditionals and four-letter words, cannot be trusted in the philosopher's study, they are still serviceable in the streets" ("Seven Strictures on Similarity," 22). For more on the relevance of this question to the history of sexuality, see Lucey, "Catégorie ou concept."

28 Gide and Mauriac, *Correspondance André Gide–François Mauriac*, 71.

29 "I know only too well how much courage it takes today to speak of me in certain circles without horrified protestations." The entire passage from which this sentence is drawn is quite interesting regarding Mauriac. It is dated July 4, 1931, and is reprinted in *Correspondance André Gide–François Mauriac*, 149–51.

30 Mauriac's article is reprinted in *Correspondance André Gide–François Mauriac*, 119–23.

31 Proust, *Correspondance*, 20:268–69.

32 Compagnon's comments are in the editorial matter to the Pléiade edition of the *Recherche*, 3:1186.

33 Mauriac would publish an article on Gide's *Saül* in June 1922 in which he uses some of the same tropes we find in his letter to Proust: "But there are certain shores on which a wise man does not land. Doubtless in a long-standing literary tradition, when all has already been said, an artist feels drawn to these unknown territories. He explores strange, sad islands and digs around in the ruins of burned cities without fearing that very God who turned into pillars of salt certain just individuals merely because they glanced back at these mysteries" [Mais il est des rives où le sage n'aborde pas. Sans doute, dans une si vieille littérature et lorsque tout a été dit, un artiste est sollicité par ces terres inconnues; il explore les îles étranges et tristes, et fouille les décombres des villes incendiées, sans craindre ce Dieu qui, pour un seul regard jeté sur leurs mystères, changea des justes en statues de sel] (*Correspondance André Gide–François Mauriac*, 126).

34 Goffman, *Forms of Talk*, 147.

35 Ibid., 148. Goffman's reference is to George Herbert Mead. See Mead's *Mind, Self, and Society from the Standpoint of a Social Behaviorist.*

36 Bourdieu, "Rites of Institution," 121.

1   Here I am recontextualizing part of a longer analysis of this novel that can be found in chapter 4 of my book *The Misfit of the Family*.

2   Balzac, *A Harlot High and Low*, 454; *Splendeurs et misères des courtisanes*, 6:840.

3   Vidocq, *Mémoires*, 823–24.

4   See Silverstein, "Indexical Order and the Dialectics of Sociolinguistic Life," 280–81.

5   The letter dates from either June 6 or 7, 1905. See Proust, *Correspondance*, 5:207–10. The letters concerning this soiree run from May 3 to June 6 (5:129–210).

6   Montesquiou, *Professionnelles Beautés*, 92–94.

7   Proust, "Un Professeur de beauté," *Les Arts de la vie*, August 15, 1905.

8   Bourdieu, "Price Formation and the Anticipation of Profits," 71.

9   Silverstein, "Indexical Order," 268.

10   Silverstein, "Metapragmatic Discourse and Metapragmatic Function," 36–37.

11   Silverstein, "Indexical Order and the Dialectics of Sociolinguistic Life," 273.

12   Trashy, but widely read in its moment. Jean Lorrain called Mendès "le Père saphiste" (see Jullian, *Jean Lorrain*, 200). In Renée Vivien's 1904 novel *Une Femme m'apparut*, the character named San Giovanni explains: "I was twenty years old before I glimpsed the inexpressible grace of feminine loves, that paleness in intense pleasure, that candid grace in temptation. Reading *Méphistophéla* opened for me the doors of unsuspected gardens, showed the path to unknown stars. I adored this book, in spite of the poor taste of certain of its chapters in which bourgeois morality marries itself officially to popular melodrama. It was then that I understood that uncertain lips could join themselves without disgust to other lips more knowing if just as timid. I understood that there could blossom on this earth magical kisses in which there was no regret and no remorse" (58–59). Aubrey Beardsley notes in a letter to André Raffalovich in 1896 that "Catulle Mendès is a great favourite of mine." He also mentions reading Rachilde and Pierre Louÿs around the same time (see Gray, *Last Letters of Aubrey Beardsley*, 29, 33, 53). Carolyn Dean speaks of Mendès's *Méphistophéla* alongside *Mademoiselle Giraud, ma femme* (1870) by Adolphe Belot, saying: "In most of these novels about Sappho (as well as those in which she does not figure), lesbianism is either associated with upper-class women seeking stimulation of already overwrought nerves or with the depravity of oversexed working-class women, especially prostitutes, whom Dr. Alexandre Parent-Duchâtelet had associated with lesbians in his comprehensive 1836 work on prostitution" (*The Frail Social Body*, 182).

13 Mendès, *Méphistophéla*, 151.

14 Chauncey's work (on the North American context) is quite helpful on these questions. See, for example, his article "Christian Brotherhood or Sexual Perversion?" in which he comments: "Indeed, the very terms 'homosexual behavior' and 'identity,' because of their tendency to conflate phenomena that other cultures may have regarded as quite distinct, appear to be insufficiently precise to denote the variety of social forms of sexuality we wish to analyze" (316).

15 Pougy, *Idylle saphique*, 27.

16 The contrast between *Méphistophéla* and *Idylle saphique* also reveals the division between a model of female same-sex desire related to "inversion" (a model that easily attracts medicalized pathologizing discourse) and a different model based on female homoeroticism in which the femininity of one or the other or both of the partners sometimes moves in the direction of androgyny but resists any full-fledged relation to masculinity.

17 Rosario, *The Erotic Imagination*, 97–98.

18 Raffalovich, *Uranisme et unisexualité*, 14. The relation of Gide's position to that of his precursor Raffalovich is evident. The contrast between *Méphistophéla* (inversion theory) and *Idylle saphique* (where neither of the women involved is markedly masculine) makes clear that this tendency to denigrate forms of same-sex sexuality involving gender inversion in one of the partners in favor of those forms of same-sex sexuality in which both partners remain either "masculine" in the case of men or "feminine" in the case of women is a tendency that existed among certain practitioners of both male and female same-sex desire.

19 Cited by Deffoux, in *J.-K. Huysmans sous divers aspects*, 96–97. When Raffalovich published the letter in 1904, he did not provide the name of the letter's author. It was apparently written in 1896. Raffalovich wrote a reply to Huysmans, which can be found in Sewell, *Two Friends*. In his reply, he claims never to have visited a gay bar such as the one Huysmans describes because he could never bear to be in the company of a whole group of people given over to sensuality—be they unisexual or heterosexual—all at the same time.

20 Silverstein, "The Limits of Awareness," 382.

21 Gide, *The Journals of André Gide*, 3:337; *Journal II: 1926–1950*, 515.

22 Louÿs, *Aphrodite*, 78–79.

23 Rachilde, "Les Romans," *Mercure de France*, July 1902, 184.

24 Rachilde, "Les Romans," *Mercure de France*, June 1902, 750, 752.

25 A letter from Colette to Rachilde in May 1902 makes it perfectly clear that Rachilde, whatever she said in print, did in fact know who the principal author of the novel was. See Colette, *Lettres à ses pairs*, 143.

26 Bourdieu, "The Economy of Symbolic Goods," 112.

27 Nearly every biography of Colette tells of her struggle to establish her

rights to the intellectual property of the books she wrote while married to Willy, books initially published under his name. For a brief summary of the "paradoxes" of Colette's self-presentation as a woman author, see Courtivron, " 'Never Admit!': Colette and the Freedom of Paradox," in the helpful collection edited by Chadwick and Latimer, *The Modern Woman Revisited*. This volume includes a useful appendix on "The Napoleonic Civil Code of 1804," which gives a chronology of the various modifications to the code affecting women's legal status. In *The Other Enlightenment*, Hesse situates Colette in a long line of literary women struggling with the terms of the Napoleonic Code. See esp. 67–78.

28 Ghéon and Gide, *Correspondance*, 443.

29 One can find Lorrain writing in a similar manner on similar subjects as early as 1889. See Angenot, *Le Cru et le faisandé*, 16–17, 123, 125n24.

30 Jullian, *Jean Lorrain*, 69, 258. On de Max, see Lorrain, *La Ville empoisonnée*, 226–28.

31 Lorrain, for instance, cites Gide's *Fruits of the Earth* (1897) in his own *Monsieur de Phocas* (1901), 232–33.

32 Gide, *Journal I*, 340. These passages are not available in the published English translation of Gide's journal.

33 Bourdieu, "L'Illusion biographique," 71.

34 For a discussion of the concept of the literary field, see Bourdieu, *The Rules of Art*, 181–84.

35 Cited in Plat, *Lucie Delarue-Mardrus*, 94–95. Delarue-Mardrus is making reference to a play that Gide had published in 1901, *Le Roi Candaule*.

36 Delarue-Mardrus, who would separate from her husband in 1914, and who both during her marriage and subsequently established intimate relationships with other women, is perhaps now best known for her novel *The Angel and the Perverts* (1930), which portrays an intersexed character interacting with various members of different Parisian same-sex cultures. See Anna Livia's introduction to her translation of the novel for an account of Delarue-Mardrus in relation to the alternative sexual cultures of Paris in the early twentieth century.

37 Ghéon and Gide, *Correspondance*, 439–40. The correspondence with Ghéon contains evidence of other reactions to *The Immoralist* among Gide's friends and acquaintances. The letter Gide writes Ghéon telling him of Gide's experience reading the manuscript of *The Immoralist* aloud to Jacques-Emile Blanche is particularly noteworthy. See the introduction to the Ghéon-Gide correspondence, 51–55, and Gide's letter to Ghéon on September 27, 1901, 362–63.

38 Lorrain's memory of Belot's novel is a bit faulty. Mademoiselle Giraud dies in her bed. It is her female lover whom the husband drowns.

39 See, for example, Galopin's *Les Enracinées*, from 1903, which repro-

duces what it presents as authentic letters written by incarcerated women. The book claims that its goal is to demonstrate the deleterious effects of a women's prison on girls who are sent there as minors. Galopin includes a long section of letters from lesbians to their prison lovers. For example: "My dear, I've devoted myself to a little project for you and it has taken me a little time, as you'll be able to see. You know the nasty books that they offer us here. I've read twenty of them and none of them was any good. So I've made an effort to get some from outside. . . . So here it is: one morning someone slipped me a book I had asked for especially for you, my dearest, because I've already read it, but I read it again before sending it along to you. . . . Yesterday, Sunday, I asked for a book; when I got it, I removed its covers and slipped your special book into them. I sewed it back together carefully with thread so that you'll be able to read it in your cell without anyone being the wiser. They'll think you're reading one of the books from here. You'll see how interesting it is. Just the title should get your juices going: *Mademoiselle Giraud, ma femme*. You'll really enjoy your reading, and you'll think of me especially at those passages I've marked for you with a pencil, my precious and adored little girl . . . Mademoiselle Yolande, Ta femme" (224–25). Galopin's book is mentioned in Francesca Canadé Sautman's helpful article "Invisible Women."

40 Colette, *Oeuvres*, 3:1791.

41 For instance, in a book from 1996, a recent critic remarks of Montesquiou: "Despite his passion for Baudelaire, this gentleman finds no appeal in the seductions of squalor. Montesquiou is no Jean Lorrain; he cannot be counted among those aristocrats and rich members of the bourgeoisie who sample the racy pleasures of slumming in frequent visits to the lower depths of the modern Babylon" [En dépit de sa ferveur pour Baudelaire, le gentil-homme ne ressent aucun attrait pour les séductions de la misère. Montesquiou n'est pas Jean Lorrain; il ne se range nullement parmi les aristocrates et riches bourgeois qui goûtent les plaisirs piquants de l'encanaillement en fré-quentant les bas-fonds de la moderne Babylone] (Bertrand, *Les Curiosités esthétiques de Robert de Montesquiou*, 2:509).

42 Many of Lorrain's novels are also burdened by this baggage, although it is much less prevalent in his late and in many ways most interesting ones, even if they are not the best known: *La Maison Philibert* (1904), *Le Tréteau* (1906), and *Maison pour dames* (1908), for instance.

43 Lorrain, *La Maison Philibert*, 322.

44 Cited by Compagnon in the editorial matter for *Sodome et Gomorrhe* in Proust, *À la recherche du temps perdu*, 3:1187.

45 Cited by Compagnon in ibid.

46 Proust, *Recherche*, 3:955.

47 In a letter she wrote to Francis Carco to praise a text he had written called *Le Possédé*, Colette asked: "Is *Le Possédé* something other than pure (or

rather impure) imagination? If Jean Lorrain were still alive, he would be kneeling in front of you, if you'll permit the expression" [Est-ce que le *Possédé* est autre chose que de l'imagination pure, ou mieux impure? Si Jean Lorrain vivait, il serait déjà à vos genoux,—si j'ose écrire] ("Lettres à ses pairs," 16:285). In *Mes apprentissages* (*My Apprenticeships*), she writes: "Merely by pointing to some detail in the way I did my hair, or to the narrow tie I wore, and saying 'No, not like that, like this. That's better. And don't put red round your neck. Try and find a colour that matches your eyes,' he had given me real pleasure" (111) [Rien qu'à me dire, en indiquant un détail de ma coiffure, et une petit cravate à mon cou: «Non, pas comme ceci; là, c'est mieux. Et pas de rouge autour du cou, cherchez plutôt la même couleur que vos yeux», Jean Lorrain m'avait fait plaisir (*Oeuvres*, 3:1059)].

48   Colette, "A Fable: The Tendrils of the Vine," in *The Collected Stories of Colette*, 100–101; *Les Vrilles de la vigne*, in *Oeuvres*, 1:960–61.

3 ꧁ Colette, the Moulin Rouge, and *Les Vrilles*

1   Colette, *Oeuvres*, 1:994. I will indicate future references to this volume parenthetically in the text. Where no English translation is indicated, the translations are my own. A fair amount of Colette's writing remains untranslated into English, including much of *Les Vrilles de la vigne*.

2   See Thurman, *Secrets of the Flesh*, 163–66; Caradec, *Feu Willy*, 178–90; Pichois and Brunet, *Colette*, 125–26; Francis and Gontier, *Colette*, 191–202. There are many biographies of Colette. Along with those by Thurman, Pichois and Brunet, and Francis and Gontier, I have consulted that of Michèle Sarde. It should be noted that, for all its verve, the biography by Francis and Gontier has been severely criticized for its lack of accuracy. (See, for instance, Claude Pichois's review of it in *Cahiers Colette* 19 [1997]: 250–52.) It seems best not to trust it for details that cannot be confirmed elsewhere.

3   The French original of this text was published as Colette Willy, "Une Lettre," *La Vie Parisienne*, August 14, 1909, 503. A certain number of the texts by Colette that I will be citing in this chapter (including this one) can be found in translation in *The Collected Stories of Colette*, edited by Robert Phelps. For this citation, see 46. I will indicate future references to this volume parenthetically with the abbreviation CSC; I will frequently have made small adjustments to the translation.

4   For information on female nudity in art, literature, photography, and onstage at this time, see Waldberg, *Eros in la Belle Époque*.

5   In the chapter on Colette's *Le Pur et l'impur* in *Another Colette*, Lynne Huffer instructively pursues "the question of [Colette's] persona as a writer and the textual markings through which she inscribes herself as a gendered,

sexual subject." She is interested in the ways "Colette's text transcribes or translates certain semiotic systems (individual dress and behavior, social inter-actions, literary texts) that are culturally coded according to the intersecting categories of sexuality and gender. Those categories, in turn, reveal the struc-tures of power and transgression that define subjects through those semiotic systems as gendered, sexual beings" (74). Also helpful is Flieger, *Colette and the Fantom Subject of Autobiography*, on the way Colette's "tales deploy the writing 'I' as heroine and create a textual identity in the process, a fantom who both is and is not the historical woman herself" (ix–x). In particular, see her first chapter, "Fictional Autobiography: The Spectral Subject," in which Flieger discusses the "palimpsest" (8) of Colette's first-person writing in her novel *La Naissance du jour* (*Break of Day*). On context, see Ross Chambers, *Loiterature*: "It's clear that no context can ever be the whole context—the existence of 'a' context necessarily depends on their being at least one 'other' context—the context in light of which the first context becomes 'a' (an incomplete) context" (12).

6   Willy was the pen name of Henry Gauthier-Villars, a fixture of Parisian turn-of-the-century journalism, especially music criticism, who was also known for his second-rate novels, ones that usually pushed the limits of propriety in some way or another. Calling them "his" novels is probably a bit of an exaggeration, as he had a constant stream of ghost writers working for him, the most famous of whom was Colette, whose "Claudine" novels were originally published under his name. Colette's early fame as a personality was built upon the popularity of the eponymous protagonist of those novels— *Claudine à l'école* (1900), *Claudine à Paris* (1901), *Claudine en ménage* (1902), *Claudine s'en va* (1903)—a character who would often be confused with Col-ette herself, a confusion encouraged by Willy's publicity strategies. Willy dressed Colette up as Claudine on occasion. There was a play based on the novels, in which the actress Polaire would originally star. There were product tie-ins: Claudine outfits, Claudine perfumes and soaps, Claudine postcards (in which both Colette and Polaire would pose as Claudine), and so on. See Pichois and Brunet, *Colette*, 90–100.

7   They were married in 1893, when Colette was twenty years old and Willy thirty-three. Their divorce would be finalized in 1910. See the helpful "Chronologie" by Jacques Frugier in Colette, *Oeuvres*, 1: cxxiii–cxlix.

8   The key events of this period in her personal, artistic, and literary life all follow closely on each other's heels: her stage career begins in 1906, the year she separates from Willy and begins a relationship with Missy. The scandal at the Moulin Rouge is in January 1907. She publishes *La Retraite sentimentale* in February 1907. She becomes a regular contributor to *La Vie Parisienne* in April of the same year. She publishes *Les Vrilles de la vigne* in late 1908, made up in part of texts written since 1905, but largely of texts written since she began contributing to *La Vie Parisienne* in 1907. In 1909, she published under

the name Colette Willy the novel *L'Ingénue libertine*, a combined version of two earlier publications, *Minne* and *Les Égarements de Minne*, that had been published under Willy's name in 1904 and 1905. She published the novel *La Vagabonde* in 1910. In 1911 her relationship with Missy drew to a close, and she began a relationship with Henry de Jouvenel, who would become her second husband.

9   On Montmartre, see Chevalier, *Montmartre du plaisir et du crime*, and Weisberg, *Montmartre and the Making of Mass Culture*.

10   For a recent look at this culture, see Griffin, *The Book of the Courtesans*.

11   *Le Matin* was one of the four large-circulation Parisian dailies at the time. (The others were *Le Journal, Le Petit Parisien*, and *Le Petit Journal*.) Its political line is hard to characterize, being dependent on the shifting likes and dislikes of its owners. See Albert, "La Presse française de 1871 à 1940," 310–14.

12   Missy, for instance, was close friends with Alfred Edwards, who owned *Le Matin* until 1899. See ibid., 309–10, and Francis and Gontier, *Mathilde de Morny*, 218–20. Willy worked for *L'Écho de Paris* and published in other papers as well.

13   The phrase is cited in a letter that Meg Villars wrote to Willy's son, Jacques Gauthier-Villars, describing the evening. See d'Hollander, *Colette*, 360–64.

14   *Le Cri de Paris* established the genre of the "journal d'echos," the gossip rag, which focused on both artistic and political celebrities. Albert suggests that it was the model for today's *Le Canard Enchaîné* ("La Presse française de 1871 à 1940," 386).

15   As this article in *Le Journal* makes clear, the performance of the pantomime, *Le Rêve d'Égypte*, in public at the Moulin Rouge on January 3, 1907, had been preceded by performances of other pantomimes by the couple in less public circumstances (even if the "private" performances were covered by large-circulation daily newspapers). It was also preceded by an unquestionably public appearance together at the Moulin Rouge in *La Romanichelle* (The Gypsy Girl) in mid-December 1906. Apparently Missy's antagonists had not yet, at the time of that performance, organized themselves to protest her new hobby. See Colette, *Oeuvres*, 1:xci–xcii on the performance at the Moulin Rouge in December. For further evidence that Colette, Willy, and, to a lesser extent, Missy, were orchestrating the publicity for the event in order to produce a scandal from which they intended to profit, see Bonal and Remy-Bieth, *Colette intime*, 117, 126, 132.

16   *Gil Blas* was quite successful in its early years, but had lost most of its steam by the turn of the century. Even after a makeover in 1903, it would never fully succeed in building up a new readership. By 1911, it was being published in only 5,000 copies, and it ceased publication in 1914. See Albert, "La Presse française de 1871 à 1940," 346, 380–81.

17 See Chalon, *Liane de Pougy*, 43–76.

18 Missy had apparently, in an earlier period of her life, owned a pair of horses she named Vanilla and Garlic. The word for a vanilla bean in French is also *gousse*. A fair number of slang references to lesbianism have to do with the word for "garlic": *ça sent l'ail, bouffer de l'ail, cuisine à l'ail*—"it smells like garlic," "to wolf down garlic," "to cook with garlic." See Thurman, *Secrets of the Flesh*, 153.

19 The socialist daily *L'Humanité* doesn't give the event much coverage at all, just a short article on January 5, 1907, in which it is noted that "The noise redoubled when Colette Willy, returning to life in her sarcophagus, arose to mime a love scene with her partner Mme de Belbeuf. 'Throw them out,' people cried . . . along with insults we cannot record; from the front of the theater women threw a variety of projectiles onto the stage." The conclusion of the journalist in *L'Humanité* is the same as that we see everywhere else: "People in high places seem to want to ensure that the marquise de Morny will not appear onstage."

20 *L'Intransigeant* had gone through a good number of political shifts since its founding in 1880. In the years 1905 to 1909 it was in a state of financial crisis, and there were disagreements between its two main directors. It had nonetheless clearly established itself as a right-wing journal that followed the party line of the nationalist Ligue de la Patrie Française. In late 1909, it would add a literary column whose regular contributors would include Alain-Fournier, Max Jacob, and Guillaume Apollinaire (Albert, "La Presse française de 1871 à 1940," 341–42).

21 On cucumbers in travel narratives, see chapter 5, "The Psychomorphology of the Clitoris," in Traub, *The Renaissance of Lesbianism in Early Modern England*, esp. 199, 206.

22 Earlier in the same issue (January 12, 1907, 23), in a column called "Les On-dit" (News of the town), *La Vie Parisienne* explicitly makes fun of the misplaced pride of "aristocratic" families: "In the galleries of the Music Hall packed with people eager to attend the debut performance of the Marquise, a long-haired gentleman wanders about indifferently. He is not at all concerned with the exhibition of the niece of an emperor. He has other reasons for being there. His role is to offer titles of nobility to spectators who lack them so that they too might become indignant at seeing one of their own acting like a Liane de Pougy or a Suzanne Derval. He hands us a flyer. We read: ' . . . A great number of our contemporaries are still unaware that, dating from the reign of Louis XIV, all the notable families of France, even bourgeois families, are possessed of a registered coat of arms, thanks to a royal edict of November 20, 1696, the originals of these coats of arms being preserved in the Office of Titles.' So it is that the Herald-at-Arms, as he calls himself, offers his services, quite economically, to search out these arms. . . . If the reproduc-

tion of the royal decrees is not sufficient satisfaction for his clients, he points out that it is unquestionably interesting in other ways, for manufacturers and merchants 'could make use of the traditional emblem of their race as a trademark.'" In other words, almost anyone, if willing to pay for the research, can find a family coat of arms, which would allow them to be outraged should a family member ever decide to appear onstage at the Moulin Rouge, following in the footsteps of well-known courtesans such as Liane de Pougy. And if it turns out they don't like their coat of arms, or if they are ever short on cash, they can rent it out for advertising—as it is assumed Missy has done.

23   The author of the article is here probably making reference to a story in circulation to the effect that Colette had been seen of late wearing a dog collar made of gold and engraved with the words "I belong to Missy." The description of her almond-shaped eyes may also be a passing reference to Lucie Delarue-Mardrus, another member of "Paris-Mytilène," sometimes called "La Princesse Amande." Delarue-Mardrus was well known for her travels in North Africa with her husband, and for the photographs of her taken there in various kinds of outfits.

24   "La Première de 'Lysistrata,'" in *La Vie Parisienne*, January 12, 1907, 52–54.

25   Goffman, *Frame Analysis*, 9.

26   On the Ligue de la Patrie Française, see Roux, *Nationalisme et conservatisme*; Watson, "The Nationalist Movement in Paris"; and Alexander, "Jules Lemaître and the Ligue de la Patrie Française." Syveton seems to have been caught up simultaneously in a personal scandal and in an effort to discredit the Republican government then in power for its secret efforts to weed out opponents from the hierarchy of the French military. There was speculation immediately after Syveton's death that he had been murdered for his role as a serious thorn in the government's side, but the hypothesis that he committed suicide for personal reasons is the one that prevailed. His death when he was at the center of political controversy provoked a great deal of public emotion (rioting at his funeral) and press coverage of his own case and, of course, of the nationalist movement. This was in late 1904 and early 1905. For information on the way the Ligue positioned itself in French intellectual culture (principally in opposition to the Ligue des Droits de l'Homme) and on the affiliations of various intellectual and literary types within it, see Compagnon, *Connaissez-vous Brunetière?*, 176–93.

27   The word *métèque* was in fact rather common in French nationalist discourse of the time. It seems to have been used to express a combined anti-German sentiment (given that France had lost Alsace and Lorraine to the Germans in 1870), anti-English sentiment, and an antisemitism recently fueled by the Dreyfus Affair. The word was used by people like Maurras, and also by Noilhan's friend Syveton, one of the university professors who

founded the Ligue de la Patrie Française, and who liked to excoriate the French professorate for being pro-German and antimilitary. In 1899, Syveton published an article titled "Le Complot des métèques"(The Plot of the Metics) in which he complained that such people wanted to "deform the French spirit and bend it to their foreign ideal, to transform France according to the model of their homeland and the land of their predilection, England or Germany" (cited in Bonnamour, *Gabriel Syveton*, 202). Watson writes that "antisemitism played almost no part in the official policy of the Patrie Française although they agreed on joint candidatures with several antisemites, and 'à bas les juifs' seems to have been a common slogan shouted at their meetings. But in spite of attacks on Jewish high finance they opposed any measures of exception directed against Jews, and concentrated rather on the danger of foreigners within France" ("The Nationalist Movement," 64–65).

28 Pierre Noilhan seems to have been a second-tier figure within the Ligue de la Patrie Française. He was certainly friends with many of the major figures who wrote the main opinion columns for the *Annales de la Patrie Française*: Syveton, Jules Lemaître, Maurice Barrès, François Coppée, and others. One can read in the *Annales* of speeches Noilhan made to local branches of the Ligue.

29 Alexander informs us that there were many notable Bonapartists in the Ligue de la Patrie Française and explains how this complicated the Ligue's party line ("Jules Lemaître and the Ligue de la Patrie Française," 148).

30 It was also known as the Cercle Victor Hugo because it was located on the Avenue Victor Hugo in Paris. See Francis and Gontier, *Colette*, 189; Pichois and Brunet, *Colette*, 119–21.

31 Francis and Gontier, *Mathilde de Morny*, 228.

32 Pichois and Brunet, *Colette*, 140.

33 Léopard, "La Panthère," *Fantasio*, January 1, 1908, 604.

34 In the days after the scandal at the Moulin Rouge, Willy would lose his job at *L'Écho de Paris*. It turns out that a number of the key people in the Ligue de la Patrie Française were associated with *L'Echo de Paris*. Pierre Albert tells us that around 1900 it became "the unofficial voice of the Ligue de la Patrie Française, launching itself into the heart of the anti-Dreyfusard campaign, and welcoming a good part of the clientele of the *Figaro*" (346–47). Many of the people associated with the Ligue would write for *L'Écho*: Barrès and Bourget, for example. By 1906, Albert writes, "the formerly lightweight gossip rag had become the extremely academic organ of the catholic and nationalist right" (347). The Ligue's platform included the typical elements of a right-wing nationalist group of the moment: praise for the army, denunciations of left-wing intellectuals, insistence on the importance of submission to collective authority. It took a position against "alcoholism, immorality, and depopulation" and gave voice to a stereotypical notion of a woman's duty: to transmit

to her children "une âme française" [a French soul], and to "make her sons into true children of the race, to give to her daughters the virtues of their foremothers and thereby prepare the generation that will be the strength of French life of tomorrow" (see Roux, *Nationalisme et conservatisme*, 32, 76). To the extent that *L'Écho de Paris* intended to be a vehicle for this sort of nationalist ideology, it might appear to be an odd place for someone like Willy, who seemed committed to a life on the edge of scandal. Yet it would also seem that if he sustained his position there up until 1907, it must be because it wasn't until 1907 that someone intervened personally to see him removed. That is, his removal would probably have been not on the basis of ideological principle (nationalist discourse and music criticism by a man of dubious morals who wrote trashy novels could easily coexist on different pages of the same newspaper), but on the basis of a kind of personal vengeance on the part of someone—say someone affiliated with the Ligue de la Patrie Française or with the Jockey Club—who felt dishonored by the events at the Moulin Rouge and who could bring the appropriate kind of pressure to bear upon the administration of the newspaper. Here again, the response to the events at the Moulin Rouge would seem as much or more a question of offended aristocratic (or national?) honor than a question of a phobic response to two women kissing.

35 Thurman, *Secrets of the Flesh*, 162.

36 The conjunction of sexual nonconformity with right-wing political tendencies and an aristocratic social positioning is a notable characteristic in French cultural history. In the cases of figures such as Missy or Jacques d'Adelswärd-Fersen, one might even say that the forms of activism they undertook on behalf of their right to express their own sexuality grew out of a sense of their own aristocratic privilege. On Fersen, see Peyrefitte, *L'Exilé de Capri* and Lucien, *Akademos*.

37 Foucault, *The History of Sexuality, Volume 1*, 119.

38 Reprinted in Lorrain, *Une Femme par jour*, 75–76.

39 See Francis and Gontier, *Mathilde de Morny*, 149–56, 167–78.

40 Francis and Gontier note that the life of the young Missy was, indeed, quite scandalous. At the moment Rachilde's novel was published, she was, they claim, too occupied with certain shocking events from her real life to pay much attention to or take action against the novel: "She had fallen in love with a young woman, a gardener from Brittany and had a short, passionate affair with her. In a moment of raging passion, Missy had excised her clitoris with her teeth. The young woman was threatening to sue. The marquise needed a large sum of money to buy her silence" (149). Again, one wishes the biographers were clearer about their sources for their information.

41 Francis and Gontier suggest in *Mathilde de Morny* that it was Missy who sued Lorrain for defamation (127, 178–79). They are incorrect in this assertion.

42 Lorrain, *Correspondance*, 144.

43 "Justice et Morale," *Le Courrier Français*, February 7, 1892, 8.

44 The article in which *L'Écho de Paris* recounts its day in court and provides a description of its lawyer's arguments can be found on the first two pages of the issue of February 5, 1892. For a useful general account of this whole period, see Albert, *Saphisme et décadence*.

45 See Terrou, "L'Evolution du droit de la presse de 1881 à 1840."

46 There is a collection of poems by d'Alençon, *Sous le masque*, published in 1918, that includes, in the section called "Énigme," love poems to another woman.

47 On Proust's use of Vigny's poem and of Sodom and Gomorrah more generally, and on the criticisms of his version of Gomorrah by people such as Colette and Natalie Clifford Barney, see Ladenson, "Colette for Export Only" and *Proust's Lesbianism*. In *Proust's Lesbianism*, Ladenson comments that "it was Proust who made Gomorrah a recognized euphemism for female homosexuality" (35), but it would appear Proust had some help from Mendès, even if Mendès does misquote Vigny (putting Sodom where Gomorrah should be, and vice versa).

48 We might, thinking in historical terms, theorize that Mendès in these columns is making a claim that practices of female homoeroticism which in the past may not necessarily have been thought of as related to *le vice lesbien*, or which simply may not have been thought of as much of anything at all, now must be associated with all other kinds of female same-sex sexuality. On the distinction between female homoeroticism and lesbian sex, see Sharon Marcus's work on Victorian English culture in "Reflections on Victorian Fashion Plates." Marcus comments that "Victorians' relative unfamiliarity with the lesbian as the pathological type later defined by sexologists made for a society in which the absence of recognizable lesbians promoted the acceptance of female homoeroticism." She continues: "Precisely because Victorians saw lesbian sex almost nowhere, they could embrace female homoeroticism almost everywhere. . . . For Victorian women, homoeroticism encompassed companionship, love, caretaking, self-sacrifice, admiration, longing, obsession, physical intimacy, and intense excitement and passion. . . . It would be as absurd to think that in practice female homoeroticism never led to sex between women as it would be to think that it always did so" (5–6). The French materials I am considering make it clear that it was possible (for someone like Mendès) to make a distinction between female homosexual eroticism and lesbianism, but it was also possible to challenge that distinction. Yet it also seems clear that a well-developed culture of women sexually involved with other women (and fully conscious of being so) existed in France throughout much of the nineteenth century, and that women affiliated around the ques-

tion of same-sex desires even as they recognized clear distinctions between various sets of practices through which those desires were enacted.

49 There seems even to have been a certain competition regarding this topic. In a number of his letters from 1889 to Edmond Magnier, Lorrain worries over the fate of one of the columns he has recently sent in to *L'Événement* (of which Magnier was the editor). The article appears to be on a lesbian topic, and Lorrain worries about its fate because on October 19, 1889, *L'Événement* has published a front page article by someone else called "Sapho Raison Sociale." That article describes a marketing campaign for a certain brand of soap. The campaign seems to be directed specifically to lesbians, for it includes a dialogue in verse between Sappho and Mlle. Giraud, heroine of Belot's notorious novel, *Mademoiselle Giraud, ma femme.* The author ironizes that if lesbians are already perceived as a niche market, soon sodomites will be too: "If Lesbians already make up a small world that merchants of today cannot ignore, then probably Sodomites form a slightly smaller one, but also quite respectable (please don't misunderstand my use of the word) in number." See Lorrain, *Soixante-huit lettres à Edmond Magnier*, 20, 24, 26, 78.

50 It is not only journalists who enact this cultural division. Liane de Pougy herself gives voice to it in her diary, *My Blue Notebooks*, in 1926: "I shall never understand that kind of mistake: wanting to look like a man, sacrificing feminine grace, charm and sweetness. To help the illusion, Missy used to flatten her breasts under a wide rubber band. How horrible to crush and damage such a charming gift of Nature! And cutting off one's hair when it can be a woman's most beautiful adornment! It's a ridiculous aberration, quite apart from the fact that it invites insult and scandal" (111). She would say as much again in 1933: "We were passionate, rebels against a woman's lot, voluptuous and cerebral little apostles, rather poetical, full of illusions and dreams. We loved long hair, pretty breasts, pouts, simpers, charm, graces; not so much masculine women. 'Why try to resemble our enemies?' Nathalie-Flossie used to murmur in her little nasal voice" (253).

51 Richard O'Monroy, "Nos Charmeuse: Liane de Pougy," *Fantasio,* November 1, 1906, 288–90.

52 Cited in Colette, *Oeuvres*, 2:1285.

53 Ibid., 2:5–6.

54 Franc-Nohain, "Une Nouvelle Etoile: Colette Willy," *Fantasio,* November 1, 1906, 274–76.

55 Jammes, for instance, friend of Gide as well as Colette, knew Gide wouldn't take kindly to the idea of Jammes writing a preface for Colette's book. He wrote to Gide, in a letter of October 17, 1904, "You will reply perhaps, that you would never have deigned to write a preface to this book. And I would then tell you that I find it perfect and that the preface is a

wonderful occasion for me to broadcast my own name more widely" (cited in Colette, *Oeuvres*, 2:1285). In some ways, Gide's *La Nouvelle Revue Française*, which published its first issue in 1908 and began regular publication in 1909, set itself up in opposition to the literary world of Mendès, Lorrain, and thus also Colette, as well as in opposition to the *Mercure de France*, where some of Colette's first works, as well as Gide's *The Immoralist*, would be published, and where Rachilde was one of the ruling forces. In April 1909, rather quickly after Catulle Mendès's death in February, Gide published a sarcastic article in the NRF that shocked some of his contemporaries, "Moeurs littéraires: Autour du tombeau de Catulle Mendès" (Literary Morals: At the Tomb of Catulle Mendès), in which he wrote: "This sad, degrading poet, who ruined or sullied every genre it occurred to him to try out, will perhaps be of use in provoking a salutary rebound away from that false literature with which we are encumbered, away from a decrepit romanticism." As for who belongs to this "false literature," given his comments (quoted in chapter 1) on the Moulin Rouge scandal, one might assume Gide would include Colette. Consider the report André Germain gives of Gide's grudging expression of admiration more than a decade later for Colette's *Chéri*: "In a coquettish manner, blushing a bit, Gide spoke to us—it was as if at the age of fifty he was still somehow slightly virginal or embarrassed—about a book he apologized for having read, but that unfortunately he was obliged to find admirable. Telling us all of this, with a kind of ecclesiastical gluttony, he moved about sinuously, like a serpent offering an apple" (Germain, *Les Clés de Proust*, 236).

56 See Francis and Gontier, *Mathilde de Morny*, 250–53. They note, for instance, that Missy escorted Colette, together with Liane de Pougy, to the glamorous opening of the Théâtre Réjane on December 14, 1906, where they were much in view. As for the possibility that Willy wrote the article in *Fantasio*, Francis and Gontier are unclear as to what evidence supports this speculation.

57 On Mayol, see page xv of the photographic insert on "Chansons" in Eribon, *Dictionnaire des cultures gays et lesbiennes*, and see also the article Hazera, "Chansons" (103–6 in the same volume). Mayol was famous for the elaborate gestural play that went into his performances of songs about women. Public images of him make no secret of his effeminacy. Colette would, in the months ahead, appear in the same music hall programs as Mayol, her pantomime sometimes apparently coming immediately after one of Mayol's numbers. She mentions this fact with some displeasure—perhaps not desiring too close an association with parts of popular culture she deemed *too* popular or vulgar—in a draft for one of the texts in *Les Vrilles de la vigne*. See Colette, *Oeuvres*, 1:1569–70. For examples of other drawings of Missy and Colette by Sem, see Bonal and Remy-Bieth, *Colette intime*, 100, 107, and 119.

58 Le Vitrioleur, "La Marquise," *Fantasio*, December 15, 1906, 416–17.

For a study of rhetorics of degeneration at this time, see Nye, "Degeneration and the Medical Model of Cultural Crisis in the French *Belle Epoque*."

59 Francis and Gontier (*Colette*, 224) tell us that toward the end of 1907, Sem painted a mural at Maxim's representing celebrities in the Bois de Boulogne and included a carriage being driven by Willy in which Missy and Colette were passengers involved in some kind of an embrace. Willy would sue for defamation this time and would lose.

60 The book, devoted in large part to the Eulenburg affair, would be a bestseller for a few months after its publication in February of that year. See Rivers, *Proust and the Art of Love*, 128.

61 Typical examples from the late nineteenth century would be the volume by Martineau mentioned in the previous chapter, *Les Déformations vulvaires et anales*, or Fiaux, *Les Maisons de tolérance*, with its chapter 10: "Comment les maisons servent la morale publique.—Les maisons publiques repaires de tribadisme, de pédérastie et de bestialité."

62 Judith Halberstam's *Female Masculinity* is helpful on the functioning of this distinction and others. See especially the chapter called "Perverse Presentism: The Androgyne, the Tribade, the Female Husband, and Other Pre-Twentieth-Century Genders." She writes, for instance: "The androgyne . . . represents a different form of gender variance than the masculine woman, and although the androgyne may have faced some kind of social opprobrium, it probably did not come in the form of a response to gender confusion. The androgyne represents some version of gender mixing, but this rarely adds up to total ambiguity; when a woman is mistaken consistently for a man, I think it is safe to say that what marks her gender presentation is not androgyny but masculinity. . . . I propose that we consider the various categories of sexual variation for women as separate and distinct from the modern category of lesbian. . . . There are likely to be many examples of masculine women in history who had no interest in same-sex sexuality. . . . There is probably a lively history of the masculine heterosexual woman to be told" (57). In Colette's cultural circles, and in her writing, the androgynous woman drawn to other women, the feminine woman drawn to other women, and the masculine woman drawn to other women are sometimes held distinct, and sometimes assimilated to each other, just as they sometimes affiliated with each other and sometimes did not feel able to do so. Colette moved between and in and out of all these categories in the years 1900–10. It was in some ways the interactive context of her relation to Missy and of her attempts to create a particular profile for herself as a certain kind of woman writer that made her *femininity* particularly salient. Halberstam also helps us to understand the importance not only of gender variance but of chosen sexual *practices* in providing form for a variety of female same-sex sexual identities. She writes: "Before the emergence of what we now understand as 'lesbian' identities, same-sex desire

worked through any number of different channels. If it seems both obvious and undeniable that probably many models of same-sex desire did exist, then why have we not busied ourselves in imagining their variety?" (50). We can see all these different channels in operation in French culture of Colette's moment. We can also see, in commentary on and representations of these channels by Colette and her contemporaries, both a practical knowledge of the distinctions and even tensions between them and an ability to lump them all together as part of "Paris-Lesbos" or "Paris-Mytilène." Thus *saphisme, tribadisme, lesbianisme,* and then *homosexualité* and *inversion* could in some contexts be made to function as synonyms, and in others be used to make distinctions; and the distinctions could have to do with the gender identities of the participants, the degree of exclusivity of their focus on women, the particular sexual practices they engaged in, and probably other factors as well.

63   See, for example, the remarks of Munholland, in "Republican Order and Republican Tolerance": "Increasingly radical republican politicians demanded that the police and the censors impose 'good taste' upon the music halls and cafés. A nationalist attack upon a prominent republican politician, Camille Pelletan, and his wife during a show staged at La Scala music hall caused radical politicians, normally defenders of press liberty, to insist that their minister of interior enforce the state's censorship laws. In his own newspaper, *L'Aurore,* which had staunchly defended the rights of Captain Dreyfus, Clemenceau asked why the 'reactionary filth' of the music halls and the cabarets was permitted. This complaint marked Clemenceau's political trajectory from mayor of Montmartre during the Commune to the apostle of law and order during his tenure as prime minister from 1906 to 1909, when he became known as a strike breaker and the nation's 'number one cop.' The posters advertising the pleasures of Montmartre came under attack from the director of primary education for the city of Paris who denounced the 'abominable imagery' that had appeared on the walls of the city, claiming that it had a corrupting effect" (30).

64   Lowe, *Critical Terrains,* 8.

65   I take the phrase "the essential qualities of their race" from Gabriel Syveton's "Le Complot des métèques," reprinted in Bonnamour, *Gabriel Syveton,* 269–70. *Race* at this moment in French history cannot be understood as having any simple or even primary relation to "whiteness" and its others, although this situation would shift dramatically in the course of the following decade. See, for instance, Tyler Stovall, "National Identity and Shifting Imperial Frontiers."

66   Foucault, *"Society Must Be Defended,"* 80–81. For a challenging reading of the place of race in Foucault's thought, and in these lectures in particular, see Stoler, *Race and the Education of Desire.*

67   See *Fantasio,* April 15, 1907, 215.

68 See *"Society Must Be Defended,"* 77, 189. Lisa Lowe says something related about orientalist discourse in the helpful introduction to her *Critical Terrains*, where she writes: "I argue for a conception of orientalism as heterogeneous and contradictory; to this end I observe, on the one hand, that orientalism consists of an uneven matrix of orientalist situations across different cultural and historical sites, and on the other, that each of these orientalisms is internally complex and unstable." Lowe is particularly interested in points where "orientalism is refunctioned and rearticulated against itself," in "junctures at which narratives of gendered, racial, national, and class difference complicate and interrupt the narrative of orientalism" (5). The evening of January 3, 1907, at the Moulin Rouge could conceivably count as one such juncture.

69 Stoler, *Race and the Education of Desire*, 124, citing Weber, *Peasants into Frenchmen*, 3,6,7.

70 Cited in Thurman, *Secrets of the Flesh*, 7, and Francis and Gontier, *Colette*, 9.

71 Cited in Francis and Gontier, *Colette*, 9. Francis and Gontier wish to establish the truth of the rumors regarding Colette's mixed-race heritage (9–17). Pichois and Brunet point out in their biography (13) that while it is true that one branch of Colette's family lived in Martinique for a certain period in the seventeenth and eighteenth centuries, Francis and Gontier are not actually able to construct a family tree for Colette that shows at what point a mixed-race coupling would have occurred. See also Pichois's review of the Francis and Gontier biography in *Cahiers Colette* 19 (1997), where Pichois comments that while they perhaps make a mixed-race hypothesis seem reasonable (*vraisemblable*), they never actually prove it (251–52). What we can conclude is that Francis, Gontier, Pichois, and Brunet all demonstrate that racialized habits of thought, exploited by Colette in the early years of the twentieth century, can still structure certain kinds of writing about her.

72 For a slightly earlier period, see Pao, *The Orient of the Boulevards*.

73 A notable exception would be Madeleine Dobie, who situates this pantomime in a long sequence of French literary representations of mummies in her interesting book, *Foreign Bodies*. See her chapter 5, "The Modernist Turn in Orientalism: Gautier's Egyptian Tales."

74 On Napoléon's occupation of Egypt, see Colla, " 'Non, non! Si, si!' " On the ongoing European fascination for ancient Egypt, see Colla's dissertation, "Hooked on Pharaonics."

75 See Bonnamour, *Gabriel Syveton*, 277. On May 15, 1903, the *Annales de la Patrie Française* would editorialize against the recent visit of the English King Edward to France. The editorialist would wonder how the French people could be expected to tolerate such a visit while their hearts were still suffering from the French disgrace at Fachoda.

76   See on this topic the introduction to Ladenson's *Proust's Lesbianism*.

77   The edition of *Les Vrilles de la vigne* in print today is one that dates from 1934, when Colette reordered the texts, dropping some and adding others. There was an intermediate edition in 1923, mostly the same as the 1908 edition, except that the final text of the 1908 edition, "Printemps de la Riviera," was dropped. The Pléiade edition of Colette's *Oeuvres* reprints the 1934 edition of *Les Vrilles*, but includes all of the texts from 1908 that were later dropped from *Les Vrilles* as appendixes. The eighteen texts from 1908, listed in the order of that edition, are: "Les Vrilles de la vigne," "Nuit blanche," "Jour gris," "Le Dernier Feu," "Nonoche," "La Dame qui chante," "Toby-Chien parle," "Dialogue de bêtes," "Toby-Chien et la musique," "Belles-de-Jour," "De quoi est-ce qu'on a l'air?" "La Guérison," "Le Miroir," "En marge d'une page blanche I," "En marge d'une page blanche II," "Partie de pêche," "Music-Halls," "Printemps de la Riviera." I will be including in my analysis a number of texts Colette published in 1909 that seem to me to continue the project of *Les Vrilles de la vigne*. (I mention here only those texts from Colette's 1909 output to which I make specific reference. A full bibliography for 1909 can be found in Colette, *Oeuvres*, 1:1678–79.) Those texts are: "Le Sémiramis-Bar" (from *La Vie Parisienne*, March 27, 1909), "Impressions de danse" (from *Fantasio*, April 15, 1909), "Gitanette" (from *La Vie Parisienne*, May 1, 1909), "En voyage" (from *La Vie Parisienne*, July 10, 1909), "Une Lettre" (from *La Vie Parisienne*, August 1, 1909), and "Dans la dune" (from *La Vie Parisienne*, October 2, 1909).

78   See Chevalier, *Montmartre du plaisir et du crime*, 226.

79   See Colette, *Lettres à ses pairs*, 202.

80   See Thurman, *Secrets of the Flesh*, 528n18.

81   *Cinaedus* and *pathicus* in fact seem to have been used synonymously in ancient Rome to designate passive male homosexuals.

82   See Wanda, "L'Hérésie sentimentale," *Fantasio*, May 1, 1909, 647–48. The Bulton scandal was widely covered in the Parisian press in late March and early April 1904. See, for instance, *Le Journal* starting on March 21. In subsequent days, the police raided the apartments of the men they had arrested at Bulton's party and, when concerned friends hadn't got there first, seized correspondences and other personal papers. Given that the men arrested, after having their names published in the papers, were slowly released by the police, and given that the story disappears from the newspapers by the first days of April, one can imagine that the initial zealousness of the police was calmed down due to orders from higher up—out of concern for who might be implicated were the investigation to be allowed to expand its purview inordinately.

83   Colette, "Le Sémiramis Bar," *La Vie Parisienne*, March 27, 1909, 223–

26. An English version can be found in *The Collected Stories of Colette*. For this citation, see 53.

84 Colette, "Gitanette," *La Vie Parisienne*, May 1, 1909, 320–21.

85 Carco, *Envoûtement de Paris*, 25–26.

86 See, for instance, her review of *La Retraite sentimentale*, in which she writes, addressing the character Claudine: "As you are, as you forever will be, there is a kind of fatality about you, and also most certainly a utility, for such exceptions are necessary if we are to endure the weight of the solemn rules of our old prejudices. Praise be to you, then, Claudine, for the closing pages of your book, in which, lying on the earth damp both with the morning dew and your tears, you speak of dying with the dignity of a truly superior being. From the rotting of leaves and of cadavers you are able to extract the enduring perfume of the nourishing earth, the earth that turns the better to give repose to the dead. You, more than any other poet, have found the sacred words an old humanity needs in order to remember the dawn of its virtues" (Rachilde, "Les Romans," *Mercure de France*, March 1, 1907, 114).

87 Rachilde, "Les Romans," *Mercure de France*, January 1, 1909, 108–9.

88 On the question of the date of the composition of the second half of the text, see the editors' speculations in Colette, *Oeuvres*, 1: 1534–35, 1537. On 1:1554, the editors suggest that the second half of the text had originally been published in *La Vie Parisienne* before having been included in *Les Vrilles de la vigne*. They do not give a date for this earlier appearance, and I have not found any trace of it.

89 "Nuit blanche" was first published in *La Vie Parisienne*, on June 8, 1907, but in that version it included neither the dedication nor the final sentence with its unequivocal past participle. June 1907 was still only a few months after the incident at the Moulin Rouge. Was someone worried about causing too much more scandal at this point, and had those fears been allayed by late 1908, when *Les Vrilles de la vigne* was published? Or had Colette simply not yet written that final sentence? In the earliest printings of the *Vie Parisienne* edition of *Les Vrilles de la vigne* every selection except for "Les Vrilles de la vigne" and "Le Miroir" was dedicated to someone or other. Even Willy and Miss Meg V . . . were among the dedicatees. Only "M . . ." received more than one dedication. In later printings of this same edition (which seems to have remained in print for well over a decade) most of the dedications were removed. The dedication "Pour M . . ." was one of the few to remain, but it would remain only for "Jour gris" and "Le Dernier Feu." The dedication would be removed from "Nuit blanche"—at whose behest and for what reasons remaining a matter for speculation. We might also note that another of Colette's texts, "Dans la dune," first published in *La Vie Parisienne* on October 2, 1909, also bears the dedication "Pour M . . ." and also deals with

Missy and Colette's relationship together in Le Crotoy. Elaine Marks's classic essay "Lesbian Intertextuality" includes a commentary on the concluding sentences of "Nuit blanche" (364–65).

90 Recently, for instance, in Julia Kristeva's *Le Génie féminin, tome III: Colette*, filled with dishearteningly predictable psychoanalytic gestures that enforce the most reactionary of gender ideologies and reveal a fair amount of homophobia as well.

91 Colette, *Claudine Married*, 381, translation modified. I cite the French from *Oeuvres*.

92 *Vrille* in this usage seems no longer to be current in French. Along with Lacassagne's dictionary, it is attested in Napoléon Hayard's *Dictionnaire d'argot-français* of 1907, which simply defines it as "tribade" (39). (On the complications involved in understanding what tribade might mean in different times and places, see Halberstam, *Female Masculinity*, 59–65, and Traub, *The Renaissance of Lesbianism*, 191–228.) *Vrille* also occurs, as we saw in the last chapter, in Lorrain's *La Maison Philibert*. It can also be found in Charles-Etienne's *Notre-Dame de Lesbos* (1924). The September 15, 1906, issue of *Fantasio* mentions a novel (apparently pornographic) by "La Vrille" titled *Les Mémoires d'une masseuse*. I have been unable to locate a copy.

93 We could speculate that Colette is here imagining that just as in certain cultures a man can have sex with both men and women without being marked as nonnormative as long as he retains an identity as a penetrator, so a woman can have sex with both women and men without being marked as nonnormative as long as she is the "feminine" partner. But we have earlier seen Liane de Pougy suggesting a different model—that what was for her "acceptable" was two women taking pleasure in each other's femininity—with this being an episode contained within a sexual career that also included relations with men.

94 It probably bears mention that the text which immediately follows the group of texts "Pour M . . ." is a third-person narration about a cat, Nonoche, and the text immediately following that, "La Dame qui chante" is a first-person narration, but by a man. There follow two dialogues between Toby-Chien and Kiki-la-Doucette, and an interview of Toby-Chien by his mistress, before a series of texts in which the first-person figure of Colette tells of her relation with Valentine.

4 🐚 Gide and Posterity

1 Many such private texts circulated, especially among Gide's friends. See, for instance, Alibert, *Le Fils de Loth* and the preface to that volume by Eribon. Alibert was among those to whom Gide read *Corydon*. See Gide and

Alibert, *Correspondance 1907–1950*, including the helpful introduction by Claude Martin. Alibert supported the idea of Gide publishing *Corydon*. See his letter to Gide on August 13, 1909, 26–27. Among those opposed to its publication was another of the privileged few to hear it read, Eugène Rouart. See David H. Walker's postface to Gide, *Le Ramier*. Marcel Drouin was also vociferous in his opposition to *Corydon* once Gide had read it to him. See Sheridan, *André Gide*, 237, Gide and Copeau, *Correspondance*, 1:334, and Gide's fascinating journal entry for December 21, 1923: *The Journals of André Gide*, 338–41; *Journal I*, 1234–37.

2 Ghéon and Gide, *Correspondance*, 930.

3 The hero of Ghéon's *L'Adolescent* was named Guillaume Arnoult (Gide's initials reversed), and clearly the work involved transpositions of intimate situations Gide and Ghéon had lived through together. See the introduction to their correspondence (60–93) and also the correspondence itself (esp. 678–84). Sheridan gives a useful account of the rapport between Gide and Ghéon. See *André Gide*, 166–306. Monique Nemer's work in progress, *L'Effet Corydon*, promises to be immensely helpful to anyone interested in Gide's activities in the years he was thinking about and working on *Corydon* and related texts.

4 See Ghéon and Gide, *Correspondance*, 94–95 and 678–79.

5 Gide, *Les Nouvelles Nourritures*, 253. On the date of composition of this passage, see the "Notice" on *Les Nouvelles Nourritures*, 1492–1502.

6 The pages in Gide's journal concerning this crisis in his relationship with his wife have been incorporated into the latest Pléiade edition of the *Journal* but were not included in earlier editions. Gide reserved them for *Et nunc manet in te*, a volume devoted to his wife that Gide had published shortly after his death. It is titled *Madeleine* in the English translation. The passage cited here is thus not to be found in *The Journals of André Gide*, but can be found on page 69 of *Madeleine*.

7 Gide gives one account of this crisis in *Et nunc manet in te*. Other points of view can be found in Schlumberger, *Madeleine et André Gide*, and in a document written by Alibert and published as an appendix to his correspondence with Gide, 477–81. An earlier version of the present chapter was presented at a conference devoted to Gide's 1918 trip to Cambridge with Allégret, and the published proceedings of that conference include many helpful contributions dealing with this period in Gide's career: Segal, *Le Désir à l'oeuvre*.

8 This passage was published for the first time only in the 1996 Pléiade edition of Gide's journal edited by Eric Marty. (That is, it had never been published earlier, even in *Et nunc manet in te*.) It might seem a paradoxical suppression from earlier editions: why censor the sentence that expresses the possibility of not (or no longer) censoring the "revelatory" texts, *Corydon* and *Si le*

grain ne meurt? That, as of 1996, we can finally read the entire November 24, 1918, entry in Gide's *Journal* in its sequentially appropriate place in the text (previously, only the shortened version of that day's entry printed in *Et nunc manet in te* was available) poses another kind of question: how, in our own editorial practices, do we instantiate a notion of "literary posterity" and an evolving notion of privacy in regards to sexuality and intimate relations, as we produce exact, complete, well organized editions of texts such as Gide's *Journal*?

9   See Sheridan, *André Gide*, 319. On Gide's reading to his wife more generally, see Armstrong, " 'Je lis à Em.' "

10   Gide, *Madeleine*, 68.

11   Gide and Martin du Gard, *Correspondance*, 1:157–58.

12   Martin du Gard, *Journal*, 2:171–72, emphasis added.

13   Ibid., 2:172.

14   The bracketed sentences are listed as a manuscript variant in the notes to the Pléiade edition. See 1688–89.

15   Bourdieu, "L'Illusion biographique," 71.

16   Gide and Martin du Gard, *Correspondance*, 1:177–78.

17   Bourdieu, "L'Illusion biographique," 72.

18   I have written a bit about Gide's relation to Proust and Wilde in this regard in the introduction to *Gide's Bent* (8–16), and to Proust in chapter 1 above. As for Dostoyevsky, Gide's lectures on him (published in 1923) make it clear not only how important his thinking about Dostoyevsky was in conceptualizing his own novelistic project in *Les Faux-Monnayeurs*, but also how fruitful reflection on Dostoyevsky was in conceptualizing his own personal practice of and investment in literature. To show the complex interrelations between his thoughts on Dostoyevsky and everything else that was going on in his personal and his literary life would take at least an essay in its own right, but several passages from his lectures show reasonably clearly some of the forms of identification at work: "He [Dostoyevsky] is particularly attached to disconcerting cases, to people who rise up as challenges to accepted morality and psychology. Obviously, he himself does not feel at ease with the morality and psychology current in his day" [Il s'attache particulièrement aux cas déconcertants, à ceux qui se dressent comme des défis, en face de la morale et la psychologie admises. Evidemment dans cette morale courante et dans cette psychologie, il ne se sent pas lui-même à l'aise] (*Dostoievski*, 146). Or, writing of Dostoyevsky's epilepsy: "At the origin of every great moral reform, if we seek carefully, we will always find a small physiological mystery, a dissatisfaction of the flesh, a disquietude, an anomaly. . . . I do not believe that one could find, among those who would propose to humanity new values, a single reformer in whom one could not discover a flaw" [A l'origine de chaque grande réforme morale, si nous cherchons bien, nous trouverons toujours un petit mystère physiologique, une insatisfaction de la chair, une inquiétude,

une anomalie. . . . Je ne sache pas qu'on puisse trouver un seul réformateur, de ceux qui proposèrent à l'humanité de nouvelles évaluations, en qui l'on ne puisse découvrir . . . une tare] (209–10).

19 Martin du Gard, *Journal*, 2:294. Another version of this passage can be found in Martin du Gard's *Notes sur André Gide*, 44–48.

20 I am using "ethos" in a way suggested by Bourdieu, in a passage from *The Rules of Art* in which he is, in fact, discussing Gide and his group: "The gathering together of the authors and, secondarily, of the texts that make up a literary review has as its genuine principle, as we see, social strategies close to those governing the constitution of a salon or a movement—even though they take into account, among other criteria, the strictly literary capital of the assembled authors. And what these strategies themselves have as a unifying and generative principle is not something akin to the cynical calculation of a banker with symbolic capital (even if André Gide is also that, objectively . . .) but rather a common habitus, or, better still, an ethos which is one dimension of it and which unites the members of what one calls 'the nucleus' " (273).

21 I discuss all of these texts at greater length in *Gide's Bent*.

22 Anglès, *André Gide et le premier groupe de* La Nouvelle Revue Française, 3:312.

23 Ibid., 2:480.

24 Anglès's chapter titled "Vers le vrai roman" (2: 456–85) is especially interesting in this regard. Gide's confrontation with Claudel is recounted in the chapter "Orage sur Sodom" (3:302–52).

25 Gide, *Dostoievski*, 146. On the general topic of Gide and children, see David H. Walker's thorough and helpful "Gide, les enfants et la loi."

26 Anglès, *André Gide et le premier groupe de* La Nouvelle Revue Française, 2:462. Gide's *Les Caves du Vatican* is dedicated to Copeau.

27 Gide, *Dostoievski*, 135–36.

28 Proust, *Lettres à André Gide*, 24–25.

29 Not that Gide is without noteworthy competitors. In 1913, the NRF publishes Valery Larbaud's *A. O. Barnabooth*, Alain-Fournier's *Le Grand Meaulnes*, and part of Roger Martin du Gard's *Jean Barois*. In April 1914, it publishes the final installment of *Les Caves du Vatican*. In June and July of 1914, it publishes two sets of excerpts from Proust's *À la recherche du temps perdu*. The NRF had earlier turned down a chance to publish *Du côté de chez Swann* and had been smarting from its mistake ever since the group gained a closer acquaintance with the volume when it was published by Grasset. Various members of the group worked to convince Proust to forgive them and to agree to have subsequent volumes published by the NRF. It is also likely that, given what the NRF was publishing at that moment, given their efforts to think about the future of the French novel, and given that they would publish a novel with a character like Lafcadio in it, there was no place Proust would rather have been

published. He switched over to the NRF in 1914. (See Anglès, *André Gide et le premier groupe de* La Nouvelle Revue Française, 3:226–29, 266–70, 289–90, 310–31, 336–38, 369–79, 421–32.)

30 In *Gide's Bent* (117–42), I discuss how *inconséquence* is crucial to the implicit theorization of sexuality found in Gide's *Les Faux-Monnayeurs* as well.

31 See Anglès, *André Gide et le premier groupe de* La Nouvelle Revue Française, 3:300 and 322.

32 Martin du Gard, *Journal*, 2:295–96, emphasis added.

33 As well as being a collection of journal passages about Madeleine that Gide had not previously allowed to be published, *Et nunc manet in te* also includes a set of reflections on Gide's relation to his wife written in the years following her death.

34 Schlumberger, *Madeleine et André Gide*, 250.

35 Martin du Gard, *Notes sur André Gide*, 129, emphasis added. Segal uses this passage as one of the epigraphs to her intriguing book *André Gide: Pederasty and Pedagogy*. I've taken the liberty of citing her translation (xii).

36 Gide and Martin du Gard, *Correspondance*, 1:453–54, emphasis original. The French idiom "un veau à cinq pattes" is used to refer to something odd or abnormal. It recurs frequently in the correspondence between Gide and Martin du Gard when the matter at hand is sexuality.

37 Ibid., 1:627, emphasis original.

38 Martin du Gard's text is reproduced in Gide, *Journal I*, 1690.

39 The following is from a letter he left for the friend to whom he confided the manuscript of his childhood memoirs. One sees here again the links between this obsessive figure of posterity and a certain kind of future literary critic: "It appears that these confidences concerning my childhood, if they are published after my death, and before—long before—my complete biography be known with the publication of my *Journal* . . . seriously risk falsifying the judgment of critics. . . . *Their publication should thus be delayed* until such time as I have authorized the Bibilothèque Nationale to open the case that contains my *Journal* and other biographical documents. Thus I beg you to append a copy of the present interdiction to the manuscript that you have so that, if you should happen to pass away before the publication of my *Journal*, none of your inheritors might commit the indiscretion of publishing the confidences of these *Souvenirs d'enfance*." See the first volume of his *Journal*, 45–46.

40 Gide and Martin du Gard, *Correspondance*, 1:105.

41 Sartre, *Qu'est-ce que la littérature?*, 87.

42 For an interesting set of responses to Gide in 1968, including one by Rochefort, see "Gide vu par . . . ," *Magazine littéraire* 14 (January 1968): 23–25.

1 Proust, *Time Regained*, 191–92; *À la recherche du temps perdu*, 4:401. Future references to the various volumes of Proust's novel will be given parenthetically.

2 Genette, "Proust and Indirect Language," 274 and 293n136.

3 Of the many passages in Freud one might think of in regard to figural transformations of language, I'll merely recall the passage, from *Jokes and Their Relation to the Unconscious*, about a "piece of sophistry which has been much laughed over, but whose right to be called a joke might be doubted": "A. borrowed a copper kettle from B. and after he had returned it was sued by B. because the kettle now had a big hole in it which made it unusable. His defence was: "First, I never borrowed a kettle from B. at all; secondly, the kettle had a hole in it already when I got it from him; and thirdly, I gave him back the kettle undamaged" (100).

4 Foucault, *Death and the Labyrinth*, 183–84 (translation modified).

5 Genette, *Narrative Discourse*, 234–36. Genet's novels, as well as his theater, exploited this technique of metalepsis, even a few years before Robbe-Grillet, when his characters proved able, having first appeared only within the fantasy world, the imagination, of an already existing character, to enter the novel at a later point as free-standing characters in their own right.

6 See chapter 2 of Gray, *Postmodern Proust*, esp. 40–44.

7 On Proust's reuse of material, developed in fragmentary form, see Fraisse, *Le Processus de la création chez Marcel Proust*, 418–33; see also Finn, *Proust, the Body and Literary Form*, 155–67.

8 Wilde, "Balzac in English," 30–31.

9 Wilde, "The Decay of Lying," 970.

10 Compare some comments by Jenny Cook-Gumperz and John J. Gumperz: "verbal communication of all kinds presupposes shared background knowledge. Speakers, if they want to be understood, must be able to assess the hearer-interactants' social position within a known or knowable social universe. Where participants are not known to each other, ritualization reflects the need for the inevitably present yet often unpredictable parameters of power and social relations to be made safe and otherwise neutralized through politeness formulae" ("The Politics of a Conversation," 373). For a compelling analytical look at the pragmatic uses of the difference between statement and utterance, see Chambers, *Untimely Interventions*. For instance: "The statement meaning of any language-use answers the question: what is this language-use *about*? Thus 'It's raining' is a statement about the weather. As an utterance, however, the statement about the weather might mean something like: I don't feel up to going to the movies tonight, let's stay indoors and snuggle in front of the TV. The utterance meaning of a language-use answers the questions: why

is this utterance being proffered? and (hence) what are the 'contextual' circumstances that make its utterance meaningful?" (38).

11　On the way material moves from Proust's correspondence into the *Recherche*, see Compagnon, *Proust entre deux siècles*, esp. chap. 5, "Tableaux vivants dans le roman," 127–52. See also Finn, *Proust, the Body and Literary Form*, 104–17, esp. 114: "The letter can also be the initial point of inscription of important episodes that appear in *A la recherche*, as though personal correspondence were not the devalued and impersonal genre Proust paints it to be, but an important staging area, or an *avant*-textual waystop, in the process by which fictional writing evolves." On the particular letters I have just mentioned and their relation to the evolution of Proust's writing plans, see Rivers, *Proust and the Art of Love*, 144–52.

12　Proust, *Correspondance*, 8:112–13.

13　Ibid., 8:123–24n5. Sedgwick's comments on this crucial moment (1908–9) in the genesis of the *Recherche*, and on the article Proust is discussing (the one on which it seems Dreyfus was frowning) provoked much of my thinking for this chapter. The article was apparently a version of "La Race maudite," parts of which would later be incorporated into the first section of *Sodom and Gomorrah*, "The First Appearance of Men-Women" (Première apparition des hommes-femmes). Sedgwick writes: "It makes all the sense in the world that it was exactly the invention . . . of the Baron de Charlus, in the sentimental matrix of 'La Race maudite' in 1909, that should . . . have had the power to constitute for the first time as a speaker of more than fragmentary and more than sentimental narrative the thereby disembodied interlocutor whose name is probably not Marcel" (*Epistemology of the Closet*, 223). Relevant details of the textual history of this part of the *Recherche* are helpfully laid out by Compagnon in the explanatory matter of the Pléiade edition. See esp. 3:1196–1204 and 1215–21.

14　This letter is cited and discussed in Rivers, *Proust and the Art of Love*, 144–50. I have borrowed Rivers's English translation here.

15　These passages on Balzac—which return to this same confusion of the levels of reality and representation—may help us to see the more social implications of the confusion in question. If Vivian is haunted by Lucien in his moments of pleasure, the haunting by a fictional character may well be a sign of the awareness that the nonnormative nature of one's sexuality produces a vulnerability to social violence, and that the moment of enforcement of this violence is not foreseeable. Thus to prefer to stay at home with Lucien is to favor an alternative reality in which queer sexuality might be valorized. To mourn Lucien's death interminably is to recognize, in a nearly psychologically disabling way, that no such alternative reality is available in any sustained way.

16　Proust, *Against Sainte-Beuve*, 56; *Contre Sainte-Beuve*, 228. I will give future page references to these editions parenthetically. On what Proust calls Balzac's vulgarity, see also Finas, *Le Toucher du Rayon*, 36, 39, 43–44.

17   Within the section of *Contre Sainte-Beuve* called "Sainte-Beuve and Balzac," there is a pointed interest in the parts of Balzac's work that have to do with nonnormative sexualities. The person speaking, in one brief passage, mentions the sexual secrets of la Princesse de Cadignan, the relations of Vautrin and Lucien, the story "Sarrasine," the intricate sexual plot of *La Fille aux yeux d'or*, and the further sexual intricacies surrounding Vautrin in a couple of novels written by Charles Rabou after Balzac's death and passed off as Balzac novels. (Proust apparently accepted them—*La Famille Beauvisage* and *Le Comte de Sallenauve*—as authentically Balzacian. See Lucey, *The Misfit of the Family*, 229–37.) See *Against Sainte-Beuve*, 69–70; *Contre Sainte-Beuve*, 264–65. Given that the Proustian young man of *Contre Sainte-Beuve* is ostensibly speaking to his mother, it is hardly surprising that the interest in sexuality will be mentioned often through euphemism: "So in reading Balzac we shall continue to feel and almost to satisfy those passions from which the best literature ought to cure us" (61) [Aussi continuerons-nous à ressentir et presque à satisfaire, en lisant Balzac, les passions dont la haute littérature doit nous guérir (242)]. Or: "He hides nothing; he tells everything" (the passage is not in the English translation) [Il ne cache rien, il dit tout (248)]. Yet Balzac and Wilde turn out to be good excuses also to speak directly of homosexuality to the mother. The young man tells his mother of Wilde's foolhardy words about Lucien (65–66; 256–57) and speaks to her of "Vautrin and all his kind" and even uses the word "homosexualité" (66; 258). Proust himself, in his correspondence, had discussed *Splendeurs et misères des courtisanes* with his mother, and written about how moving Lucien's death was. His mother replied with what we might think of as some kind of rebuke: that she found Esther's death more moving than Lucien's. (Esther is the beautiful young courtesan who willingly kills herself to assure Lucien's success. See *Correspondance*, 2:133.)

18   Proust, *Lettres à André Gide*, 25.

19   On the meeting between Vautrin and Lucien, see Finas, *Le Toucher du rayon*, 46–56. See also Kempf, *Sur le corps romanesque*, 133–89. Critics have often noted that the scene in *Le Côté de Guermantes* in which Charlus offers to guide the narrator to success in life contains many echoes of the scene at the end of *Illusions perdues*. See Borel, *Proust et Balzac*, 37–38. See also Eribon, *Insult and the Making of the Gay Self*, 147–48, 180.

20   See Murat, "«Proust, Marcel, 46 ans, rentier»."

21   Genette, *Narrative Discourse*, 258.

22   Finn, in a recent contribution to discussions of the "je" of the *Recherche*, writes, "And in this bundling of component selves into one voice, Proust clearly moves close to the multiple but integrated identity to which he

aspires" (173; see also 168–77). My reading suggests rather that in relation to either Charlus or Swann, the "bundling" or "integration" of the "je" is not necessarily the endpoint of the process, that some of the apparent univocality in the *Recherche* is merely an appearance.

6 🐚 Sodom and Gomorrah

1 *Sodom and Gomorrah* is divided into two parts, which I will refer to as *Sodom and Gomorrah I* and *Sodom and Gomorrah II*. *Sodom and Gomorrah II* is quite lengthy and is divided into four chapters. *Sodom and Gomorrah I* is made up of a single short chapter.

2 For a recent account of how the Dreyfus Affair figures in the novel, how Jewishness also figures in the novel and is a problem for the narrator in much—but not exactly—the same way that same-sex sexuality is, see Freedman, "Coming Out of the Jewish Closet with Marcel Proust." Freedman comments, for instance, that "biographically, Proust seems to have been far more out—far more open in his dealings—with his sexuality than with his Jewishness, for in the circles he wished to enter, it was the latter, not the former, that conveyed a touch of exoticism, a whiff of deviancy" (531).

3 Genette, *Narrative Discourse*, 35.

4 See Proust, *Recherche*, 3:919–33.

5 See ibid., 3:936–38.

6 On the dates of the various typescripts and the moments when Proust made corrections to them, see ibid., 3:1250–51, 1261–63.

7 See ibid., 3:1262.

8 Genette, *Narrative Discourse Revisited*, 78. See also *Narrative Discourse*, 195, 197, 203–210. "Paralepsis" is for Genette when more information is given by a narrative instance than the conventions of verisimilitude that define that instance should allow. As Genette nicely summarizes it in *Narrative Discourse*, "we could say that between a tonal (or modal) system with respect to which all infractions . . . can be defined as alterations, and an atonal (amodal?) system where no code prevails anymore and where the very notion of infraction becomes outworn, the *Recherche* illustrates quite well an intermediary state: a plural state, comparable to the polytonal (polymodal) system ushered in for a time, and in the very same year, 1913, by the *Rite of Spring*. One should not take this comparison too literally; let it at least serve us to throw light on this typical and very troubling feature of Proustian narrative, which we would like to call its *polymodality*" (210).

9 See Cohn, "Proust's Generic Ambiguity," for a thorough recent consideration of the generic status of narration and narrator in Proust's novel. She

considers the question of reliability (a term developed by Wayne Booth) on 73–77.

10   Indeed, this groom seems a kind of avant-garde stagehand, farcically entering a scene to put in place a prop that is about to come in handy even though it has no real reason for being there. As for what the Guermantes's absence has to do with the ladder's presence, it is hard to say, except that the master/servant tension hinted at resonates with the social tensions present elsewhere in these pages, and that it reminds us that if the narrator, like the ladder, is not in the place he would usually be, this is also an effect of the Guermantes's absence.

11   As when he writes: "For from what I heard . . . which was only a series of inarticulate sounds, I imagine that few words had been exchanged. It is true that these sounds were so violent that, if they had not always been taken up an octave higher by a parallel plaint, I might have thought that one person was slitting another's throat within a few feet of me, and that subsequently the murderer and his resuscitated victim were taking a bath to wash away the traces of the crime" (12) [Car d'après ce que j'entendis . . . et qui ne furent que des sons inarticulés, je suppose que peu de paroles furent prononcées. Il est vrai que ces sons étaient si violents que, s'ils n'avaient pas été toujours repris un octave plus haut par une plainte parallèle, j'aurais pu croire qu'une personne en égorgeait une autre à côté de moi et qu'ensuite le meurtrier et sa victime ressuscitée prenaient un bain pour effacer les traces du crime (3:11)].

12   There are many helpful discussions of the significance of the imbricated relation between the first and third persons in novelistic narration. Bakhtin, for instance, in "Forms of Time and Chronotope in the Novel," relates the third person to public life: "Public life—any event that has any social significance—tends toward making itself public (naturally), necessarily presuming an observer, a judge, an evaluator; and a place is always created for such a person in the event, he is in fact an indispensable and obligatory participant *in* the event" (122–23). Bakhtin goes on to note that the novel gradually develops third person access to *private* life via figures of eavesdropping and spying ("the literature of private life is essentially a literature of snooping about" [123]), and via devices such as Apuleius's ass: "For the spying and eavesdropping on private life, the position of Lucius the Ass is most advantageous. For this reason, tradition has reinforced such a position, and we encounter it in a multitude of variations in the later history of the novel. What is preserved of the metamorphosis-into-ass is precisely this specific placement of the hero as a 'third person' in relation to private everyday life, permitting him to spy and eavesdrop" (124). In *Vanishing Points*, Audrey Jaffe has a helpful introduction regarding the imbrication of the first and third persons in nineteenth-century British fiction. She notes that "the narrator's mobility

and freedom" exists only in relation to "the character's bound and embodied condition" (11). The omniscient narrator, she notes, is "a fantasy of knowledge, mobility and authority" that "can come into being only in contrast to limitation, which is constructed in the form of character" (12). Both Bakhtin's comments on the importance of eavesdropping and Jaffe's on the relation of a fantasy of omniscience to the portrayal of embodied character are helpful to keep in mind when thinking about Proust. A thorough and relevant discussion of the problematic relation between first-person narration and omniscience in Proust can be found in Lavagetto's *Chambre 43*, about which I will say more in the main body of the text. See also Compagnon's review of Lavagetto's book: "La Dernière Victime du narrateur."

13   Lavagetto, *Chambre 43*, 115.

14   Compagnon, "La Dernière Victime du narrateur," 143–44.

15   Proust, *Correspondance*, 20: 542. The letter is cited by Rousset in *Narcisse romancier*, 9.

16   The actual dating of events and sections within the *Recherche* is notoriously difficult. For one discussion of this, see Genette, *Narrative Discourse*, 90–92.

17   See *Recherche*, 3:955, 1536, 1813.

18   See, for instance, Rivers, *Proust and the Art of Love*, 150–51; Sedgwick, *Epistemology of the Closet*, 216–17; Eribon, *Insult and the Making of the Gay Self*, 146–49. See also Compagnon's remarks in the Pléiade edition of the *Recherche*, 3:1199–1202.

19   See Pollard, *André Gide*, 121–37, for information on various trials and scandals of the time.

20   Steakley, "Iconography of a Scandal," 254.

21   See ibid., 238, 247.

22   This final sentence, one of those seemingly profound but also slightly ridiculous pearls of wisdom for which Proust's narrator is too well known, is interesting in that it offers a kind of alibi for the way the novel "cheats" regarding omniscience—offering a vaguely mystical hypothesis having to do with what is known in the depths of one's psyche as a cover for the novel's need for information to be presented in a certain fashion or at a certain time. Thanks to Tim Hampton for pointing this out.

23   Sedgwick writes of the "by now authentically banal exposure of Proust's narrator as a closeted homosexual" (*Epistemology of the Closet*, 223). For examples of such exposures, see Lavagetto's *Chambre 43* or Guenette, "Le Loup et le Narrateur." In a slightly different vein, on the workings of the relations between Charlus and the narrator at an earlier moment in the novel, see Schehr, "Gaydar."

24   It is the narrator's own language that may cause us to hesitate regarding the nature of the encounter for him: "I felt so urgent a need for M. de Charlus

to listen to the stories I was burning to tell him that I was bitterly disappointed to think that the master of the house was perhaps in bed, and that I might have to go home to work off by myself my verbal intoxication" (757) [J'avais un tel besoin que M. de Charlus écoutât les récits que je brûlais de lui faire, que je fus cruellement déçu en pensant que le maître de la maison dormait peut-être et qu'il me faudrait rentrer cuver chez moi mon ivresse de paroles (2:840)]; or, as he tramples Charlus's hat: "There was in him, in my view, only pride, while in me there was only fury. . . . this fury could contain itself no longer. I felt a compulsive desire to strike something, and, a lingering trace of discernment making me respect the person of a man so much older than myself, and even, in view of their dignity as works of art, the pieces of German porcelain that were grouped around him, I seized the Baron's new silk hat, flung it to the ground, trampled it, picked it up again, began blindly pulling it to pieces, wrenched off the brim, tore the crown in two" (766) [Il n'y avait en lui, selon moi, que de l'orgueil, en moi il n'y avait que de la fureur. . . . cette fureur ne se contint plus. D'un mouvement impulsif je voulus frapper quelque chose, et un reste de discernement me faisant respecter un homme tellement plus âgé que moi, et même, à cause de leur dignité artistique, les porcelaines alle-mandes placées autour de lui, je me précipitai sur le chapeau haut de forme neuf du baron, je le jetai par terre, je le piétinai, je m'acharnai à le disloquer entièrement, j'arrachai la coiffe, déchirai en deux la couronne (2:847)].

25 We have come across this kind of dissymmetry or discrepancy before. It conceivably characterizes the construction Colette gives to her relationship with Missy. It probably characterizes the relations between Gide and many of his passing sexual partners, recalling the kinds of distinctions that came to light in chapter 1 between a practicing pederast, a nonpracticing pederast, and a practicing nonpederast—the person who engages in pederasty without "being" one.

26 If this speaking position has seemed so implausible to those critics who have felt compelled to uncover a hidden homosexuality in the narrator, this is perhaps not so much because such a speaking position is incredible in and of itself, as it is due to the characteristics of the market in credibility around issues of sexuality that came into predominance in the years around the novel's writing and that still holds in the minds of many today. On the different matter of the narrator's position regarding female same-sex relations, see Ladenson, *Proust's Lesbianism.*

27 I have learned a lot from two recent sociological accounts of the *Recherche* and have a great deal of admiration for both of them: Dubois, *Pour Albertine,* and Sprinker, *History and Ideology in Proust.* In spite of my admira-tion, it seems to me that they both stumble in their thinking about sexuality, mistaking, in Dubois's case, the representation of the particular well-defined and long-established practices of a given sexual culture for a diagnosis of a

social trend. Dubois writes that Proust's fear in his novel "is that the wide field of the social economy should have its laws dictated to it by a deviant sexual economy, thereby becoming perverted. . . . Less concerned with class barriers, sexual deviance is all the more susceptible of transposing its anarchic economy to the general field, thereby threatening it with anomie" (150). Dubois here simply gives voice to a persistent theme in the ambient ideology of hostility to same-sex relations of which Proust's novel is much more critical. Similarly, Sprinker mistakes a representation of a shift in the amount of cover provided for nonnormative sexual behavior by aristocratic privilege for a naturalistic diagnosis of social decadence. He mistakenly asserts that "homosexuality is taboo in the Faubourg Saint-Germain" and goes on to deduce, erroneously, that "homosexuality . . . is a sign of aristocratic decadence; it constitutes a threat to the nobility's class solidarity and indicates that its hold over social power is loosening" (124). Again this is to confuse an ambient ideology regarding same-sex relations that is represented in the novel with the novel's own more sophisticated analysis of sexuality. It also instrumentalizes the function of the representation of same-sex sexualities in the novel in a reductive way.

28 Compare Marcus's analysis of the figure of the *portière* for nineteenth-century French apartment houses in *Apartment Stories: City and Home in Nineteenth-Century Paris and London*, esp. 42–50, 71–80.

29 Lavagetto, *Chambre 43*, 43.

30 Châtellerault had appeared several times in *Le Côté de Guermantes*, where his hopes to make an advantageous marriage were a topic of conversation. Charlus mentions him again in a later volume, *La Prisonnière*, accusing him of amusing women in salons with scandalous tales of male homosexuality —including stories about Charlus. As for the doorman, Maurice Sachs writes that he was modeled on none other than Albert Le Cuziat, the fellow who later in life would become the proprietor of the brothel in which the police would find Marcel Proust in 1918. See Sachs, *Le Sabbat*, 194–96.

31 Dorrit Cohn has already pointed to this passage in mentioning the "repeatedly foregrounded omission" of the narrator's names. See "Proust's Generic Ambiguity," 61.

32 This kind of sociological mapping regarding the circulation of certain kinds of knowledge at the party, we might add, is not only relevant to the circulation of knowledge about same-sex sexual practices. It also bears upon who is pro- or anti-Dreyfus, and upon who is in the know about that, or upon who is involved in adulterous opposite-sex affairs with whom. Further, as illustrated by the case of the two sons of Mme. de Surgis-le-Duc whom we meet at the party, and about whom there is a certain amount of surprise or admiration attached to the fact that they both have the same father, and that the father is actually Mme. de Surgis-le-Duc's husband, it has to do with the

modalities of the circulation of information about the official and unofficial family trees of various members of the aristocracy, with an ongoing accounting of both their licit and illicit couplings and the offspring of those couplings (120–21, 3:88).

33 Compare Sedgwick's remarks in *Epistemology of the Closet*: "To the extent that any child's ability to survive in the world can be plotted through her wavering command of a succession of predicate adjectives (important milestones might include the ability to formulate 'I must be tired,' 'X is violent,' 'Y is dying,' 'Z must be stupid,' 'A and B are quarrelling,' 'C is beautiful,' 'D is drunk,' 'E is pregnant'), so that the assignment of adjectives and the creation of reliable adjectival communities become ached-for badges of the worldly, the framing of the homosexual scene by Proust's young-old narrator must both disorient and reassure the reader, disorient almost in proportion as she already finds the scene familiar; the stripping away of the consistencies by which she would normally find her way through it seems also a kind of reassurance of the narrator's high descriptive hand" (229).

Epilogue

1 Van Rysselberghe, *Les Cahiers de la petite dame*, 99.

2 See Gide's journal entry for October 3, 1921: "I write, almost without any difficulty, two pages of the dialogue with which I hope to open my novel. But I shall not be satisfied unless I succeed in getting still farther from realism. It matters little, moreover, if, later on, I am to tear up everything I write today. The important thing is to get accustomed to living with my characters" (2:271) [J'écris, sans presque aucune peine, deux pages du dialogue par quoi je pense ouvrir mon roman. Mais je ne serai satisfait que si je parviens à m'écarter du réalisme plus encore. Peu m'importe, du reste, si je dois, par la suite, déchirer tout ce que j'écris aujourd'hui. L'important c'est de m'habituer à vivre avec mes personnages (1136)].

3 Van Rysselberghe reports these comments as part of the same conversation in which Gide mentions Proust's comment about his third person (99). It is a group conversation, and Gide's mention of the word *avarice* seems to set him and his interlocutors onto a train of thought about Proust's "Jewishness," and what that means in opposition to Gide's Protestant identity. In general, Van Rysselberghe's notebooks for these years are a good place to observe certain racist reflexes prevalent in Gide and his circle.

4 See Litvak, "Strange Gourmet."

5 He wrote to her a letter of praise in which he noted, "I am myself completely astonished to be writing to you, completely astonished by the great pleasure I've had in reading you" (cited by Thurman, *Secrets of the Flesh*, 300).

6 The French can be found in Gide, *Journal II*, 751. Colette would read the passage in 1946 and call Gide to thank him for writing it, which would give him a chance to make another note in his journal that shows him still keeping his distance: "Doubtless I shall respond to her call, but knowing well, alas, that immediately after the first effusions we shall have nothing to say to each other" (4:266) [Sans doute vais-je répondre à son appel; mais sachant bien, hélas! que, sitôt après les premières effusions, nous ne trouverons rien à nous dire (*Journal II*, 1029)].

7 Cited in Colette, *Oeuvres*, 3:1503.

8 Colette, *Ces plaisirs . . .* , 121–22. Colette reworked and reprinted this book in 1941 as *Le Pur et l'impur*. She made no changes to the passage I cite here, and so I have cited the English translation of *The Pure and the Impure*, 139. This is a much-commented-on book and passage. See Marks, "Lesbian Intertextuality"; chap. 3 of Huffer, *Another Colette*; chap. 4 of Flieger, *Colette and the Fantom Subject of Autobiography*; and the particularly helpful dissection of what Colette is up to here in Ladenson, "Colette for Export Only." Huffer returns to this particular passage in " 'There Is No Gomorrah,' " foregoing a consideration of the context of the 1920s and 1930s when the passage was first written and published in order to situate it first in the context of the catastrophes of World War II contemporaneous with and following its republication in *Le Pur et l'impur* and then in the context of the intellectual debates within feminist and queer theory of the late twentieth century.

9 "By *identity* we can understand a subjective intuition that one belongs to a particular social category of people, with certain potentials and consequences of this belonging. Frequently the intuition suggests participation in ritual occasions and socializing in certain ways in variously institutionalized forms to make our identity clear to ourselves and to others on a continuing basis. This already suggests a kind of temporality to the way identity is, as it were, practiced" (Silverstein, "The Whens and Wheres—as Well as Hows—of Ethnolinguistic Recognition," 532).

10 Colette, *Ces plaisirs . . .* , 103–4. Again this is a passage that was not rewritten for *The Pure and the Impure*. In the English translation, which I have modified slightly, it is on 115–16.

11 This topic will be central to the sequel to the present volume that I plan to write, covering the remainder of the twentieth century. I hope to give a longer treatment of some of Colette's later texts in that volume. For an initial look at this odd situation in which one might be allowed to speak for a certain sexuality only if one can also demonstrate no identitarian attachment to it, see my article "Sexuality, Politicization, May 1968."

12 Deleuze and Guattari, *A Thousand Plateaus*, 80, translation modified.

Works Cited

Agamben, Giorgio. *Homo Sacer: Sovereign Power and Bare Life*. Translated by Daniel Heller-Roazen. Stanford, Calif.: Stanford University Press, 1998.

Albert, Nicole G. *Saphisme et décadence dans Paris fin-de-siècle*. Paris: La Martinière, 2005.

Albert, Pierre, "La Presse française de 1871 à 1940." In *Histoire générale de la presse française. Tome III: De 1871 à 1940*. Edited by Claude Bellanger, Jacques Godechot, Pierre Guiral, Fernand Terrou, 135–622. Paris: Presses Universitaires de France, 1972.

Alençon, Emilienne d'. *Sous le masque*. Paris: Edouard Sansot, 1918.

Alexander, V. Cleve. "Jules Lemaître and the Ligue de la Patrie Française." PhD diss., Indiana University, 1975.

Alibert, François-Paul. *Le Fils de Loth*. Edited by Emmanuel Pierrat. Preface by Didier Eribon. Paris: La Musardine, 2002.

Angenot, Marc. *Le Cru et le faisandé: Sexe, discours social et littérature à la Belle Époque*. Éditions Labor, 1986.

Anglès, Auguste. *André Gide et le premier groupe de La Nouvelle Revue Française*. 3 vols. Paris: Gallimard, 1978–86.

Anscombe, G. E. M. "The First Person." In *Metaphysics and the Philosophy of Mind*, 21–36. Minneapolis: University of Minnesota Press, 1981.

Armstrong, Christine Latrouitte. " 'Je lis à Em.' " In *Le Désir à l'oeuvre: André Gide à Cambridge 1918, 1998*, edited by Naomi Segal, 83–95. Amsterdam: Rodopi, 2000.

Artières, Philippe, ed. *Le Livre des vies coupables: Autobiographies de criminels (1896–1909)*. Paris: Albin Michel, 2000.

Bakhtin, M. M. "Forms of Time and Chronotope in the Novel." In *The Dialogic Imagination: Four Essays*, edited by Michael Holquist. Translated by Caryl Emerson and Michael Holquist, 84–258. Austin: University of Texas Press, 1981.

Balzac, Honoré de. *Splendeurs et misères des courtisanes*. In *La Comédie humaine*. Vol. 6, edited by Pierre-Georges Castex. Paris: Gallimard (Pléiade), 1977. Translated by Rayner Heppenstall as *A Harlot High and Low* (Harmondsworth: Penguin, 1970).

Banfield, Ann. *Unspeakable Sentences: Narration and Representation in the Language of Fiction*. Boston: Routledge & Kegan Paul, 1982.

——. "Where Epistemology, Style, and Grammar Meet Literary History: The Development of Represented Speech and Thought." In *Reflexive Language: Reported Speech and Metapragmatics*, edited by John A. Lucy, 339–64. Cambridge: Cambridge University Press, 1993.

Barthes, Roland. *Roland Barthes par Roland Barthes*. Paris: Seuil, 1975. Translated by Richard Howard as *Roland Barthes by Roland Barthes* (New York: Hill and Wang, 1977).

Beckett, Samuel. *L'Innommable*. Paris: Minuit, 1953.

Benveniste, Emile. *Problems in General Linguistics*. Translated by Mary Elizabeth Meek. Coral Gables: University of Miami Press, 1971.

Berry, Walter. "Du côté de Guermantes." *Nouvelle Revue Française*, January 1923, 77–80.

Bertrand, Antoine. *Les Curiosités esthétiques de Robert de Montesquiou*. 2 vols. Geneva: Droz, 1996.

Bonal, Gérard, and Michel Remy-Bieth. *Colette intime*. Paris: Phébus, 2004.

Bonnamour, George. *Gabriel Syveton 1864–1904*. Neuilly-sur-Seine: L'Auteur, 1907.

Borel, Jacques. *Proust et Balzac*. Paris: José Corti, 1975.

Borrillo, Daniel. "Droit." In *Dictionnaire des cultures gays et lesbiennes*, edited by Didier Eribon, 163–64. Paris: Larousse, 2003.

Bourdieu, Pierre. "Le Champ littéraire." *Actes de la recherche en sciences sociales* 89 (1991): 4–46.

——. "Description and Prescription: The Conditions of Possibility and the Limits of Political Effectiveness." In *Language and Symbolic Power*, edited by John B. Thompson, translated by Gino Raymond and Matthew Adamson, 127–36. Cambridge, Mass.: Harvard University Press, 1991.

——. "The Economy of Symbolic Goods." In *Practical Reason: On the Theory of Action*, translated by Randal Johnson, 92–126. Stanford, Calif.: Stanford University Press, 1998.

——. "L'Illusion biographique." *Actes de la recherche en sciences sociales* 62–63 (1986): 69–72.

——. *Outline of a Theory of Practice*. Translated by Richard Nice. Cambridge: Cambridge University Press, 1977.

——. "Price Formation and the Anticipation of Profits." In *Language and Symbolic Power*, edited by John B. Thompson, translated by Gino Raymond and Matthew Adamson, 66–89. Cambridge, Mass.: Harvard University Press, 1991.

——. "Rites of Institution." In *Language and Symbolic Power*, edited by John B. Thompson, translated by Gino Raymond and Matthew Adamson, 117–26. Cambridge, Mass.: Harvard University Press, 1991.

——. *The Rules of Art: Genesis and Structure of the Literary Field*. Translated by Susan Emanuel. Stanford, Calif.: Stanford University Press, 1996.

——. "Social Space and the Genesis of 'Classes.' " In *Language and Symbolic Power*, edited by John B. Thompson, translated by Gino Raymond and Matthew Adamson, 229–51. Cambridge, Mass.: Harvard University Press, 1991.

Bourdieu, Pierre, ed. *La Misère du monde*. Paris: Seuil, 1993. Translated by Priscilla Park Ferguson, Susan Emanuel, Joe Johnson, and Shoggy T. Waryn as *The Weight of the World: Social Suffering in Contemporary Society* (Cambridge, U.K.: Polity, 1999).

Butor, Michel. *Répertoire I*. Paris: Minuit, 1960.

——. *Répertoire II*. Paris: Minuit, 1964.

Caradec, François. *Feu Willy, avec et sans Colette*. Paris: Carrere, 1984.

Carco, Francis and René-Jacques. *Envoûtement de Paris*. Paris: Nathan, 1988.

Dr. Cazanove, "La Dépravation sexuelle chez les relégués à Saint-Jean-du-Moroni (Guyane française)," *Archives d'anthropologie criminelle* 21 (1906): 44–58.

Chalon, Jean. *Liane de Pougy: Courtisane, princesse et sainte*. Paris: Flammarion, 1994.

Chambers, Ross. *Loiterature*. Lincoln: University of Nebraska Press, 1999.

——. *Untimely Interventions: AIDS Writing, Testimonial, and the Rhetoric of Haunting*. Ann Arbor: The University of Michigan Press, 2004.

Charle, Christophe. *Paris fin de siècle: Culture et politique*. Paris: Seuil, 1998.

Chauncey, George. "Christian Brotherhood or Sexual Perversion? Homosexual Identities and the Construction of Sexual Boundaries in the World War I Era." In *Hidden from History: Reclaiming the Gay and Lesbian Past*, edited by Martin Bauml Duberman, Martha Vicinus, and George Chauncey Jr., 294–317. New York: New American Library, 1989.

——. *Gay New York: Gender, Urban Culture, and the Making of the Gay Male World, 1890–1940*. New York: Basic Books, 1994.

Chevalier, Louis. *Montmartre du plaisir et du crime*. Paris: Laffont, 1980.

Cicourel, Aaron V. "The Acquisition of Social Structure: Towards a Developmental Sociology of Language and Meaning." In *Cognitive Sociology: Language and Meaning in Social Interaction*, 42–73. Harmondsworth: Penguin, 1973.

Cohn, Dorrit. "Proust's Generic Ambiguity." In *The Distinction of Fiction*, 58–78. Baltimore: Johns Hopkins University Press, 1999.

Colette. *Ces plaisirs . . .* Paris: Le Livre Moderne Illustré, 1934.

——. *Claudine Married*. In *The Claudine Novels*. Translated by Antonia White. London: Penguin Books, 1987.

——. *The Collected Stories of Colette*, edited by Robert Phelps, translated by Matthew Ward, Antonia White, Anne-Marie Callimachi, and others. New York: Farrar, Straus and Giroux, 1983.

——. *Lettres à ses pairs*. In *Oeuvres complètes de Colette*. Vol. 16, edited by Claude Pichois. Paris: Flammarion, 1973.

——. *My Apprenticeships and Music Hall Sidelights*. Translated by Helen Beauclerk and Anne-Marie Callimachi. London: Secker and Warburg, 1957.

——. *Oeuvres*, edited by Claude Pichois et al. 4 vols. Paris: Gallimard (Pléiade), 1984–2001.

——. *The Pure and the Impure*. Translated by Herma Briffault. Intro. Judith Thurman. New York: New York Review Books, 2000.

Colla, Elliott. "Hooked on Pharaonics: Literature and the Appropriation of Ancient Egypt." PhD diss., University of California, Berkeley, 2000.

——. " 'Non, non! Si, si!': Commemorating the French Occupation of Egypt (1798–1801)." *MLN* 118 (2003): 1043–69.

Compagnon, Antoine. *Connaissez-vous Brunetière? Enquête sur un antidreyfusard et ses amis*. Paris: Seuil, 1997.

——. "La Dernière Victime du narrateur." *Critique* 53 (March 1997): 131–46.

——. *Proust entre deux siècles*. Paris: Seuil, 1989.

Courtivron, Isabelle de. " 'Never Admit!': Colette and the Freedom of Paradox." In *The Modern Woman Revisited: Paris between the Wars*, edited by Whitney Chadwick and Tirza True Latimer, 55–64. New Brunswick, N.J.: Rutgers University Press, 2003.

Dean, Carolyn J. *The Frail Social Body: Pornography, Homosexuality, and Other Fantasies in Interwar France*. Berkeley: University of California Press, 2000.

Deffoux, Léon. *J.-K. Huysmans sous divers aspects*. Paris: Mercure de France, 1942.

Delarue-Mardrus, Lucie. *The Angel and the Perverts*. Translated by and intro. Anna Livia. New York: New York University Press, 1995.

Deleuze, Gilles. "Cinq propositions sur la psychanalyse." In *L'Île déserte et autres textes: Textes et entretiens 1953–1974*, edited by David Lapoujade, 381–90. Paris: Minuit, 2002.

Deleuze, Gilles, and Félix Guattari. *A Thousand Plateaus: Capitalism and Schizophrenia*. Translated by Brian Massumi. Minneapolis: University of Minnesota Press, 1987.

Dobie, Madeleine. *Foreign Bodies: Gender, Language, and Culture in French Orientalism*. Stanford, Calif.: Stanford University Press, 2001.

Douglas, Mary. "Rightness of Categories." In *How Classification Works: Nelson Goodman among the Social Sciences*. Edited by Mary Douglas and David Hull, 239–71. Edinburgh: Edinburgh University Press, 1992.

Dubois, Jacques. *Pour Albertine: Proust et le sens du social*. Paris: Seuil, 1997.

Ducrot, Oswald. *Dire et ne pas dire: Principes de sémantique linguistique*. Paris: Hermann, 1972.

Duvert, Tony. *La Parole et la fiction: A propos du «Libera»*. Paris: Minuit, 1984. Reprinted from *Critique*, no. 252 (1968).

Dwight, Eleanor. *Edith Wharton: An Extraordinary Life*. New York: Harry N. Abrams, 1994.

Eribon, Didier. *Insult and the Making of the Gay Self*. Translated by Michael Lucey. Durham, N.C.: Duke University Press, 2004.

Eribon, Didier, ed. *Dictionnaire des cultures gays et lesbiennes*. Paris: Larousse, 2003.

Erlich, Gloria C. *The Sexual Education of Edith Wharton*. Berkeley: University of California Press, 1992.

Fiaux, Louis. *Les Maisons de tolérance: Leur fermeture*. Second edition. Paris: G. Carré, 1892.

Finas, Lucette. *Le Toucher du rayon: Proust, Vautrin et Antinoüs*. Paris: Nizet, 1995.

Finn, Michael R. *Proust, the Body and Literary Form*. Cambridge: Cambridge University Press, 1999.

Flieger, Jerry Aline. *Colette and the Fantom Subject of Autobiography*. Ithaca, N.Y.: Cornell University Press, 1992.

Foucault, Michel. *Death and the Labyrinth: The World of Raymond Roussel*. Translated by Charles Ruas. Garden City, N.Y.: Doubleday, 1986.

——. *Dits et écrits, 1954–1988*, edited by Daniel Defert and François Ewald. 4 vols. Paris: Gallimard, 1994.

——. *The History of Sexuality. Volume 1: An Introduction*. [*La Volonté de savoir*]. Translated by Robert Hurley. New York: Vintage, 1990.

——. *"Society Must Be Defended": Lectures at the Collège de France, 1975–1976*. Translated by David Macey. New York: Picador, 2003.

Fraisse, Luc. *Le Processus de la création chez Marcel Proust: Le Fragment expérimental*. Paris: José Corti, 1988.

Francis, Claude, and Fernande Gontier. *Colette*. Paris: Perrin, 1997.

——. *Mathilde de Morny: La Scandaleuse Marquise et son temps*. Paris: Perrin, 2000.

Freadman, Anne. *The Machinery of Talk: Charles Peirce and the Sign Hypothesis*. Stanford: Stanford University Press, 2004.

——. "When the King and Queen of England Came to Town: Popular Entertainment, Everyday Life, and the Teaching of 'Culture.'" Inaugural Lecture in the University of Melbourne, November 23, 2004. Available at www.fritss.unimelb.edu.au/staff/kingqueen.html.

Freadman, Anne, and Amanda Macdonald. *What Is This Thing Called "Genre"? Four Essays in the Semiotics of Genre*. Mount Nebo, Australia: Boombana, 1992.

Freedman, Jonathan. "Coming Out of the Jewish Closet with Marcel Proust." *GLQ* 7 (2001): 521–51.

Freud, Sigmund. *Jokes and Their Relation to the Unconscious*. Translated by James Strachey. Harmondsworth: Penguin, 1976.

Galopin, Arnould. *Les Enracinées*. Paris: A. Fayard, 1903.

Genette, Gérard. *Narrative Discourse: An Essay in Method*. Translated by Jane E. Lewin. Ithaca, N.Y.: Cornell University Press, 1980.

——. *Narrative Discourse Revisited*. Translated by Jane E. Lewin. Ithaca, N.Y.: Cornell University Press, 1988.

——. "Proust and Indirect Language." In *Figures of Literary Discourse*. Translated by Alan Sheridan. Introduction by Marie-Rose Logan, 229–95. New York: Columbia University Press, 1982.

Germain, André. *Les Clés de Proust*. Paris: Sun, 1953.

Ghéon, Henri, and André Gide. *Correspondance*, edited by Jean Tipy. 2 vols. Paris: Gallimard, 1976.

Gide, André. *Ainsi soit-il ou Les Jeux sont faits*. Paris: Gallimard, 1952. Translated by Justin O'Brien as *So Be It or The Chips Are Down* (New York: Knopf, 1959).

——. *Corydon*. Paris: Gallimard, 1924. Translated by Richard Howard as *Corydon* (New York: Farrar, Straus and Giroux, 1983).

——. *Dostoievski: Articles et causeries*. Paris: Plon, 1923.

——. *Et nunc manet in te, suivi de Journal intime*. Neuchâtel: Ides et Calendes, 1951. Translated by Justin O'Brien as *Madeleine* (New York: Knopf, 1952).

——. *Journal I: 1887–1925*, edited by Éric Marty. Paris: Gallimard (Pléiade), 1996.

——. *Journal II: 1926–1950*, edited by Martine Sagaert. Paris: Gallimard (Pléiade), 1997.

——. *The Journals of André Gide*. 4 vols. Translated by Justin O'Brien. New York: Knopf, 1947–1951.

——. *Les Nouvelles Nourritures*. In *Romans, récits et soties; oeuvres lyriques*. Paris: Gallimard (Pléiade), 1958.

——. *Oscar Wilde*. Paris: Mercure de France, 1913. Translated by Bernard Frechtman as *Oscar Wilde: In Memoriam* (New York: Philosophical Library, 1949).

——. *Le Ramier*. Foreword by Catherine Gide. Preface by Jean-Claude Perrier. Postface by David H. Walker. Paris: Gallimard, 2002.

——. *Si le grain ne meurt*. Paris: Gallimard (Folio), 1985. Translated by Dorothy Bussy as *If It Die . . .* (London: Penguin, 1977).

Gide, André, and François-Paul Alibert. *Correspondance 1907–1950*, edited by Claude Martin. Lyon: Presses Universitaires de Lyon, 1982.

Gide, André, and Jacques Copeau. *Correspondance*, edited by Jean Claude. 2 vols. Cahiers André Gide 12 and 13. Paris: Gallimard, 1987.

Gide, André, and Roger Martin du Gard. *Correspondance*, edited by Jean Delay. 2 vols. Paris: Gallimard, 1968.

Gide, André, and François Mauriac. *Correspondance André Gide–François Mauriac, 1912–1950*, edited by Jacqueline Morton. Cahiers André Gide 2. Paris: Gallimard, 1971.

Goffman, Erving. *Forms of Talk*. Philadelphia: University of Pennsylvania Press, 1981.

——. *Frame Analysis: An Essay on the Organization of Experience*. Boston: Northeastern University Press, 1986.

——. "On Face-Work." in *Interaction Ritual: Essays on Face-to-Face Behavior*, 5–45. New York: Pantheon, 1967.

Goodman, Nelson. "On Likeness of Meaning." In *Problems and Projects*, 221–30. Indianapolis: Bobbs-Merrill, 1972.

——. "Seven Strictures on Similarity." In *How Classification Works: Nelson Goodman among the Social Sciences*, edited by Mary Douglas and David Hull, 13–23. Edinburgh: Edinburgh University Press, 1992.

——. *Ways of Worldmaking*. Indianapolis: Hackett, 1978.

Goodman, Nelson, and Catherine Z. Elgin. *Reconceptions in Philosophy and Other Arts and Sciences*. Indianapolis: Hackett, 1988.

Gray, John, ed. *Last Letters of Aubrey Beardsley*. London: Longmans, Green, and Co., 1904.

Gray, Margaret E. *Postmodern Proust*. Philadelphia: University of Pennsylvania Press, 1992.

Griffin, Susan. *The Book of the Courtesans: A Catalogue of Their Virtues*. New York: Broadway Books, 2001.

Guenette, Mark D. "Le Loup et le Narrateur: The Masking and Unmasking of Homosexuality in Proust's 'A la recherche du temps perdu.'" *Romanic Review* 80 (1989): 229–46.

Gumperz, John J., and Jenny Cook-Gumperz. "Introduction: Language and the Communication of Social Identity," in *Language and Social Identity*, edited by John J. Gumperz, 1–21. Cambridge: Cambridge University Press, 1982.

——. "The Politics of a Conversation: Conversational Inference in Discussion," in *What's Going on Here? Complementary Studies of Professional Talk*, edited by Allen D. Grimshaw, Peter J. Burke, and Aaron V. Cicourel, 373–95. Norwood, N. J.: Ablex, 1994.

Halberstam, Judith. *Female Masculinity*. Durham, N.C.: Duke University Press, 1998.

Halperin, David. "Homosexuality." In *Gay Histories and Cultures*, edited by George E. Haggerty, 45–55. New York: Garland, 2000.

Hayard, Napoléon. *Dictionnaire d'argot-français*. Paris: Hayard, 1907.

Hesse, Carla. *The Other Enlightenment: How French Women Became Modern*. Princeton, N.J.: Princeton University Press, 2001.

Hollander, Paul d'. *Colette: Ses apprentissages*. Montréal: Presses de l'Université de Montréal, 1978.

Huffer, Lynne. *Another Colette: The Question of Gendered Writing*. Ann Arbor: University of Michigan Press, 1992.

———. "'There Is No Gomorrah': Narrative Ethics in Feminist and Queer Theory." *differences* 12, no. 3 (2001): 1–32.

Jaffe, Audrey. *Vanishing Points: Dickens, Narrative, and the Subject of Omniscience*. Berkeley: University of California Press, 1991.

Jakobson, Roman. "Shifters and Verbal Categories." In *On Language*, edited by Linda R. Waugh and Monique Monville-Burston, 386–92. Cambridge, Mass.: Harvard University Press, 1990.

Jansiti, Carlo. *Violette Leduc*. Paris: Grasset, 1999.

Jullian, Philippe. *Jean Lorrain, ou le Satiricon 1900*. Paris: Fayard, 1974.

Kempf, Roger. *Sur le corps romanesque*. Paris: Seuil, 1968.

Kristeva, Julia. *Le Génie féminin, tome III: Colette*. Paris: Fayard, 2002.

Lacassagne, Jean, and Pierre Devaux. *L'Argot du "Milieu."* Preface by Francis Carco. 2nd ed. Paris: Albin Michel, 1935.

Ladenson, Elisabeth. "Colette for Export Only." *Yale French Studies* 90 (1996): 25–46.

———. *Proust's Lesbianism*. Ithaca, N.Y.: Cornell University Press, 1999.

Landy, Joshua. "'Les Moi en Moi': The Proustian Self in Philosophical Perspective." *New Literary History* 32 (2001): 91–132.

———. "Proust, His Narrator, and the Importance of the Distinction." *Poetics Today* 25, no. 1 (2004): 91–135.

Lavagetto, Mario. *Chambre 43: Un Lapsus de Marcel Proust*. Translated by Adrien Pasquali. Paris: Belin, 1996.

Leduc, Violette. *Thérèse et Isabelle*, edited by Carlo Jansiti. Paris: Gallimard, 2000.

Lejeune, Philippe. *Je est un autre: L'Autobiographie de la littérature aux médias*. Paris: Seuil, 1980.

———. *Moi aussi*. Paris: Seuil, 1986.

———. *Le Pacte autobiographique*. Nouvelle édition augmentée. Paris: Seuil-Points, 1996.

Lindon, Mathieu. "Le Lecteur impossible." *Minuit* 16 (November 1975): 65–71.

Litvak, Joseph. "Strange Gourmet: Taste, Waste, Proust." In *Novel Gazing: Queer Readings in Fiction*, edited by Eve Kosofsky Sedgwick, 74–93. Durham, N.C.: Duke University Press, 1997.

Lorrain, Jean. *Correspondance: Lettres à Barbey d'Aurevilly, François Coppée, Oscar Méténier, Catulle Mendès, Edmond Deschaumes, Mecislas Golberg, etc., suivies des articles condamnés*. Paris: Baudinière, 1929.

——. *Une Femme par jour*, edited by Michel Desbruères. Saint-Cyr-sur-Loire: Christian Pirot, 1983.

——. *La Maison Philibert*. Paris: Librairie universelle, 1904.

——. *Monsieur de Phocas*, edited by Hélène Zinck. Paris: Flammarion, 2001.

——. *Soixante-huit lettres à Edmond Magnier*. Poitiers: Au Paréiasaure philatéliste. 1998.

——. *La Ville empoisonnée: Pall-Mall Paris*. Paris: Éditions Jean Crès, 1936.

Louÿs, Pierre. *Aphrodite*. 1896. Paris: Fasquelle, 1928.

Lowe, Lisa. *Critical Terrains: French and British Orientalism*. Ithaca, N.Y.: Cornell University Press, 1991.

Lucey, Michael. "Catégorie ou concept: Balzac et la sexualité." In *Conférences litter*, by Leo Bersani, David M. Halperin, and Michael Lucey, 7–40. Paris: EPEL, 2005.

——. *Gide's Bent: Sexuality, Politics, Writing*. New York: Oxford University Press, 1995.

——. *The Misfit of the Family: Balzac and the Social Forms of Sexuality*. Durham, N.C.: Duke University Press, 2003.

——. "Sexuality, Politicization, May 1968: Situating Christiane Rochefort's *Printemps au parking*." *differences* 12 (2001): 33–68.

Lucien, Mirande. *Akademos: Jacques d'Adelswärd-Fersen et «la cause homosexuelle»*. Lille: GayKitschCamp, 2000.

Manalansan, Martin F., IV. *Global Divas: Filipino Gay Men in the Diaspora*. Durham, N.C.: Duke University Press, 2003.

Marcus, Sharon. "Reflections on Victorian Fashion Plates." *differences* 14 (2003): 4–33.

Marin, Louis. *Pascal et Port-Royal*. Paris: PUF, 1997.

Marks, Elaine. "1929: 'Odor di Femina' [Sic]." In *A New History of French Literature*, edited by Denis Hollier, 887–91. Cambridge, Mass.: Harvard University Press, 1989.

——. "Lesbian Intertextuality." In *Homosexualities and French Literature: Cultural Contexts, Critical Texts*, edited by George Stambolian and Elaine Marks, 353–77. Ithaca, N.Y.: Cornell University Press, 1979.

Martin du Gard, Roger. *Journal*, edited by Claude Sicard. 3 vols. Paris: Gallimard, 1992.

——. *Notes sur André Gide, 1913–1951*. Paris: Gallimard, 1951.

Martineau, L. *Les Déformations vulvaires et anales produites par la masturbation, le saphisme, la défloration et la sodomie*. 1884. 3rd ed. Paris: Vigot, 1905.

Mead, George Herbert. *Mind, Self, and Society from the Standpoint of a Social Behaviorist*, edited by Charles W. Morris. Chicago: University of Chicago Press, 1934.

Mendès, Catulle. *Méphistophéla*. 1890. Paris: Séguier, 1993.

Merleau-Ponty, Maurice. *Phenomenology of Perception*. Translated by Colin Smith. London: Routledge and Kegan Paul, 1962.

Mertz, Elizabeth. "Beyond Symbolic Anthropology: Introducing Semiotic Mediation." In *Semiotic Mediation: Sociocultural and Psychological Perspectives*, edited by Elizabeth Mertz and Richard J. Parmentier, 1–19. Orlando, Fla.: Academic, 1985.

Miller, D. A. *Jane Austen, or The Secret of Style*. Princeton, N.J.: Princeton University Press, 2003.

Montesquiou, Robert de. *Professionnelles Beautés*. Paris: F. Juven, 1905.

Munholland, John Kim. "Republican Order and Republican Tolerance in Fin-de-Siècle France: Montmartre as a Delinquent Community." In *Montmartre and the Making of Mass Culture*, edited by Gabriel P. Weisberg, 15–36. New Brunswick, N.J.: Rutgers University Press, 2001.

Murat, Laure. "«Proust, Marcel, 46 ans, rentier»: Un individu «aux allures de pédéraste» fiché à la police." *La Revue Littéraire* 2, no. 14 (May 2005): 82–93.

Nye, Robert A. "Degeneration and the Medical Model of Cultural Crisis in the French *Belle Epoque*." In *Political Symbolism in Modern Europe: Essays in Honor of George L. Mosse*, edited by Seymour Drescher, David Sabaen, and Allan Sharlin, 19–41. New Brunswick, N.J.: Transaction Books, 1982.

Pao, Angela. *The Orient of the Boulevards: Exoticism, Empire, and Nineteenth-Century French Theater*. Philadelphia: University of Pennsylvania Press, 1998.

Peirce, Charles S. "Pragmatism (1907)." In *The Essential Peirce: Selected Philosophical Writings, Volume 2 (1893–1913)*, 398–433. Bloomington: Indiana University Press, 1998.

Peyrefitte, Roger. *L'Exilé de Capri*. Paris: Flammarion, 1959.

Pichois, Claude, and Alain Brunet. *Colette*. Paris: Fallois, 1999.

Plat, Hélène. *Lucie Delarue-Mardrus: Une Femme de lettres des années folles*. Paris: Grasset, 1994.

Pollard, Patrick. *André Gide: Homosexual Moralist*. New Haven, Conn.: Yale University Press, 1991.

Pougy, Liane de. *Idylle saphique*. (1901). Paris: Éditions des femmes, 1987.

——. *My Blue Notebooks*. Translated by Diana Athill. New York: Harper and Row, 1979.

Proust, Marcel. *Against Sainte-Beuve and Other Essays*. Translated by John Sturrock. London: Penguin, 1988.

——. *À la recherche du temps perdu*, edited by Jean-Yves Tadié. 4 vols. Paris: Gallimard (Pléiade), 1987.

——. *The Captive; The Fugitive*. Translated by C. K. Scott Moncrieff, Terence Kilmartin, and D. J. Enright. New York: Modern Library, 2003.

——. *Contre Sainte-Beuve*, edited by Bernard de Fallois. 1954. Paris: Gallimard (Idées), 1979.

——. *Correspondance*. 21 vols., edited by Philip Kolb. Paris: Plon, 1970–1993.

——. *The Guermantes Way*. Translated by C. K. Scott Moncrieff, Terence Kilmartin, and D. J. Enright. New York: Modern Library, 2003.

——. *Lettres à André Gide*. Neuchatel: Ides et Calendes, 1949.

——. "Un Professeur de beauté," *Les Arts de la vie*, August 15, 1905.

——. *Sodom and Gomorrah*. Translated by C. K. Scott Moncrieff, Terence Kilmartin, D. J. Enright. New York: Modern Library, 2003.

——. *Time Regained*. Translated by C. K. Scott Moncrieff, Terence Kilmartin, D. J. Enright. New York: Modern Library, 2003.

Raffalovich, Marc-André. "Les Groupes uranistes à Paris et à Berlin," *Archives d'anthropologie criminelle* 19 (1904): 926–36.

——. "*Les Hors Nature*, par Mme Rachilde," *Archives d'anthropologie criminelle* 12 (1897): 321–24.

——. *Uranisme et unisexualité: Etude sur différentes manifestations de l'instinct sexuel*. Paris: Masson, 1896.

Régis, P. "Un Cas de perversion sexuelle à forme sadique," *Archives d'anthropologie criminelle* 14 (1889): 399–419.

Rivers, J. E. *Proust and the Art of Love: The Aesthetics of Sexuality in the Life, Times, and Art of Marcel Proust*. New York: Columbia University Press, 1980.

Rosario, Vernon A. *The Erotic Imagination: French Histories of Perversity*. New York: Oxford University Press, 1997.

Rousset, Jean. *Narcisse romancier: Essai sur la première personne dans le roman*. Paris: José Corti, 1972.

Roux, Jean-Pierre. *Nationalisme et conservatisme: La Ligue de la Patrie Française 1899–1904*. Paris: Beauchesne, 1977.

Rupp, Leila J. "Toward a Global History of Same-Sex Sexuality." *Journal of the History of Sexuality* 10 (April 2001): 287–302.

Sachs, Maurice. *Le Sabbat: Souvenirs d'une jeunesse orageuse*. Paris: Gallimard, 1960.

Sarde, Michèle. *Colette, libre et entravèe*. Paris: Stock, 1978.

Sarraute, Nathalie. *L'Ère du soupçon: Essais sur le roman*. Paris: Gallimard, 1956.

Sartre, Jean-Paul. *Qu'est-ce que la littérature?* Paris: Gallimard, 1978.

Sautman, Francesca Canadé. "Invisible Women: Lesbian Working-class Culture in France, 1880–1930." In *Homosexuality in Modern France*, edited by Jeffrey Merrick and Bryant T. Ragan Jr., 177–201. New York: Oxford University Press, 1996.

Schehr, Lawrence R. "Gaydar: A Proustian Anatomy of Cruising." In *Proust in Perspective: Visions and Revisions*, edited by Armine Kotin Mortimer and Katherine Kolb, 172–85. Urbana: University of Illinois Press, 2002.

——. *The Shock of Men: Homosexual Hermeneutics in French Writing*. Stanford, Calif.: Stanford University Press, 1995.

Schlumberger, Jean. *Madeleine et André Gide*. Paris: Gallimard, 1956.

Sedgwick, Eve Kosofsky. *Epistemology of the Closet*. Berkeley: University of California Press, 1990.

Segal, Naomi. *André Gide: Pederasty and Pedagogy*. Oxford: Oxford University Press, 1998.

——, ed. *Le Désir à l'oeuvre: André Gide à Cambridge 1918, 1998*. Amsterdam: Rodopi, 2000.

Sewell, Brocard. *Two Friends: John Gray and André Raffalovich*. Aylesford, U.K.: Saint Alberts, 1963.

Sheridan, Alan. *André Gide: A Life in the Present*. Cambridge, Mass.: Harvard University Press, 1999.

Silverstein, Michael. "Indexical Order and the Dialectics of Sociolinguistic Life." *Symposium about Language and Society—Austin* 3 (1995): 266–95.

——. "Language and the Culture of Gender: At the Intersection of Structure, Usage, and Ideology." In *Semiotic Mediation: Sociocultural and Psychological Perspectives*, edited by Elizabeth Mertz and Richard J. Parmentier, 219–59. Orlando, Fla.: Academic, 1985.

——. "The Limits of Awareness." In *Linguistic Anthropology: A Reader*, edited by Alessandro Duranti, 382–401. Oxford: Blackwell, 1990.

——. "Metapragmatic Discourse and Metapragmatic Function." In *Reflexive Language: Reported Speech and Metapragmatics*, edited by John A. Lucy, 33–58. Cambridge: Cambridge University Press, 1993.

——. "Shifters, Linguistic Categories, and Cultural Description." In *Meaning in Anthropology*, edited by Keith H. Basso and Henry A. Selby, 11–55. Albuquerque: University of New Mexico Press, 1976.

——. "The Whens and Wheres—as Well as Hows—of Ethnolinguistic Recognition." *Public Culture* 15 (2003): 531–57.

Sprinker, Michael. *History and Ideology in Proust:* A la recherche du temps perdu *and the Third French Republic*. Cambridge, U.K.: Cambridge University Press, 1994.

Steakley, James D. "Iconography of a Scandal: Political Cartoons and the Eulenburg Affair in Wilhelmin Germany." In *Hidden from History: Reclaiming the Gay and Lesbian Past*, edited by Martin Bauml Duberman, Martha Vicinus, and George Chauncey Jr., 233–63. New York: New American Library, 1989.

Stoler, Ann Laura. *Race and the Education of Desire: Foucault's* History of Sexuality *and the Colonial Order of Things*. Durham, N.C.: Duke University Press, 1995.

Stovall, Tyler. "National Identity and Shifting Imperial Frontiers: Whiteness and the Exclusion of Colonial Labor After World War I." *Representations* 84 (2003): 52–72.

Terrou, Fernand. "L'Evolution du droit de la presse de 1881 à 1840." In

Histoire générale de la presse française, Tome III: De 1871 à 1940, edited by Claude Bellanger, Jacques Godechot, Pierre Guiral, Fernand Terrou, 5–57. Paris: Presses Universitaires de France, 1972.

Thurman, Judith. *Secrets of the Flesh: A Life of Colette*. New York: Knopf, 1999.

Traub, Valerie. *The Renaissance of Lesbianism in Early Modern England*. Cambridge: Cambridge University Press, 2002.

Urban, Greg. "The 'I' of Discourse." In *Semiotics, Self, and Society*, edited by Benjamin Lee and Greg Urban, 27–51. New York: Mouton de Gruyter, 1989.

Van Rysselberghe, Maria. *Les Cahiers de la Petite Dame, 1918–1929*. Cahiers André Gide 4. Paris: Gallimard, 1973.

Vidocq, Eugène-François. *Mémoires: Les Voleurs*, edited by Francis Lacassin. Paris: Laffont, 1998.

Vivien, Renée. *Une Femme m'apparut*. (1904). Paris: Régine Deforges, 1977.

Waldberg, Patrick. *Eros in la Belle Epoque*. Translated by Helen R. Lane. New York: Grove, 1969.

Walker, David H. "Gide, les enfants et la loi." In *Le Désir à l'oeuvre: André Gide à Cambridge 1918, 1998*, edited by Naomi Segal, 303–25. Amsterdam: Rodopi, 2000.

Warner, Michael. *Publics and Counterpublics*. New York: Zone Books, 2002.

Watson, D. R. "The Nationalist Movement in Paris, 1900–1906." In *The Right in France 1890–1919: Three Studies*, edited by David Shapiro, 49–84. Carbondale: Southern Illinois University Press, 1962.

Weber, Eugen. *Peasants into Frenchmen*. Stanford, Calif.: Stanford University Press, 1976.

Weisberg, Gabriel P., ed. *Montmartre and the Making of Mass Culture*. New Brunswick, N.J.: Rutgers University Press, 2001.

Wilde, Oscar. "Balzac in English." In *The Artist as Critic: Critical Writings of Oscar Wilde*, edited by Richard Ellmann, 29–32. New York: Random House, 1969.

——. *The Decay of Lying*. In *The Complete Works of Oscar Wilde*, 970–92. New York: Harper and Row, 1989.

Wittig, Monique. *The Straight Mind and Other Essays*. Boston: Beacon Press, 1992.

Index

Mauriac, François, 31, 51–54, 268 nn.29, 33
Mayol, Felix, 126, 282 n.57
Mendès, Catulle, 25, 87, 108, 123, 126, 156, 280 n.48; *Méphistophéla*, 67–71, 80, 85, 120–22, 269 n.12, 270 n.16
Mercure de France, 32–33, 76–77, 85, 100
Merleau-Ponty, Maurice, 164
Mertz, Elizabeth, 21
Missy. *See* Mathilde de Morny
Montesquiou, Robert de, 9, 11, 53, 61–64, 66–67, 72, 81, 86, 91, 260, n.10, 272 n.41; *Professionelles Beautés*, 90
Mortier, Pierre, 107–8
Murat, Princess, 48–49

Names and Naming. *See* Nomenclature
Narrative metalepsis, 198–99
Noilhan, Mlle. (The Panther), 110–12, 116–17, 137
Nomenclature: for homosexuality, 7–8, 29, 36–39, 42–43, 46–47, 73–74, 230, 267 nn.21, 22, gousse, 109, 159; slang, 58–59, 152; tante, 58–63, 66, 88–89; vrille, 88–89, 92, 93; 155–56. *See also* Homosexuality; Lesbianism; Sexuality: social categories of
Nouvelle Revue Française, La, 25, 178–79, 182, 291 n.29
Nouvel Observateur, Le, 11

Otéro, Caroline, 120, 138–40, 160

Pederasty. *See* Nomenclature
Peirce, Charles, 20
Pinget, Robert, 15–16
Posterity: and literary reputation, 170, 173, 176, 183; and sexuality, 178, 181–82, 190–92
Pougy, Liane de, 71–72, 80, 84, 88, 100, 108, 111, 115, 120, 123, 125,

137, 160, 276 n.22, 281 n.50, 288 n.93
Pragmatism, 20–23, 26, 36; meta-pragmatics, 64, 68
Pronouns, 17–18; abstract approach to, 19–20, sexuality and, 18; as shifter, 15–16. *See also* First person
Proust, Marcel, 4–7, 9, 11, 17, 23–25, 27, 30–31, 46–47, 51–56, 58, 61–64, 66, 81, 86, 90, 165, 216–17, 220–22, 228–34, 247–50, 253–54, 256–58, 262 n.23, 263 n.34, 264 n.38, 295 n.17, 298 n.22; *À la recherche du temps perdu*, 9, 15, 18–19, 26, 35, 48, 195–96, 294 nn.11, 13; Balzac and, 201–10, 212–13; Charlus, 200, 202, 206, 210–13, 216, 220–29, 232–41, 298 nn.23, 24, 299 n.26, 300 n.30; *Contre Sainte-Beuve*, 90, 202, 207–8, 211, 213, 229, 295 n.17; Gide and, 46–56, 250–53, 258, 301 n.3; *The Guermantes Way*, 48, 218–22, 234–35, 300 n.30; homosexuality of, 196; *Sodom and Gomorrah*, 9, 48, 54, 90, 121, 202, 206, 210, 214–17, 218–22, 228–30, 232–34, 236–47, 251–55, 297 nn.10, 11; Swann, 215–17; *Le Temps retrouvé*, 193–95, 197; vulgarity of, 252; Wilde and, 201–10, 213

Queer culture: affiliation with, 80–83, 85–93, 139–41, 146–49, 151, 161, 195

Race, 126, 131–32, 134, 137–38, 284 n.65, 285 n.71. *See also* Colette: race and
Rachilde, 25, 32–33, 37, 86, 119, 126, 150, 165; on Colette, 77–80; on Gide, 77–80, 85
Rafflovich, Marc-André, 37, 72–74, 269 n.12, 270 nn.15, 19

320   Index

MICHAEL LUCEY is a professor of French and comparative literature at the University of California at Berkeley. He is the author of *The Misfit of the Family: Balzac and the Social Forms of Sexuality* (2003) and *Gide's Bent: Sexuality, Politics, Writing* (1995).

Library of Congress Cataloging-in-Publication Data
Lucey, Michael, 1960–
Never say I : sexuality and the first person in Colette, Gide, and Proust / Michael Lucey.
p. cm. — (Series Q)
Includes bibliographical references and index.
ISBN-13: 978-0-8223-3857-4 (cloth : alk. paper)
ISBN-10: 0-8223-3857-2 (cloth : alk. paper)
ISBN-13: 978-0-8223-3897-0 (pbk. : alk. paper)
ISBN-10: 0-8223-3897-1 (pbk. : alk. paper)
1. French literature—20th century—History and criticism.
2. Homosexuality and literature—France. 3. Homosexuality in literature. 4. Lesbianism in literature. 5. Self in literature.
6. Autobiography in literature. 7. Colette, 1873-1954—Criticism and interpretation. 8. Gide, André, 1869-1951—Criticism and interpretation. 9. Proust, Marcel, 1871-1922—Criticism and interpretation. I. Title. II. Series.
PQ307.H6L83 2006
840'.9353—dc22   2006011058